D1297743

lon

Grand Canyon NATIONAL PARK

AVON LAKE PUBLIC LIBRARY
32649 ELECTRIC BOULEVARD
AVON LAKE, OHIO 44012

Loren Bell, Jennifer Rasin Denniston

PLAN YOUR TRIP

ON THE ROAD

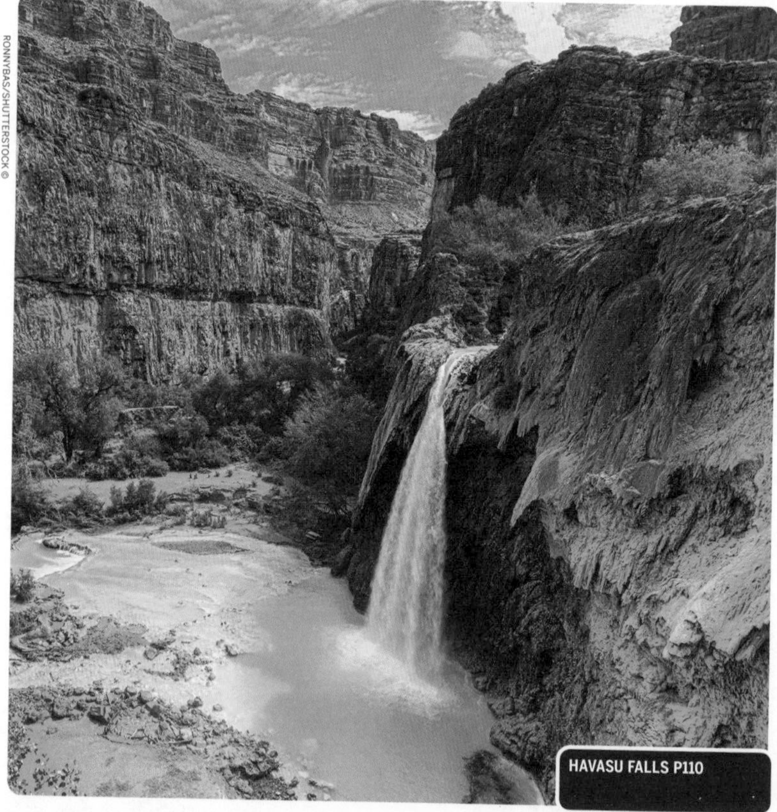

HAVASU FALLS P110

RONNYBAS/SHUTTERSTOCK ©

Contents

MATHER POINT P81

COYOTE P205

COVID-19

We have re-checked every business in this book before publication to ensure that it is still open after 2020's COVID-19 outbreak. However, the economic and social impacts of COVID-19 will continue to be felt long after the outbreak has been contained, and many businesses, services and events referenced in this guide may experience ongoing restrictions. Some businesses may be temporarily closed, have changed their opening hours and services, or require bookings; some unfortunately could have closed permanently. We suggest you check with venues before visiting for the latest information.

Welcome to Grand Canyon

The Grand Canyon embodies the scale and splendor of the American West, captured in dramatic vistas, dusty trails, and stories of exploration, exploitation and preservation.

Sublime Vistas

We've all seen images of the canyon in print and on-screen, but there is nothing like arriving at the edge and taking it all in – the immensity, the depth, the light. Descend into the canyon depths, amble along the rim or simply relax at an outcrop – you'll find your own favorite Grand Canyon vista. Though views from both rims are equally stunning, the South Rim boasts many more official and dramatic overlooks. One of the most beautiful in its simplicity, however, is the view that whispers from the Grand Canyon Lodge's patio on the canyon's quieter north side.

Native American & Pioneer History

Ancestral Puebloans lived in and near the Grand Canyon for centuries, and its pioneer history is full of wild and eccentric characters who wrangled this intimidating expanse for profit and adventure. Their stories echo in the weathered trails they built; the iconic mule-train traditions that lured 19th-century tourists; and the stone and timber buildings constructed by the railroads. Ranger talks and South Rim museums explore the park's native history, showcase indigenous dwellings and crafts, and tell inspiring tales of intrepid adventurers.

Hiking an Inverted Mountain

You don't have to be a hard-core hiking enthusiast to taste the park's inner-canyon splendor. Even a short dip below the rim gives a stunning appreciation for its magnificent scale and awesome silence; descend deeper for a closer look at a mind-boggling record of geologic time. The park's raw desert climate and challenging terrain demand a slower, quieter pace, and that's just perfect, because it's exactly that pace that is best for experiencing the Grand Canyon in all its multisensory glory.

Two Billion Years of Rocks

One look at the reds, rusts and oranges of the canyon walls and the park's spires and buttes, and you can't help but wonder about the hows and whys of the canyon's formation. Luckily for laypeople with rock-related questions, the South Rim has answers, primarily at Yavapai Point and Geology Museum and the Trail of Time installation, and both rims offer geology talks and walks given by the park's knowledgeable rangers. For a more DIY experience, hike into the canyon with a careful eye for fossilized marine creatures, animal tracks and ferns.

Why I Love the Grand Canyon

By Jennifer Rasin Denniston, Writer

I came to Grand Canyon for the first time with my toddler and newborn in tow. Frazzled and exhausted, and always the skeptical traveler, I was prepared to be underwhelmed. But seconds after walking onto the veranda of the North Rim lodge, I understood. My canyon isn't about the view alone, which I knew from postcards and books, photographs and oil paintings. Its power lies in the grounding silence and dusty quiet, the smells of ponderosa and desert, the clarity that comes from feeling so very small. We return year after year.

For more about our writers, see p256.

Above: Toroweap Point (p144)

Grand Canyon National Park

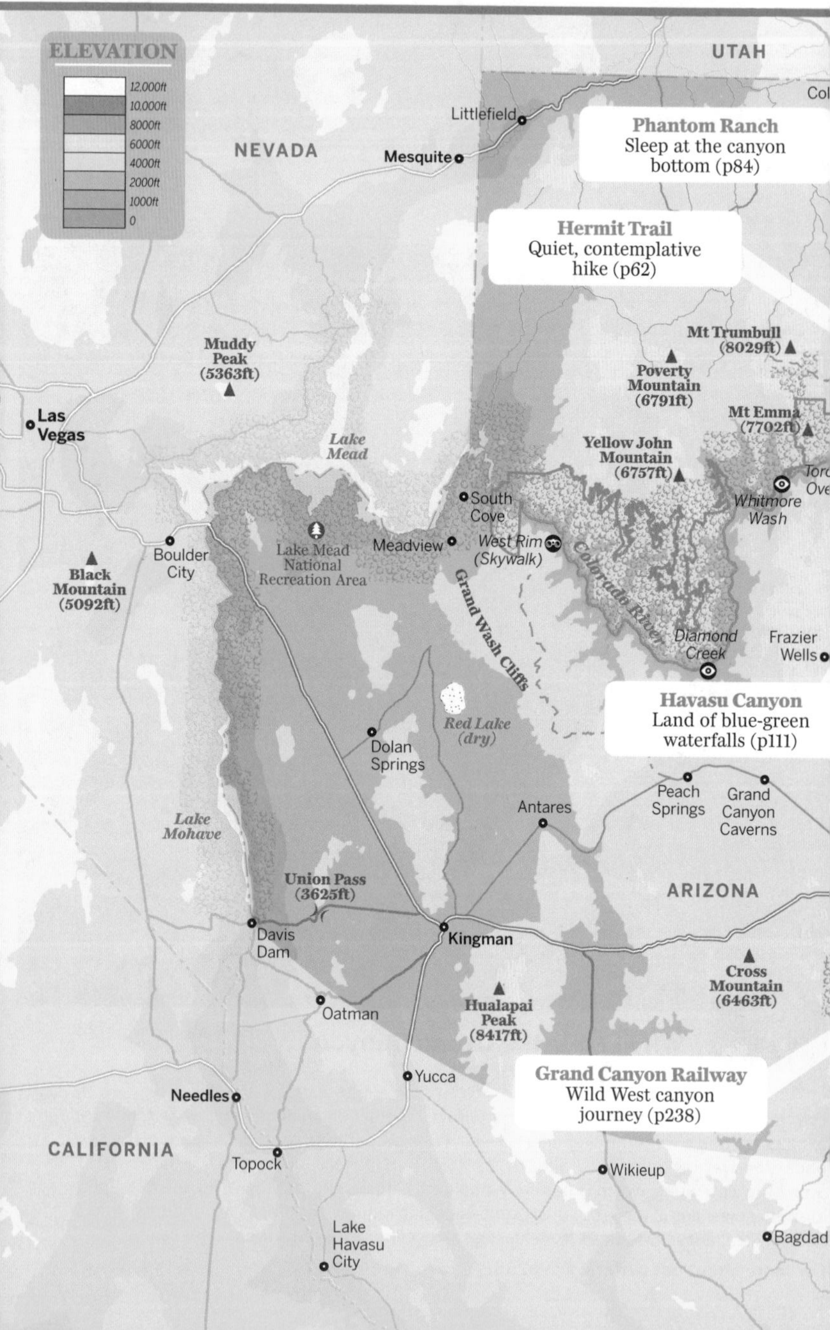

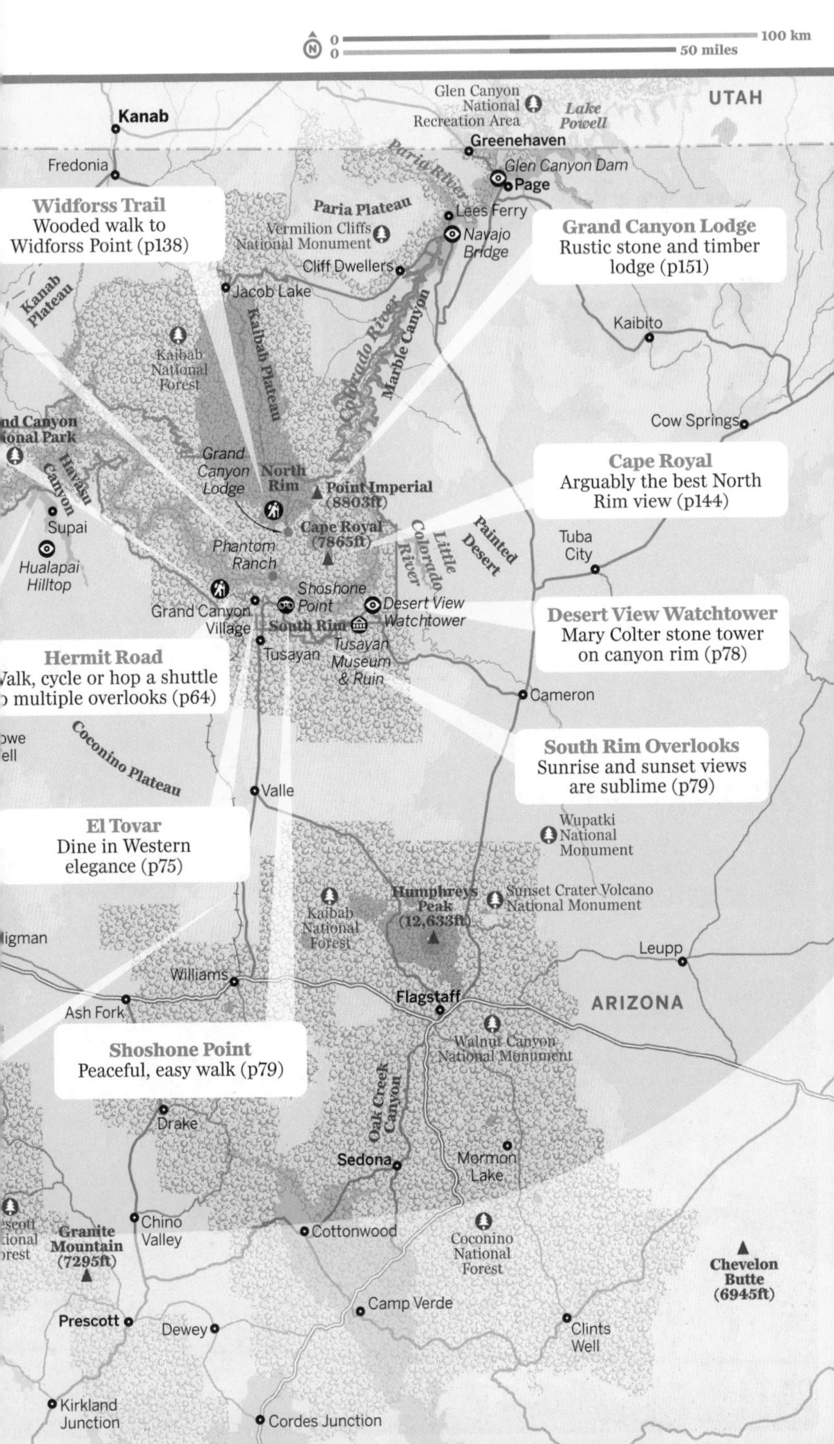

0 100 km
0 50 miles
UTAH
Glen Canyon National Recreation Area
Lake Powell
Kanab
Greenehaven
Fredonia
Paria River
Glen Canyon Dam
Page
Widforss Trail
Wooded walk to Widforss Point (p138)
Paria Plateau
Lees Ferry
Vermilion Cliffs National Monument
Navajo Bridge
Grand Canyon Lodge
Rustic stone and timber lodge (p151)
Cliff Dwellers
Kanab Plateau
Jacob Lake
Kaibab Plateau
Colorado River
Marble Canyon
Kaibito
Kaibab National Forest
Cow Springs
Grand Canyon Lodge
North Rim
Point Imperial (8803ft)
Cape Royal
Arguably the best North Rim view (p144)
Havasu Canyon
Supai
Cape Royal (7865ft)
Little Colorado River
Painted Desert
Tuba City
Hualapai Hilltop
Phantom Ranch
Shoshone Point
Desert View Watchtower
Grand Canyon Village
South Rim
Desert View Watchtower
Mary Colter stone tower on canyon rim (p78)
Tusayan
Tusayan Museum & Ruin
Hermit Road
Walk, cycle or hop a shuttle to multiple overlooks (p64)
Cameron
Coconino Plateau
South Rim Overlooks
Sunrise and sunset views are sublime (p79)
Valle
Wupatki National Monument
El Tovar
Dine in Western elegance (p75)
Humphreys Peak (12,633ft)
Sunset Crater Volcano National Monument
Kaibab National Forest
Leupp
Williams
Ash Fork
Flagstaff
ARIZONA
Walnut Canyon National Monument
Shoshone Point
Peaceful, easy walk (p79)
Oak Creek Canyon
Drake
Sedona
Mormon Lake
Granite Mountain (7295ft)
Chino Valley
Cottonwood
Coconino National Forest
Chevelon Butte (6945ft)
Camp Verde
Prescott
Dewey
Clints Well
Kirkland Junction
Cordes Junction

Grand Canyon's Top 20

1

South Rim Overlooks

1 The canyon doesn't have a photographic bad side, but it has to be said that the views from the South Rim (p52) are stunners. Each has its individual beauty, with some unique angle that sets it apart from the rest – a dizzyingly sheer drop, a view of river rapids or a felicitous arrangement of jagged temples and buttes. Sunrises and sunsets are particularly sublime, with the changing light creating depth and painting the features in unbelievably rich hues of vermilion and purple. Below left: Sunrise over Yavapai Point (p76)

Hiking Rim to Rim

2 There's no better way to fully appreciate the grand of Grand Canyon than hiking through it, rim to rim. The classic corridor route descends the North Rim on the North Kaibab (p227), includes a night at Phantom Ranch or Bright Angel Campground at the bottom of the canyon, crosses the Colorado River and ascends to the South Rim on Bright Angel trail. A popular alternative rim-to-rim route (p66) is to descend from the South Rim on the South Kaibab trail (pictured below) and ascend via the North Kaibab trail.

MATTEO COLOMBO/GETTY IMAGES ©

2

PATRICK J. ENDRES/GETTY IMAGES ©

Havasu Canyon

3 The people of the blue-green waters, as the Havasupai call themselves, take their name from the otherworldly turquoise-colored waterfalls and creek that run through the canyon. Due to limestone deposits on the creekbed, the water appears sky blue, a gorgeous contrast to the deep red of the canyon walls. The only ways into and out of Havasu Canyon (p111) are by foot, horse or helicopter, but those that make the 10-mile trek are richly rewarded by the magic of this place, epitomized by spectacular Havasu Falls.

Grand Canyon Lodge

4 Perched at 8000ft on the canyon rim, this granddaddy of national-park lodges (p151) promises a high-country retreat like nothing else in the Grand Canyon. Completed in 1928, the original structure burned to the ground in 1932. It was rebuilt in 1937, and in the early days staff greeted guests with a welcome song and sang farewell as they left. Today, you'll find that same sense of intimate camaraderie, and it's easy to while away the days at a North Rim pace.

5

6

Widforss Trail

5 This gentle North Rim hike (p138) rises and dips along the plateau, veering toward a side canyon and meandering 5 miles to Widforss Point. It's a mild, gentle amble, with canyon views whispering rather than screaming from the edges, plenty of shade and room for children to run among wildflowers. A picnic table at the end makes a lovely lunch spot, and at the overlook you can sit on a stone jutting over the Grand Canyon, dangling your feet above the rocky outcrop just below, listening to the silence.

Phantom Ranch

6 After descending to the canyon bottom, it's a delight to ramble along a flat trail, past a mule corral and a few scattered cabins to Phantom Ranch (p242), where you can relax with a lemonade and splash in the cool waters of Bright Angel Creek. This lovely stone lodge, designed by Mary Colter and built in 1922, continues to be the only developed facility in the inner canyon. Mule trips from the South Rim include one or two nights here, and hikers can enter the lottery for accommodations 15 months in advance.

7

JOHN ELK/GETTY IMAGES ©

8

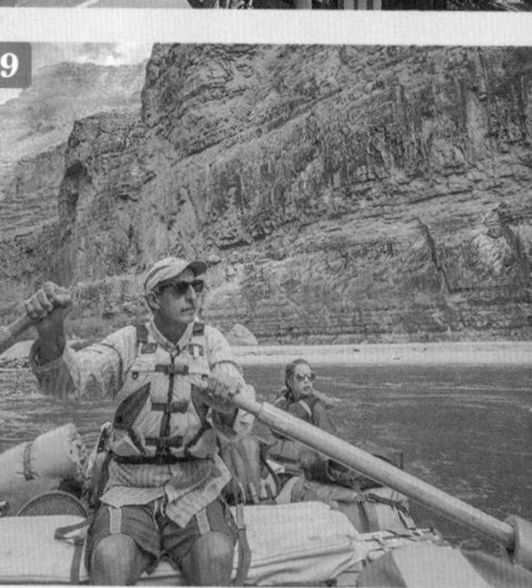

9

Hermit Trail

7 The name seems apropos, even today, as you are unlikely to encounter many hikers and backpackers on the Hermit Trail (p63). Though easily accessible from South Rim shuttles and tourist hub, it feels marvelously remote. Day hikers connect with the Dripping Springs Trail to reach a little oasis where water seeps down from a small overhang festooned with maidenhair fern. Take a moment to imagine the quiet life of Louis 'The Hermit' Boucher, the prospector who made this spot his home for many years.

Kolb Studio

8 Perched on the South Rim at the top of Bright Angel Trail, tiny Kolb Studio (p74) was built as a home and photography studio in 1905 by Ellsworth and Emery Kolb. For years the intrepid Kolb Brothers ran a successful photography business at the canyon, originally developing their film using cow pond water and building a primitive darkroom 4.5 miles below the rim at Indian Garden. Ellsworth moved to Los Angeles in 1924, but Emery remained here until his death in 1976. Today, changing exhibits include artifacts, photos and film from the life and work of the brothers, and Grand Canyon–inspired art.

Rafting the Colorado River

9 Considered the trip of a lifetime by many river enthusiasts, rafting (p38) the Colorado is a wild ride down a storied river, through burly rapids past a stratified record of geologic time and up secretive side canyons. Though riding the river is the initial attraction, the profound appeals of the trip reveal themselves each day and night in the quiet stretches on smooth water, side hikes to hidden waterfalls, the musicality of ripples and birdsong, and the vast solitude of this awesome place.

ape Royal Point

0 A pleasant drive through woods with teasing canyon views leads to e trailhead for this most spectacular of orth Rim overlooks. It's an easy 0.5-mile alk to Cape Royal (p144) along a paved ail with signs pointing out facts about e flora and fauna of the area. The walk is iitable for folks of all ages and capabili-es. Once at the point, the expansive view cludes the Colorado River below, Flag-aff's San Francisco Peaks in the distance id stunning canyon landmarks in both rections.

Grand Canyon Railway

11 Things start out with a bang at the Wild West shootout in Williams, and then the 'sheriff' boards the train to make sure everything's in its place. Is it hokey? Maybe a little. Fun? Absolutely. Riding the historic Grand Canyon Railway (p238) to the South Rim takes a bit longer than if you were to drive, but you avoid traffic and disembark relaxed and ready to explore the canyon. The train drops you off a few minutes from the historic El Tovar and canyon rim.

10

11

Mule Rides

12 There's something classically Grand Canyon about riding a mule (p227) into the canyon, a time-honored tradition that began with turn-of-the-century pioneering tourists. While less strenuous than hiking the canyon, mule rides are a physically active experience that require a sense of adventure. If you want to ride to the Colorado River, head to the South Rim for an overnight trip to Phantom Ranch. From the North Rim, you can descend into the canyon on a half-day ride down the North Kaibab, and both rims offer jaunts above the rim.

Grandview Trail

13 Developed by prospector Pete Berry, whose crumbling stone cabin still sits on Horseshoe Mesa 6.2 miles below the rim, the rugged and steep Grandview Trail (p64) is a South Rim favorite of experienced hikers visiting in the fall or spring. The path descends quickly, with switchbacks of cobblestone. After crossing a couple of narrow saddles to Horseshoe Mesa, you'll find open mine shafts speaking silently of the canyon's past. Pace yourself on the hike out, taking time to take in the grand views.

14

15

lagstaff

14 Flagstaff (p99) is (give or take): one part granola, one part wild game, ne part craft brew, one part espresso, ne part mountain man, one part medicine oman. But unscientific formulas aside, ne sum of Flagstaff is fun stuff. It's a uni-ersity town with a Route 66 flavor and pedestrian-friendly downtown, where ailway history, astronomy and culinary harms contribute as much to the town's eitgeist as its haunted hotels and its New ear's pinecone drop. Come for the can-on and stay for Flag.

Splashing in Oak Creek

15 Winding through Sedona's spectacular red-rock landscape and riparian Oak Creek Canyon (p112), the cold and clear waters of gentle Oak Creek make a marvelous antidote to summer heat. Sedona offers several places to access its shallow tumbles and deep swimming holes, including East Fork Trail, Grasshop per Point, Midgley Bridge and Red Rock Crossing. Several upscale inns nestle against its shores, and popular Slide Rock State Park offers family-perfect rock slides along the creek.

Shoshone Point

16 For a leisurely walk away from the South Rim circus, hiking through the ponderosa to Shoshone Point (p59) does the trick. The soundtrack to this mostly flat 1-mile walk is that of pine needles crunching underfoot and birdsong trilling overhead, and lacy shadows provide cover from the sun. Upon reaching the rim, you'll trace the edge for a short while to the stone point jutting out over the canyon depths. Shoshone Point, or the picnic area at the end of the trail, is perfect for a peaceful lunch.

Dinner at El Tovar

17 No one goes to the Grand Canyon for an epicurean adventure, but the finest dining on the South Rim is mor than fine. Part of the dinner experience is sitting in this historic lodge (p75), absorbing a little of its bygone glamour and rustic architectural elegance. Relaxing over venison and a glass of wine in these environs feels especially decadent after a dusty afternoon walking miles from overlook to overlook along the canyon rim or days hiking the canyon interior. Allow tim for people-watching over a cocktail on th back porch.

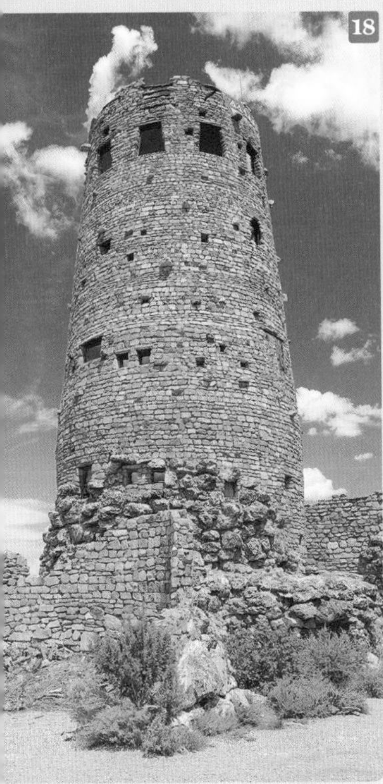

RADIUS IMAGES/ALAMY STOCK PHOTO ©

MICHELEVACCHIANO/GETTY IMAGES ©

Desert View Watchtower

18 At the eastern edge of the South Rim, Desert View Watchtower (p78) could almost pass as an American Indian ruin, but it's an amalgamation of Mary Colter's imagination and myriad American Indian elements. This circular tower encases a spiral stairway that winds five stories to the top floor, with walls featuring a Hopi mural and graphic symbols from various American Indian tribes. From its many windows on all sides, you can see mile upon magnificent mile of canyon ridges, desert expanse, river and sky.

Best Friends Animal Sanctuary

19 Angel Canyon, where dozens of old Westerns were shot, is now home to the US' biggest no-kill animal shelter (p160). Nestled in over 30,000 acres of spectacular red-rock landscape sit seven idyllic sanctuaries for lost, sick and abandoned animals rescued from natural and human disasters around the world. At any given time, about 1700 animals, including cats, dogs, rabbits, horses, pigs, birds and more, call this canyon home. Free tours are given daily, there are a handful of casitas for overnight stays and, with advance arrangements, volunteers are always welcome.

Kaibab National Forest (North)

20 Spreading miles across the Kaibab Plateau and towering over vast desert expanses of the seemingly endless Arizona Strip, the North Kaibab National Forest (p157) hugs Grand Canyon to the north and offers the traveler gentle respite from searing summer heat. Lush meadows are home to deer and buffalo, hiking trails wind through the aspen and ponderosa forests, and remote canyon overlooks lure adventurous travelers. You can camp anywhere for free, but after the first major snowfall the 44-mile road through the Kaibab to the North Rim closes.

Need to Know

For more information, see Survival Guide (p221)

Entrance Fees

$35 per car, $30 per motorcycle, $15 per person entering on foot, bicycle, train, shuttle or raft; valid at both rims for seven days

Number of Visitors

6.3 million (2017)

Money

The South Rim's Chase Bank (p231) offers limited currency exchange and will cash travellers cheques for Chase Bank customers. Credit and debit cards are widely accepted.

Cell Phones

Cell-phone reception on the South Rim is generally available in Grand Canyon Village along and immediately below the rim, but is otherwise spotty to nonexistent. Do not expect cell-phone service on the North Rim or inner canyon.

Driving

Some South Rim roads closed to private vehicles. Fuel available at North Rim Campground and South Rim's Desert View.

When to Go

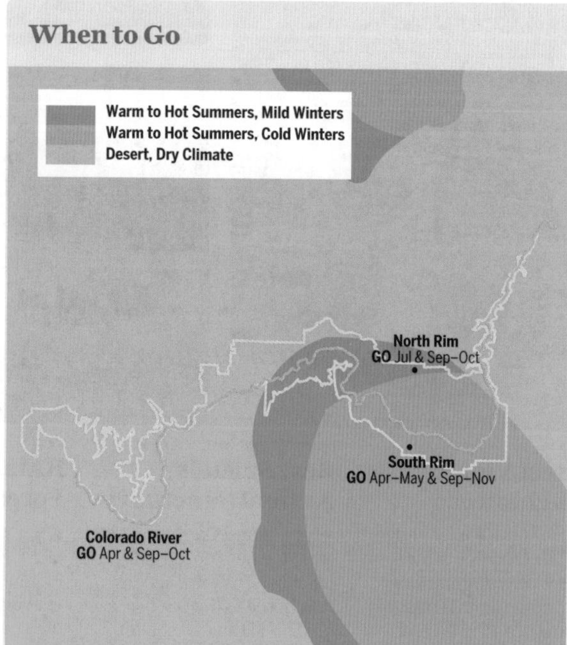

High Season

(May–Sep)

➡ Bone-dry inner-canyon temperatures hover above 100°F (38°C) during summer peak; August brings monsoon rains.

➡ Accommodations bookings increase and sell out further in advance.

➡ North Rim facilities open mid-May and close mid-October.

Shoulder

(Mar–Apr & Sep–Oct)

➡ Cooler and fluctuating temps; South Rim can see snow as late as April.

➡ March is packed with spring-break crowds.

➡ North Rim Campground open with backcountry permit.

Low Season

(Nov–Feb)

➡ The stream of South Rim visitors slows to a trickle.

➡ Snowfalls bring frosted vistas, but also treacherous roads and trails.

➡ The first snow closes Hwy 67 to the North Rim.

Important Numbers

For long-distance and toll-free calls, dial 1 followed by three-digit area code and seven-digit local number. For emergencies on either rim, call 911.

Grand Canyon National Park Headquarters	☎928-638-7888
Grand Canyon Lodge (North Rim)	☎928-638-2611
Grand Canyon South Rim Switchboard	☎928-638-2631
Xanterra (South Rim)	☎888-297-2757
Emergency Search and Rescue	☎928-638-2477

Useful Websites

National Park Service (www.nps.gov/grca) Hiking, river-running and backcountry details, below-the-rim camping permits, useful links and park alerts.

Lonely Planet (www.lonelyplanet.com/usa/arizona/grand-canyon-national-park) Destination information, hotel bookings, traveler forums and more.

Xanterra/Grand Canyon Lodges (www.grandcanyonlodges.com) South Rim and Phantom Ranch accommodations and dining, bus tours and mule trips.

Visit Grand Canyon (www.visitgrandcanyon.com) South Rim pet-friendly lodge and RV Park.

Grand Canyon Association (www.grandcanyon.org) Grand Canyon's nonprofit website; best online bookstore and map resource, details on tours, classes and events.

Grand Canyon Lodge (www.grandcanyonlodgenorth.com) North Rim accommodations, mule trips and dining.

Daily Costs

Budget: $40–100

- Camping: free to $25
- Groceries and cheap eats: $20-35
- Tusayan to South Rim Shuttle (March through September): free
- Hiking and ranger talks: free

Midrange: $100–250

- Double room in motel: $100–250
- South Rim bicycle rental: $45
- Car rental: $50

Top End: More than $250

- Double room in B&Bs and three-star hotels: $250–350
- Dinner with wine at El Tovar: $90–170
- Mule ride from South Rim to/from Colorado River with meals and night at Phantom Ranch: $606

Exchange Rates

Australia	A$1	$0.71
Canada	C$1	$0.76
China	Y10	$1.46
Euro zone	€1	$1.16
Japan	¥100	$0.90
Mexico	MXN10	$0.52
New Zealand	NZ$1	$0.65
UK	£1	$1.29

For current exchange rates, see www.xe.com.

Opening Dates

South Rim

Open year-round, 24 hours a day.

North Rim

Open May 15 to October 15, 24 hours a day.

You can drive or hike into the park after it officially closes, but the 44-mile State Hwy 67 from Jacob Lake to the rim is not plowed; visitors may enter on foot, skis, snowmobile or snowshoes. Park entrance fees are collected until November 30; all lodging, dining and visitor services, with the following exceptions, are closed October 15 to May 15.

- A year-round on-site NPS ranger.
- The rim-to-rim shuttle (p235) runs until November 15 (weather permitting).
- The North Rim Campground (p228) takes reservations through October 31, and is open year-round as primitive camping for campers with a backcountry permit secured in advance.
- Sometimes the gift shop next to the lodge stays open until October 31.
- Self-service gas is available until December 1, or until State Hwy 67 closes.

Park Policies & Regulations

- The use of drones is prohibited anywhere at Grand Canyon National Park.
- Wood or charcoal fires of any type are prohibited in the backcountry, including anywhere below the rim.
- Fires are allowed in grills at above-the-rim established campgrounds, but it is against park regulations to collect wood. Go to www.nps.gov/grca for current fire restrictions.
- On the South Rim, bicycles are allowed on paved or unpaved roads and the Greenway Trail (p239); on the North Rim, they are allowed on blacktop roads, the 17-mile dirt road to Point Sublime, and the Bridle Trail.
- It's illegal to feed wildlife.

If You Like...

Hiking

North Kaibab Trail The 14-mile trail from high-country North Rim to the Colorado River passes two campgrounds. (p145)

South Kaibab Trail At just over 6 miles from the South Rim to the river, this stunning hike is the shortest and steepest corridor trail. (p62)

Widforss Trail This peaceful amble among the pines and aspen of the North Rim winds past quiet canyon vistas to an excellent picnic perch on the rim. (p138)

Rim Trail The South Rim's most popular trail follows the canyon rim for 13 miles, passing historic buildings, museums and more than a dozen overlooks. (p227)

Hermit Trail One of the South Rim's most quiet canyon descents, the Hermit makes an excellent day hike and offers backcountry camping. (p63)

Sedona A mecca for day hikers, with spectacular red-rock surrounds and alluring Oak Creek. (p112)

Flagstaff Excellent variety of easily accessible trails and multiple outdoor shops with experienced advice. (p99)

Dramatic Views

You can't really go wrong anywhere along or below the rim; early-morning and late-afternoon light add depth, color, dimension and drama.

Grand Canyon Lodge Settle into a rimside Adirondack chair for a sunset glass of wine. (p227)

Moran Point Named for the painter whose depiction helped secure national-park status. (p79)

Mohave Point Sublime South Rim viewpoint for sunrise or sunset – listen for Hermit Rapid. (p79)

Rim Trail Dirt and paved trail winds along 13 miles of canyon edge on South Rim. (p227)

South Kaibab Trail Well maintained inner-canyon trail descends from South Rim. (p62)

Bright Angel Point Walk along a North Rim fin to a point surrounded by vast views. (p151)

Cape Royal Trail Easy paved trail to one of the North Rim's best views. (p227)

Tuweep Area Long and rough road leads to sheer cliff that's hours from tourist hubs. (p144)

American Indian Culture

Both the largest American Indian reservation and the most remote (the Navajo and Havasupai, respectively) exist within and around the Grand Canyon, and the region is rich in Puebloan history.

Hopi Reservation One of the oldest continuously occupied villages on the continent sits on the Hopi Reservation. (p171)

Museum of Northern Arizona Craftsman-style Flagstaff museum with excellent exhibits on American Indian art and guided tours to Grand Canyon. (p101)

Walnut Canyon Moderate trails to American Indian cliff dwellings inhabited from AD 1100 to 1250. (p102)

Wupatki National Monument Remains of one of the region's largest Puebloan cultures and home to the Wupatki less than 850 years ago. (p102)

Tusayan Ruins Explore American Indian Grand Canyon history at the small ruins and museum on the South Rim. (p78)

Top: An Arizona road on Route 66 (p98)

Bottom: Rafting the Colorado River (p178)

Scenic Drives

The ever-changing landscape goes from bizarre red-rock formations to ponderosa forest to high desert flatlands – and the grandest canyon.

Desert View Drive Arriving through the South Rim's east entrance introduces the canyon gradually and elegantly, with multiple incredible canyon overlooks. (p227)

Hermit Road Seven-mile drive passes some of the park's best overlooks; open to private vehicles December through February only, and by shuttle the rest of the year. (p227)

Oak Creek Canyon Wind through riparian landscape from Flagstaff to Sedona. (p117)

North Kaibab National Forest Driving through alpine meadows, ponderosa forest and aspen groves to the North Rim. (p93)

Route 66 Back roads evoke nostalgia in spades and buckets of kitsch. (p98)

Water

Especially precious in the dry climate of the Southwest, the waterways of the Grand Canyon region offer some of the most unique experiences in the world – rafting the Colorado River being the most obvious, but not the only one.

Rafting the Colorado The trip of a lifetime, with dozens of white-water rapids, day hikes to waterfalls and nights camping along the river. (p38)

Smooth-water Floats through Glen Canyon Motorized trips on the Colorado, from Glen Canyon Dam to Lees Ferry. (p227)

Oak Creek Cool, clear creek tumbles through red-rock landscape and wooded canyon around Sedona; several parks and trails offer access. (p117)

Kayak Lake Powell Explore the peaceful hidden side-canyons of Lake Powell using your own paddle power. (p166)

Havasu Canyon Famous inner-canyon blue-green waterfalls and swimming holes on Havasupai Reservation. (p110)

Black Canyon A 30-mile smooth-water Colorado River float on designated National Water Trail close to Las Vegas. (p122)

Lake Mead Massive lake formed by Hoover Dam, popular for water sports, fishing, houseboating and swimming. (p121)

Arts

Kolb Studio Small museum dedicated to the pioneering Grand Canyon photographic expeditions of the adventurous Kolb brothers. (p74)

Grand Canyon Music Festival Live music of varying genres livens up the cultural scene at the South Rim. (p25)

Grand Canyon Celebration of Art Includes a plein air painting festival with a timed 'quick draw' event. (p25)

Sedona Upscale galleries and an annual film festival in picture-perfect red-rock country. (p112)

Architecture

'National Park Rustic' style was born when Mary Colter, hired by the railroad, designed South Rim buildings to blend harmoniously with the indigenous landscape, incorporating local materials and elements of American Indian design.

Hermits Rest This cozy stone resthouse, with its gigantic fireplace, is something of a tribute to its hermit namesake. (p75)

Lookout Studio Sits on the edge of the South Rim with a terraced path below. (p76)

Hopi House Inspired by and modeled after Hopi Puebloan dwellings. (p77)

Desert View Watchtower Circular tower at South Rim's East Entrance affords views from all sides. (p78)

Phantom Ranch Down at the bottom of the canyon, this stone lodge and canteen is still the center of inner-canyon civilization. (p242)

Grand Canyon Lodge Stone and timber masterpiece perches on the North Rim, with plate-glass windows for canyon-viewing perfection. (p227)

El Tovar South Rim exception to Colter, this elegant timber lodge offered some of park's earliest accommodations. (p75)

Bicycling

Sorry, mountain bikers: bombing down Grand Canyon trails is strictly verboten.

Rainbow Rim Trail This 18-mile single track outside North Rim weaves through forest with side-canyon viewpoints along the way. (p157)

Sedona Slickrock and single track amid red-rock monuments, fins and spires. (p112)

Greenway Trail Multiuse paved trail is a fantastic, easy and relaxing way to enjoy South Rim overlooks. (p239)

Flagstaff There's great high-elevation mountain biking in Flagstaff; check out woodsy Mt Elden for a start. (p99)

Bootleg Canyon Single-track course in bone-dry surrounds, particularly popular for its black-diamond descents. (p121)

Hermit Road Some of the South Rim's most memorable overlooks dot this 7-mile road. (p227)

Wildlife

North Kaibab National Forest Deer and buffalo frequent the meadows between Jacob Lake and the North Rim. (p93)

Best Friends Animal Sanctuary An animal rescue that focuses on cats and dogs but also nurtures birds, bunnies and other critters. (p160)

South Kaibab Trailhead It's not unusual to see elk loping along the rim here, helping themselves to gulps from the water-bottle filling station. (p62)

Marble Canyon Though you can spot the California condor from the canyon rim (particularly around Grand Canyon Village), pause to look for them at Navajo Bridge on the drive from rim to rim. (p170)

Bearizona Not exactly wildlife, but a chance to see native North American animals in a quasi free-range setting. (p95)

Historic Hotels & Intimate Inns

Grand Canyon Lodge Historic North Rim lodge with magnificent public spaces and cabin accommodations. (p227)

Hotel Monte Vista (p105), Flagstaff

El Tovar Grande Dame of national-park lodges. (p227)

Bright Angel Lodge Stick to rimside cabins if you're looking for historic charm. (p228)

El Portal Friendly, gracious, handsome and dog-friendly Sedona favorite. (p116)

Briar Patch Inn Acres of grass and shade in low-key compound on Oak Creek. (p116)

Hotel Monte Vista Quirky downtown Flagstaff landmark with iconic neon sign and eclectic rooms. (p105)

Lodge on Route 66 Beautifully restored Route 66 adobe-style drive-up motel in Williams. (p97)

Food

Though the park itself is not known for its food, the Grand Canyon is surrounded by go-to hot spots for creative dining with a commitment to organic and local produce.

Sedona Of the city's many foodie delights, Elote Cafe shines as a regional jewel for fresh and tasty Mexican. (p112)

Flagstaff Offers a plethora of excellent coffee shops, markets, cafes and upscale eateries in historic downtown. (p99)

Rocking V Cafe An oasis of low-key fine dining in tiny Kanab. (p164)

Indian Gardens Cafe & Market Boho gathering spot for outdoor types flocking to Oak Creek Canyon. (p117)

Las Vegas Buffet extravaganzas, elaborate high-end splurges and celebrity chefs. (p122)

Month by Month

TOP EVENTS

Grand Canyon Star Party, June

Flagstaff Fourth, July

Grand Canyon Music Festival, September

Grand Canyon Celebration of Art, September

Flagstaff Festival of Science, September

February

According to some, this is the best time of year to visit – an empty South Rim (North Rim is still closed for winter), with snow often frosting the canyon features.

Sedona International Film Festival

Founded in 1994, this international film festival (www.sedonafilmfestival.org) is hosted by Sedona, whose red-rock backdrop has starred in numerous films. Takes place from late February to early March.

June

Summer is in full swing, with temperatures rising, day-tripping crowds flocking to the South Rim, and lodges and campgrounds on both rims filling to capacity.

Grand Canyon Star Party

Annual Star Parties (www.nps.gov/grca/planyourvisit/grand-canyon-star-party.htm) illuminate the week following summer solstice. Organized by local astronomy clubs, the North Rim Star Party is hosted on the Grand Canyon Lodge veranda; on the South Rim find the party at the Grand Canyon Visitor Center.

Hullabaloo

Billed as a 'celebration of all things Flagstaff,' this quirky community and family-friendly festival (www.flaghullabaloo.com) includes a street fair with local vendors, regional microbrew booths, music, a crazy-costume contest and circus performers. Held early June.

July

One of the best months to visit the North Rim. Be cautious hiking slot canyons during this time and through August, as monsoons bring flash floods. Searing inner-canyon temps and lightning storms demand extra caution.

Flagstaff Fourth

Marking both the Fourth of July and the founding of Flagstaff, festivities include a parade, concerts, rodeo and fireworks (www.flagstaffarizona.org/fourth/).

Hopi Festival of Arts & Culture

At Flagstaff's Museum of Northern Arizona, this well-established celebration of Hopi art, dance and food has been running since the 1930s. Arts and cultural demonstrations include storytelling and basket weaving. (p101)

August

Summer temperatures are still at their peak, as are South Rim crowds, both of which are bearable if you have a game plan. Or head to the North Rim for less of both.

Navajo Festival of Arts & Culture

American Indian cultural festival at the Museum of Northern Arizona in Flagstaff, this early-August event features weaving demonstrations, dancing and a juried art show. (p101)

Heritage Days

During early and mid-August, this North Rim festival (www.nps.gov/grca) celebrates several local American Indian tribes with cultural and historical ties to the Grand Canyon; events showcase their music, art and food.

Western Legends Roundup

Tiny Kanab, known as Little Hollywood for its film-making heydays, hosts all things cowboy and silver-screen Westerns, with cowboy poetry and wagon trains (www.westernlegendsroundup.com).

September

September softens the harshness of the desert; autumn brings brilliant colors and a respite from the oppressive heat and the crush of crowds.

Grand Canyon Music Festival

Chamber music, American Indian flutes and other tunes enhance the aural dimensions of the South Rim in late August and early September (www.grandcanyonmusicfest.org).

Grand Canyon Celebration of Art

Plein air painters do their thing at the South Rim as they engage with visitors. Though the events organized by the Grand Canyon Association happen in September, the art exhibition extends through January. (p231)

Flagstaff Festival of Science

Showcasing and celebrating science research in and around Flagstaff, this 10-day festival (www.scifest.org) features guided hikes, star parties and archaeological field trips, with opportunities for children to join scientists in labs, observatories and in the field.

Fall Color

From now through mid-October, brilliant yellows, reds and oranges transform the landscape, and it's a perfect time for hiking, cycling and scenic drives. Best spots for autumn splendor are the North Rim, Flagstaff and Sedona's Oak Creek Canyon.

October

Though North Rim services close mid-month, the earlier half of October is a fantastic time to visit. The days remain warm and sunny, but by the end of the month it's not unusual to see snow.

Celebraciones de la Gente

Held at the same time of year as Día de los Muertos (Day of the Dead), this late-October festival at the Museum of Northern Arizona in Flagstaff celebrates Mexican cultural traditions. (p42)

Sedona Plein Air Festival

Open-air painters from all over the country and the world are invited to visit Sedona's spectacular natural setting in late October to paint and show off their works. A week-long celebration (www.sedonapleinairfestival.com) with paint-offs, art sales, and wine and food events.

Sedona Arts Festival

This arts fest (www.sedonaartsfestival.org), held in the high school in early October, showcases more than 100 artists from around the country and includes cuisine and entertainment.

December

Grand Canyon might not be the first place you associate with the holidays, but the region's elevation makes it a winter wonderland. The South Rim and surrounds feel festive but relaxed.

Festival of Lights

Thousands of luminaria light up Tlaquepaque in Sedona in mid-December, accompanied by hot cider, a visit from Santa and other holiday festivities (www.tlaq.com). Live music is a Sedona-style mix: from traditional carolers to wandering mariachis.

Polar Express

In Williams, the Grand Canyon Railway makes its magical trips to the 'North Pole.' Kids sip hot cocoa, nibble cookies, hear stories and best of all: meet Santa. Reserve very early; Polar Express trains begin running in November and continue into January. (p238)

Itineraries

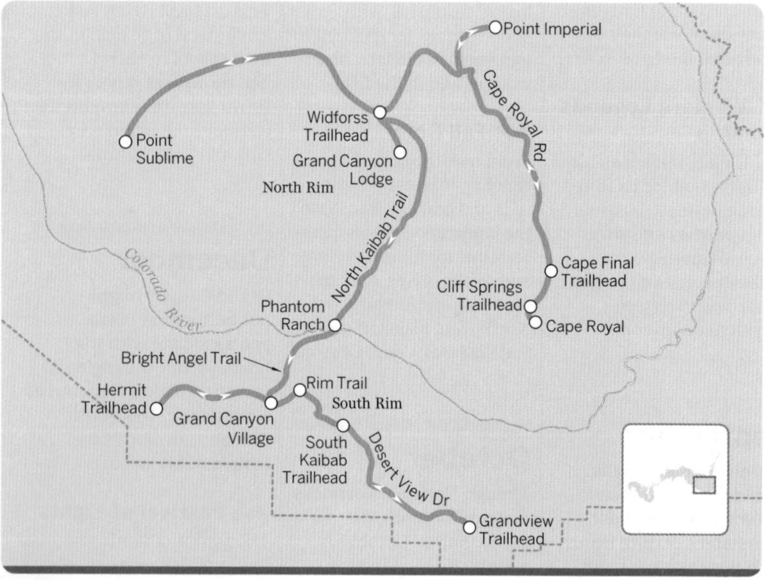

Rim to Rim

Grand Canyon National Park includes three distinct tourist regions (South Rim, North Rim and Below the Rim), each with its own personality and perspective. This leisurely rim-to-rim expedition covers all three, offering travelers the breadth of the park's sights and activities. Accommodation at Phantom Ranch, on the canyon floor, is available by lottery 15 months in advance of arrival.

Begin with several nights in a Western Cabin at **Grand Canyon Lodge**, on the bucolic and intimate North Rim. Drive to **Point Sublime**, **Point Imperial** and **Cape Royal**, hike the **Widforss Trail**, **Cape Final Trail** and **Cliff Springs Trail**, attend a ranger talk and stargaze on evening strolls. Relax with a glass of wine on the lodge's rim-side veranda, and eat dinner in its spectacular rim-side restaurant. Hike 14 miles down the **North Kaibab Trail**, spend a couple of nights by the river at **Phantom Ranch**, and start at dawn for the 10-mile haul up the **Bright Angel Trail** to the South Rim. Reward yourself with a hearty dinner at **El Tovar**, and spend four or five nights taking in South Rim hikes, overlooks, museums and historic buildings. Walk the **Rim Trail**, take a bus tour of **Desert View Drive**, and day-hike the **Hermit Trail**, **South Kaibab Trail** and **Grandview Trail** before catching a shuttle back to the North Rim.

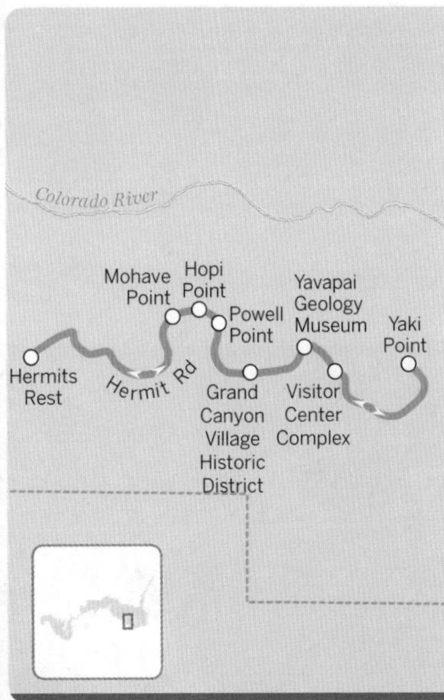

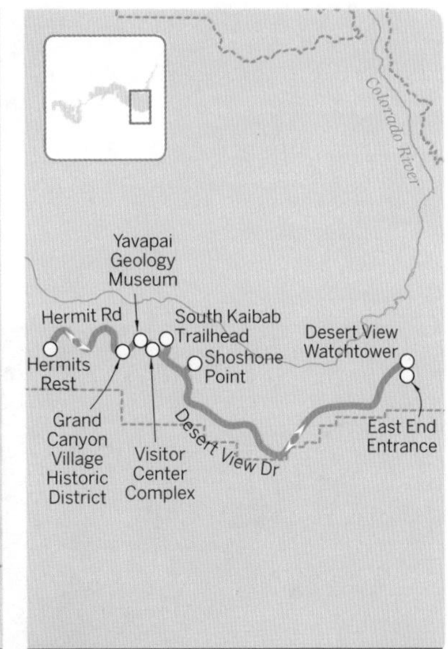

South Rim in an Afternoon

A full half-day includes lunch at an historic lodge, a rimside stroll and a quiet sunset.

Start with views, museums and historic buildings in **Grand Canyon Village Historic District**. Admire the classic park architecture of **El Tovar** over lunch in the dining room, check out American Indian art at **Hopi House** and stroll west along the Rim Trail. Stop at the History Room in Bright Angel Lodge, the Lookout Studio and Kolb Studio before descending far enough down the Bright Angel Trail to marvel at the canyon's scale from the first tunnel, below the rim.

Catch a Hermit Rd shuttle to **Powell Point**, walk the rim to **Hopi Point** and **Mohave Point**, hop a shuttle to **Hermits Rest** and sit quietly in the picnic area with a snack before heading back to the village. Then stroll east along the rim, pausing at the installations along the Trail of Time and visiting the **Yavapai Geology Museum**, then hop a shuttle to the **Visitor Center Complex**. Grab a sandwich to go at Bright Angel Bicycles & Cafe, hop on a shuttle to **Yaki Point**, wander away from the parking lot and find a spot from which to enjoy the evening light or sunset.

South Rim in a Day

In one full day, you can take in the highlights of the South Rim, including museums, hikes, overlooks and a ranger talk.

Arrive at the park before breakfast – park at **Grand Canyon Visitor Center Complex**, grab a breakfast burrito and a snack for your pack at Bright Angel Bicycles and catch a shuttle to the head of the South Kaibab Trail for a 1.5 mile hike down the **South Kaibab** to Cedar Ridge. Remember to bring plenty of water. Shuttle to **Yavapai Geology Museum,** and walk west along the Rim Trail through the Trail of Time. Relax over lunch at **El Tovar** and pop into museums in **Grand Canyon Village Historic District**. Fill up your water bottles, and take an afternoon stroll along the Rim Trail to overlooks along Hermit Rd, hopping on the shuttle whenever you get tired. At **Hermits Rest**, pause for a moment to relax in the silence of the Hermit Trail before taking a shuttle back to the village to connect with a village shuttle to your car. Take Desert View Drive east to exit the park at the **East End Entrance**, stopping at scenic overlooks including **Shoshone Point** and **Desert View Watchtower**.

DANIELA CONSTANTINESCU/SHUTTERSTOCK ©

Above: Views from Yaki Point (p79)

Left: Mather Point (p81)

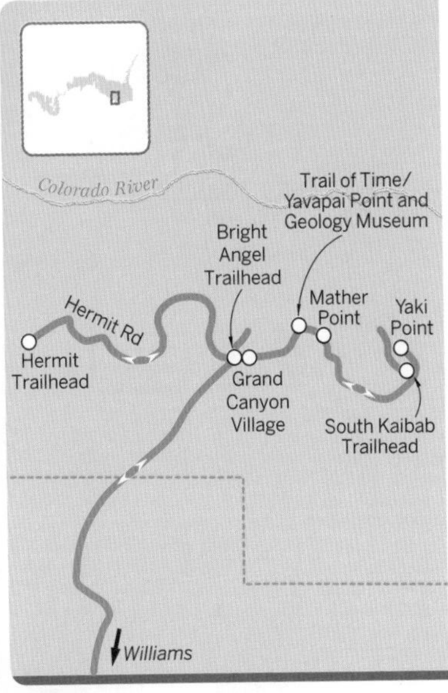

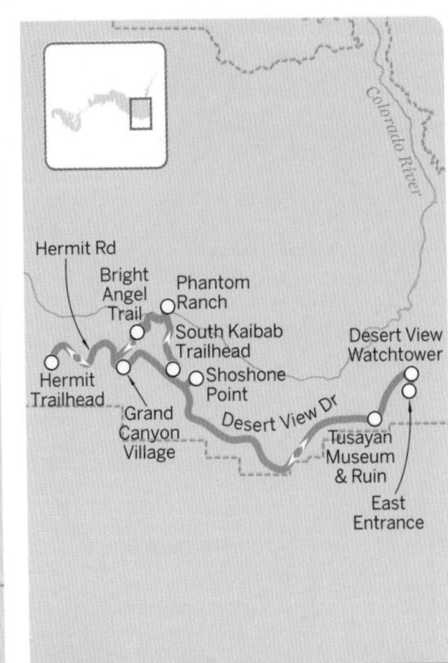

South Rim in Three Days

Three days without a car allows a leisurely pace.

Catch the Wild West shoot-out and board the **Grand Canyon Railway** train in Williams. Upon arrival at **Grand Canyon Village**, check into a cozy Bright Angel Lodge cabin or a room at El Tovar, both just steps from the canyon edge. Meander through the village, stopping at historic buildings and museums, stroll the **Trail of Time** to **Yavapai Point and Geology Museum**, continue on the Rim Trail to **Mather Point**. Rent a bike and ride along the rim to the trailhead of the **South Kaibab Trail** and **Yaki Point**, and enjoy dinner at **El Tovar**.

The next day, wake up early and head down **Bright Angel Trail**. Hike and shuttle overlook-to-overlook along Hermit Rd, descend into the canyon just a bit on the **Hermit Trail** and shuttle back to the village. Sip a cocktail as you wait for a table at the **Arizona Room**, and attend an evening ranger talk. On your final day, hike the South Kaibab Trail to **Cedar Ridge** for a picnic lunch, and catch the 3:30pm train back to Williams.

South Rim in One Week

This trip requires a car and advanced planning for overnight mule trips and accommodation at Phantom Ranch.

Enter Grand Canyon at the **East Entrance**, climb the spiral staircase for spectacular views at **Desert View Watchtower**, and explore overlooks along **Desert View Dr**. Learn about the canyon's human history at **Tusayan Museum & Ruin**, before picnicking at **Shoshone Point**. Spend a few nights at a Grand Canyon Village lodge or campground to enjoy South Rim attractions and activities. Check out Mary Colter architecture and museums in **Grand Canyon Village Historic District**, walk the Rim Trail to the **South Kaibab Trailhead**, and attend a few ranger walks and evening programs.

Catch the pre-dawn Hikers' Express Shuttle to the South Kaibab Trailhead, and hike (or take a mule ride) down the **South Kaibab** to **Phantom Ranch**; spend a night or two, and then hike out on **Bright Angel**. If you have camping gear, you can camp at Bright Angel Campground. On your last full day, walk or bike to overlooks along **Hermit Rd** and **Hermit Trail**, and catch a sunset from the canyon edge.

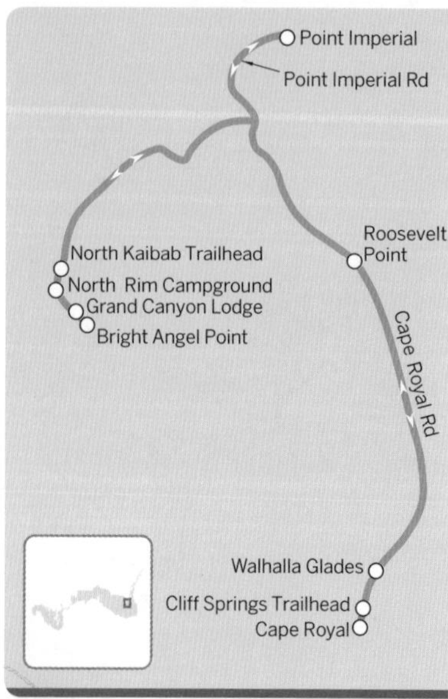

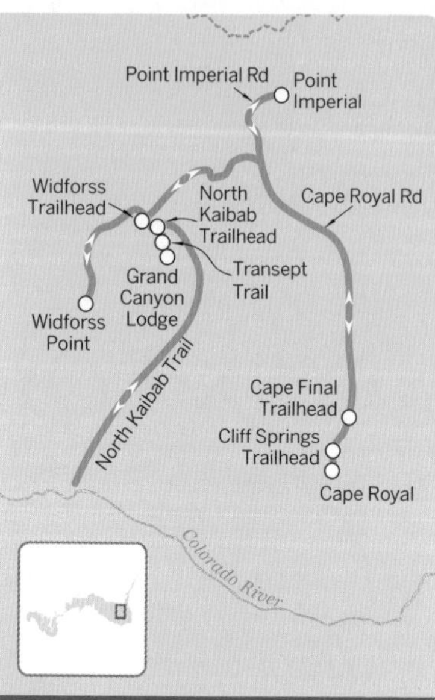

1 DAY North Rim in a Day

For a day at the North Rim, you'll want to spend two nights at **Grand Canyon Lodge** or the **North Rim Campground**.

Wake up with the sun and hike (or ride a mule) into the canyon on the **North Kaibab Trail.** Pause at Coconino Overlook and relax at Redwall Bridge, 2.6 miles from the rim, before tackling the haul back out of the canyon in time for lunch. Take your tray from Deli in the Pines to the lodge's sun porch and kick back in the Adirondack chairs, soaking in the view. Once you've refueled, head out to Cape Royal Rd. Pull over for a rim-side stroll at **Roosevelt Point** and a scramble to **Cliff Springs Trail**; on the way check out ancient Puebloan ruins at **Walhalla Glades** and, at the road's end, walk out to Angel's Window and **Cape Royal**. On the drive back, detour a few miles to **Point Imperial** before returning to the lodge. Grab a beer from the Rough Rider Saloon, amble out to **Bright Angel Point** and watch the sun set over the canyon. After dinner at the lodge, take in an evening ranger talk and collapse into bed.

4 DAYS North Rim in Four Days

Grand Canyon's North Rim transports even the most wearied spirits from harried lives of emails and deadlines into a slower time. With four days you can settle into a slow-paced groove that returns folks to the real world feeling just a little bit less weary and a little more inspired.

On the North Rim, it's easy to find a quiet place to be alone with the canyon. Plan ahead for a Western Cabin at **Grand Canyon Lodge**. Enjoy one day taking in sights along Cape Royal Rd to **Cape Royal** and driving to **Point Imperial**; another hiking through meadow and woods along **Widforss Trail** to **Widforss Point**; a third day hiking or riding a mule down the **North Kaibab Trail;** and a fourth hiking **Cliff Springs** and **Cape Final** trails. Spend an evening walking the **Transept Trail**, perhaps catching the sunset over the side canyon; have a dinner or two in the lodge. Pepper in ranger talks on stargazing and condors, long stretches reading on the lodge's rim-side sun porch and picnic lunches among the aspen, and you'll have experienced some of the best the Grand Canyon has to offer.

Campers beside the Colorado River (p174)

Plan Your Trip

Activities

Technically, it only takes a second to 'see' the Grand Canyon, but you'll definitely want to 'experience' it. Whether it's a South Rim stroll, a mule ride, an inner-canyon hike, or catching a ranger talk, the canyon gives back in proportion to the time you invest in it.

Hike Classifications

The park service classifies canyon terrain and trails into the following specific zones:

Corridor Zone

Grand Canyon's corridor trails refer to the South Rim's South Kaibab and Bright Angel Trails, and the North Rim's North Kaibab Trail. Heavily trafficked and well marked, sometimes with water available, these are the only inner-canyon trails that are maintained and regularly patrolled by National Park Service personnel.

Threshold Zone

More rugged, less-traveled trails, with little or no water, and few if any facilities. Recommended for experienced hikers.

Primitive Zone

Little-used, unmaintained paths requiring route finding. These areas are for very experienced canyon hikers looking to take it to the next level.

Wild Zone

Only expert Grand Canyon explorers who know what they're doing should venture out here. Don't expect to find trails. Or water. Not recommended during summer months.

Hiking

The best way to truly experience the Grand Canyon is to take a hike. If you think the view from the rim is exhilarating, wait until you see how it looks while standing on top of the Redwall, or when you become one of those tiny specks walking the Tonto Trail. Hikes range from wheelchair-accessible paved paths to primitive, unmaintained treks that will challenge backcountry experts; all open up new windows into this complex landscape.

Even a short stroll along the edge gives you a better perspective on the canyon as you notice a tiny flower clinging to a cliff, or find a 450-million-year-old fossil embedded in the rocks. Relatively flat trails on the North Rim amble through meadows and pine forests to secluded chasm peeks, while the South Rim's Rim Trail provides great views for little challenge.

We're told that just 1% of park visitors stray below the rim. To be fair, descending into the canyon is like no hiking on earth. Routes invariably involve precipitous declines of switchback after switchback, rocky terrain, and sharp drops from the trail edge. But the opportunities for solitude, exploration and adventure are unparalleled, and not to be missed.

Unique Environment

Hiking in the Grand Canyon is extremely rewarding and should be on everyone's list, but know what to expect before you go. Hiking here is like nothing you've done before: the sheer terrain is uniquely challenging, made even more so by the extreme environment and variable climate. The relentless sunshine saps the water from your body making dehydration a constant danger. Rainstorms on distant hillsides can send flash floods down quiet, sunny side canyons.

And then there's the effects of altitude and massive elevation changes you can't quite comprehend until you experience them. Most inner-canyon trails begin with sharp descents, which translate into equally steep ascents at the end of a hike – when you're most exhausted. Even professional athletes hiking into the canyon for the first time suffer burning muscles, aching knees and numb feet on a scale they've never felt before.

Many hikers beat the heat by planning winter trips, and while the crisp blue skies and snow dusted temples are spectacular, the colder season comes with its own set of challenges. Shaded trails are often perilously icy, requiring crampons (available throughout the South Rim) to minimize your chances of ice-skating off a cliff. Weather can change rapidly – we've started trips at the river in shorts only to reach the top in 2ft of snow – so pack accordingly.

All of these challenges can be met it you prepare properly and hike smart. Honestly assess – and respect – your limitations and the terrain, and select hikes that best match your ability.

A hiker surveys the canyon

Difficulty Level

From first timers to veteran hikers, everyone will find suitable trails within the park. Most routes are out-and-backs (meaning you retrace your steps), making it easy to tailor a hike to your abilities. Rangers cite average hiking speed as 2mph going down and 1mph climbing up; no matter how fast you hike, plan on twice as long for the uphill.

Generally, hikes are organized into four difficulty levels, but note that a single trail can have several ratings, depending on which segment you plan to hike.

Easy Even, possibly paved, terrain, with little elevation gain or loss.

Moderate Some elevation change (500ft to 1000ft) and longer or more exposed than those rated 'easy.' Generally fine for most ability levels.

Difficult Significant elevation change and longer mileage. Requires more hiking experience.

Very Difficult Tough hikes, involving the greatest exposure and mileage, as well as substantial elevation change (2500ft to 4000ft). Suitable for the fittest, most experienced hikers only.

Day Hikes

The easy hikes in the Grand Canyon are limited to a handful of those above the rim, many of which are short strolls out to viewpoints, or longer relatively flat trails.

The South Rim's Rim Trail (p227) hugs the canyon edge for much of its 13 miles, connecting tourist hubs of museums, restaurants and hotels with isolated post-card-perfect overlooks you can't access by vehicle. Explore any of the pleasantly approachable forest trails on the North Rim for mellow walks in the woods, but we're particularly fond of the Widforss Trail (p138), which leads to one of our favorite picnic spots.

Alternatively, many hikers choose to tackle short segments of more challenging trails that descend into the canyon – an excellent choice, if done responsibly. Perennial favorites include the well-maintained corridor trails: Bright Angel (p227), South Kaibab (p62) and North Kaibab (p227). Though they may feel like superhighways in summer, plan on hiking at least one of these magnificent trails – if only for a short distance. Consider the Hermit Trail (p63) to the cool alcove of Dripping Springs for a more intimate inner-canyon day hike on the South Rim.

Overnight Hikes

Until you've fallen asleep to a froggy serenade along Bright Angel Creek, or watched the sunrise from the Tonto platform, you have not truly experienced the Grand Canyon. Provided you plan an appropriate route and itinerary that is within the capabilities of every member of your group, and you take your time, anyone with basic camping and hiking savvy can experience the majesty of the inner gorge.

Before setting out on any overnight hikes check trail conditions, the weather forecast and water availability at the **Backcountry Information Center** (☎928-638-7875; www.nps.gov/grca; Grand Canyon National Park, PO Box 129, Grand Canyon, AZ 86023; ⏲8-5pm daily, seasonal variation) on the North or South Rim.

Permit Information

Overnight backpacking at Grand Canyon National Park requires a permit from the Backcountry Information Center. The sole exceptions are hikers or mule riders with reservations at Phantom Ranch (the park's only non-camping accommodations below the rim).

The park limits camping to protect resources and maintain unparalleled opportunities for solitude, and demand often far exceeds available slots. If you're caught camping in the backcountry without a permit, expect a hefty fine and possible court appearance.

➡ Applications are accepted in person or by mail or fax beginning on the 20th of the fifth month prior to the planned trip; for instance, if you'd like to hike the Bright Angel in June, you can – and should – apply as early as January 20.

➡ Permits cost a flat $10, plus $8 per person per night; the nonrefundable fee is payable by check or credit card.

➡ Go to www.nps.gov/grca/planyourvisit/backcountry-permit.htm for the downloadable backcountry-permit application, and detailed instructions; allow three weeks for the permit to be mailed to you.

➡ Permits are valid only for trip leader, itinerary, number of people and dates specified on the permit.

➡ Once a permit is granted, itinerary changes are not allowed, except for emergencies.

➡ Increase your chances of securing a spot by listing alternative dates and routes in your application.

A small number of last-minute permits are held for corridor campgrounds (Indian Garden, Bright Angel and Cottonwood) for same- or next-day departures. Apply in person at the Backcountry Information Center on either rim. If nothing is available you may be placed on a waiting list which requires showing up at 8am every day to maintain your position. Waits can take up to a week (with longer times on the South Rim).

Rim to River

Several trails lead from the rim to the Colorado River, but hikers new to the area should focus on the well-maintained and well-traveled Kaibab and Bright Angel Trails. The South Kaibab (p62) and Bright Angel (p227) descend from the South

COOL TRAILS FOR A HOT DAY

Looking for a reprieve from the scorching sun? Take on one of the following shade-filled trails. All are on the North Rim, except Shoshone Point, which is on the South Rim.

Shoshone Point (p79) An almost entirely shaded ramble through a patch of South Rim ponderosa pine forest ending at a quiet, secluded overlook.

Cliff Springs Trail (p139) Short and sweet, this trail starts out as a sunny downhill into the canyon interior before dipping beneath overhangs and ends at a misty, fern-fringed oasis.

Transept Trail (p142) Wending along the rim of its namesake canyon, this popular trail connects the North Rim campground to the lodge.

Widforss Trail (p138) One of the longer offerings, this day hike meanders through the forests along the rim to a viewpoint turnaround that's great for a picnic.

Rim, and the North Kaibab (p227) drops in from the North. All three converge on Bright Angel Campground and the air-conditioned Phantom Ranch, 0.3 miles apart on the north side of the canyon just up from the Colorado River.

Combine these routes to create multi-night, inner-canyon backpacking itineraries, or head down by foot (or, from the South Rim only, by mule) in one day, spend a night or two at the ranch or campground, and hike back out from river to rim in one day. From March through September, you'll want to hit the trail early to avoid hiking in dangerous heat. **Do not attempt to hike to the river and back in a single day.**

You'll need to plan in advance for a rim-to-river trek. Secure a backcountry permit (p83) to camp at Bright Angel (p239), Indian Garden (p242) or Cottonwood (p152) Campgrounds and/or a reservation for overnight accommodations at Phantom Ranch (p242). If you want to hike rim-to-rim (down from one rim and back up to the opposite rim), arrange for shuttle transport back to your starting point, or complete an epic rim-to-rim-to-rim by returning the way you came.

Responsible Backcountry Use

To help preserve the ecology and beauty of Grand Canyon National Park, strive to leave absolutely no evidence of your backcountry visit. For more information on low-impact backpacking, learn and live the seven principles of the Leave No Trace ethic at www.lnt.org.

Trash

- Pack out all waste, including food scraps and biodegradable items like orange peels.
- Don't bury trash; not only will it take years to decompose, but it's detrimental to the health of the animals that will likely dig it up.
- Pick up any trash you find left by others who aren't as savvy as you.

Human Waste

- Where there are no toilets, bury solid human waste in a cathole (about 6in deep) at least 200ft from trails, campsites or water sources. In snow, dig down to the soil.
- Pack out your toilet paper in a double ziplock bag; do not burn or bury toilet paper.
- Urinate 200ft from water, preferably on sand or rock.
- When camping along the Colorado River, the sheer volume of water makes urinating in the river an acceptable option. However, this applies to the Colorado only, and not to the creeks flowing into it.

Washing

- Never use soap in a creek or spring; even biodegradable soap requires soil to properly break down.
- Disperse waste water at least 200ft away from any water source, scattering it widely to allow the soil to filter it fully.
- When washing dishes and utensils, try using sand or snow rather than detergent.

Erosion

- The fragile desert soil is prone to erosion. Stay on existing trails and avoid shortcuts.

RIM TO RIVER IN A DAY

Canyon newbies are often tempted to hike from the rim to the river and back in a single day. Don't. This extreme undertaking involves close to 9000ft of elevation change, and no matter how early you start, how many previous miles you've logged, or how many energy bars you eat, it's just a bad idea – and it makes no difference if you're a fit 25-year-old or a 65-year-old trail veteran.

DON'T HORSE AROUND WITH THE MULES

Day hikers on the corridor trails are bound to encounter mules, which always have the right of way. As a mule train approaches, stand quietly on the uphill side of the trail, turn your pack away from the animals, and listen for directions from the guide. Be especially careful if you're hiking with kids – being pushed off the edge of the trail by a mule can have disastrous consequences.

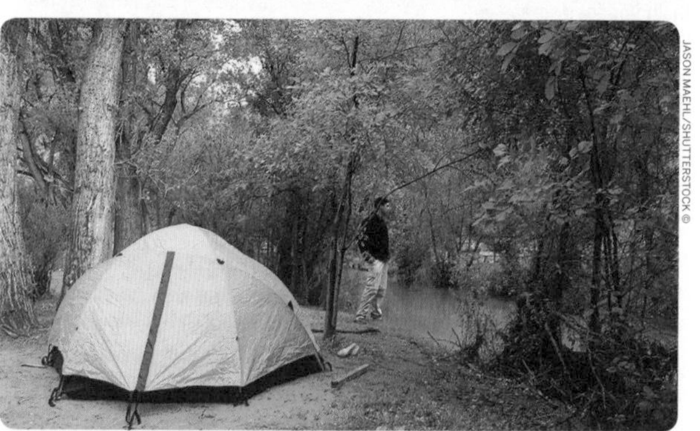

JASON MAEHL/SHUTTERSTOCK ©

Above: Hiking in Grand Canyon National Park

Left: Camping in Havasupai Reservation (p110)

➡ Where a well-used trail passes through a mud patch, walk through the mud so as not to widen the trail.

➡ Do not remove or trample the plant life that keeps topsoils in place.

➡ Never trench around your tent; if rain is forecast, pick a suitable place where water will drain away from you naturally.

Fires & Low-Impact Cooking

➡ Open fires are prohibited in Grand Canyon National Park except at established campgrounds on the rims.

➡ Where fires are allowed, keep them in established fire rings or grills. Never leave fires unattended; extinguish them thoroughly with water.

➡ Collecting dead wood is prohibited; purchase firewood at Canyon Village Marketplace or the North Rim General Store.

➡ Cook on a lightweight kerosene, alcohol or white-gas stove; avoid the waste of disposable butane canisters.

Wildlife Conservation

➡ Discourage nuisance wildlife by packing out all food scraps; watch out for ravens – they're brave, clever and opportunistic.

➡ Keep all food and fragrant items (soap, deodorant, toothpaste etc) sealed away in your pack and hang it from a tree overnight to keep critters at bay.

➡ While dispersed camping, try to camp at least 100ft away from water sources.

Hiking Outfitters & Groups

Descending into the unknown can be intimidating, and first-time hikers might better enjoy the experience with a group and a knowledgeable guide. Catch a free, can't-miss, ranger-led walk or hike on either rim to add new perspective to your visit. For a more intimate experience, join a naturalist-led hike or backpacking trip offered by the highly regarded Grand Canyon Association Field Institute (p234). These reasonably priced trips cater to all skill levels and last from a few hours to several days.

Many local outfitters offer a range of guided hiking excursions in the park, sometimes combining hiking with cycling and rafting. Trips, prices, dates and styles vary widely, so definitely contact a few before making your choice. Make reservations at least five months in advance.

EMERGENCY CONTACT

Cell service below the rim is typically nonexistent. Before departing on an overnight hike into the canyon, be sure to leave your hiking itinerary, backcountry permit number, final destination and date of your return with a contact person who will not be hiking. They should also take note of the Park's Search & Rescue number (928-638-2477) as an emergency resource if you do not return as planned.

Pick up a full list of accredited backcountry guide services at the park's visitor centers or on the National Park Service website (www.nps.gov/grca/planyourvisit/guided-hikes.htm). The following list is just a sampling of outfitters.

Four Season Guides (☎928-525-1552; www.fsguides.com; 506 N Grant St, Suite O, Flagstaff, AZ 86001; 3-day hike South Kaibab to Bright Angel per person $850) Straight outta Flagstaff, this local and professional outfit offers day and multiday hikes catering to a variety of abilities and preferences, including the rim-to-rim hike and Havasu Canyon.

All-Star Grand Canyon Tours (p103) Private and group day and overnight hikes with hotel pick-up in Flagstaff, Las Vegas, Sedona and a handful of towns near the South Rim.

Backroads (☎800-462-2848; www.backroads.com; per person 6 days & 5 nights from $2800, double occupancy) Cycling and hiking tours to both rims, including combination trips to Grand Canyon, Bryce and Zion National Parks.

Just Roughin' It Adventure Co (☎480-857-2477; www.justroughinit.com; 8658 E Shea Blvd, Suite 175, Scottsdale, AZ 85260) Scottsdale, AZ, outfit catering to hikers of all levels looking to challenge themselves.

Pygmy Guides (☎928-707-0215; www.pygmy-guides.com; South Rim day hikes per person incl pickup at Flagstaff, Williams or Tusayan $490 for 2 people) Excellent local outfit guiding everything from day hikes to rim-to-rim hikes.

Wildland Trekking (☎928-379-6383, 800-715-4453; www.wildlandtrekking.com; all-day hikes $135-235, 3-day trips from $990) Regular hiking or backpacking tours guided by experts – or design your own adventure.

Bicycling

Bicycles are only allowed on three trails within the park: the South Rim's paved Greenway Trail and the North Rim's Bridle and Arizona Trails. Bikes are, however, welcome on all roads, paved or unpaved – though know that most are winding and narrow with limited shoulders. Don't count on drivers to be watching where they're going: there's a rather scenic canyon that's quite distracting.

Bicycle and backpacker campsites (closed to vehicles) are available at both North Rim and Mather campgrounds, and South Rim shuttles have two- to three-capacity bicycle racks. You can rent two-wheeled chariots on the South Rim at Bright Angel Bicycles (p239), which also runs cycling tours.

Outside the Park

Just outside the South Rim, great mountain-biking trails in Kaibab National Forest include a 16-mile trail running from the Tusayan Trailhead to the Grandview Lookout Tower. Stop at the Tusayan Ranger Station (p240) for trail maps and directions.

On the North Rim, mountain bikers flock to the 18 miles of smooth singletrack of the Rainbow Rim Trail (p157) in the Kaibab National Forest which contours between five fingers jutting above the Grand Canyon. Pick up a map and information at the Kaibab Plateau Visitor Center (p240) in Jacob Lake.

Also in the forest: hundreds of miles of washboard roads providing endless gravel-grinding opportunities through old-growth ponderosa pines, steep-sided canyons, aspen groves and velvety meadows.

River Rafting

Rafting the Colorado ranks among the top outdoor adventures of a lifetime – not just for the thrill (the water is BIG), but also for the epic scenery and exploration. It's a placid geological journey through time, an adrenaline rush, a jagged desert landscape and lush riparian paradise all rolled into one phenomenal ride.

Most experience the river on a commercial rafting trip between mid-April and September (for motorized boats) or November (for oared vessels). Though the park carefully regulates the number of rafts on the Colorado, during this high season you won't be alone, often sharing hikes and beaches with other trips.

For those on tight schedules, commercial motorized tours can show you half the canyon in four days, or the full thing in seven. This is a bit like watching your favorite movie on fast-forward: you'll get

PREVENT DEADLY DEHYDRATION & HYPONATREMIA

Both dehydration and its related cousin hyponatremia are very real dangers while being active in the Grand Canyon. The first results from not drinking enough water, while the second comes from not eating enough salt. Prevent these life-threatening conditions.

➡ Sip water constantly, drinking 0.5 to 1 quart per hour. Though there are a handful of seasonal water stations in the main corridor, pipelines can break. Bring a backup water-treatment option.

➡ Replenish electrolytes by snacking on salty high-carbohydrate foods even if you're not hungry. Avoid sugar.

➡ Wear a wide-brimmed hat, sunglasses and loose cotton clothing that retains moisture and keeps you cool through the slow evaporation of sweat. Soak your clothes at any water source you pass.

➡ Irritability is a common sign of dehydration. If you find yourself snapping at your fellow travelers over minor issues, drink more.

➡ Avoid activity during the hottest part of the day (10am to 4pm). Hide under a rock overhang or a shady tree. Remember: the deeper you go in the canyon, the hotter it gets.

the general idea, but miss everything that makes it great. The longer you can spend, the better.

A few hundred private rafting excursions are allowed on the river as well; they launch year-round after securing permits (p239) via a lottery. Some people wait decades for the right opportunity.

While there are no day trips through Grand Canyon National Park itself, there are two options outside the park. The Hualapai Reservation offers a white-water day trip that includes bus pickup in Williams, a drive to the canyon bottom, and a helicopter ride back out of the canyon. Several tour operators offer half-day smooth-water trips (p72) between Glen Canyon Dam and Lee's Ferry.

ARIZONA TRAIL

Stretching the length of Arizona from Mexico to Utah, the Arizona Trail covers 800 continuous miles of nonmotorized trail connecting the best of Arizona's diverse landscapes, including Grand Canyon National Park. Sections of the AZ Trail make excellent day hikes, and bicycles are allowed except below the rim – though some through riders strap their bikes to their backs and hike the rim-to-rim portion.

Find more information, maps and current news on the trail at www.aztrail.org.

Mule Rides

Mule trains have been making their way down Bright Angel and other trails into the canyon for over a century, carrying delighted tourists and ferrying supplies in and out of the canyon. Traveling the trails on the backs of these mellow, sure-footed creatures is an iconic tradition that makes for a memorable – if dusty – trip.

But don't plan a mule trip assuming it's the easiest way to travel below the rim. It's a bumpy adventure on a hard saddle, and unless you regularly ride a horse, you will be saddle-sore afterwards. Those scared of heights or big animals – gentle and cute though they may be – are best off exploring the canyon by other means.

South Rim trips (p71) include half-day above-rim rides, and the epic overnight descent to Phantom Ranch. North Rim (p150) mules also offer short forest rides, and three-hour trips down the North Kaibab Trail to Supai Tunnel. At the Havasupai Reservation, four hours from the South Rim, you can arrange in advance for either a personal or gear-only mule down to Supai Village or Havasu Falls Campground.

Depending on the trip, riders must be at least 4ft 7in tall, speak good English and weigh no more than 200lb.

Mule-Ride Reservations

South Rim Reservation requests for rides to Phantom Ranch are assigned by lottery 15 months before the stay date; spaces unfilled by lottery are available by phone 13 months in advance. Contact Grand Canyon Mule Rides (p227). Wait-list available.

North Rim North Rim mule trips, offered through Canyon Trail Rides (p151), can often be booked at the mule desk in the Grand Canyon Lodge the day before.

Havasu Falls Reserve up to one week in advance of arrival with the **Havasupai Tourism Office** (☎928-448-2180).

Horseback Riding

Horseback riding is offered outside the park. Near the North Rim, try Allen's Outfitters (p161) in Kanab. Just outside the South Rim, near Tusayan, Apache Stables (p93) offers group rides along the piney trails of the Kaibab and campfire rides (BYO hot dogs and s'mores).

Rock Climbing

Rock climbing is allowed anywhere in the Grand Canyon – except above established trails (for obvious reasons) – but while Arizona is rife with climbing areas, scaling the canyon is not popular. That being said, almost any boulder or wall is begging to be scaled, just beware of loose, dirty and chalky rock.

Most climbers tend to target the canyon's remote temples (spires carved by

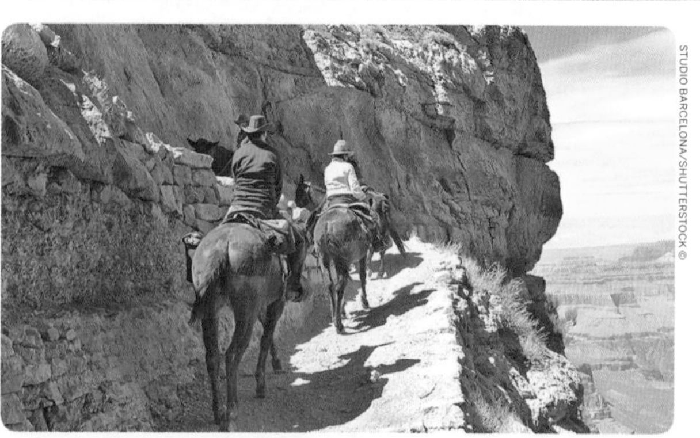

STUDIO BARCELONA/SHUTTERSTOCK ©

Above: Rafting in the Grand Canyon

Left: Mule ride ascending the Grand Canyon

converging side canyons) which can involve multiday approaches and creative route-finding. Mountaineers who plan to hike in and camp will need a backcountry permit (p83). Bolting is not allowed inside the park.

Stop by Flagstaff Climbing (p103) in Flagstaff for info on climbing throughout the region. Stewart M Green's *Rock Climbing Arizona* (Falcon, 1999) is a comprehensive guide to prime Arizona crags and includes topographical maps and detailed route information.

Cross-Country Skiing & Snowshoeing

Schussing from one frosty overlook to the next certainly sounds idyllic, but to pull it off requires creativity, self-sufficiency and good timing.

North Rim

The North Rim definitely gets the snow (around 150in annually) opening up miles of snow-covered forest roads and a patchwork of wide meadows for those willing to make the trek. There are no designated trails, but you can go virtually anywhere.

However, the big caveat is that the road from Jacob Lake to the canyon rim closes at the first snowfall, making it a 44-mile multiday ski or snowshoe trek just to get to the North Rim. Those who tackle this route often then hike rim to rim, as that can be easier than skiing back.

Camping anywhere on the North Rim in the winter season requires permits available from the Backcountry Information Center (p34).

South Rim

South Rim snows are unpredictable and fleeting. There are no groomed routes, but park residents sometimes break trails to favorite viewpoints.

You can rent skis in Flagstaff, where you'll find groomed cross-country trails at the popular Flagstaff Nordic Center (p103), plenty of ungroomed trails throughout Kaibab and Coconino National Forests, and downhill skiing at Arizona Snowbowl (p103).

Helicopter & Airplane Tours

Over 100,000 flights take almost a million passengers over the canyon each year. And while the noise pollution likely bothers wildlife and definitely annoys hikers seeking solitude below, for some visitors the overflight experience defines their Grand Canyon vision.

Flights over the national park are limited to certain times of day, must follow narrow, predefined paths, and are not allowed to fly below the rim – so don't expect to be zooming between cliffs performing Hollywood-style acrobatics.

Hualapai tribal land on the West Rim (p118), however, does not have these restrictions. As a result, the constant traffic – around 400 flights a day – makes the place feel like a war zone. One helicopter every five minutes touches down by the river. If you're interested in a mellow and scenic flight, you're better off avoiding this mayhem.

Contact companies for routes and rates, as each offers several options, but note that their prices are fairly competitive; airplane rides tend to cost less than helicopter trips and cover more distance. For a 45-minute scenic airplane tour departing from the South Rim, expect to pay about

OVER THE EDGE: DEATH IN GRAND CANYON

Before heading to the park, it's worth reading some or all of Michel Ghiglieri and Thomas Myers' gripping *Over the Edge: Death in Grand Canyon*. Each chapter is dedicated to various ways in which people have died in the canyon, offering detailed stories from the park's early history to today. It's morbidly fascinating, and a stark reminder this place isn't an amusement park, but nature at its most raw and consequential.

On average, 12 people die every year in Grand Canyon. Even in the park's most developed areas a moment of foolhardiness born from the illusion of safety can lead to tragic consequences.

$150; for a similar itinerary in a helicopter, it'll be closer to $300. Flights from the West Rim cost a bit less. If you're dead set on a ride, insist that your aircraft uses Quiet Technology, something the NPS has tried to encourage, but does not yet require.

Most air tours operate out of airports in Tusayan, Las Vegas, Phoenix, Sedona, Page and the Hualapai Reservation (West Rim). Pop in to the **National Geographic Visitor Center & IMAX Theater** (☎928-638-2468; www.explorethecanyon.com; 450 Hwy 64, Tusayan; ⏰8am-10pm Mar-Oct, 10am-8pm Nov-Feb) in Tusayan on the South Rim to arrange last-minute reservations.

Guided Tours

It can be hard to wrap your brain around the size, ecological diversity and history of the Grand Canyon. Having someone point out overlooked features and help spot elusive wildlife can add an invaluable layer to your visit. Tour operators offer everything from narrated bus drives to hikes to bicycle rides. Among the best organized tours are those offered as classes through Grand Canyon Field Institute (p234) and **Museum of Northern Arizona** (Map p100; ☎928-774-5211; www.musnaz.org; 3101 N Fort Valley Rd, Flagstaff, AZ 86001).

Dozens of companies offer a wide variety of options for one- and multiday tours from nearby cities, primarily departing from Las Vegas, Flagstaff and Sedona as well as from further afield (Los Angeles and San Francisco, for example). Some stay above t rim, while others descend into the canyon Options include bus, hiking, mule, rafting cycling and scenic aerial tours; themed tr include yoga, photography, geology and history.

From Flagstaff, Williams & Tusayan

Most tour operators operating out of Flag-staff will also pick people up in Williams – and vice versa. Tusayan is on the way fro both, so you're likely good to go if they hav room, even if they don't explicitly list Tusa as a pickup point.

From Las Vegas

Air packages are a popular way to do day tours of the canyon from Las Vegas, but be sure to check the itinerary very closely. Ma of them are trips to the West Rim (p118), o the Hualapai Reservation and not part of Grand Canyon National Park; there are no sights beyond the handful of overlooks, it i very busy with bus and helicopter tours an because it sits several thousand feet lower than either rim, views are less grand. Don' expect much in the way of charm or chara-ter from tours starting in the big city.

From Kanab

Tour options from Kanab are limited, and tend to only hit the North Rim. If you're interested in South Rim tours, head to Flag staff or Tusayan first.

Plan Your Trip

Travel with Children

From lazy days fossil-hunting along rocky trails to white-water adventures down the Colorado, the iconic family road trip to the Grand Canyon makes for memories that imprint not only into photos but into the spirit. All it takes is a little planning, and a lot of patience and flexibility.

Best Activities for Kids

Ranger Programs

Stargazing talks around the fire, activity books and kid-friendly lectures.

Rafting

White-water trips through the canyon, perfect for older kids and teens, and calm-water floats along the Colorado River from Glen Canyon Dam to Lees Ferry for children four and older.

Hiking

Scrambles through desert scrub, rambles through aspen and meadows, and overnight expeditions down to the Colorado River; Grand Canyon offers plenty of fantastic hiking opportunities for young children and teenagers alike.

Mule Rides

Overnight treks to the canyon bottom are offered from the South Rim; half-day rides from the North Rim give a taste of the canyon interior and follow a less precipitous trail. Children must be aged nine or over for all South Rim trips and 10/seven or over for North Rim rides below/above the rim.

Grand Canyon for Kids

Long drives, precarious canyon overlooks, crowded shuttles and stifling summer heat can be a challenge. The rewards, however, rest in the most mundane of activities – a sunset picnic at Cape Royal, a bicycle ride along the rimside Greenway Trail, hot chocolate under the stars, snuggling into an Adirondeck chair on the patio of the North Rim's Grand Canyon Lodge. And the canyon's geology, human history and wildlife, accessible in concrete ways at every turn, make the park the world's largest classroom – kids learn without even trying.

While the South Rim has more sights, inner-canyon trails, museums and a broader variety of ranger-led interpretive programs designed for children, the chaos and crowds can be intimidating and exhausting. The intimacy of the North Rim attracts families looking for a quieter vacation.

Ranger Programs

In the **Junior Ranger Program**, geared toward children aged four to 14, children pick up an activity book from the visitor center on either rim, complete three pages and attend a ranger program. Upon completion, a ranger solemnly swears them in as junior rangers and the child receives a certificate and a badge. While the whole thing sounds rather hokey, a leisurely afternoon completing the project just might be the highlight of your six-year-old's visit.

Download a seasonal schedule of ranger programs on the park's website (www.nps.gov/grca/learn/kidsyouth/beajuniorranger.htm). National monuments surrounding the park offer Junior Ranger and kid-friendly ranger programs as well.

Hiking

Both rims offer opportunities for kids to get dirty and dusty on the trails, but each offers a distinct experience.

With miles of rimside rambles and several opportunities to descend into the canyon, hiking on the South Rim is particularly suited for older kids. The constant danger of the rim and rocky interior precipices can be nerve-wracking for parents of little ones; Rim Trail stretches of the Greenway Trail (p239) make a lovely bicycle ride.

On the quieter North Rim, the grassy meadows, shaded trails and elevation offer relief from the summer sun, and it's almost guaranteed that you'll see mule deer or wild turkeys. Several above-the-rim trails make lovely rambles for all ages, or you can take a day hike (or mule ride) into the canyon on the North Kaibab Trail (p227).

The paved Rim Trail (p227) on the South Rim is suitable for strollers, but if you plan on more extensive hiking, consider a front carrier for infants or a backpack carrier for toddlers. You can rent a jogging stroller at the bike rental in the gas station on the North Rim; at the South Rim, Bright Angel Bicycles (p239) rents bicycles with pull-along trailers, children's bicycles and strollers.

The Grand Canyon Association Field Institute (www.grandcanyon.org) offers excellent small-group family-friendly hikes spanning from an afternoon to multiday, inner-canyon treks. Children should be aged eight or older. Guided by Grand Canyon experts, these trips focus on park ecology, history and geology, among other things; see website for specialized hikes and details.

Children's Highlights

Family Hikes

Rim Trail (South Rim ; p227) Popular path to museums and overlooks, with multiple spots to stretch out with a picnic.

Shoshone Point (South Rim; p79) Easy, wide, wooded dirt road to picnic area and a quiet overlook.

Bright Angel (South Rim; p227) Below-the-rim hike with limited trailside drop-offs.

North Kaibab (North Rim; p227) A 3-mile round-trip descent to Coconino Overlook makes an excellent day hike for older kids.

Widforss Trail (North Rim; p138) Gentle ramble through woods and meadows to the canyon rim.

Cape Final (North Rim; p142) Jutting canyon view rewards a mild hike.

Children 12 & Under

IMAX Grand Canyon, Tusayan (p93) Amazing aerial canyon footage on massive movie screen.

Junior Ranger (p227) Activity books, ranger talks and hands-on fun throughout the park.

Trail of Time (p75) (South Rim) Geologic timeline with rocks excavated from the canyon.

Cape Royal Dr (p151) (North Rim) Picnic at Greenland Lake, stroll out to Cape Royal (p151) Point and visit Ancient Puebloan ruins on this short, scenic drive.

Desert View Watchtower (South Rim; p78) Children love climbing the spiral staircase and taking in the view at this Mary Colter classic on the South Rim.

Grand Canyon Railway (South Rim; p238) Ride the historic rails from Williams to the South Rim.

Tweens & Teens

Raft the Colorado (p38) Float the rapids on a multiday rafting and camping trip through the canyon.

Mule Treks Overnights from the South Rim to Phantom Ranch (p227), half-day trips down the North Kaibab (p151) from the North Rim, and short above-the-rim rides on both the North and the South Rims.

Rim to Rim (p26) Huff it down one side of the canyon and out the other on an overnight hike;

IN THE CAR

You can't avoid long stretches in the car when you're traveling to the Grand Canyon, particularly if you're headed to the isolated North Rim. But with the right frame of mind and some smart packing, here's how you can minimize backseat whining.

➡ Try not to squeeze too much in. Endless hours in the car rushing from overlook to overlook, sight to sight, can result in grumpy, tired kids and frustrated parents. After a while, canyon views start to look alike.

➡ Stop often and stay flexible.

➡ Remember sunshades for the window, and a football, soccer ball or Frisbee – any grassy area or meadow is a potential playing field.

➡ Surprise the kids with a Grand Canyon trip bag filled with canyon books (www.grandcanyon.org), a special treat, a car-friendly toy and game.

➡ Bring a journal, an enlarged Xeroxed map and colored pencils (crayons melt!) for each child. Kids can follow along on their map as you drive, drawing pictures of what they see and do, and record the trip in their journal.

➡ Pack music and audiobooks, or download in advance. Unlike videos and video games, which require staring at a screen, kids can listen to stories or music and still take in the dramatic natural surrounds.

backcountry camping permit or reservations at Phantom Ranch required.

Cycling, South Rim (p239) Rent a bike at Bright Angel Bicycles and cruise to overlooks along Hermit Rd; picnic at Hermits Rest (p75).

Grand Canyon Association Field Institute (p234) Expert guided day and overnight hikes designed especially to be family friendly.

Planning

While any trip should allow plenty of time for serendipitous discoveries, anything more than a day trip requires some advanced planning. If possible, try to come to the park during the fall, after the summer crowds of school-aged children ebb and the gripping desert heat softens, but before that teasing hint of winter becomes a full-fledged snowstorm. It's the best time to be here, but remember, the North Rim closes October 15 (though you can still camp here until snow closes access).

For all-around information and advice, check out Lonely Planet's *Travel With Children*.

Before You Go

It's possible to cruise into the South Rim, check out the museums and hike the trails on a whim, but for the following canyon highlights you'll need to make plans in advanced; for high-season overnight mule rides and Phantom Ranch accommodations, you'll need to plan 15 months ahead!

➡ White-water rafting trips on the Colorado River through the Grand Canyon (www.nps.gov/grca/planyourvisit/river-concessioners.htm).

➡ Family trips with the Grand Canyon Field Institute (www.grandcanyon.org).

➡ Overnight stays at Phantom Ranch, on the canyon bottom (www.grandcanyonlodges.com).

➡ Accommodations at the North Rim's Grand Canyon Lodge (www.grandcanyonlodgenorth.com).

➡ Grand Canyon Railway (www.thetrain.com).

➡ South Rim lodges and overnight mule treks from the South Rim to Phantom Ranch (www.grandcanyonlodges.com).

➡ South Rim pet-friendly lodge (www.visitgrandcanyon.com).

➡ Volunteering at Best Friends Animal Sanctuary outside Kanab, Utah (86 miles north of North Rim) and spending a night with a borrowed cat, dog or pot-bellied pig (www.bestfriends.org).

Accommodations

Reservations for park lodges on either rim are accepted up to 13 months in advance and you can cancel without penalty up to 48 hours in advance. Phantom Ranch (p242) can be reserved by lottery only, and requests must be submitted between the 1st and 25th day of the 15th month prior to desired stay month. Children must be at least six to stay in Phantom Ranch dorm accommodations.

If you travel with lots of gear, you might prefer to stay at the single-story Yavapai West (p227) on the South Rim, as it's the only place on the South Rim where you can park directly outside your door. Bright Angel Lodge (p228) offers two-room cabins, and El Tovar (p227) has several suites. On the North Rim, Grand Canyon Lodge's (p227) Pioneer Cabins sport two rooms and sleep six.

Children under 16 stay free at all Grand Canyon lodgings, using existing bedding, but there is a $10-per-day charge for cribs and cots.

Most accommodations outside the park do not charge extra for children under 12, and many have suites and pools. Bed and breakfasts often do not welcome children. In Flagstaff, Little America Hotel (p106) borders acres of forest, has a grass-surrounded outdoor pool and playground, and offers spacious rooms.

Dining

Even the fanciest restaurants in and around the park welcome families, and both rims offer cafeterias and plenty of picnic spots. There's a full grocery store on the South Rim and a limited general store on the North Rim. Most rooms in the park have refrigerators, but coolers are useful. There's free ice behind the visitor center on the North Rim and you can buy ice on both rims.

SAFETY

It's easy to forget, as you're waiting in line for a shuttle or walking a rim trail with hundreds of other folk, that this is a wilderness. In most areas, there are no guardrails along the rim, and even where there are, there is room for a small child to slide through. Children and adults alike have plummeted to their deaths engaging in the most mundane activities in the most populated parts of the park. Secure toddlers in backpacks, always clutch young children's hands, and absolutely do not allow anyone to run and scramble along the rim or beyond formal overlooks.

Hikes into the canyon can be treacherous – consider carefully before bringing children under 10 years old. If you do descend below the rim, do not let children run or scamper about off the trail. Because trails are not cordoned off, and there are tempting rocks for climbing and finding that perfect view, this can be a challenge. It's easy to stumble on the park's sandy-trailed descents, and when icy or muddy they become particularly slippery. When faced with a mule train, follow the wrangler's instructions, and always turn backpacks to the canyon wall to allow the mules to pass; there have been incidents of a mule bumping a pack and knocking a hiker off the trail into the canyon.

Beyond falling, the main safety issues when traveling to Grand Canyon with children include dehydration, sunburn and altitude sickness. During the summer months, children should sip water all day, and you should consider bringing electrolyte replacements on any kind of extended hike. Remember, park rangers recommend noting how long it takes you to hike into the canyon, and allowing twice that for the hike back out.

Arizona law requires that children five years old and younger sit in a car seat except on public transportation. Most car-rental agencies rent rear-facing car seats (for infants under one year old), forward-facing seats and boosters for about $10 per day, but you must reserve these in advance.

Note that the North Rim is isolated and the closest medical facilities are 1½ hours away in Kanab, but basics like children's tylenol and first-aid supplies are easily available at both rims and Phantom Ranch on the canyon bottom.

Beyond the Park

Families with children of all ages could spend several days, even weeks, exploring the mountains and desert surrounding Grand Canyon National Park. Remember, however, that distances are long, particularly in and around the North Rim.

Las Vegas, a convenient place to fly into if heading to either the South or North Rim, makes a great place to indulge in a fancy resort with luxurious pools. For visits to the South Rim, Phoenix is an easy drive and offers a range of kid-friendly activities and accommodations; consider breaking the trip from Phoenix to the South Rim with a few days in Sedona. In the summer, rates in both Las Vegas and Phoenix plummet.

Around the South Rim

Flagstaff (p99) With excellent parks, outdoor family movies and a pedestrian-friendly downtown, this mountain college town is an exceptionally kid-friendly base for the region.

Williams (p95) Touristy Route 66 retro-fun, with zipline over the town.

Bearizona (p95) Drive-through wildlife park and walk-through zoo outside Williams.

Grand Canyon Deer Farm (p95) Feed the deer and get up close to critters at this throwback roadside attraction.

Slide Rock State Park (p113) Slide down natural slickrock of Oak Creek just outside Sedona.

Walnut Canyon National Monument (p102) Explore ancient Puebloan cliff dwellings.

Red Rock Crossing (p112) In Sedona, splash in the the creek, hike through red-rock country and picnic.

Sunset Crater National Monument (p102) Hike through the striking black basalt of a lava flow.

Around the North Rim

North Kaibab National Forest (p93) Gentle trails, meadows, Aspen and high-country overlooks.

Kanab (p160) Small and quiet red-rock Utah town with kitschy Western fun; zipline over.

Best Friends Animal Sanctuary (p160) Visit critters in the nation's largest no-kill animal shelter.

Lake Powell (Page; p166) Houseboat or kayak on the cold clear waters of this massive desert reservoir.

Glen Canyon (Page; p227) Smooth-water day trip along the Colorado River from Glen Canyon Dam to Lees Ferry

Marble Canyon (p170) Excellent fly-fishing in stunning surrounds; a handful of outfitters offer guided day trips suitable for kids.

Park & Poke from the South to North Rim

Sometimes the best times are had by simply parking the car and poking around – no charge, no destination, no agenda. Break up the four-hour drive around the canyon from the South to North Rim with a few park and pokes.

Little Colorado Gorge (Hwy 64, east of South Rim's East Entrance) Peruse Navajo crafts and take in the view.

Cameron Trading Post (p121) Shady green gardens and tourist trinkets in Cameron.

Balanced Rocks (Lees Ferry; p170) Scramble and hike among giant boulders in Marble Canyon; just west of Navajo Bridge, head north a mile or so on Lees Ferry Rd.

Navajo Bridge (Hwy 89A, Marble Canyon; p170) Walk over the Colorado River, look for condors and pop into the Interpretive Center.

Historic Lees Ferry (p170) Picnic in the apricot orchard at Lonely Dell Ranch.

Jacob Lake Inn (p160) Grab a milkshake for the last leg to the North Rim.

Plan Your Trip

Travel with Pets

While it's certainly possible to enjoy a trip to Grand Canyon with your pet, summer heat and park restrictions can be challenging. A little advanced planning will go a long way to making the trip smoother and happier for both you and your four-legged friend.

Best Spots for Dogs

Rim Trail (South Rim)

The 13-mile Rim Trail allows you to walk the dog and take in some of the best canyon views at the same time.

Shoshone Point (South Rim)

It's about a mile's walk along through the ponderosa to a picnic area and spectacular views at Shoshone Point.

North Rim, Desert View and Mather (North and South Rim campgrounds)

The park's three above-the-rim developed campgrounds provide plenty of space for wooded walks. Of the three, the North Rim is best for summer visits because it is cooler and more shaded.

Rules & Regulations

➡ Dogs and cats are allowed at campgrounds on both rims, South Rim's Yavapai Lodge (p227) and Trailer Village (p228), and throughout the park's developed areas, but cannot go below the rim, ride the shuttles or enter any other hotels, stores or restaurants on either rim.

➡ Dogs must be leashed at all times and you must clean up after your dog; it is illegal to leave a dog tied up alone at a campground.

➡ Official service animals are welcome throughout the park; register at the backcountry office before taking them below the rim.

Health & Safety

The environment can be harsh on pets, and mountain lions, rattlesnakes, scorpions and other critters are prevalent in the region. Prepare for weather extremes. In the summer, do not leave them in the car or RV unattended at any time. Think twice before taking pets on desert hikes in the summer, as it's excruciatingly hot and the sand burns tender paws. Always bring a portable water bowl. The only complete pet-supply shops in the region are Flagstaff's **Petsmart** (Map p100; ☎928-213-1737; 1121 S Plaza Way, University Plaza Shopping Center; ⏰9am-9pm Mon-Sat, to 7pm Sun) and **Petco** (☎928-526-4934; www.petco.com; 5047 East Marketplace Dr; ⏰9am-9pm Mon-Sat, 10am-7pm Sun).

BEST SPOTS FOR DOGS BEYOND THE PARK

North Kaibab National Forest (p93) With miles of trails and dirt roads, no leash laws and plenty of big meadows, the national forest that borders Grand Canyon National Park to the north is dog heaven. Even in summer, the high elevation and thick shade of the Kaibab Plateau keeps it cool.

Kanab (p160) Down the road from the nation's largest no-kill animal shelter, this tiny Utah town a 1½-hour drive from the North Rim is particularly dog friendly. Just about every hotel takes dogs, and most restaurants and shops have water bowls and dog treats.

Flagstaff (p99) A high-altitude college town with a soft spot for four-legged friends; there are a handful of dog parks, and most sidewalk cafes welcome dogs. Though few allow dogs inside, downtown's Hops on Birch (p108), a friendly neighborhood hangout with loads of quirky microbrews, is a delightful exception.

Remember that dogs, like humans, need to be in good shape before taking off on extended hikes, and are susceptible to altitude sickness and dehydration. When walking near the rim, be sure to keep dogs leashed and close to your side.

Dog-Friendly Trails

In the Park

Dogs are allowed at all above-the-rim trails and overlooks on the South Rim. On the North Rim, the only trail that allows dogs is the 1.9 mile Bridle Path connecting the North Kaibab Trailhead to Grand Canyon Lodge. Dogs must be leashed at all times.

Beyond the Park

In general, trails in and around Flagstaff are excellent for dogs.

North Kaibab National Forest (p157) Just outside the park's North Rim gate; all the trails and dirt roads allow dogs and they are not required to be leashed.

Paria Canyon (p172) Dogs are welcomed on this five-day wilderness hike, but you must pay $5 per day and pick up special dog-doo bags at the Paria Contact Station.

Buffalo Park (p103) An open mesa outside Flagstaff with a lovely 2-mile gravel loop trail. Leashed dogs only.

Dog-Friendly Accommodations

In the Park

Yavapai Lodge (p227) South Rim

North Rim Campground (p228) North Rim

Desert View Campground (p228) South Rim

Mather Campground (p228) South Rim

Trailer Village (p228) South Rim

Beyond the Park

Several motels just outside Grand Canyon National Park, including just about every hotel in Kanab, UT, welcome dogs and cats in some or all rooms. You may have to pay a daily or one-time fee. Best options include the following.

Kaibab Lodge (p159) The closest pet-friendly accommodations to the North Rim, about a half-hour drive from Grand Canyon Lodge on the canyon edge; pet-sitting services available and a $15 one-time fee.

Drury Inn & Suites (p106) Clean and modern chain motel within easy walking distance to restaurants and bars in Flagstaff's historic downtown; pets $35 per night.

El Portal (p116) Exquisitely handsome boutique inn nestled in Sedona that warmly welcomes pets into rooms and the dining area.

Four Seasons (p127) Elegant non-casino hotel on Vegas Strip near the airport.

Best Western Plus Inn (p97) Just off I-40 in Williams, with bright and welcoming lobby and renovated rooms.

Kennel Services

If taking the Grand Canyon Railway from Williams to the South Rim, you can leave your pet for the day or overnight at the Railway Pet Resort (p97) in Williams, and there is a basic kennel (p90) on the South Rim. There is no kennel on the North Rim.

Several high-quality kennels in Flagstaff offer the best option for travelers looking for somewhere to board their dog while they are at the park.

Horse Trails & Equestrian Facilities

In the Park

Horses and pack animals are allowed in the park, including on several trails above the rim and corridor trails. No permits are required for day-use, but you must check in at the Backcountry Information Center (p227) and the mule-ride concessionaires on each rim before descending.

Visit www.nps.gov/grca/planyourvisit/private-stock.htm for details and regulations.

Overnight Accommodations

Four campgrounds and one horse camp within Grand Canyon National Park offer overnight equestrian facilities; backcountry permit required everywhere except Mather.

North Rim Horse Camp One site with a small corral is open to visitors from May 15 to November 1; maximum six equines and six people.

Bright Angel Campground (p239) Accepts one equine group per night.

Cottonwood Campground (p152) Accepts one equine group per night.

Mather Campground (p228) Two sites with corrals accommodate six equines and six people each; first-come first-served.

Phantom Ranch (p242) Guests must have one person sleep with the animals.

Beyond the Park

The Kaibab National Forest (p93) that borders the North Rim offers excellent riding opportunities with all trails open to horses, and miles of dirt roads. Ranchers who run cattle in the Kaibab have a permit to use corrals within the forest, and while they welcome riders passing through, you need to call or stop by the Kaibab Plateau Visitor Center (p240) in Jacob Lake for locations and current information.

In the Coconino National Forest just outside of Flagstaff, Little Elden Springs Horse Camp (p105) is a campground designated only for people with horses. It offers 15 horse-friendly campsites with hitching posts but no corrals. From here, riders can access more than 100 miles of equestrian trails. To get to Little Elden, head 5 miles northeast of Flagstaff on Hwy 89. Turn west on FR 556 (Elden Springs Rd) and drive 1.5 miles to campground.

In Flagstaff, 90 minutes from the South Rim, board your horse at **MCS Stables** (☎928-774-5835; www.mcsstables.com; 8301 S Highway 89A; per night from $25). You're welcome to camp on-site at no extra charge. The closest horse facility to the North Rim is Paria River Ranch (http://pariariverranch.com/index.html), 30 miles west of Page, about a two-hour drive from the park.

On the Road

South Rim

928 / ELEV 7000FT

Includes ➡

Why Go?

Easily accessible, well developed and open year-round, the South Rim offers iconic canyon views, almost two dozen official overlooks, historic buildings, multiple trails, museums and ranger talks. Though its accessibility means sharing your experience with many others, particularly in summer, there are all kinds of ways to commune with the canyon and its wildlife, and enjoy its sublime beauty, one on one. Escaping the crowds can be as easy as tramping a hundred yards from an official scenic overlook. And in the evening, when day-trippers have left, you don't have to wander far at all to feel completely alone on the canyon edge.

Infrastructure is abundant: you'll find several lodgings, restaurants, cafeterias, bookstores, libraries and a supermarket. Shuttles ply one of the park's two scenic drives, and the flat and often paved 13-mile Rim Trail allows the mobility-impaired and stroller-pushers to take in the dramatic, sweeping canyon views.

Best Activities

- ➡ Hermit Road (p227)
- ➡ Desert View Drive (p227)
- ➡ Rim Trail (p58)
- ➡ South Kaibab Trail (p62)
- ➡ Bright Angel Bicycles (p71)
- ➡ Mule Ride (p71)

When to Go

South Rim

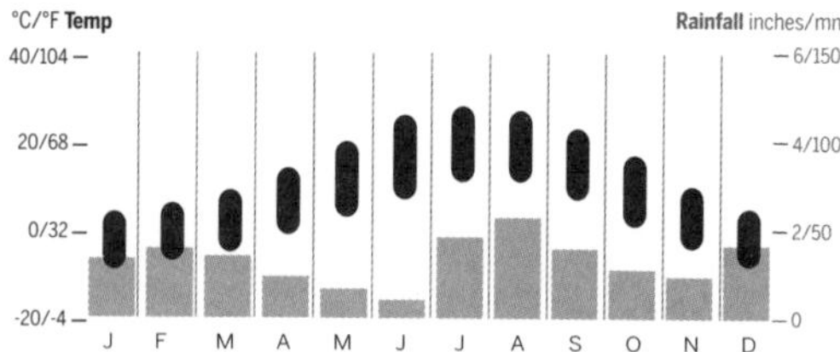

Mar–Apr Cooler, fluctuating temps; South Rim can see snow til April. March sees spring-break crowds.

May–Sep Inner canyon temperatures above 100°F (38°C) in summer peak; August brings rain.

Nov–Feb The stream of South Rim visitors slows to a trickle.

Best Places to Stay

- ➡ Bright Angel Lodge (p84)
- ➡ El Tovar (p85)
- ➡ Bright Angel Campground (p83)
- ➡ Kachina & Thunderbird Lodges (p84)

Entrances

The South Rim has two park entrances: the South Entrance, 74 miles north of Flagstaff on Hwy 180, and the East Entrance on Hwy 64, 32 miles west of Cameron and 82 miles north of Flagstaff. Most visitors enter from the South Entrance. After tackling summer queues (upwards of 45 minutes), visitors then head a few miles north to the mayhem of Grand Canyon Village – home to the park's tourist facilities, including hotels, restaurants and the visitor center.

If possible, enter the park through the East Entrance. As you drive the 25 miles to Grand Canyon Village, stopping at overlooks along the way, your first glimpses of the canyon will be more dramatic and much less hectic.

DON'T MISS

As in life, the best things at the South Rim are free. Watch a sunrise or sunset at an overlook along Desert View Dr (p227), stroll along the Rim Trail (p58) from Powell Point to Mohave Point, enjoy a picnic in a quiet spot along the canyon rim, descend into its depths on the South Kaibab (p62), and climb the winding staircase of the Desert View Watchtower (p78). Learn about the park's geology at the Trail of Time (p75) and its tourist beginnings at the History Room inside Bright Angel Lodge (p75), and take in a ranger program (p72).

Only slightly more expensive is renting a bike at Bright Angel Bicycles (p71) for a spin along the rim followed by prickly-pear margaritas on the porch swing at El Tovar (p86).

When You Arrive

➡ Admission to the Grand Canyon National Park costs $35 per vehicle, $30 per single motorcycle and $20 per individual arriving by foot, bicycle, bus, trail or raft, and is valid for seven days at both rims. Individuals 15 years old and younger enter free; bus and train passengers may pay a lesser fee or have it included in the tour price.

➡ Avoid summer wait times by prepaying for your park ticket at the National Geographic Visitor Center & IMAX Theater (p233) in Tusayan, which allows you to cruise through in a special lane.

Practical Tip

If you plan to do some hiking and don't want to leave laptops, passports or other valuables in the car, Bright Angel Lodge (p84) offers a storage service on a space-available basis.

LAST MINUTE

Because of the flexible cancellation policy, it's not unusual to secure last-minute rooms even during summer peak season. For more information see p82.

Fast Facts

➡ Rim Trail length: 13 miles

➡ Highest elevation: 7461ft

➡ Elevation change: 4420ft

Reservations

➡ Fifteen months before going, enter the lottery for Phantom Ranch (p84) accommodations and make reservations for overnight mule rides (p71).

➡ Reserve lodge accommodation as early as 13 months in advance (the earliest date reservations are accepted). Multiday rafting trips should also be reserved now.

Resources

National Park Service (www.nps.gov/grca) Best resource for current information, including backcountry permits, lodging and tours.

Grand Canyon National Park Lodges (www.grandcanyonlodges.com) Most lodging, mule trips, Phantom Ranch lottery information and bus tours.

Discover Grand Canyon National Park (www.visitgrandcanyon.com).

South Rim Chamber and Visitors Bureau (www.grandcanyoncvb.org)

South Rim

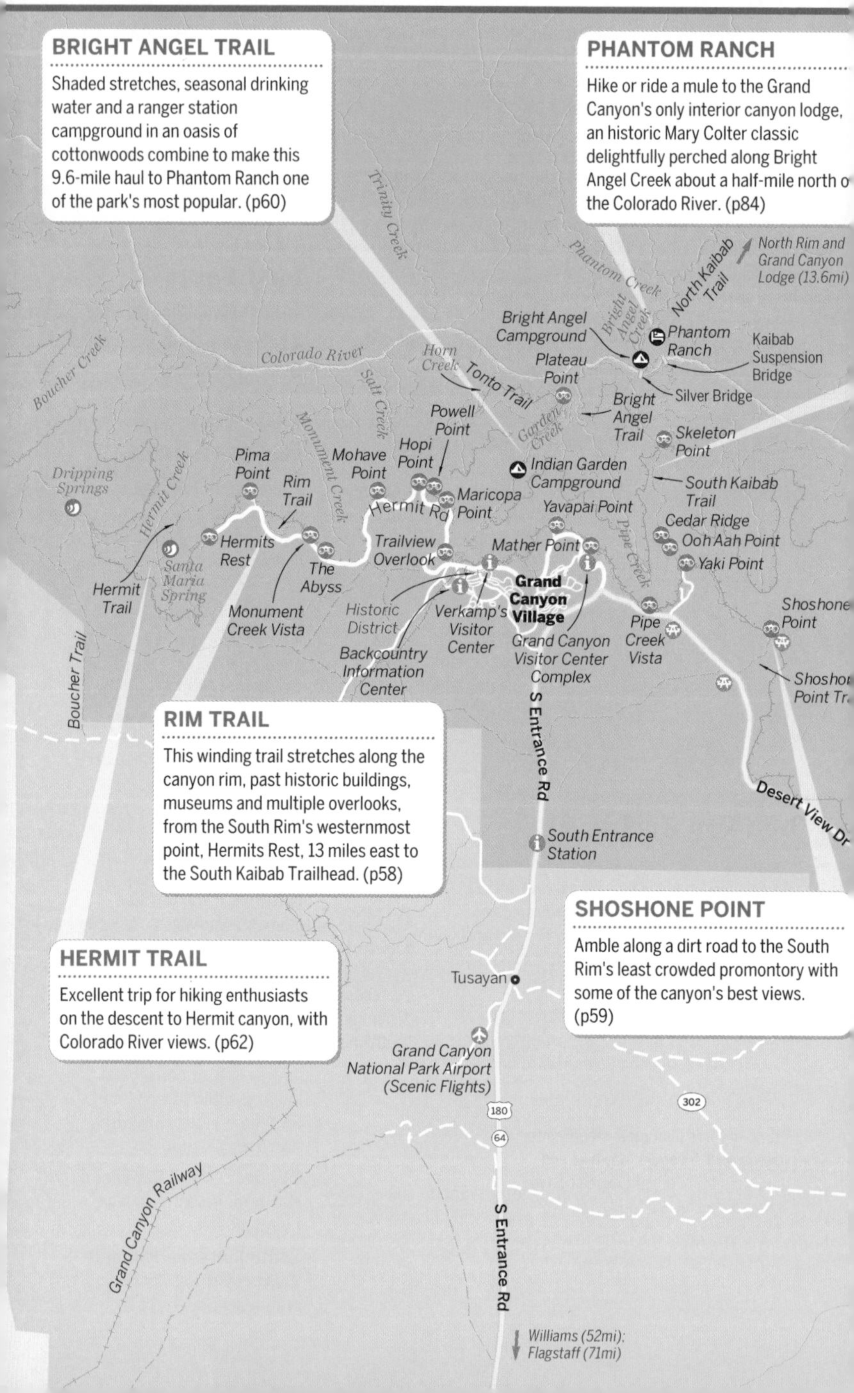

BRIGHT ANGEL TRAIL

Shaded stretches, seasonal drinking water and a ranger station campground in an oasis of cottonwoods combine to make this 9.6-mile haul to Phantom Ranch one of the park's most popular. (p60)

PHANTOM RANCH

Hike or ride a mule to the Grand Canyon's only interior canyon lodge, an historic Mary Colter classic delightfully perched along Bright Angel Creek about a half-mile north o the Colorado River. (p84)

North Rim and Grand Canyon Lodge (13.6mi)
Trinity Creek
Phantom Creek
North Kaibab Trail
Bright Angel Creek
Bright Angel Campground
Phantom Ranch
Kaibab Suspension Bridge
Silver Bridge
Colorado River
Boucher Creek
Horn Creek
Tonto Trail
Plateau Point
Salt Creek
Garden Creek
Bright Angel Trail
Skeleton Point
Powell Point
Monument Creek
Hopi Point
Mohave Point
Pima Point
Rim Trail
Dripping Springs
Hermit Creek
Indian Garden Campground
South Kaibab Trail
Maricopa Point
Hermit Rd
Yavapai Point
Pipe Creek
Cedar Ridge
Ooh Aah Point
Yaki Point
Mather Point
Trailview Overlook
Hermits Rest
The Abyss
Santa Maria Spring
Hermit Trail
Monument Creek Vista
Historic District
Verkamp's Visitor Center
Grand Canyon Village
Grand Canyon Visitor Center Complex
Pipe Creek Vista
Shoshone Point
Shoshone Point Tr
Backcountry Information Center
Boucher Trail
S Entrance Rd
Desert View Dr

RIM TRAIL

This winding trail stretches along the canyon rim, past historic buildings, museums and multiple overlooks, from the South Rim's westernmost point, Hermits Rest, 13 miles east to the South Kaibab Trailhead. (p58)

South Entrance Station

SHOSHONE POINT

Amble along a dirt road to the South Rim's least crowded promontory with some of the canyon's best views. (p59)

HERMIT TRAIL

Excellent trip for hiking enthusiasts on the descent to Hermit canyon, with Colorado River views. (p62)

Tusayan
Grand Canyon National Park Airport (Scenic Flights)
302
180
64
Grand Canyon Railway
S Entrance Rd
Williams (52mi); Flagstaff (71mi)

SOUTH KAIBAB TRAIL

Exposed crest line descends 7 miles to the Colorado River and Phantom Ranch, offering dramatic panoramic views. (p61)

TONTO TRAIL

While the entire 95-mile Tonto winds midway down the canyon's south face parallel to the Colorado River, shorter stretches of this wild and desolate ribbon can be accessed through South Rim Trails. (p62)

GRANDVIEW TRAIL

Bone-dry trail plummets steeply into the canyon, a popular day hike and backcountry overnight expedition for experienced hikers. (p63)

HIKING IN SOUTH RIM

To experience the full majesty of the canyon, hit the trail. It may look daunting, but there are options for all levels of skill and fitness. Though summer is the most popular season for day hikes experienced canyon hikers know that it's much more pleasant in the spring and fall, when there

NAME	START LOCATION	DESCRIPTION	DIFFICULTY
Bright Angel Trail			
To Mile-and-a-Half Resthouse (p60)	Bright Angel Trailhead	Short, rewarding hike along the Grand Canyon's most popular inner-canyon trail	moderate
To Three-Mile Resthouse (p60)	Bright Angel Trailhead	Following Bright Angel Fault, this trail zigzags to a shaded resthouse with panoramic views	moderate-difficult
To Indian Garden (p61)	Bright Angel Trailhead	The grueling switchbacks of Jacob's Ladder lead to the leafy bliss of Indian Garden	moderate-difficult
To Plateau Point (p61)	Bright Angel Trailhead	Not recommended for summer day hikes; leads to the edge of Tonto Plateau	difficult
Grandview Trail			
To Coconino Saddle (p64)	Grandview Trailhead	This steep, rocky challenge winds up at a shady spot with phenomenal views	difficult
To Horseshoe Mesa (p64)	Grandview Trailhead	Stay on the steep and narrow on this, one of the park's most exposed hikes	difficult
Hermit Trail			
To Santa Maria Spring (p63)	Hermit Trailhead	Beautiful and serene day hike along a steep wilderness trail to small cliffside spring	difficult
Dripping Springs (p63)	Hermit Trailhead	Peaceful and challenging hike to Louis 'The Hermit' Boucher's favorite hangout	difficult
To Hermit Camp (p69)	Hermit Trailhead	Hard but beautiful hike to a sublime, cliffside camping spot	difficult-very difficult
South Kaibab Trail			
Ooh Ahh Point (p62)	South Kaibab Trailhead	Excellent choice for a taste of inner-canyon hiking	moderate
To Cedar Ridge (p62)	South Kaibab Trailhead	Steep descent along a ridge crest	moderate-difficult
To Skeleton Point (p62)	South Kaibab Trailhead	Panoramic views	difficult
To Phantom Ranch (p67)	South Kaibab Trailhead	Tough but rewarding hike to Colorado River	difficult-very difficult
Rim to Rim (p66)	South Kaibab Trailhead	Classic rim-to-rim corridor hike; can also be started from the North Rim or from Bright Angel Trailhead	difficult-very difficult
Rim Trail (p58)	Multiple	Popular paved and dirt point-to-point trail connects South Rim overlooks	easy
Shoshone Point (p59)	Shoshone Point Trailhead	Cool, shady walk to one of the South Rim's most spectacular viewpoints	easy
Tonto Trail (p62)	South Kaibab Trailhead	Long, tough loop down the South Kaibab, across the mid-canyon Tonto and up Bright Angel	very difficult

  *Wildlife Watching*  *View*   *Great for Families*   *Wheelchair Accessible*  *Restrooms*

are also fewer visitors. In winter, you will need crampons to navigate icy trails. For short, easy-to-print trail descriptions (with mileages, turnaround points and basic maps) check out the Plan Your Visit section of the park website (www.nps.gov/grca); click through to Backcountry Hiking.

DURATION	ROUND-TRIP DISTANCE	ELEVATION CHANGE	FEATURES	FACILITIES
2-3hr	3 miles	1120ft		
5hr	6 miles	2120ft		
7hr	9.2 miles	3040ft		
8-10hr	12.2 miles	3040ft		
2-4hr	2.2 miles	1600ft		
4-8hr	6.2 miles	2699ft		
3hr	4 miles	1760ft		
5hr	6.2 miles	1040ft		
2 days	15.4 miles	3660ft		
1-2hr	1.8 miles	760ft		
2-3hr	3 miles	1120ft		
6hr	6 miles	2040ft		
2-3 days	18.6 miles	4714ft		
3 days	20.9 miles	5770ft		
5hr	13 miles	200ft		
40min	2 miles	50ft		
7-9hr	13.1 miles (one way)	3260ft		

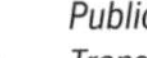 *Public Transportation to Trailhead*  *Drinking Water*   *Ranger Station*  *Backcountry Campsite*

DAY HIKES

Hiking along the South Rim is among park visitors' favorite pastimes, with options for all levels. The popular river-bound corridor trails (Bright Angel and South Kaibab) follow paths etched thousands of years ago by geologic faults and water drainages. Several turnaround spots make these trails ideal for day hikes of varying lengths. Though the Bright Angel and South Kaibab trails can be packed during the summer with foot and mule traffic, more solitude can be found on less trodden trails like Hermit or Grandview.

Most of the trails start with a series of super-steep switchbacks that descend quickly to a dramatic ledge of Coconino sandstone about 2 miles beneath the rim. Hike another 3 miles and you'll hit the sun-baked Tonto Platform, which after another couple of miles opens up to inner gorge vistas. Day hikers will want to stay above the Tonto Platform.

Day hiking requires no permit, just preparation and safety. Day hike routes extend into overnight excursions, but overnight hiking requires either a reservation at Phantom Ranch (p84), on the canyon bottom and available by lottery only, or a permit for backcountry camping in advance of departure; do not set off for a day hike and then decide en route that you would like to stay below the rim overnight.

The Rim Trail and Shoshone Point hikes are excellent for families, as neither involve significant elevation change.

Above the Rim

Rim Trail

Duration Five hours one-way

Distance Varies (up to 13 miles one way)

Difficulty Easy

Start Hermits Rest

Finish South Kaibab Trailhead

Nearest Town Grand Canyon Village

Transportation Shuttle

Summary The Rim Trail can be walked in its entirety in a day with stops at overlooks, or explored in short segments.

Stretching from Hermits Rest on the rim's western edge through Grand Canyon Village to South Kaibab Trailhead, the **Rim Trail** (www.nps.gov/grca; ; Village, Kaibab/Rim, Hermits Rest, Mar 1-Nov 30) connects a series of overlooks and is hands-down the easiest long walk in the park. By no means a nature trail, the central leg includes the tourist hub of Grand Canyon Village, and long swaths are accessible to wheelchairs. It's paved for most of the 6.7 miles between Powell Point east through the Village to South Kaibab Trailhead, and for the 2.8 miles between Monument Creek Vista and Hermits Rest.

Flexibility is a big draw, with the shuttles making it simple to jump on for a segment and hike for as long as you like. Each of the overlooks along the way is accessed by one of three shuttle routes, which means you can walk to a vista and shuttle back, or shuttle to a point, walk to the next and shuttle from there. A helpful map at the visitor center shows the shuttle stops and hiking distances along each segment of the trail, and each leg is clearly marked along the trail.

The trail passes many of the park's historical sights, including **El Tovar**, **Hopi House**, **Kolb Studio**, **Lookout Studio** and **Verkamp's Visitor Center**. The 3 miles or so that wind through the village are usually crowded with people, but the further west you venture, the more you'll break free. Out there the trail runs between Hermit Rd and the rim, and though some segments bump up against the road, you're typically alone to amble along the rim.

One very pretty and quiet stretch is the 3.7-mile leg from Powell Point to Pima Point. Heading west from **Powell Point**, the trail turns rocky, not suited to strollers, hugging the rim and offering incredible views and peaceful spots along the 0.5 miles to **Hopi Point**. Here, the canyon opens majestically to the west and down to the Colorado River. Continuing the 0.8 miles to **Mohave Point**, the trail passes a wonderful rim-side picnic table with expansive views and relative isolation, and from Mohave Point to the The **Abyss** (1.1 miles) and on to **Monument Creek Vista** (0.9 miles) there are a couple more picnic-perfect tables. From Monument Creek, it's 1.7 miles to **Pima Point** and another 1.1 miles through piñon-juniper woodlands to **Hermits Rest**.

Continuing west to Hermits Rest, it's just a few minutes' walk to a wide, wooden, rim-side bench, a peaceful spot before reaching the swirling activity of Hermits Rest. About halfway between Pima and Hermits Rest another bench offers panoramic views west down the Colorado, a perfect spot for a quiet sunset.

The 2.8 miles between Hermits Rest and Monument Creek Vista and the 1.9 miles

Above the Rim – Day Hikes

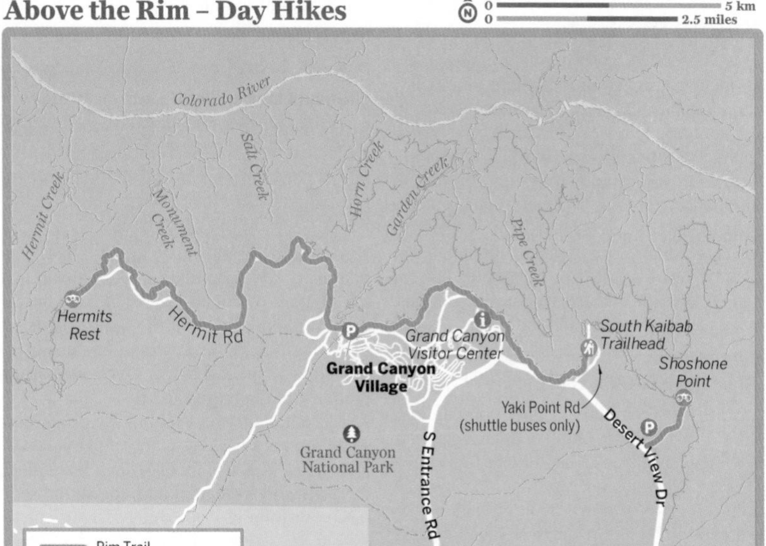

just west of the South Kaibab Trailhead are part of the park's designated Greenway Trail (p71). These wide, paved stretches can be enjoyed on bicycle; rent one at Bright Angel Bicycles (p71). Leashed pets are allowed on the entire trail.

Shoshone Point

Duration 40 minutes round-trip

Distance 2 miles round-trip

Difficulty Easy

Start/Finish Shoshone Point Trailhead

Nearest Town Grand Canyon Village

Transportation Car

Summary With an elevation change of only 50ft and a sandy trail through ponderosa forest, Shoshone Point puts solitude within easy reach.

The gentle and cool amble out to Shoshone Point, accessible only by foot, can be a welcome pocket of peace during the summer heat and crowds. This little-known hike is also ideal for children. Chances are you won't see another person, which means you can have the spectacular views all to yourself.

The walk starts from a dirt pullout along Desert View Dr, 1.2 miles east of Yaki Point or 6.3 miles west of Grandview Point. There's no official trailhead or signpost, so look for the dirt road barred by a closed and locked gate. The park service deliberately downplays this trail, and makes it available from May to October for weddings and other private events. If the parking lot is full of cars, refrain from hiking there, out of respect for any private events taking place. When it hasn't been reserved for a special gathering, and during winter months, hikers are welcome on the trail.

It's a fast and mostly flat out-and-back walk along the wide forested trail, which weaves through fragrant ponderosa pines before reaching a clearing. This is a great spot for a family gathering, as you'll find picnic tables, BBQ grills (advanced permit from National Park Service required) and portable toilets. Nearby Shoshone Point juts out into the canyon, offering magnificent views of the North Rim's full sweep. Unlike the other scenic points, there are no safety railings here. You can walk to the tip of the slender plateau and its Easter Island *moai*-like formation, where it feels almost possible to reach out and touch **Zoroaster Temple** rock formation.

Below the Rim

In winter and early spring the upper reaches of the Bright Angel, South Kaibab, Grandview and Hermit trails can be icy and dangerous. In the summer, temperatures easily soar above 100°F (38°C). Between mid-May and mid-September, it's recommended that you stay off interior canyon trails between 10am and 4pm. Plan to start hiking at first light (4:30am in summer, and 6:30am in spring and fall). Even if you're heading into the canyon for just for a short day hike, check weather conditions, bring plenty of water and hike smart.

Bright Angel Trail

A wide, well-maintained and popular corridor trail, **Bright Angel** (www.nps.gov/grca; Rim Trail, Grand Canyon Village Historic District; ; Village, Hermits Rest, Mar 1-Nov 30) winds 7.8 miles and 4460ft down from the rim to the Colorado River. Short day hikes lead 1.5 and 3 miles to two stone resthouses, Long day hikes, safe for September through May only, descend 4.6 miles to Indian Garden (a popular campground) and from there 1.5 miles along a spur trail to spectacular views at Plateau Point. Overnight hikers continue into the canyon from Indian Garden 3.1 miles to the River Trail, another 1.6 miles to Bright Angel Campground and a final 0.3 miles to Phantom Ranch.

In contrast to the steeper and shorter South Kaibab descent, Bright Angel offers shady resthouses with seasonal drinking water and stretches along a delightful creek. Note, however, that water-line breaks are becoming an increasing problem and drinking water may not be available. Check the bulletin board at the trailhead for current water availability along the trail, and never depend on a below-the-rim drinking water source.

The trailhead is on the Rim Trail smack in Grand Canyon Village, directly west of Kolb Studio and a two-minute walk from Bright Angel Lodge. Restrooms and a water-bottle filling station sit by the shuttle stop and parking lot.

BRIGHT ANGEL TRAIL – SHORT DAY HIKE

Duration Mile-and-a-Half Resthouse two to three hours round-trip; Three-Mile Resthouse four to five hours round-trip

Distance 3 miles round-trip; 6 miles round-trip

Difficulty Moderate-difficult

Start/Finish Bright Angel Trailhead

Nearest Town Grand Canyon Village

Transportation Shuttle, car or foot

Summary Test out your canyon legs with a hike to two historic stone resthouses, where you can relax in the shade before returning to the rim.

Bright Angel Trailhead (6860ft) is both exhilarating and intimidating. The canyon unfolds before you in all its glory, hikers bustle around making last-minute adjustments to their backpacks, and wranglers acquaint first-time mule riders (is there any other kind?) with the curious beasts.

The piñon-fringed trail quickly drops into some serious switchbacks as it follows a natural break in the cliffs of Kaibab limestone, the Toroweap formation and Coconino sandstone. Start slowly. If you suffer vertigo, look to the left for a while – the first five minutes are the hardest. Before you know it, you'll grow accustomed and the trail gets interesting.

The trail soon passes through two tunnels – look for the Native American **pictographs** on the walls of the first. Just after passing through the second tunnel you'll reach **Mile-and-a-Half Resthouse** (5720ft), about an hour from the trailhead. Anyone starting late or hiking for the first time should turn around here. It has restrooms, an emergency phone and, from May to September, drinking water.

Continuing downward through different-colored rock layers, more switchbacks finally deposit you at **Three-Mile Resthouse**, which has seasonal water and an emergency phone but no restrooms. Down below, you'll see the iridescent green tufts of Indian Garden, a campground 1.6 miles further, as well as the broad expanse of Tonto Platform, a nice visual reward before beginning the ascent back to the rim.

BRIGHT ANGEL TRAIL – LONG DAY HIKE

Duration Indian Garden five to seven hours round-trip; Plateau Point eight to 10 hours round-trip

Distance 9.2 miles round-trip; 12.2 miles round-trip

Difficulty Difficult

Start/Finish Bright Angel Trailhead

Nearest Town Grand Canyon Village

Transportation Shuttle, car

Below the Rim – Day Hikes

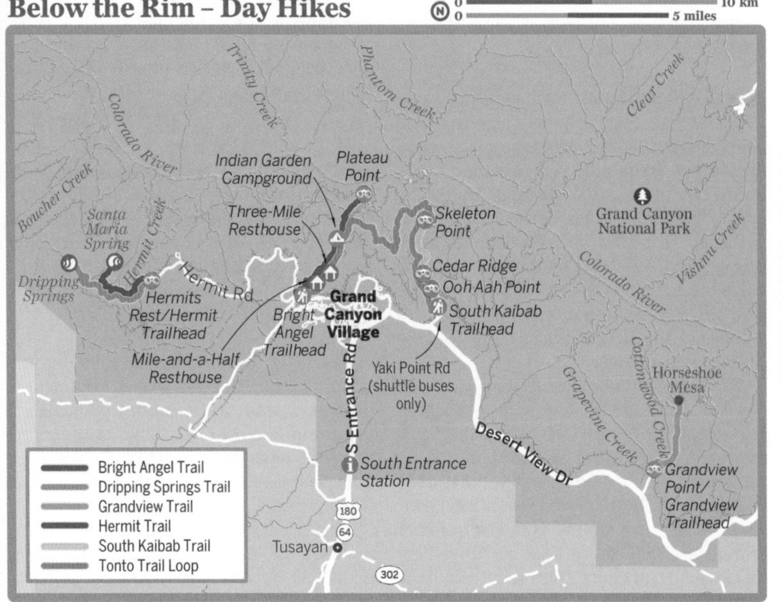

Summary Continuing down the Bright Angel brings you to the shady oasis of Indian Garden; for a more challenging and very exposed hike to expansive views of the inner gorge, cross Tonto Platform along a spur trail to reach Plateau Point.

Follow the Short Day Hike (p60) and continue from Three-Mile Resthouse using the following hike description.

After Three-Mile Resthouse, you'll soon hit a demanding set of switchbacks known as **Jacob's Ladder** which twist through Redwall limestone cliffs into the cool leafiness of **Indian Garden** (3760ft). Havasupai farmed here until a century ago, and these days it's a popular campground, with a ranger station, toilets, year-round drinking water, shaded picnic tables and a mule corral.

If this is your day-hike destination, linger in the soothing, albeit crowded, spot: eat lunch under a cottonwood, nap on the grass and splash your feet in the creek. With an elevation gain of 3040ft, it's a hard and hot 4.6-mile climb back up to the rim – particularly the thigh-burning Jacob's Ladder. The round-trip takes about seven hours with a rest here.

From the campground, if you turn left and head west across Garden Creek, you'll soon reach the **Plateau Point Trail** junction, a spur off the Tonto Trail (a 95-mile inner-canyon trail that parallels the Colorado River). This ribbon of a trail unfurls north for just under a mile over the barren and yucca-studded **Tonto Plateau**, which is not as flat as it looks from above. The trail dead-ends at **Plateau Point** (3140ft below the rim) for a stunning view of the inner gorge.

Though Plateau Point is a popular destination for strong day hikers, do not make the round-trip trek from May through September. The long, exposed stretch can be searingly hot, with the 12.2-mile round-trip from the rim taking up to 12 hours.

South Kaibab Trail

Duration Ooh Aah Point one to two hours round-trip; Cedar Ridge two to three hours round-trip; Skeleton Point six hours round-trip

Distance 1.8 miles round-trip; 3 miles round-trip; 6 miles round-trip

Difficulty Moderate; moderate–difficult

Start/Finish South Kaibab Trailhead

Nearest Town Grand Canyon Village

Transportation Shuttle

Summary Unlike other interior-canyon

trails, the South Kaibab follows a ridgeline rather than a side canyon, offering the park's most expansive views.

Blasted out of the rock by rangers in the mid 1920s, the steep, stark and sun-drenched **South Kaibab** (www.nps.gov/grca; Kaibab/Rim) offers unparalleled panoramic views and is one of the park's prettiest trails. The lack of shade and water, however, combined with the sheer grade and exposure to steep drop-offs make ascending the South Kaibab particularly dangerous in summer, and the trail sees a fair number of rescues. Take advantage of the Hikers' Express Bus (p91) to hit the trail at dawn.

From the South Kaibab Trailhead the trail starts out at a gentle decline, before spiraling steeply down to **Ooh Aah Point** (0.9 miles from the rim) and **Cedar Ridge**, 1.5 miles from the rim and a descent of 1140ft. A dazzling spot, particularly at sunrise, Cedar Ridge is the turn-around point for summer day hikers. The ascent back up from here takes one to two hours. During the rest of the year, the continued trek to **Skeleton Point** (5200ft), 1.5 miles beyond Cedar Ridge, makes for a fine day hike, though the climb back up is a beast in any season.

The trailhead, located at the eastern-most point of the Rim Trail, cannot be reached by private vehicle. You must ride either the Kaibab/Rim Route Shuttle or the early-morning Hikers' Express Bus. Alternatively, cycle along Desert View Dr and Yaki Rd or walk along the Rim Trail; it's about a 2-mile walk from the Visitor Center Plaza to the trailhead.

There are toilets and a water-bottle filling station at the trailhead.

Tonto Trail: Down South Kaibab, up Bright Angel

Duration Seven to nine hours one way

Distance 13.4 miles one way

Difficulty Very difficult

Start South Kaibab Trailhead

Finish Bright Angel Trailhead

Nearest Town Grand Canyon Village

Transportation Shuttle

Summary A stellar choice for strong hikers seeking solitude, this full-day excursion links two popular corridor trails along a peaceful, winding section of the Tonto Trail – but time it right to avoid charring your epidermis and brain. Distance and duration given for this hike are from start to finish; the hike description, however, details only the section linking the South Kaibab and Bright Angel trails.

This 4.1-mile section of the Tonto linking the South Kaibab and Bright Angel (p60) trails jumps up and down as it follows the contours and canyon faults. The segment described here – from the Tipoff on South Kaibab to Indian Garden on Bright Angel – is considered the central portion and is officially referred to as the Tonto Trail.

From the South Kaibab Trailhead it's a bone-jarring, hot 4.4-mile descent beyond Skeleton Point to the Tonto Trail junction, dropping 3260ft in elevation to the edge of the Tonto Platform. Just past the junction there's an emergency telephone and a toilet, a final reminder you're about to set foot on wilder terrain.

Heading west on the Tonto, you'll hug the contours as the trail crosses the agave-dotted plateau and darts in and out of gulches. Deep in a canyon fold, the trail skirts through a canopy of cottonwoods near a drainage; just past here on the left is a terrific spot for camping.

The trail remains in shade through midmorning. As the day progresses, however, the Tonto bakes and the surrounding landscape is completely parched – you don't want to be caught here midday, so it's imperative to time your start accordingly. After about two hours you'll stumble into lush **Indian Garden**, 8.8 miles from the hike's beginning at the South Kaibab trailhead and the perfect shady oasis for cooling off before the 4.6 mile haul up to the rim; or, with an advanced backcountry permit, you can camp at Indian Garden.

Though technically a day hike, this is a long, difficult backcountry haul that is not suited for summer, regardless of skill level or experience.

Hermit Trail (to Santa Maria Spring)

Duration Three to four hours round-trip

Distance 4 miles round-trip

Difficulty Moderate–difficult

Start/Finish Hermit Trailhead

Nearest Town Grand Canyon Village

Hermit Trail

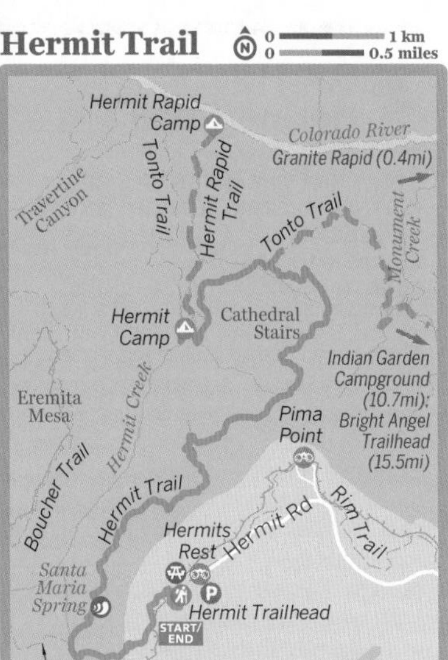

Transportation Shuttle, bicycle (year-round), car (December 1 to February 28)

Summary Unmaintained Hermit Trail winds down into the often shady and usually unpopulated Hermit Canyon, connecting with several other trails to secluded canyon treks.

This wilderness **trail** (www.nps.gov/grca; Hermit Rd, Mar 1-Nov 30) descends into lovely Hermit Canyon. It's a rocky trip down, with some knee-wrenching switchbacks and long traverses that wend through the Supai cliffs. But if you set out early in the morning and take it slow, the Hermit offers a wonderfully serene day hike and glimpses into hidden corners.

The best destination for day hikers is Santa Maria Spring. For a shorter but still worthwhile hike, turn around at the **Waldron Trail junction**, a round-trip of 2.6 miles with 1240ft of elevation change. The upper section of the Hermit is well shaded in the morning, making it a cool option in summer.

The rocky trail weaves down Hermit Basin toward Hermit Creek along a cobblestone route indented with steps and fraught with washouts. You'll reach the rarely used Waldron Trail (jutting off to the south) after about 1.3 miles, followed some 30 minutes later by the spur trail headed for Dripping Springs. The trail then traces over some flat rocks (a perfect picnic spot) before descending steeply to **Santa Maria Spring**, a cool, shady haven, marked by a pretty stone shelter adorned with green foliage and a welcome wooden bench. The lush scene belies the spring, however, which is actually more of a trickle. You can drink the water provided you treat it.

The Hermit Trailhead is at Hermits Rest, 7 miles west of Grand Canyon Village. From March through November, private cars are not allowed on the road here and you must take the Hermits Rest Route Shuttle, walk the Rim Trail or cycle to the trailhead.

Dripping Springs Trail

Duration Five to seven hours round-trip

Distance 6.2 miles round-trip

Difficulty Moderate–difficult

Start/Finish Hermit Trailhead

Nearest Town Grand Canyon Village

Transportation Shuttle, bicycle (year-round), car (December 1 to February 28)

Summary An excellent day hike with an elevation change of 1040ft, Dripping Springs is an isolated spur trail off Hermit Trail.

For the first 2 miles you are on the Hermit Trail. At the junction with the Dripping Springs Trail, turn left and head west along the narrow path as it climbs and meanders along the slope's contours. After 1 mile you'll hit the junction with the Boucher Trail; turn left here to continue following the Dripping Springs Trail as it winds up toward the water source, which sprouts from an overhang not far beneath the rim. Droplets shower down from the sandstone ceiling, misting a myriad maidenhair ferns.

Grandview Trail

Duration Coconino Saddle two to four hours round-trip; Horseshoe Mesa four to eight hours round-trip

Distance 2.2 miles round-trip; 6.2 miles round-trip

Difficulty Difficult

Start/Finish Grandview Trailhead (Grandview Point)

Nearest Town Grand Canyon Village

Transportation Car

Summary The unmaintained Grandview plummets about 2600ft over 3.1 miles from the rim to Grandview Mesa.

One of the steepest trails in the park – dropping 2500ft in the first 3.0 miles – **Grandview** (www.nps.gov/grca; Desert View Dr) is also one of the finest day hikes. The payoff following the stunning (and grueling) descent is an up-close look at one of the inner canyon's sagebrush-tufted mesas and a wonderful sense of solitude. The trail spirals down to a sprawling horseshoe-shaped mesa, where Hopi people once collected minerals.

In 1892 miner Pete Berry improved the former Native American route and constructed the current trail to access his Last Chance Mine at Horseshoe Mesa. For the next 15 years mules carted high-grade copper from there to the rim, even after Berry established his Grand View Hotel in 1897 and guided mule tours into the canyon.

Because there is no water on the very exposed trail, and the climb out is a doozy, do not day-hike to Horseshoe Mesa in the summer. Instead, hike to Coconino Saddle and turn around there. Though it's only a 2.2-mile round-trip, it packs a quick and precipitous punch as you plunge 1000ft over about 1 mile. With the exception of a few short level sections, the Grandview is a rugged, narrow and rocky trail, and the steep drop-offs can be a bit scary. This is not a good choice for those skittish of heights.

Steep from the start, the trail first winds down the north end of Grandview Point, passing through Kaibab limestone along cobbled and cliff-edged rock stairs fringed with occasional flowers like fiery orange Indian paintbrush, straw-yellow arnica and blue delphinium. The views from the trailhead and just below are extraordinary, so even if you don't plan to hike, do walk down the trail a short way to take in the vistas. After about 30 minutes, you'll reach the **Coconino Saddle**, where the trail crosses the slender spur between Hance and Grapevine Canyons.

The saddle is a stunning overlook and a nice leafy spot for a snack and a rest in the shade. From here the trail is more exposed and eventually narrows to a ribbon as it traverses the ruddy Supai sandstone. A little over 2 miles past Coconino you'll hit a second saddle, connecting to **Horseshoe Mesa**, then a short dip later you reach pit toilets and remnants of an old miners' camp cookhouse. There are traces of mining all

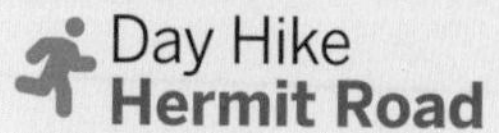

Day Hike Hermit Road

START GRAND CANYON VILLAGE HISTORIC DISTRICT (BRIGHT ANGEL TRAILHEAD)
END HERMITS REST
LENGTH 7.8 MILES; THREE HOURS

This popular scenic walk along a stretch of the Rim Trail (p58) meanders along the canyon edge, sometimes winding away from the edge for stretches through the piñon and juniper, and sometimes hugging the road. The trail is mostly dirt, but the final 2.8 miles from Monument Creek Vista to Hermits Rest is a paved multi-use path open to bicycles. Though the main attractions are the eight official park overlooks along the way, there are excellent views all along the walk, and plenty of benches and quiet, flat rocks to relax with a rim-side sandwich.

From March through November, the park's westbound Hermit Rest Route Shuttles stop at each of the overlooks detailed here. During this time, you can walk some stretches and hop on a shuttle for others. Bring plenty of water: the only water sources are the water-filling station by 1 **Bright Angel Trail** at the walk's start and at Hermits Rest, and the only bathrooms are at Hopi Point and Hermits Rest. Hermit Rd is open to private vehicles December 1 to February 28, during which time this tour can be taken as a scenic drive; there is a parking lot at each overlook.

From Hermit Rd Gate, it is 0.7 mile incline to 2 **Trailview Overlook**. From here, there is a great view of Bright Angel Trail, the lush vegetation at Indian Garden and Grand Canyon Village on the rim to the east. If you arrive early in the morning, you may see the tiny specks of a faraway mule train descending into the canyon.

Continue along the rough trail 0.7 miles to Maricopa Point. In 1890, prospector Daniel Lorain filed a mining claim for an area 1100ft below the rim, and 4 acres on the rim, and set about making his fortune in copper. After more than 40 years of minimal success, Hogan realized that the real money at the canyon was in tourism, so in 1936 he built tourist cabins, a trading

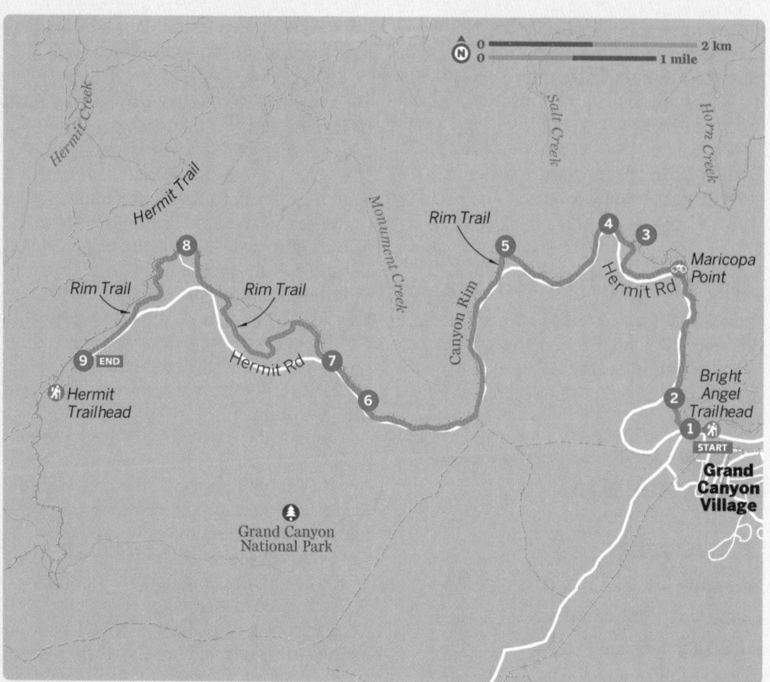

post and a saloon on the rim. In 1947 he sold the property to Madelaine Jacobs, who would end up making the fortune Hogan never did – in uranium, not copper.

It's a gentle 0.5 mile uphill stroll from Maricopa to spectacular views at 3 **Powell Point**. Here, you will find the Powell Memorial, erected in 1915 in honor of John Wesley Powell, the intrepid one-armed Civil War veteran, ethnologist and geologist who led the first white-water run through the canyon on the Colorado in 1869. The park was officially dedicated at this spot in 1920.

The trail continues 0.3 miles to 4 **Hopi Point**, jutting out further than any other overlook along Hermit Rd and offering huge, spectacular views of plateau upon plateau and the Colorado River a mile below. From Hopi, the remainder of the walk is mostly flat and downhill, beginning with a 0.8-mile walk to 5 **Mohave Point**. This is an an exceptional place to see the Colorado, as three rapids – Salt Creek, Granite and Hermit – are visible below, downstream. If you're doing the Grand Canyon speed-demon tour and only have time for a couple of stops, make them count at Hopi Point and Mohave Point.

From Mohave, it's 1.1 miles to the aptly named 6 **The Abyss**, a beautiful example of how steep some canyon drop-offs can be. If you're at all acrophobic, consider walking past this viewpoint, as the sheer cliffs drop 2600ft to the Redwall limestone below. Continuing along the trail westward you'll pass several excellent spots to (carefully) check out the dizzying drop on the 0.9-walk to 7 **Monument Creek Vista**. From here, the trail turns paved and mostly winds through the desert shrub away from the rim.

In 1.7 miles you will reach 8 **Pima Point**. Here, the overwhelming grandeur of the Grand Canyon can truly be appreciated, as it offers clear panoramic views for miles to the west, north and east. The walk concludes with a final 1.1 miles to 9 **Hermits Rest**, one of the 13 canyon features named after one of the park's most famous residents, Louis Boucher (aka 'The Hermit').

Buy a cold drink or an ice-cream and wander behind Hermits Rest to find a quiet spot to enjoy the canyon before catching a shuttle back to the Village.

over the mesa, from the speckled soil to old machinery and mine shafts. Although the many hollowed-out caves may look enticing, it's forbidden, not to mention very dangerous, to enter them.

The trailhead is at Grandview Point (p79), 12 miles east of the village on Desert View Dr, with year-round parking.

OVERNIGHT HIKES

Unless you have advanced reservations at Phantom Ranch (p84), on the canyon bottom, you must secure a backcountry permit (p83) for all overnight hiking at Grand Canyon.

Below the Rim

Rim to Rim

Duration Two to three days one way

Distance 21 miles one way

Difficulty Difficult

Start South Kaibab Trailhead (South Rim)

Finish North KaibabTrailhead (North Rim)

Nearest Town Grand Canyon Village

Transportation Shuttle, car, bicycle

Summary Descend 6.9 miles along the panoramic ridge of the South Kaibab, sleep in the canyon depths and climb 14 miles back out the canyon to the North Rim.

PATROLLED CAMPGROUNDS BELOW THE RIM

Bright Angel (p60), the park's most popular corridor trail, offers the only patrolled inner-canyon campground between the South Rim and the Colorado River: Indian Garden Campground (p84), 4.6 miles down from the trailhead. Bright Angel Campground (p83) and Phantom Ranch (p84) are a further 4.7 and 5 miles, respectively.

From Bright Angel Campground, it is 7.2 miles up the North Kaibab Trail to Cottonwood (p152), open mid-May to mid-October, and then a final 6.8 miles to the North Rim.

Advanced backcountry permits (p227) are required for camping at all corridor campgrounds.

The three-day South Kaibab to North Kaibab trek is the classic Grand Canyon rim-to-rim hike and one of the finest trips in the canyon. For those hikers beginning on the South Rim, most descend the South Kaibab (p62) 6.9 miles and cross the Colorado River on the Kaibab Suspension Bridge to **Bright Angel Campground** (or another 0.3 miles up to **Phantom Ranch**). From Bright Angel Campground, it's 7.2 miles up the North Kaibab to **Cottonwood Campground** for the second night, and a final 6.8-mile climb up to the North Rim, 1000ft higher in elevation than the South Rim.

Alternatively, descend from the South Rim 9.3 miles to Phantom Ranch along the Bright Angel Trail (p60), or begin the hike from the North Rim. Because the climb up the South Kaibab is the hottest and most exposed in the park, it's best to ascend via the Bright Angel Trail when hiking from north to south.

You'll need a backcountry permit (p83) to camp below the rim (or, if you plan on hiking down one day and out the second, reservations at Phantom Ranch) and will need to arrange a ride back to your starting point. Between mid-May and mid-October, the nifty Trans-Canyon Shuttle (p235) departs twice daily (7am and 2pm) from Grand Canyon Lodge (p227) on the North Rim for the 4½-hour drive to the South Rim. From South Rim to North Rim, it departs Bright Angel Lodge (p84) at 8am and 1:30pm. There is only one shuttle daily, weather permitting, from mid-October through November 15. It also offers private custom shuttle services, as does Grand Canyon Shuttle Service (p236).

Think through your schedule carefully. If you emerge from the canyon without a pre-arranged same-day shuttle pick-up, you'll need a place to spend the night, and the only accommodations on the North Rim are Grand Canyon Lodge or the North Rim Campground (p228). Kaibab Lodge (p159), about 16 miles away from the North Rim, is the closest alternative, and it offers shuttle pick-up at the North Kaibab Trailhead.

Facilities on the North Rim are closed between mid-October and mid-May, and the weather is unpredictable – you could leave warm, sunny skies on the South Rim and walk into a blizzard on the North Rim. There is a year-round ranger station that can provide shelter if you turn left at the North

Kaibab Trailhead and walk about a mile, but if you turn right at the trailhead, you will encounter a whole lotta nothing for 43 miles.

There is no public transportation from the North Kaibab Trailhead to Grand Canyon Lodge (1.2 miles) and cell-phone service is unreliable.

South Kaibab to Phantom Ranch, up Bright Angel

Duration Two to three days

Distance 16.5 miles

Difficulty Difficult

Start South Kaibab Trailhead

Finish Bright Angel Trailhead

Nearest Town Grand Canyon Village

Transportation Shuttle, bicycle

Summary Iconic inner-canyon loop descends steeply along one of the park's most spectacular trails.

If you only have time to spend one night in the canyon, or you want to start and finish on the South Rim, this hike is an ideal choice. It's 6.9 miles down the South Kaibab (p62) to Bright Angel Campground, just beyond the Colorado River, and 9.3 miles back up along Bright Angel (p60). Phantom Ranch sits 0.3 miles beyond Bright Angel Campground. Enter the lottery for ranch lodging 15 months in advance of your descent; or, for camping at Bright Angel, submit a backcountry permit five months in advance.

From the mule corral by the South Kaibab Trailhead (7000ft) the trail starts out deceptively gentle, with a long, well-graded switchback that leads to the end of a promontory about 20 minutes from the top. Here the cliff-hugging trail opens up to Ooh Aah Point, a shaggy promontory, which juts off the elbow of a switchback and offers a sweeping panorama of the purplish Tonto Platform far below. The ledge is a nice spot for rest and refreshment.

Soon after, things turn serious, as the trail takes a sharp nosedive and begins to zigzag down a series of steep, tight switchbacks, making its way down the red sandstone. After about 30 minutes, the trail straightens out some when it hits the gorgeous Cedar Mesa and its namesake Cedar Ridge (6060ft), a striking red-tinged mesa. Stop long enough for a snack and perhaps a visit to the pit toilet, and linger to enjoy the lovely vast views of Bright Angel Canyon, Devil's Corkscrew and the North Rim.

The trail then meanders off the mesa toward O'Neill Butte, wraps around to the east, then levels out onto another plateau known as **Skeleton Point** (5200ft), where you can enjoy views of the Colorado River while you refuel with a snack. From here, the trail continues its precipitous drop over scree and through the Redwall cliffs, eventually opening up onto the Tonto Platform.

Traverse the agave-studded plateau past the Tonto Trail junction, then take a long pause and a deep breath at the **Tipoff** (3870ft), which provides an emergency phone and pit toilet, and marks the beginning of the steep descent into the inner gorge. After hiking another challenging 1.5 miles and drinking in pretty views of Phantom Ranch, you'll reach the intersection of the River Trail, which skirts the south side of the Colorado River and connects up with the Bright Angel Trail. Soon you'll go through a short tunnel and cross the river via the skinny black **Kaibab Suspension Bridge**, built in 1928 by the National Park Service and spanning 440ft across the Colorado.

At the other side of the river, turn left past an ancient Puebloan dwelling (do not enter the site), Boat Beach below and the grave of Rees B Griffiths, who died building the Tipoff, and head less than a mile to the intersection with the River Trail. Here you'll find drinking water, a restroom and a circa 1934 ranger station now used as a residence. Follow Bright Angel Creek north a few minutes to Bright Angel Campground, and just past that is Phantom Ranch. Designed by Mary Colter in 1922, the lovely stone lodge is the only developed facility in the inner canyon. Riders heading into the canyon on mule, as

PRIMITIVE TRAILS

For highly experienced hikers with knowledge in route-finding and wilderness desert extremes, the South Rim offers two unmaintained primitive-zone trails that descend from the rim into the canyon: **Tanner Trail** and **New Hance Trail** (www.nps.gov/grca; Desert View Dr). Expect eroded trails, steep descents and complete isolation. There is no water until the Colorado River; bring a filtration system. You must have a topographical map before attempting these trails, and a backcountry permit for at-large camping.

South Kaibab to Bright Angel

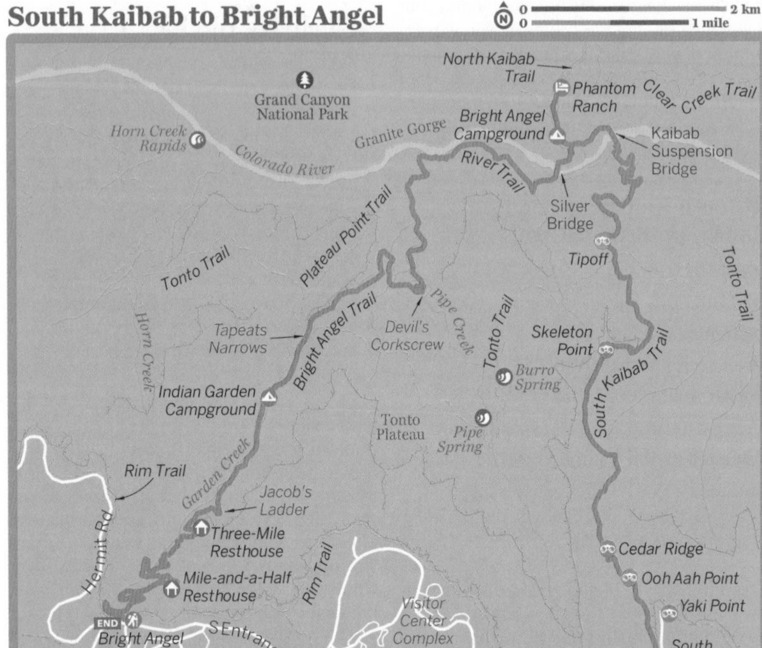

well as hikers with advanced reservations, spend the night at Phantom Ranch, and the canteen here is welcome air-conditioned bliss. Relax over a beer and board games, or kick back in the cool, clear waters of Bright Angel Creek.

From May through September, you'll want to start the return to the rim at dawn to avoid hiking in the searing sun. It's 9.6 miles from the ranch to the South Rim via Bright Angel. Cross the Colorado River on the **Silver Bridge**, and take the River Trail just over 1 mile to Bright Angel Trail; from here, the 7.7-mile ascent takes between six and nine hours.

The River Trail's desert vegetation and slogging sand soon give way to willows and cottonwoods as the trail follows loosely along Pipe Creek, and then begins the grueling and exposed switchbacks of **Devil's Corkscrew**. As the name implies, this is one of the most daunting stretches – the trail winds up and up 1000ft through the desert landscape of the Vishnu schist, ending in another sweet sigh of riparian landscape surrounding Garden Creek.

The trail then passes through **Tapeats Narrows**, Here, where the Vishnu schist meets the Tapeats, the rocks sit atop one another like a pile of flapjacks. Continuing up the canyon, you soon arrive at Indian Garden Campground (3760ft), 5 miles from Phantom Ranch, where you'll find water, toilets, a ranger station and a popular campground. Provided you have planned ahead, you could break up your climb from Bright Angel Campground (or Phantom Ranch) to the South Rim with a night here. It's a popular and lovely spot, with plenty of shade and the cool waters of Garden Creek.

You'll want to relax and refuel at Indian Garden, as the final stretch to the rim is a doozy. The trail stretches 1.6 miles through the upper Tonto Platform to **Jacob's Ladder,** another set of grueling switchbacks, and through the distinctive Redwall Limestone to the stone **Three-Mile Resthouse**.

From May through September, there is drinking water, but because of increasingly frequent waterline breaks it's best not to depend on it. Wander behind the building to take in the view out over the Redwall to Indian Garden and Plateau Point.

The **Mile-and-a-Half Resthouse**, 1.5 miles later, offers another welcomed respite in the cool of the 1936 stone cottage, as well as seasonal water and compost toilets, before the final 1.5 miles to the South Rim. You'll pass under two tunnels – at the second one, look to the right for Native American pictographs painted onto the canyon wall.

Upon emerging on the bustling rim, take a moment to congratulate yourself, and head left to El Tovar for a well-deserved beer and bison chile on the rim-side patio.

Hermit Trail to Hermit Camp and Hermit Rapid

Duration Two days round-trip

Distance 15.4 miles round-trip (to Hermit Camp), 18.4 miles round-trip (to Hermit Rapid)

Difficulty Difficult

Start/Finish Hermit Trailhead

Nearest Town Grand Canyon Village

Transportation Shuttle, car, bicycle

Summary Tracing the path of the Hermit, this steep but rewarding out-and-back hike leads to a backcountry campground on the site of one of the park's earliest tourist accommodations.

DAY 1: HERMIT TRAIL HEAD TO HERMIT CAMP

4-6 HOURS/7.7 MILES

From the Hermit Trailhead a steep, rocky path descends 2 miles to **Santa Maria Spring**, a lovely day hike. Backpackers continue past the spring as the trail levels for a mile or so before zigzagging over loose rocks. Note that the Hermit Trail hasn't seen a maintenance crew in over 80 years, and it's showing signs of the same erosion that created the canyon. The Supai section of the trail (just below Santa Maria Spring) has deteriorated to the point where hikers need to scramble over rocks and it can be difficult to find the trail.

Soon after descending the Redwall via a series of extremely steep, compressed switchbacks known as the **Cathedral Stairs** (keep an eye out for fossils in the bottom sections of this formation), the Hermit eventually hits the cross-canyon Tonto Trail (6.4 miles from the trailhead, at 3210ft).

Turn left (west) to merge with the Tonto; in 1 mile you'll reach the stone remnants of the old **Hermit Camp** (2800ft), one of the original Fred Harvey tent accommodations. Just beyond the ruins, the cliff-rimmed backcountry campground (with pit toilets and seasonal water) makes a glorious place to sleep.

From the campground it's another 1.5 miles to the Colorado River, which you can reach by following your nose down the creek right from the campground; alternatively, the river is a bit closer if you turn down Hermit Creek just before Hermit Camp.

Down at the river, the canyon walls are exquisite black Vishnu schist shot through with veins of pink Zoroaster granite. **Hermit Rapid**, a major Colorado River rapid, marks the confluence of Hermit Creek and the Colorado. There's a backcountry campground, but no facilities.

DAY 2: HERMIT CAMP TO HERMIT TRAILHEAD

6-8 HOURS/7.7 MILES

To return to Hermits Rest, retrace your steps for the arduous climb back to the trailhead. For a longer wilderness excursion, with advanced backcountry permits, you can pick up the eastbound Tonto and intercept the Bright Angel.

Tonto Trail: Down the Hermit Trail, Up Bright Angel

Duration Three to four days one way

Distance 26.9 miles one way

Difficulty Difficult

Start Hermit Trailhead

Finish Bright Angel Trailhead

Nearest Town Grand Canyon Village

Transportation Shuttle, bicycle

Summary For experienced canyon hikers, this stunning trek may require some route finding – particularly along the undulating and unmaintained Tonto – but you'll find plenty of backcountry camping spots.

DAY 1: HERMIT TRAILHEAD TO MONUMENT CREEK

5-7 HOURS/9.3 MILES

Descend the Hermit Trail 4.4 miles past Santa Maria Spring, and turn right at the Tonto Trail junction for the 14.5-mile eastbound passage to the Bright Angel Trail. From the

TONTO TRAIL CAUTION

Tonto Trail, the longest in the canyon, is a 95-mile east–west primitive-zone trail along the entire length of the Tonto Platform. It parallels the Colorado River on the south side of the canyon, intersecting with several rim-to-river trails and serving as a primary vein for complicated inner-canyon treks. Unlike the corridor trails, the Tonto does not extend to the rim, and it does not involve significant elevation change, remaining around 4000ft. Most folks hike specific sections of the Tonto, descending the South Rim on, for example, the Grandview, cutting west on the Tonto, and ascending back to the South Rim on the South Kaibab. There are several backcountry campsites along the way, as well as spurs to the river.

The Tonto is an unpatrolled wilderness area with no facilities along its undulating, sunbaked desert terrain. Under no circumstances is this route an option for inexperienced hikers, and the NPS recommends that no one hike the Tonto from May 1 through September. Contact the Backcountry Information Center (p90) for details.

junction it's just over 4 miles to **Monument Creek** (2995ft), providing water and designated trailside campsites. Alternatively, you can spend the first night at Hermit Camp Campground, just over 1 mile west beyond the junction, then backtrack to embark on the Tonto your second morning. Do not hike the Tonto without securing an NPS map and guide.

For a side trip, head 2 miles down the drainage to Granite Rapid, one of the bigger rapids on the Colorado and a designated backcountry campsite.

DAY 2: MONUMENT CREEK TO INDIAN GARDEN

4-6 HOURS/10.7 MILES

The Tonto snakes along the contour with a mild elevation change of 600ft, reaching **Cedar Spring** after 1.3 miles and **Salt Creek** in another 30 minutes; both are approved for backcountry camping. From there it's just under 5 miles to **Horn Creek** – don't even think about drinking the water here (even after filtering it), as it's been found to be highly radioactive. You can backcountry camp at Horn Creek, but in under an hour you'll be at verdant Indian Garden (p84), a popular corridor campground with treated water available year-round and a ranger station.

DAY 3: INDIAN GARDEN TO BRIGHT ANGEL TRAILHEAD

3-5 HOURS/4.6 MILES

Load up on water at the campground before beginning the hot grind on the Bright Angel 4.6 miles back to the South Rim. The trail meanders along Garden Creek for a couple of miles, and two resthouses between the campground and the rim provide drinking water from June through August. Get a very early start so that you're still in the shade for the grueling Jacob's Ladder switchbacks.

Water-pipe breaks, increasingly common throughout Grand Canyon, can happen at any time, and when they do inner-canyon water sources go dry. Never descend into the canyon without enough water to last the duration of your trip.

BICYCLING

Cyclists have limited options inside the park, as bicycles are only allowed on paved roads, dirt roads that are open to the public and the multi-use Greenway Trail. Though primarily a utilitarian path through the Village, there are a couple sections where the Greenway and Rim Trail converge, offering the chance to cycle in and out of rim views and pause at canyon overlooks.

Hermit Rd offers a scenic ride west to Hermits Rest (p75), about 7 miles from the Village. Shuttles ply this road every 15 minutes between March and November (the rest of the year, traffic is minimal). They are not permitted to pass cyclists, so for the first 4 miles you'll have to pull over each time one drives by. However, starting from Monument Creek Vista (p81), the Greenway Trail overlaps with the Rim Trail and it is a lovely 2.8-mile ride to Hermits Rest on the western edge of the South Rim.

The second Rim Trail section of the Greenway Trail is the short and easy 2.5 mile ride from the visitor center to the South Kaibab Trailhead (p62); from here, you can ride about a mile to Yaki Point (p79).

Alternatively, you could ride out to the East Entrance along Desert View Dr, a 50-mile round-trip from the Village. The route is largely shuttle-free but sees a lot of car traffic in summer. Just off Desert View Dr, the 1-mile dirt road to Shoshone Point (p79) is an easy, nearly level ride that ends at this secluded panoramic vista, one of the few places to escape South Rim crowds.

Bright Angel Bicycles & Cafe at Mather Point CYCLING

(Map p76; ☎bike shop 928-638-3055, reservations 928-679-0992; www.bikegrandcanyon.com; Grand Canyon Visitor Center Complex; 24hr rental adult/child 16yr & under $45/30, 5hr rental $30/20, wheelchair $10, s/d stroller up to 8hr $18/31; ⏲7am-5pm Mar-Jan; 👪; 🚌Village, 🚌Kaibab/Rim) Bicycle rental and tours. Reserve in advance online or by phone; with the exception of the peak stretch from June through mid-August, however, walk-ins can usually be accommodated. Helmets included, add-on pull-along trailer options available. The recommended seasonal two-hour **Hermit Shuttle Package** (adult/child $34/25) shuttles riders from the shop to Hopi Point (p79), and picks them up at Hermits Rest (p75).

This allows you to avoid the traffic of busy Grand Canyon Village and the initial Hermit Rd incline so you can focus your time and energy on a leisurely and mostly flat 5.5-mile cruise along Hermit Rd's most beautiful stretch of canyon overlooks.

For folks with limited time or small children, the **Orange Route** is a moderate ride that heads east on a 7-mile round-trip from Bright Angel Bicycles to the South Kaibab Trailhead and Yaki Point. It's a lovely winding cruise through the piñon, past some canyon-view picnic spots and spectacular overlooks. The only traffic is the short stretch between South Kaibab Trailhead and Yaki Point, where you share the road with Yaki Point Rd shuttles.

Guided tours of Yaki Point (adult/child $52/42) or Hermit Road (adult/child $62/47) are offered seasonally multiple times daily.

The bike rental also serves as one of the South Rim's best cafe (p85) options for grab-and-go breakfast burritos, sandwiches, snacks and coffee.

Greenway Trail CYCLING

(Map p76; www.nps.gov/grca; Grand Canyon Village; 👪; 🚌Village, 🚌Kaibab/Rim, 🚌Hermit, Mar 1-Nov 30) A multi-use trail open to cyclists and hikers. From Monument Creek Vista 2.8 miles west to Hermits Rest and from the Visitor Center Plaza 2.5 miles east to the South Kaibab Trailhead, the Greenway Trail and the Rim Trail are the same thing. These paved stretches wind gently through piñon-dotted landscape and offer several lovely picnic spots and excellent views.

You can rent bikes, including trailers for little ones, at Bright Angel Bicycles. From here, the ride to the South Kaibab Trailhead is especially nice for families, as it is easily accessible from the visitor center and does not include any steep inclines.

Beyond that, the Greenway Trail is less a scenic bike ride than a convenient bike path through and around Grand Canyon Village and up to the Visitor Center. You can also ride along the Greenway Trail from Visitor Center Plaza 6.6 miles south to the IMAX in Tusayan, but the final 4 miles are not paved. South Rim shuttle buses can accommodate bicycles.

OTHER ACTIVITIES

Mule Rides

Visitors who want to view the canyon by **mule** (Map p76; ☎888-297-2757, next-day reservations 928-638-3283; www.grandcanyonlodges.com/plan/mule-rides/; Bright Angel Lodge, Grand Canyon Village Historic District; 2hr mule ride $143, 1-/2-night mule ride incl meals & accommodations $420/593; per 2 people $743/992; ⏲rides available year-round, hrs vary; 👪) have two choices: a two-hour above-the-rim day trip to a canyon overlook, or a two- or three-day trip to the bottom of the canyon, which includes sleeping at Phantom Ranch (p84).

The Canyon Vistas Ride ($143) meets at the livery barn in Grand Canyon Village, across from Bright Angel Lodge, and travels by bus 10 minutes to the South Kaibab Trailhead, where the mules await. Guests enjoy an interpretative ride to an overlook.

Overnight Phantom Ranch trips (one/two people $420/743) and two-night trips (one/two people $593/992) follow the Bright Angel Trail to the Colorado River, connect with the River Trail and cross the river on the Kaibab Suspension Bridge. It's a 5½-hour, 10.5-mile trip to Phantom Ranch, and a 7.8-mile return ride up the South Kaibab Trail. Overnight trips are limited to 10 riders a day and include cabin accommodations and all meals at Phantom.

For age, weight and other restrictions, consult the website.

Mule trips are popular and, especially in the summer, fill up quickly; slots, available 15 months in advance, are awarded through the online Phantom Ranch lottery only (www.grandcanyonlodges.com/lodging/

phantom-ranch). If you arrive at the park and want to join a mule trip the following day, ask about availability at the transportation desk (p90) at Bright Angel Lodge (your chances are much better during the off season). Or make tracks to the other side of the canyon: mule rides on the North Rim, available as half-day trips above or below the rim only, are usually available the day before the trip.

Ranger Programs

Rangers are fonts of information, which they happily share in free year-round **programs** (www.nps.gov/grca/planyourvisit/ranger-program.htm; Grand Canyon Village; ; Village Route) at various locations on the South Rim. Their talks and guided hikes, offered throughout the day and as nightly evening events, cover everything from canyon pioneers to fire ecology, American Indian history and constellations. Check park visitor centers or online for subjects and times of the latest offerings.

TOURS

Boat

A seasonal all-day **Smooth Water Raft Tour** (Map p76; 888-297-2757; www.grandcanyonlodges.com/plan/rafting-tours/; adult/child 4-11 $225/205; seasonal;) departs from the South Rim for a 15-mile trip on a motorized pontoon down a smooth-water stretch of the Colorado River, a beautiful float through the red-rock scenery of spectacular Glen Canyon. The trip, suitable for kids as young as four, includes a five-hour round-trip bus ride..

If you are planning to go to the Page (p166) area during your Grand Canyon visit, you can take the same river trip from there through Wilderness River Adventures (www.riveradventures.com; March to December) and avoid the five-hour round-trip bus ride from the South Rim to the Page boat launch.

Bus

Xanterra offers **bus tours** (Map p76; 888-297-2757, 928-638-3283, same-day reservations 928-638-2631; www.grandcanyonlodges.com/plan/interpretive-bus-tours/; Desert View/Hermits Rest/combination $65/36/80; children under 16 free) to key viewpoints west from the Village to Hermits Rest (two hours) and east to Desert View (four hours). Sunrise and sunset tours are also available. Stop by the Bright Angel transportation desk (p90) or ask at any lodge except Yavapai for reservations.

Driving Tour Desert View Drive

START GRAND CANYON VILLAGE VISITOR CENTER COMPLEX
END DESERT VIEW (EAST ENTRANCE)
LENGTH 25 MILES; FOUR HOURS

Desert View Drive winds through the desert woodlands past several panoramic overlooks and a Native American ruin on its way to the 1932 stone Watchtower. A leisurely drive, with plenty of time for every stop, takes about four hours, but you could zip along in much less. Desert View Drive could make an excellent bike ride if you can be dropped off or picked up at one end or if you don't mind the 50-mile round-trip. There is parking at every stop, four designated picnic areas along the road and bathrooms at Tusayan Museum & Ruin and Desert View.

Begin at the 1 **Grand Canyon Visitor Center Complex** (p91), taking a moment to peruse the displays in the visitor center; pick up a snack for the road at 2 **Bright Angel Bicycles & Cafe at Mather Point** (p85) and enjoy the spectacular views at 3 **Mather Point** (p81), about 300 yards behind the plaza. Its roomy overlooks extend to two promontories that jut out over the canyon, providing views of the Bright Angel and South Kaibab trails ribboning down into the canyon. From the visitor center, it's a short drive or a pleasant 1.3-mile walk along the Rim Trail east to roadside 4 **Pipe Creek Vista** (p81).

After taking in the views, continue the scenic drive eastward. Or, if you've walked, catch a Kaibab/Rim Route Shuttle back to your car at the Visitor Center Complex; alternatively, hop a shuttle to 5 **Yaki Point** (p79), another excellent overlook that is accessible by shuttle only, or stroll along the rim to the Kaibab Trailhead 0.8 miles east. From both Yaki Point and the South Kaibab Trailhead, you can catch a shuttle back to your car at the Visitor Center.

From Pipe Creek Vista, drive east 1.6 miles and look for the unsigned dirt parking lot on the left. If the parking lot doesn't look too crowded, make time for the wonderful 1-mile walk along a dirt road to the picnic spot and viewpoint at 6 **Shoshone Point** (p79). It's a mostly flat stroll, and the

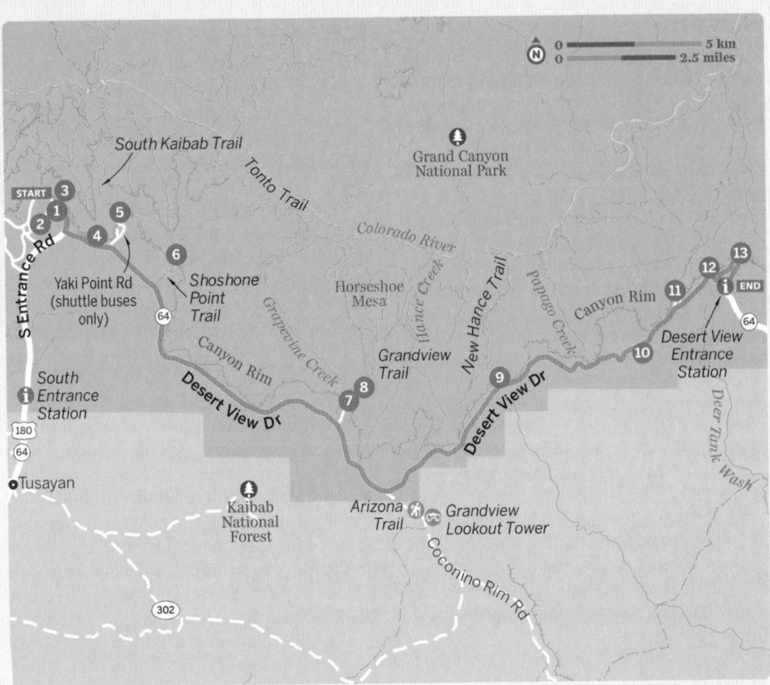

overlook is one of the quietest and best on the South Rim.

Continuing east, it's 6.9 miles to 7 **Grandview Point** (p79). Peter Berry (a prospector-turned-entrepreneur) and his partners improved a Native American trail and built the Grandview Toll Trail in 1893 to access copper claims more than 2000ft below on Horseshoe Mesa. In 1897 he constructed the Grandview Hotel here on the rim, and when he wasn't hauling copper, he led tourists into the canyon on foot and by mule. When the railroad arrived 13 miles west of here in 1901, tourists naturally gravitated toward those facilities, forcing Berry to close up shop in 1908. Today, thousands make a steep descent into the canyon via Berry's 8 **Grandview Trail** (p64), while others enjoy impressive canyon views from the spot where his hotel once thrived.

Desert View Drive winds from Grandview Point 6.8 miles to 9 **Moran Point** (p79), with incredible river views, and another 4.2 miles to 10 **Tusayan Museum & Ruin** (p78), an ancient Puebloan site and small but well-curated museum. Ask about guided tours, offered year-round. As the drive continues eastward, views to the east and south open up magnificently; on a clear day you can see the volcanic San Francisco Peaks towering on the southern horizon.

In 1.9 miles, stop and stretch your legs at 11 **Lipan Point** (p79), where you'll find a panoramic eyeful of the canyon and an unobstructed view of Unkar Rapid just to the west. To the northeast, the sheer cliffs called the Palisades of the Desert define the southeastern wall of the Grand Canyon, beyond which the Echo and Vermilion Cliffs lie in the distance. From Lipan Point, it is 1.7 miles to 12 **Navajo Point** (p81), where you'll find excellent views of several miles of the Colorado River.

The final 0.8 miles of the drive leads to 13 **Desert View Watchtower** (p78). Here, you can climb up the winding staircase to the highest point in the South Rim; take in the magnificent panorama east beyond the canyon to the desert flatness of the Navajo Reservation and the Painted Desert, and stroll along the canyon edge.

Exit the park at the East Entrance or retrace your steps back to Grand Canyon Village.

Flyovers

Companies offering scenic flyovers from the South Rim include **Grand Canyon Airlines** (Map p80; ☎702-638-3300; www.grandcanyonairlines.com; 871 Liberator Dr, Grand Canyon Village, AZ 86023; from $159), **Grand Canyon Helicopters** (Map p80; ☎Grand Canyon National Park Airport 928-638-2764, Las Vegas 702-835-8477, Page 928-645-0246; www.grandcanyonhelicopter.com; Grand Canyon National Park Airport, Hwy 64; from $259), **Maverick Helicopters** (Map p80; ☎702-261-0007, 888-261-4414; www.flymaverick.com; 107 Corsair Dr, Grand Canyon; $299 for 45 min) and **Papillon Grand Canyon Helicopters** (☎888-635-7272, 702-736-7243; www.papillon.com; 1265 Airport Rd, Boulder City, NV 89005; 45min from $124). Contact them for specific rates, as each offers several options. Most flights leave from Tusayan and Las Vegas but check itinerary and departure points carefully.

Note that Grand Canyon West is on Hualapai Tribal land and is not part of Grand Canyon National Park; the area is loud and busy with half- and full-day tours and flyovers that sometimes include landing below the canyon rim.

Jeep & Van

Several companies offer guided jeep and van tours from Tusayan to South Rim overlooks and historic sights, and some options include short hikes along the rim or into the canyon. Go to www.grandcanyoncvb.org for a full listing.

Pink Jeep Tours TOURS

(☎800-873-3662; www.pinkjeep.com; adult/child from $99/90; 👪) Offers multiple daily tours, including sunset tours, to overlooks along Desert View Drive (p227) and Hermit Road (p227), in open-air pink jeeps; all tours board at the National Geographic Visitor Center (p233) in Tusayan (accessible via free park shuttles March 1 to September 30) and some include short hikes.

Grand Canyon Jeep Tours & Safari TOURS

(☎928-638-5337; www.grandcanyonjeeptours.com; adult/child from $95/80; 👪) Open-air guided jeep tours of Grand Canyon highlights. There are five options, including a combination air-and-jeep trip and one that offers a 90-minute walk along the rim. Tours depart from the McDonalds in Tusayan; from March 1 through November 30, hop the free park shuttle to Tusayan.

SIGHTS

The Grand Canyon's natural splendor is the prime attraction, and the majority of sights are in the form of formal canyon overlooks, each more spectacular than the next. Two scenic drives wind through the desert shrub to canyon overlooks: Hermit Road, stretching 7 miles west from Grand Canyon Village, offers nine overlooks; Desert View, winding 25 miles east from Grand Canyon Village leads to seven overlooks. Grand Canyon Village itself clusters about 3 miles along the rim. You can walk to all of the Hermit Road and Village overlooks along the 13-mile Rim Trail, or catch shuttles; Desert View is accessible by car, bicycle or tour only.

In addition to scenic views, several museums and historic stone buildings illuminate the park's fascinating human history, and rangers lead a host of daily programs on subjects from geology to resurgent condors. Some of the most important buildings were designed by noted architect Mary Jane Colter to complement the landscape and reflect the local culture.

Travelers can take a **cell-phone audio tour** at sites across the South Rim. These ranger-narrated tours last two minutes and can be accessed, at no extra charge, by dialing 928-225-2907 and pressing the designated stop number. Note, however, that cellphone coverage is spotty and your service may not get any coverage at all.

Grand Canyon Village

★ **Kolb Studio** MUSEUM

(Map p76; ☎928-638-2771; www.nps.gov/grca/planyourvisit/art-exhibits.htm; Rim Trail, Grand Canyon Village Historic District; ⏰8am-7pm Mar-May & Sep-Nov, to 6pm Dec-Feb, to 8pm Jun-Aug; 🚌Village (Hermits Rest Route Transfer stop), 🚌Hermits Rest, Mar 1-Nov 30; Village Route Transfer) FREE In 1905 Ellsworth and Emery Kolb built a small photography studio on the edge of the rim, which has since been expanded and now holds a bookstore and a museum. An original Kolb brothers 1911 silent film runs continuously, show incredible footage of their early explorations of the Colorado River, and the museum displays mementos and photographs from their careers. In January and February, the NPS offers tours of their original Craftsman home, in a lower level of the studio.

★**Trail of Time** MUSEUM

(Map p76; Rim Trail, Grand Canyon Village Historic District; P 🚻; 🚌Village) This outdoor interpretative display traces the history of the canyon's formation – each meter equals one million years of geologic history, for a total of about 2.1 billion years in just over a mile. Begin with the canyon's oldest rocks and walk forward in time from Verkamp's (p77) east to the Yavapai Geology Museum (p76), or do the reverse. Rock samples from within the canyon line the trail, and specially positioned metal cylinders allow you to view these rocks on the far canyon wall.

Hermits Rest HISTORIC BUILDING, VIEWPOINT

(Map p80; ☎928-638-2351; www.nps.gov/grca/learn/photosmultimedia/colter_hermits_photos.htm; Hermit Rd; ⏲8am-8pm May-Sep, 9am-5pm Oct-Mar, 9am-6:30pm Apr-May; 🚻; 🚌Hermits Rest, Mar 1-Nov 30) Commissioned by the Fred Harvey Company and designed by Mary Colter in 1913, this low-flung stone building is the South Rim's westernmost scenic overlook (note that the overlook remains open when the building closes). It houses a small gift shop and a walk-up window, with sandwiches, ice cream and snacks, and there are restrooms. In the back, past the bustle of visitors, you'll find a lovely picnic area in the desert scrub, quiet views and the Hermit Trailhead (p63).

Hermits Rest is named after Louis Boucher (aka 'the Hermit'), who came to the canyon from Canada in 1889 with hopes of finding his fortune as a prospector. Boucher lived at Dripping Springs, several miles below the rim, for 20 years, and offered tourists guided trips to his home and orchards there. He never did strike it rich, and eventually sold the upper portions of his trail to the Santa Fe Railroad and Fred Harvey Company, and moved to Utah.

Fred Harvey History Room MUSEUM

(Map p76; Bright Angel Lodge, Grand Canyon Village Historic District; ⏲9am-5pm; P 🚻; 🚌Village) FREE Fred Harvey's Harvey Company opened the first Harvey House in 1876 in Topeka, Kansas. In the following decades Harvey, in collaboration with the Atchison, Topeka and Santa Fe Railway and architect Mary Colter, built dozens of hotels, shops and restaurants to service the growing needs of railroad travelers, and he is widely credited with branding the American Southwest as a tourist destination. This small museum display photos, dishes, postcards and souvenirs from his early-20th-century Grand Canyon tourist industry.

Grand Canyon Village Historic District HISTORIC BUILDING, MUSEUM

(Map p76; www.grandcanyonlodges.com/historic-village/; Grand Canyon Village; P 🚻; 🚌Village) The South Rim's historic district is comprised of several early-20th-century national historic landmarks clustered along and around the rim between Hermit Rd and Yavapai Point. Most of the buildings here, including two of the park's oldest lodges, were commissioned by the NPS in collaboration with the Atchison, Topeka & Santa Fe Railroad and the Fred Harvey Company to service the park's rapidly growing tourist market. Pick up a walking tour brochure online (www.grandcanyonlodges.com) or at any visitor center.

Bright Angel Lodge HISTORIC BUILDING

(Map p76; ☎928-638-2631; www.nps.gov/grca/learn/photosmultimedia/colter_ba_photos.htm; Rim Trail, Grand Canyon Village Historic District; P 🚻; 🚌Village) Commissioned by the Fred Harvey Company, designed by Mary Colter and completed in 1935, the log-and-stone Bright Angel Lodge offered canyon travelers alternative accommodations to the luxurious El Tovar. Just off the lobby is the History Room, a small museum devoted to Fred Harvey. The fireplace uses actual canyon stones to recreate the geology of Bright Angel Trail from river to rim.

Today's Bright Angel is the latest in a series of incarnations that began after the first stagecoach arrived at the South Rim from Flagstaff on May 19, 1892. On the lodge grounds is the **Buckey O'Neill Cabin**. Built in the 1890s by William Owen O'Neill and renovated in 2007 and 2018, the cabin is the longest continually standing building on the rim. Today the lucky few who make reservations at Bright Angel Lodge (p84) well in advance can stay here.

El Tovar HISTORIC BUILDING

(Map p76; ☎928-638-2631; www.grandcanyonlodges.com/historic-village/; Rim Trail, Grand Canyon Village Historic District; P 🚻; 🚌Village) Built in 1905 as a railroad hotel, El Tovar was designed by Charles Whittlesey as a blend of Swiss chalet and the more rustic style that would come to define national-park lodges in the 1920s. With its unusual spires and dark-wood beams rising behind the Rim Trail, elegant El Tovar (p85) remains a grande dame of national park lodges, and

Grand Canyon Village

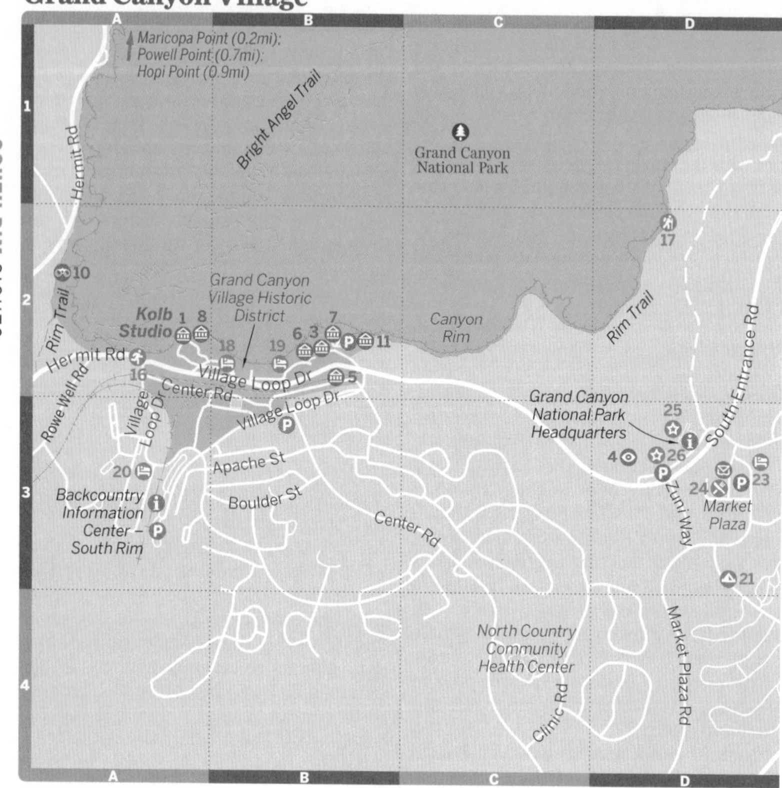

the public spaces look much as they did when the lodge opened.

Wide, inviting porches offer travelers a comfortable and elegant place to relax after a day on the trails, and in the winter the fireplace in the lobby is cozy and inviting, the interior has a classic Western feel. The lodge sits about 100 yards from the rim, and though it's thronged with tourists by day, the scene mellows considerably in the evening. The bench swing on the side porch is the best spot on the South Rim to relax with a cocktail and watch the comings and goings along the canyon rim.

Yavapai Point and Geology Museum VIEWPOINT, MUSEUM

(Map p76; 928-638-7890; www.nps.gov/grca/planyourvisit/yavapai-geo.htm; Rim Trail, Grand Canyon Village Historic District; 8am-7pm Mar-May & Sep-Nov, to 6pm Dec-Feb, to 8pm Jun-Aug; P; Kaibab/Rim) FREE Views don't get much better than those unfolding behind the plate-glass windows of this little stone building, but if weather allows be sure to enjoy the canyon splendor from the overlook just outside, where you can hear, smell and feel the canyon rather than just see it. Handy panels inside the museum identify and explain the various formations before you, and displays (including a scale model) highlight the canyon's multilayered geologic history.

From here, you can walk west along the Trail of Time (p75) about 1.5 miles to the main cluster of historic sites in Grand Canyon Village Historic District.

Lookout Studio HISTORIC BUILDING

(Map p76; www.nps.gov/grca/learn/photosmultimedia/colter_lookout_photos.htm; Rim Trail, Grand Canyon Village Historic District; 8am-sunset mid-May–Aug, 9am-5pm Sep–mid-May; Village (Hermits Rest Route Transfer stop), Hermits Rest (Hermits Rest, Mar 1-Nov 30; Village Route Transfer) FREE Like Mary Colter's other canyon buildings, Lookout Studio was modeled after stone dwellings of the Southwest Pueblo American

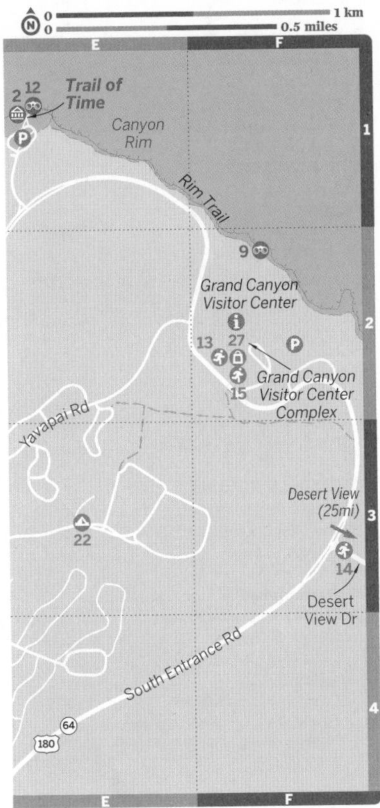

Indians. Made of rough-cut Kaibab limestone, with a roof that mirrors the lines of the rim, the studio blends into its natural surroundings. Inside is a small souvenir shop and a tiny back porch that offers coin-operated telescopes and spectacular canyon views.

Hopi House HISTORIC BUILDING

(Map p76; 928-638-2631; www.nps.gov/grca/learn/photosmultimedia/colter_hopih_photos.htm; Rim Trail, Grand Canyon Village Historic District; 8am-8pm May–Aug, 9am-6pm Sep–Apr; P; Village) Another beautiful Mary Colter–designed building, Hopi House has been offering high-quality American Indian jewelry, basketwork, pottery and other crafts since its 1905 opening. The structure was built by the Hopi from native stone and wood, inspired by traditional dwellings on their reservation, and both the exterior and the interior mimic traditional Hopi design elements. Be sure to walk upstairs to visit the Native American Art Gallery.

Verkamp's Visitor Center HISTORIC BUILDING

(Map p76; 928-638-7146; www.nps.gov/grca/planyourvisit/verkamps.htm; Rim Trail, Grand Canyon Village Historic District; 8am-8pm Jun-Aug, reduced hrs Sep-May; P; Village) FREE The arrival of the railroad in 1901 opened up the canyon to more and more tourists, and in 1905 John G Verkamp opened the Mission-style Verkamp's Curios. After running the shop for more than 100 years, Verkamp's ancestors closed down the business, and the NPS revamped the building as a small visitor center in 2008. It maintains an old-fashioned, dusty feel, and the tiny museum gives a well-presented timeline of Grand Canyon history in the context of other national events.

Grand Canyon Pioneer Cemetery CEMETERY

(Map p76; www.nps.gov/grca/planyourvisit/shrine-of-the-ages.htm; Shrine of the Ages, Market Plaza; P; Village, Shrine of the Ages stop) More than 390 people are buried at the Grand Canyon Pioneer Cemetery; the lives of many of them, including the Kolb brothers, John Verkamp, Ralph Cameron and John Hance, are intricately woven into the history of the canyon. The cemetery, which is set back from the road, removed from the park's tourist centers and surrounded by Ponderosa, makes a peaceful respite from high season crowds, and there are a few picnic tables just outside the entrance.

For details and photographs of the myriad of characters buried here, pick up a copy of *Grand Canyon Pioneer Cemetery* at the Grand Canyon Association store (p87) in Visitor Center Plaza.

Grand Canyon Train Depot HISTORIC BUILDING

(Map p76; www.thetrain.com; Grand Canyon Village Historic District; Village west-bound, Grand Canyon Railway) FREE This train depot, designed by Francis Wilson and completed in 1910, was built nine years after the first train arrived in the Village from Williams. A registered National Historic Landmark, it's one of about 14 log depots ever constructed in the US, the only one that still serves as a functioning depot, and the only train station inside a US national park.

The 1st floor was used for passenger services, and the 2nd floor was a two-bedroom apartment for the ticket agent. Today, a Grand Canyon Railway train pulls into the station daily from Williams.

Grand Canyon Village

Top Sights
1 Kolb Studio ... A2
2 Trail of Time ... E1

Sights
Bright Angel Lodge ... (see 18)
3 El Tovar ... B2
Fred Harvey History Room ... (see 18)
4 Grand Canyon Pioneer Cemetery ... D3
5 Grand Canyon Train Depot ... B2
6 Grand Canyon Village Historic District ... B2
7 Hopi House ... B2
8 Lookout Studio ... A2
9 Mather Point ... F2
10 Trailview Overlook ... A2
11 Verkamp's Visitor Center ... B2
12 Yavapai Point and Geology Museum ... E1

Activities, Courses & Tours
13 Bright Angel Bicycles & Cafe at Mather Point ... F2
Bus Tours ... (see 18)
14 Desert View Drive ... F3
Grand Canyon Mule Rides ... (see 18)
15 Greenway Trail ... F2
16 Hermit Road ... A2
17 Rim Trail ... D2
Smooth Water Raft Tour ... (see 20)

Sleeping
18 Bright Angel Lodge ... B2
El Tovar ... (see 3)
19 Kachina & Thunderbird Lodges ... B2
20 Maswik Lodge ... A3
21 Mather Campground ... D3
22 Trailer Village RV Park ... E3
23 Yavapai Lodge ... D3

Eating
Arizona Room ... (see 18)
Bright Angel Bicycles & Cafe at Mather Point ... (see 13)
Bright Angel Fountain ... (see 18)
24 Canyon Village Market ... D3
El Tovar Dining Room ... (see 3)
Harvey House Cafe ... (see 18)
Maswik Food Court ... (see 20)
Maswik Pizza Pub ... (see 20)
Yavapai Coffee Shop ... (see 23)
Yavapai Lodge Restaurant ... (see 23)

Drinking & Nightlife
Bright Angel Lounge ... (see 18)
El Tovar Lounge ... (see 3)
Yavapai Tavern ... (see 23)

Entertainment
25 McKee Amphitheater ... D3
26 Shrine of the Ages ... D3

Shopping
Canyon Village Market ... (see 24)
27 Grand Canyon Association Park Store at the Visitor Center ... F2
Hopi House ... (see 7)

Desert View

★ Desert View Watchtower — HISTORIC BUILDING, VIEWPOINT

(928-638-8960; www.nps.gov/grca/learn/photosmultimedia/mary-colter---indian-watchtower.htm; Desert View Dr; 8am-7pm May-Sep, to 6pm Oct-Mar, to 7pm Apr-May; stairs close 30min before closing; P) The marvelously worn winding staircase of Mary Colter's 70ft stone tower, built in 1932, leads to one of the highest spots on the rim. From here, slats in the tower wall offer unparalleled views of not only the canyon and a long swath of the Colorado River, but also the San Francisco Peaks, the Navajo Reservation and the Painted Desert. Hopi artist Fred Kabotie's murals depicting Hopi origin stories grace the interior walls of the 1st floor.

On the way up look for an unmarked door on the left; you can wander outside onto a rooftop patio here – a nice spot to relax with a sandwich. Outside the watchtower, a bronze plaque marks the spot as a National Historic Landmark. Just below the rim is the site of the 1956 TWA plane crash that killed 128 people and marked the beginning of modern regulations in air safety.

To find a quiet view away from the crowds, take the furthest left paved path from the parking lot to the tower and wander off among the desert scrub.

There's a small market and snack bar next door, as well as toilets and a year-round gas station.

Tusayan Museum & Ruin — MUSEUM, RUIN

(928-638-7968; www.nps.gov/grca; Desert View Dr; 9am-5pm; P) Just west of Desert View and 22 miles east of Grand Canyon Village, these small ruins and museum examine the culture and lives of the Ancestral Puebloan people who lived here 800 years ago. Only partially excavated to minimize erosion damage, it's less impressive than other such ruins in the Southwest but still worth a look. Pottery, jewelry and split-twig animal figurines on display date back 2000 to 4000 years. Guided tours offered in the summer.

Overlooks

★Shoshone Point VIEWPOINT
(park headquarters 928-638-7888; www.nps.gov/grca; Desert View Dr;) Walk about 1 mile along the mostly level and shaded dirt road to marvelously uncrowded Shoshone Point, a rocky promontory with some of the canyon's best views. Just before reaching the canyon rim, there's a grassy area with picnic tables and grills (advanced permit from NPS required). If you come for sunset, bring a flashlight for the walk back to your car. This viewpoint is unmarked; look for the small dirt parking lot about 1.2 miles east of Yaki Point.

Mohave Point VIEWPOINT
(Map p80; www.nps.gov/grca; Rim Trail, Hermit Rd; P; Hermits Rest, Mar 1-Nov 30) Mohave Point is a great spot to watch the sun rise or set. In high season, when crowds at popular overlooks can be unbearable, Mohave makes a particularly good spot because multiple overlooks offer a better chance of finding a quiet spot, and it's easy to wind your way along the rim to excellent but unofficial views.

Hopi Point VIEWPOINT
(Map p80; www.nps.gov/grca; Rim Trail, Hermit Rd; P; Hermits Rest west-bound, Mar 1-Nov 30) Spectacular Hopi Point juts further into the canyon than any other South Rim overlook, offering magnificent east–west views, making it an excellent choice for dawn and dusk. During the summer peak, however, there can be more than 1000 people waiting for shuttle pick-up after sunset; consider wandering 0.3 miles east along the dirt Rim Trail to Powell Point, which also offers spectacular sunsets and is often less crowded.

This is one of two overlooks on Hermit Rd that has toilets; the second is 5.8 miles west at Hermits Rest.

Lipan Point VIEWPOINT
(www.nps.gov/grca; Desert View Dr; P) Lipan Point offers expansive panoramas and views of both the Colorado River and the Unkar Delta, the seasonal home of the Ancestral Puebloan people from about AD850 to AD1200 (it is today an active archaeological site). Easily accessible by car, this is an excellent perch for sunset. For those particularly interested in the park's geology, Lipan Point is one of the few places where you can clearly see the tilting layered rocks that form the Grand Canyon Supergroup.

The trailhead for the Tanner Trail (p67) sits just before the car park.

Moran Point VIEWPOINT
(www.nps.gov/grca; Desert View Dr; P) With river views and an excellent panorama of the canyon's geologic history, this is one of the park's most striking and dramatic overlooks. A placard on the canyon edge identifies the layered paleozoic rocks, the Grand Canyon Supergroup and Vishnu Basement Rocks clearly visible on the horizon.

Moran Point is named after Thomas Moran, the landscape painter who spent just about every winter at the canyon from 1899 to 1920 and whose romantically dramatic work was instrumental in securing the canyon's national-park status.

Powell Point VIEWPOINT
(Map p80; www.nps.gov/grca; Rim Trail, Hermit Rd; P; Hermits Rest, Mar 1-Nov 30) This rocky peninsula cuts out over the canyon, offering some of the South Rim's most dramatic vistas. Similar to Hopi Point 0.3 miles to the west but not as crowded, Powell is a magnificent spot to catch the sunset. A granite memorial honors John Wesley Powell, the one-armed Civil War veteran who, along with his crew, is credited with being the first man to navigate the Colorado River through the Grand Canyon (1869).

Yaki Point VIEWPOINT
(Map p80; www.nps.gov/grca; Desert View Dr; ; Kaibab/Rim) With dramatic views to both the east and west, Yaki Point is one of the best spots to catch the sunrise. Because it's accessible year-round by shuttle or bicycle only, it tends to be a quieter overlook than others at the South Rim.

Grandview Point VIEWPOINT
(www.nps.gov/grca/planyourvisit/desert-view-drive.htm; Desert View Dr; P) A 1-mile spur off Desert View Dr leads to a spectacular national park highlight. Here, in 1897, pioneer miner Pete Berry built the Grandview Hotel; credited as the first Grand Canyon tourist destination, it operated until 1908. The arrival of the railroad in 1901 and the completion of El Tovar (p75) in 1903 shifted the canyon's tourist hub westward, and the Grandview Hotel was eventually dismantled. Today's Grandview Trail (p64) cuts steeply into the canyon from the overlook.

South Rim (Hermit Rd)

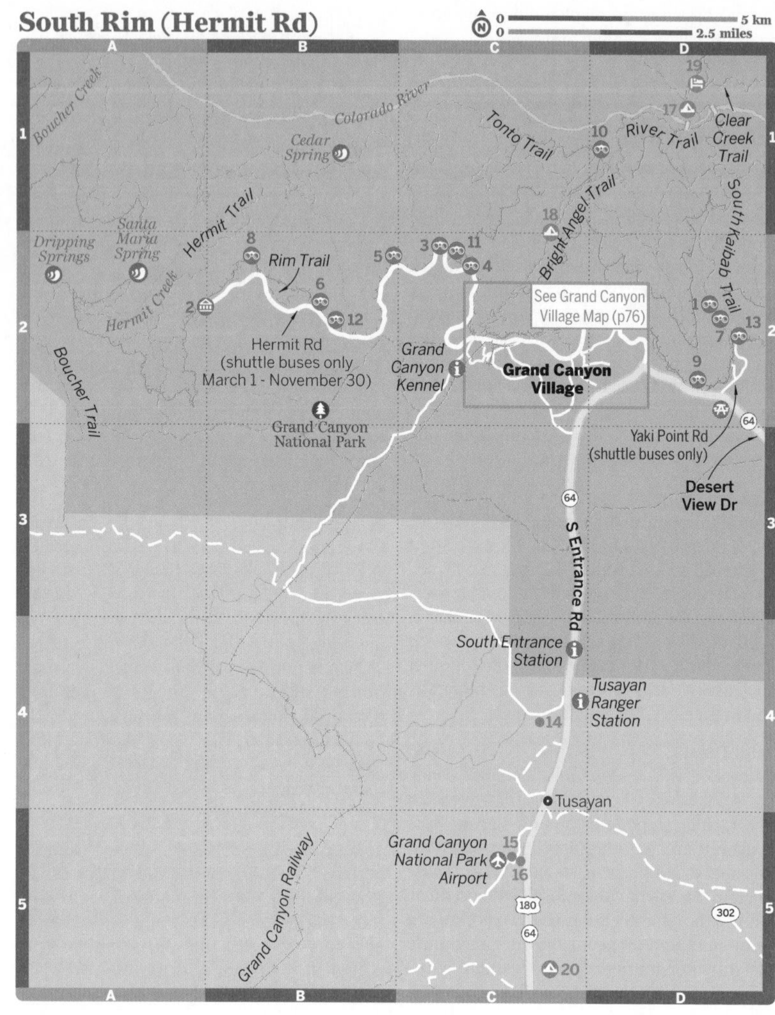

The trail, well worth a few minutes' descent, roughly follows an old Native American route that Berry and Ralph Cameron used to access their copper, gold and silver mines.

Cedar Ridge VIEWPOINT

(Map p80; www.nps.gov/grca; South Kaibab Trail) Located 1.5 miles along the challenging South Kaibab Trail (p62), with a descent of 1040ft, this large and flat red-dirt overlook offers some of the best views of the South Rim and makes an excellent destination for a day hike and below-the-rim picnic. You'll find pit toilets, but there is no shade or water along the trail or at the viewpoint – if hiking in summer, start the hike before dawn to avoid the searing heat.

Plateau Point VIEWPOINT

(Map p80; Bright Angel Trail) A spectacular overlook with incredible river views, Plateau Point is accessible via a 1.5-mile spur trail off the South Rim's inner-canyon Bright Angel Trail (p60) at Indian Garden; from the rim, it's 6 miles down to Plateau Point. Note that there is no shade here, and it is absolutely not recommended to attempt a day hike to Plateau Point during the summer.

South Rim (Hermit Rd)

Sights

Activities, Courses & Tours

Sleeping

Eating

Navajo Point VIEWPOINT

(www.nps.gov/grca; Desert View Dr; P ♿) At 7461ft, Navajo Point is the Grand Canyon South Rim's highest overlook. From here you can view a wide swath of the Colorado River, the stone Desert View Watchtower perched on the canyon rim, and the dramatic expanse of the Painted Desert stretching eastward beyond the park. Navajo Point, located about 25 miles east of Grand Canyon Village, tends to be one of the quieter overlooks, but it's every bit as spectacular as those closer to the tourist hubs.

Pima Point VIEWPOINT

(Map p80; www.nps.gov/grca; Rim Trail, Hermit Rd; P ♿; Hermits Rest, Mar 1-Nov 30) Pima Point has good views of Hermit Camp on the Tonto Platform and the Hermit Rapids on the Colorado River, as well as some sections of the Hermit Trail. If you're here when it's quiet, you can actually hear the rapids.

Ooh Aah Point VIEWPOINT

(Map p80; www.nps.gov/grca; South Kaibab Trail) This stop along the trail 0.9 miles below the rim on the South Kaibab trail, marked by a small sign and several massive boulders, makes an excellent spot to sit and take in the sweeping panorama of the Tonto Platform and is an ideal turn-around point for summer day-hikes.

Monument Creek Vista VIEWPOINT

(Map p80; www.nps.gov/grca; Rim Trail, Hermit Rd; P ♿; Hermits Rest west-bound, Mar 1-Nov 30) Excellent view of the confluence of Monument Creek and the Colorado River, known as Granite Rapid. From here westward, the bicycle- and wheelchair-friendly paved Greenway Trail overlaps with the Rim Trail, offering multiple informal overviews and resting areas along its 2.8-mile route west to Hermits Rest; the stretch from Monument Creek east to Hopi Point is one of the most scenic and least crowded.

Pipe Creek Vista VIEWPOINT

(Map p80; www.nps.gov/grca; Desert View Dr; P ♿; Kaibab/Rim) Pipe Creek Vista, an easy and pleasant 1-mile ramble along the rim, east from the Visitor Center, offers a quiet alternative to Mather Point. Views from this overlook take in Brahma Temple and O'Neill Butte, as well as Pipe Creek, naturally.

Pick up a sandwich from Bright Angel Bicycles & Cafe (p85) and pause at any of the many unofficial overlooks along the way to take in spectacular canyon views in relative silence. From here, continue another mile along the Rim Trail (p58) to the South Kaibab (p62) trailhead.

Mather Point VIEWPOINT

(Map p76; www.nps.gov/grca; Rim Trail, Grand Canyon Visitor Center Complex; P ♿; Kaibab/Rim) Mather Point is the busiest and most popular overlook at the Grand Canyon, due in large part to its close proximity to the visitor center complex and main parking lots. There are multiple vistas, which helps disperse the crowds, and if it's overwhelming simply wander in either direction along the paved rim trail and find a spot to call your own.

Mather Point is named after Stephen Mather, the first director of the National Park Service.

DUFFEL TRANSPORT

Hikers descending into the canyon for a night or two at Bright Angel Campground or Phantom Ranch (p84) can arrange to have their packs taken down (or back up, or both) on a mule. The cost is $75 one way; call **Duffel Transport Service** (Bright Angel Transportation Desk 928-638-3283, Xanterra 888-297-2757; oneway $75) a few days in advance to make arrangements.

Maricopa Point VIEWPOINT
(Map p80; www.nps.gov/grca; Rim Trail, Hermit Rd; P; Hermits Rest west-bound, Mar 1-Nov 30) Maricopa, a 1.2-mile uphill walk from Grand Canyon Village along the Rim Trail, makes a lovely sunrise spot. Just east of here are the remains of the once prolific inner-canyon Orphan Mine. During its 13 years of uranium mining, beginning with the 1951 discovery of the Cold War jewel, Orphan Mine produced 4.3 million pounds of uranium from one of the country's richest veins.

Trailview Overlook VIEWPOINT
(Map p76; www.nps.gov/grca; Rim Trail, Hermit Rd; Hermits Rest west-bound, Mar 1-Nov 30) With an excellent view of most of the Bright Angel Trail switchbacks, this is a good spot to watch hikers and mule trains ascending and descending the canyon.

The Abyss VIEWPOINT
(Map p80; www.nps.gov/grca; Rim Trail, Hermit Rd; P; Hermits Rest west-bound, Mar 1-Nov 30) The Abyss is a good place to see sheer canyon walls, with the sheer cliffs dropping 3000ft to the Redwall limestone below.

SLEEPING

With the exception of Desert View Campground, the South Rim's lodges and campgrounds cluster in the tourist hub of Grand Canyon Village. The best are along the rim in Grand Canyon Village Historic District.

Below the rim, there is one lodge, three designated campgrounds and multiple backcountry primitive campsites. Phantom Ranch, available by lottery only and accessible from the South Rim via a 7.5-mile descent on the South Kaibab or a 10-mile descent on the Bright Angel, offers dorm and cabin accommodations. Indian Garden Campground sits on Bright Angel Trail, Bright Angel Campground sits on the north canyon wall next to Phantom Ranch, and Cottonwood Campground sits along the North Kaibab Trail between the Colorado River and the North Rim.

Camping

Camping on the South Rim is prohibited outside the two developed campgrounds, run by **NPS** (877-444-6777, international 518-885-3639; www.recreation.gov). Mather (year-round) sits a couple miles away from the rim in Grand Canyon Village, and Desert View (p82) (mid-April to mid-October) is 25 miles east of the Village.

For RV camping with hook ups, the only option is Trailer Village. Both the campgrounds and the RV park allow pets.

Stays at any of the three developed campgrounds below the rim require a backcountry overnight permit. Indian Garden Campground (p84) has 15 sites and is 4.6 miles down the Bright Angel Trail, while Bright Angel Campground is on the canyon bottom near Phantom Ranch, some 9.3 miles via the Bright Angel Trail and 7 miles via the South Kaibab. Both are ranger-staffed and have water and toilets. Cottonwood Campground (p152) sits halfway up the North Kaibab Trail, between the river and the North Rim, about 16.6 miles from the South Rim. It also has water, toilets, a phone and a ranger station.

For details on backcountry permits and below-the-rim primitive camping beyond the corridor trails, contact the Backcountry Information Center (p90).

★ Desert View Campground CAMPGROUND $
(www.nps.gov/grca/planyourvisit/cg-sr.htm; Desert View, Desert View Dr; campsites $12; mid-Apr–mid-Oct; P) In the piñon-juniper 25 miles from the tourist hub of Grand Canyon Village and close to the rim, this first-come, first-served 50-site NPS campground is relatively quiet, with a spread-out design that ensures a bit of privacy. The best time to secure a spot is mid-morning, when people are breaking camp, and it usually fills by noon.

Mather Campground CAMPGROUND $
(Map p76; 877-444-6777, late arrival 929-638-7851; www.recreation.gov; Market Plaza, Grand Canyon Village; campsites $18; year-round;

; Village east-bound) South Rim's primary campground has shaded and fairly well-dispersed sites set in ponderosa forest, 1 mile from the canyon rim. There are pay showers and laundry facilities, drinking water, toilets, grills and a small general store. No hookups. Pine Loop is a good option to avoid RVs. Reservations are accepted up to six months ahead, up until the day before your arrival; from March 1 through November 30 reservations are required;from December 1 to February 28 reservations are not accepted and there is a self-pay station.

Trailer Village RV Park CARAVAN PARK $

(Map p76; 877-404-4611, same-day booking 928-638-1006; www.visitgrandcanyon.com; Market Plaza, Grand Canyon Village; full hookups $45; year-round; ; Village east-bound) A trailer park with RVs lined up tightly at paved pull-through sites on a rather barren patch of ground. You'll find picnic tables, barbecue grills and full hookups, but coin-operated showers and laundry are a half-mile walk to **Camper Services** (928-638-6350; www.visitgrandcanyon.com/trailer-village-rv-park/rv-camper-services; Market Plaza, Grand Canyon Village; hrs vary; Village). It's about a 1-mile walk along the bicycle-friendly Greenway Trail to the canyon rim.

★ **Bright Angel Campground** CAMPGROUND $

(Map p80; Backcountry Information Center 928-638-7875; www.nps.gov/grca; bottom of canyon, 9.5 miles below South Rim on Bright Angel, 7 miles below South Rim on South Kaibab, 14 miles below North Rim on North Kaibab; backcountry permit $10, plus per person per night $8; year-round) Nestled among the cottonwoods 0.5 miles north of Colorado River and 0.5 miles south of Phantom Ranch (p84), Bright Angel is a spectacular spot to hunker down after the arduous trek to the canyon bottom. Wade in the marvelously inviting Bright Angel Creek, pop into the ranch canteen for a cold drink and snacks, and reserve family-style breakfasts and dinners in advance.

Campsites, each with a picnic table and fire ring, can only be reserved through a backcountry permit request through the Backcountry Information Center (p227) and are available for a maximum of two consecutive nights (four nights November 15 to February 28).

The only way to reach Bright Angel is by hiking; most folks hike Bright Angel Trail or the South Kaibab from the South Rim, or the North Kaibab from the North Rim. These are maintained and NPS-patrolled trails. If

BACKCOUNTRY PERMITS

Camping anywhere below the rim requires a backcountry permit (except for nights at Phantom Ranch). If you're caught camping in the backcountry without a permit, expect a hefty fine and possible court appearance. There is no backcountry camping above the rim on the South Rim.

Permits cost $10, plus an additional $8 per person per night, payable by check or credit card. Permit requests are accepted by mail or fax from the 20th of the fifth month to the 1st of the fourth month prior to the planned trip. For example, for hikes beginning in January, submit request between August 20 and September 1 (5pm MST); in-person requests would be considered after October 1.

Download the Backcountry Permit Request Form online (www.nps.gov/grca/planyourvisit/backcountry-permit.htm) and fax (928-638-2125) or mail to Grand Canyon National Park, Permits Office, 1824 S Thompson St, Suite 201, Flagstaff, AZ 86001. Be sure to list your second and third itinerary choices, including alternative dates, on the form to improve your odds of snagging a spot. Backcountry rangers read all notes on the forms and will try to meet your order of preference. Faxing your request is the best way to go; it cannot be emailed.

If you arrive at the park without a permit, a limited number of last-minute permits for camping in corridor campgrounds are available at the Backcountry Information Center (p90), and when no permits are available the backcountry office keeps a waiting list. You must show up daily at 8am to remain on the list, but you'll likely hear your name called in one to four days, depending on the season and itinerary.

Email backcountry questions, including details on primitive camping outside the three established corridor campgrounds, to the office via the online email form. Staff are very helpful.

you don't want to carry your pack, you can arrange for duffel transport (p82) from the South Rim.

Indian Garden Campground CAMPGROUND $
(Map p80; Backcountry Information Center 928-638-7875; www.nps.gov/grca; Bright Angel Trail, 4.6 miles below South Rim; backcountry permit $10, plus per person per night $8; year-round) Located 3040ft below the South Rim, and a 4.6-mile hike along the Bright Angel Trail (p60), lovely Indian Garden sits along a creek surrounded by cottonwoods, with a ranger station, toilets and year-round drinking water (though pipeline breaks regularly result in closed water supplies). Each of the campground's 15 sites offers a picnic table shaded by an open-walled, roofed enclosure.

Lodging

Advance reservations for lodges, accepted up to 13 months in advance, are highly recommended. Reservations for all lodges except Yavapai are available through **Xanterra** (Grand Canyon Lodges; advanced reservations 888-297-2757, international 303-297-2757, reservations within 48hrs 928-638-2631; www.xanterra.com; 10 Albright St, Grand Canyon). For same-day reservations or to reach any lodge, call 928-638-2631. Accommodation at Phantom Ranch is by lottery only.

Children under 16 stay free at all South Rim lodges using existing bedding; cribs and cots are $10 per day.

★ **Bright Angel Lodge** LODGE $
(Map p76; advanced reservations 888-297-2757, front desk & reservations within 48hr 928-638-2631, ext 6285; www.grandcanyonlodges.com; Rim Trail, Grand Canyon Village Historic District; r with/without bath $110/89, cabins/ste $197/426; P; Village) This 1935 log-and-stone historic lodge (p75) on the canyon ledge delivers simple charm and the small public spaces bustle with activity. Buckey and Powell Lodge rooms, an excellent choice for budget accommodations, offer bright, handsome and simple rooms (refrigerator, but no TV) only steps from the rim, while rustic Rim Cabins and suites are some of the South Rim's best accommodations.

Phantom Ranch CABIN, DORMITORY $
(Map p80; advanced reservations 888-297-2757, reservations within 48hrs 928-638-3283; www.grandcanyonlodges.com; bottom of canyon, 9.9 miles below South Rim on Bright Angel, 7.4 miles below South Rim on South Kaibab, 13.6 miles below North Rim on North Kaibab; dm $49, cabin d $142; available by lottery;) Bunks at this camp-like complex on the canyon floor are in private cabins sleeping two to 10 people and four hiker-only single-sex dorms, each with five bunks. Rates include bedding, soap and towels, but meals are extra and must be reserved when booking your accommodations. Phantom is accessible by mule trip, on foot or via raft on the Colorado River.

Snacks, packed lunches, limited supplies, and beer and wine are sold at the **canteen** (Map p80; www.grandcanyonlodges.com/dine/phantom-ranch-cafe/; breakfast $23.65, dinner vegetarian stew/steak $24/48; breakfast 5am & 6:30am, Apr-Oct, 5:30am & 7am Nov-Mar, dinner 5pm & 6:30pm; canteen 8am-4pm & 8-10pm, from 8:30am Nov-Mar). You're free to bring your own food and stove.

For details of the reservation process, see p45. Children must be aged six or older to sleep in the dorms.

Kachina & Thunderbird Lodges MOTEL $$
(Map p76; advanced reservations 888-297-2757, reservations within 48hrs 928-638-2631; www.grandcanyonlodges.com; Rim Trail, Grand Canyon Village Historic District; r streetside/canyonside $234/254; P; Village) These institutional-looking lodges, built in the 1960s, sit steps away from the canyon rim, the historic charms of El Tovar, and the Bright Angel Trail (p60). Location, location, location! Though amazingly ugly on the outside, inside the rooms are bright, modern and comfortable, and canyonside rooms offer fantastic views of the Rim Trail and canyon beyond.

If staying at Kachina, check-in at El Tovar; if staying at Thunderbird, check in at Bright Angel Lodge.

Yavapai Lodge MOTEL $$
(Map p76; advanced reservations 877-404-4611, reservations within 48hr 928-638-6421; www.visitgrandcanyon.com; Market Plaza, Grand Canyon

ACCOMMODATIONS OUTSIDE THE PARK

If everything in the park is booked up, consider Tusayan (7 miles south), Valle (30 miles south) or Williams (60 miles south). Campers can pitch a tent for free in the surrounding Kaibab National Forest (p95) or reserve a site at **USFS Campgrounds** (877-444-6777; www.recreation.gov; Kaibab National Forest; sites $10; P).

Village; r $99-200; ⌚year-round; P ❄ @ 📶 🐾; 🚌Village) Sixteen motel-style buildings in the piñon and juniper forest sit about a mile from the rim. Handsome air-conditioned rooms at two-story Yavapai East sleep four to six; family rooms include bunk beds. Pet-friendly drive-up rooms in single-story Yavapai West sleep up to four, but do not have air-conditioning and are more dated.

★El Tovar LODGE **$$$**
(Map p76; ☎advanced reservations 888-297-2757, front desk & reservations within 48hr 928-638-2631, ext 6380; www.grandcanyonlodges.com; Rim Trail, Grand Canyon Village Historic District; r/ste from $228/461; ⌚year-round; P ❄ 📶; 🚌Village westbound, Train Depot stop) Perched on the Rim Trail at the canyon edge, the public spaces of this 1905 wooden lodge ooze old-world national park glamor and charm. Unfortunately, the 78 rooms and suites do not consistently share the historic aesthetic; some are lovely, with four-poster beds or a spectacular balcony, but standard rooms rival roadside motels. Stay here for the service and location.

Rooms can be reserved by phone or online 15 months in advance; suites can be reserved by phone only.

EATING

Grand Canyon Village has all the eating options you need, but nobody comes to Grand Canyon for the food! Arizona Room (p86), El Tovar (p86) and Harvey House Cafe are the only table-service restaurants on the South Rim, though several bars serve small plates and snacks. The other restaurants are cafeteria-style or fast food. You can make advanced reservations (dinner only) at Arizona Room and El Tovar.

Phantom Ranch Canteen, below the rim near the Colorado River, offers family-style breakfasts and dinners by advanced reservation only.

Grand Canyon Village: National Historic District

Bright Angel Bicycles & Cafe at Mather Point SANDWICHES **$**
(Map p76; ☎928-638-3055; www.bikegrandcanyon.com; Grand Canyon Visitor Center Complex; mains under $10; ⌚6am-8pm May-Sep, shorter hrs rest of year; 👪; 🚌Kaibab/Rim, 🚌Village) Grab-and-go sandwiches, wraps, salads, snacks and coffee drinks from the bike-shop cafe – the best spot to pick up a last-minute lunch to throw in your backpack before a hike. The cafe doubles as a bicycle rental (p71), and offers bicycle tours.

FOOD TRUCKS

From about 11am to 3pm, and until 5pm June through August, two **Food Trucks** (www.grandcanyonlodges.com/dine/food-trucks/; hot dogs, brats & snacks $3-8; ⌚Apr 1-Oct 15; 👪 🐾) station at various spots throughout the South Rim. The **Desert Dog** sells hot dogs and brats, including bison franks and elk and pork brats, with traditional and exotic toppings, while the **Fuel Your Hike Cart** offers exactly that: fruit, beef jerky, cookies, and trail mix.

Maswik Food Court CAFETERIA **$**
(Map p76; ☎928-638-2631; www.grandcanyonlodges.com/dine/maswik-cafeteria/; Maswik Lodge, 202 South Village Loop Dr; mains $8-13; ⌚6am-10pm May-Aug, hrs vary rest of year; 👪; 🚌Village) Though fairly predictable, the food here encompasses a nice variety and is filling after a day's hiking. The various food stations serve burgers, pasta, Mexican food, chili bowls and comfort food. There's a deli, grab-and-go sandwiches, beer and wine.

Bright Angel Fountain FAST FOOD **$**
(Map p76; ☎928-638-2631; www.grandcanyonlodges.com/dine/harvey-house-cafe/; Bright Angel Lodge; sandwiches $4-6; ⌚5:30-6pm May-Sep, shorter hrs rest of year; 👪; 🚌Village) Hot dogs, pre-made sandwiches and Dryers ice-cream conveniently located a few minutes' walk from Bright Angel Trail. In the morning you can grab coffee, yogurt and uninspired pastries.

Maswik Pizza Pub PIZZA **$$**
(Map p76; ☎928-638-2631, 928-638-4044; www.grandcanyonlodges.com/dine/maswik-cafeteria/; Maswik Lodge, 202 South Village Loop Dr; pizzas $18-19; ⌚11am-11pm; 👪; 🚌Village) Pick up a slice or pie to enjoy over a Grand Canyon Pilsner, or call in advance for takeout. The pizzas here have basic toppings, and there's a vegetarian pesto pie.

Harvey House Cafe AMERICAN **$$**
(Map p76; ☎928-638-2631; www.grandcanyonlodges.com/dine/harvey-house-cafe/; Bright Angel

Lodge; mains $13-21; 6am-4:30pm, 5-10pm; ; Village west-bound) Harvey House, conveniently located close to the rim, offers table-service with a standard menu of subpar burgers, fajitas, salads and pastas. The striking original graphic from the 1920s, shown on the back of today's menu and available as notecards in the gift shop, hints at the restaurant's historic charm, but the windowless basement surrounds offer nothing in way of ambiance.

Arizona Room AMERICAN **$$$**
(Map p76; 928-638-2631; www.grandcanyonlodges.com/dine/arizona-room/; Bright Angel Lodge; lunch $13-16, dinner $22-28; 11:30am-3pm & 4:30-10pm Feb-Oct, dinner only Nov-Jan; ; Village) Antler chandeliers hang from the ceiling, picture windows overlook the Rim Trail and canyon beyond, and the seasonal menu gives a Western vibe. Reservations (dinner only) are accepted online or by phone 30 days in advance, but are usually available within the week.

You can pick up a drink from the bar and take it outside to the small, informal deck and watch passersby on the Rim Trail while you wait, and you'll be buzzed when your table is ready.

★**El Tovar Dining Room** AMERICAN **$$$**
(Map p76; 928-638-2631; www.grandcanyonlodges.com/dine/el-tovar-dining-room-and-lounge/; El Tovar; mains $20-30; restaurant 6-10:30am, 11am-2pm & 4:30-10pm, lounge 11am-11pm; P ; Village) Classic national park dining at its best. Dark-wood tables are set with china and white linen, eye-catching murals spotlight American Indian tribes and huge windows frame views of the Rim Trail and canyon beyond. Breakfast options include El Tovar's pancake trio (buttermilk, blue cornmeal and buckwheat pancakes with pine-nut butter and prickly-pear syrup), and blackened trout with two eggs.

Dinner reservations are accepted up to 90 days in advance if you are staying at El Tovar (by phone or email only), or 30 days in advance online for general park visitors; during high season especially, you will need reservations. Parties of six or more can request the intimate Teddy Roosevelt Room across from the hostess desk – pop your head in to check out the mustache motif carved into the wood paneling. To avoid lunchtime crowds, eat before the Grand Canyon Railway train arrives at 11:45am.

Grand Canyon Village: Market Plaza

Canyon Village Market SUPERMARKET **$**
(Map p76; 928-638-2262; www.visitgrandcanyon.com; Market Plaza; sandwiches, pizzas $6-11; 6:30am-9pm mid-May–Sep, deli to 8pm, shorter hrs rest of year; Village) The biggest source for supplies in Grand Canyon, this massive supermarket offers everything you'd expect from your local grocery store, including fresh produce, liquor, and over-the-counter medications. A small cafeteria-style deli offers fresh-made sandwiches, thin-crust pizza, chicken wings, pasta and beer. Nothing special, but convenient.

Also sells hiking gear (p87), including boots, water sandals and apparel.

Yavapai Coffee Shop CAFE **$**
(Map p76; 928-638-4001; www.visitgrandcanyon.com; Yavapai Lodge; pastries $3-5; 7am-3pm; Village) Small quick-service coffee shop with takeaway bagels, wraps and sandwiches.

Yavapai Lodge Restaurant CAFETERIA **$**
(Map p76; 928-638-6421; www.visitgrandcanyon.com; Yavapai Lodge; breakfast $7-9, lunch & dinner $10-16; 6:30am-9pm; P ; Village) Breakfast buffet ($15) or a la carte; lunch and dinner is barbecue, hot and cold sandwiches and pizza, as well as beer and wine. Place your order on a touchscreen, pick up your drinks, and your number will be called when the food is ready. Efficient and convenient, but not much better than what you'd expect at a school cafeteria.

DRINKING

Things quiet down on the South Rim in the evening, and there aren't many options for drinking and nightlife. The best spot is the lounge at the historic El Tovar, where you sit on the rim-side back porch and enjoy a canyon-themed cocktail. All South Rim bars close by 11pm.

El Tovar Lounge BAR
(Map p76; 928-638-2631; www.grandcanyonlodges.com/dine/el-tovar-dining-room-and-lounge/; El Tovar, Grand Canyon Village Historic District; 11am-11pm; Village) Though the bar inside the historic El Tovar offers basics like nachos and sliders, the real draw is the canyon views from the back porch. Pop in for

a post-hike Grand Canyon IPA or a prickly pear margarita, and watch the comings and goings along the Rim Trail, with the canyon vista stretched beyond.

Yavapai Tavern BAR
(Map p76; ☎928-638-6421; www.visitgrandcanyon.com; Yavapai Lodge, Grand Canyon Village; ⊙3-10pm; 🚌Village) One mile from the canyon rim, with a massive window, patio roadside seating and modern interior, pleasant Yavapai Tavern serves regional craft beer, wine, cocktails, and a limited bar menu: offerings include guacamole, nachos and sliders with prickly pear barbecue sauce. Try a Grand Canyon Mule, with vodka, bitters, ginger-ale, lime and fresh mint.

Bright Angel Lounge BAR
(Map p76; ☎928-638-2631; Bright Angel Lodge, Grand Canyon Village Historic District; ⊙11am-11pm; 🚌Village) The dark, windowless bar inside Bright Angel Lodge doesn't offer much character, but it's a cozy and friendly spot for a beer and occasional live music. A limited menu offers quesadillas and wings.

☆ ENTERTAINMENT

Shrine of the Ages THEATER
(Map p76; ☎park headquarters 928-638-7888; www.nps.gov/grca; Market Plaza, Grand Canyon Village; 🚌Village) Used for performances, lectures and other public events, the 'Shrine' is also the venue for educative ranger programs (p72) on the Grand Canyon, its geology, history, flora and fauna.

McKee Amphitheater THEATRE
(Map p76; www.nps.gov/grca; Market Plaza (behind Shrine of the Ages), Grand Canyon Village; ⊙May-Sep; 🚌Village) Come here for summer-evening special events and outdoor ranger programs (p72); check at a visitor center or online for the latest details about what's on.

SHOPPING

Shopping options at the South Rim are mainly bookstores and ubiquitous gift shops. The largest and best of these is the non-profit store run by the Grand Canyon Association at the Visitor Center Complex. For hiking and camping gear, as well as over-the-counter medicines, food, beer and wine, head to the Canyon Village Market in Market Plaza.

Grand Canyon Association Park Store at the Visitor Center GIFTS & SOUVENIRS, BOOKS
(Map p76; ☎Grand Canyon Association 800-858-2808; www.grandcanyon.org; Grand Canyon Visitor Center Complex, Grand Canyon Village; ⊙8am-8pm Jun-Aug, shorter hrs rest of year; 🚌Village, 🚌Kaibab/Rim, 🚌Tusayan, Mar 1-Sep 30) An extensive collection of adult and children's books about the canyon, as well as canyon prints, T-shirts and souvenirs. The store is run by the non-profit Grand Canyon Association (p231), which supports education and research at the park and raises money to preserve and protect Grand Canyon.

Hopi House ART
(Map p76; ☎928-638-2631; www.nps.gov/grca/learn/photosmultimedia/colter_hopih_photos.htm; Rim Trail, Grand Canyon Village Historic District; ⊙8am-8pm May–Aug, 9am-6pm Sep–Apr; 🚌Village) Excellent selection of Native American designed and crafted jewelry and pottery housed in the historic Mary Colter–designed building.

Canyon Village Market CAMPING, HIKING
(Map p76; ☎928-638-2262; www.visitgrandcanyon.com; Market Plaza; ⊙6:30am-9pm mid-May–Sep, deli to 8pm, shorter hrs rest of year) In addition to grocery supplies, Canyon Village Market sells basic camping and hiking gear, including boots, rain gear and water purification systems.

ℹ Orientation

Most visitors arrive via the **South Entrance** (Map p80; ☎park headquarters 928-638-7888; South Entrance; ⊙24hr, staffed 8am-5pm Jun-Aug, 9am-5pm Sep-May), 80 miles northwest of Flagstaff, 55 miles north of Williams, about 1 mile north of Tusayan. A few miles north of the South Entrance, Grand Canyon Village (or simply the Village) is the primary hub of activity. Here you'll find lodges, restaurants, two of the three developed campgrounds, a backcountry office, visitor center, medical clinic, bank, grocery store, shuttles and other services. It is divided into three general areas – Historic Grand Canyon Village (labeled Village on the park map), Visitor Center Complex and Market Plaza – and is serviced by the free Village shuttle.

West of the Village, Hermit Rd (p227) winds along the rim for 7 miles, passing several overlooks and ending at Hermits Rest. From March to November the road is closed to private vehicles and is accessible only by tour, foot, bicycle or the free Hermit Rd shuttle.

1

LINDA HARMS/SHUTTERSTOCK ©

2

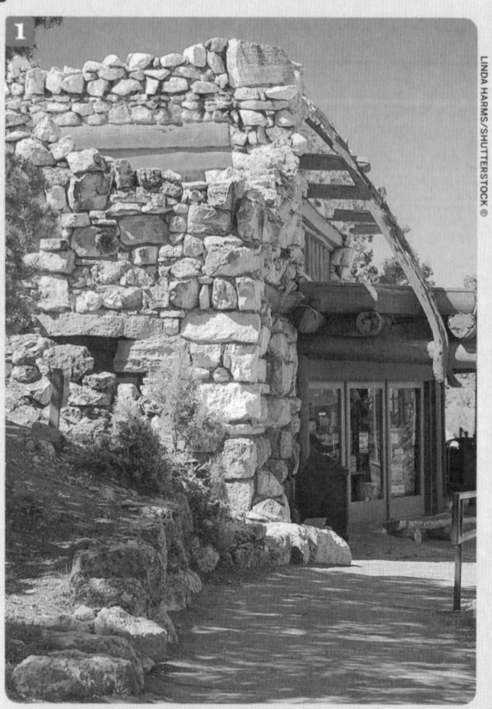

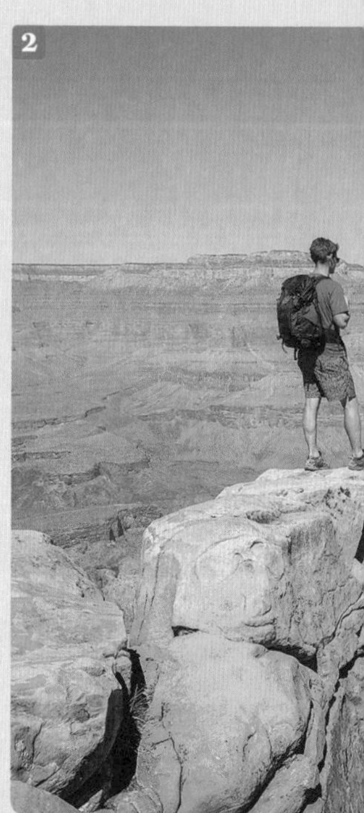

4

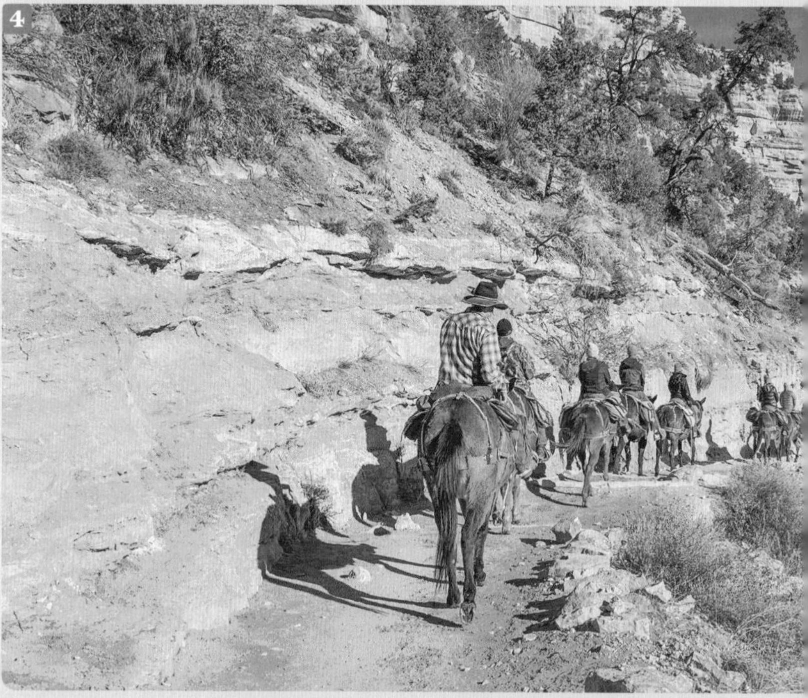

CANADASTOCK/SHUTTERSTOCK ©

BENEDEK/GETTY IMAGES ©

THOMAS TROMPETER/SHUTTERSTOCK ©

1. Hermits Rest (p75)
This cozy, stone resthouse is a tribute to its namesake Louis Boucher (aka 'the Hermit'.)

2. South Kaibab Trail (p61)
The shortest and steepest corridor trail in the Grand Canyon offers stunning views.

3. Bright Angel Lodge (p75)
Designed by Mary Colter, this log-and-stone lodge has a history room dedicated to Fred Harvey.

4. Mule rides (p39)
Mule rides are a popular activity in the Grand Canyon, and are available both on the rims and inner canyon trails.

Running east from the Village, Desert View Dr (p227) stretches 25 undeveloped miles past several overlooks to Desert View. Here you will find a small cluster of services, including a seasonal first-come, first-served campground, snack bar, general store and the park's only gas station (self-service gas year-round), as well as the **Desert View Entrance** (East Entrance; park headquarters 928-638-7888; Desert View, Desert View Dr; 24hr, staffed 8am-5pm Jun-Aug, 9am-5pm Sep-May). From here, it is 82 miles to Flagstaff and 188 miles to the North Rim.

If possible, try to enter the park at Desert View rather than at the South Entrance, especially during high season. It's a quieter entrance, and you can ease into the canyon rather than entering straight into the mayhem of the Village.

Information

INTERNET ACCESS

Most South Rim hotel lobbies offer free wi-fi; sometimes for a small fee.

Canyon Village Market (p86) Free wi-fi at the deli inside the supermarket.

Grand Canyon Community Library (928-638-2718; Grand Canyon Village Historic District; 10:30am-5pm Mon-Sat; ; Village, Village East stop) Free wi-fi and and computer terminals.

Grand Canyon National Park Research Library (928-638-7768; www.nps.gov/grca/learn/historyculture/reslib.htm; Park Headquarters, Market Plaza, Grand Canyon Village; 8am-4:30pm Mon-Thu & every 2nd Fri; ; Village) At the back of the courtyard at Park Headquarters; free wi-fi and computer terminals.

Yavapai Lodge (p84) Computer terminal with free internet access in hotel lobby.

KENNELS

Travelers can board their cat or dog at **Grand Canyon Kennel** (Map p80; 928-638-0534, for retrieval after 5pm 928-638-2631; www.nps.gov/grca/planyourvisit/pets.htm; Grand Canyon Village; dogs day/overnight $22/26; cats $18; 7:30am-5pm); proof-of-vaccination required.

MEDICAL SERVICES

North Country Community Health Center (Clinic) (928-638-2551; www.northcountryhealthcare.org; 1 Clinic Rd, Grand Canyon Village; 8am-6pm mid-May–mid-Oct, reduced hrs mid-Oct–mid-May) is a basic clinic with urgent care facilities.

POST

Post Office (928-638-2512; Market Plaza; 8:30am-3:30pm Mon-Fri; Village) Stamps are available via a vending machine from 5am to 10pm. There's a walk-up window and pay phones.

TOURIST INFORMATION

Grand Canyon Village has abundant sources of tourist information.

National Park Service (928-638-7888; www.nps.gov/grca) Comprehensive and updated information and links to all things South Rim.

Backcountry Information Center – South Rim (Map p76; 928-638-7875; www.nps.gov/grca/planyourvisit/backcountry-permit.htm; Grand Canyon Village; 8am-noon & 1-5pm, phone staffed 8am-5pm Mon-Fri; Village) Rangers, maps and backcountry permit.

Bright Angel Transportation Desk (928-638-3283; Bright Angel Lodge, Grand Canyon Village Historic District; 5am-8pm summer, reduced hrs rest of year.; Village) Phantom Ranch and mule ride information, including last-minute openings; books bus tours.

El Tovar Concierge (928-638-2631; El Tovar, Grand Canyon Village Historic District; 8am-5pm; Village) Basic information and meal reservations.

Grand Canyon Association (p87) Excellent online source, field classes and extensive South Rim bookstore.

Grand Canyon Visitor Center (Map p76; park headquarters 928-638-7888; www.nps.gov/grca/planyourvisit/visitorcenters.htm; Grand Canyon Visitor Center Plaza, Grand Canyon Village; 9am-5pm; Village, Kaibab/Rim, Tusayan, Mar 1-Sep 30) Park's main visitor center.

Grand Canyon National Park Headquarters (Map p76; 928-638-7888; www.nps.gov/grca; Market Plaza, Grand Canyon Village; 8am-5pm; Village) Organizational headquarters for NPS.

Grand Canyon South Rim Chamber and Visitors Bureau (928-638-2901; www.grandcanyoncvb.org; Hwy 64, Tusayan; 9am-5pm; Tusayan, Mar 1-Sep 30) Links to South Rim tours, accommodations and more.

Maswik Transportation Desk (928-638-2631; www.grandcanyonlodges.com; Maswik Lodge, Grand Canyon Village; 6am-7pm May-Aug, reduced hrs Sep-Apr; Village) Information on bus tours and smooth water float.

Verkamp's Visitor Center (928-638-7146; www.nps.gov/grca/planyourvisit/visitorcenters.htm; Rim Trail, Grand Canyon Village Historic District; 8am-8pm Jun-Aug, reduced hrs Sep-May; Village, Train Depot or Village East stop) Run by Grand Canyon Association, with maps and basic information.

Yavapai Transportation Desk (928-638-2631; Yavapai Lodge, Market Plaza, Grand Canyon Village) Information on bus tours and smooth water float.

Getting There & Away

The South Rim is the more accessible of the Grand Canyon's two developed tourist destinations. Grand Canyon Village, the central tourist hub, is accessed via Hwy 64 north from Williams (60 miles) or from Flagstaff (79 miles, partly on Hwy 180); alternatively, enter the park at Desert View (East Entrance) via Hwy 89 from Flagstaff (82 miles) to Cameron (30 miles) and then west from Cameron on Hwy 64.

You can book or take a scheduled shuttle (p236) from Flagstaff, Williams, Sedona and Phoenix, among other places, and there's a historic train (p238) that runs once daily from Williams to the South Rim's Grand Canyon Village Historic District.

The closest airports are Sky Harbor International Airport (p235) and Phoenix-Mesa Gateway Airport (www.gatewayairport.com) in Phoenix, and McCarran International Airport (p235) in Las Vegas. The regional Flagstaff Pulliam Airport (www.flagstaff.az.gov) offers limited weekly service to select cities. To reach the park from the airports, contact Arizona Shuttle (p236) or Grand Canyon Shuttle (p236), or rent a car.

Flights, cars and tours can be booked online at lonelyplanet.com/bookings.

Getting Around

Though the park can seem overwhelming when you first arrive, it's actually quite easy to navigate, especially when you leave it to shuttle drivers.

BICYCLE

Bicycles are allowed on all roads, and the South Rim's bicycle-friendly Greenway Trail (p71) is very convenient for accessing most restaurants and sights in Grand Canyon Village. You can rent a bicycle at Bright Angel Bicycles (p71).

CAR

Grand Canyon Village is very congested from March through September. Don't bother trying to find your way with a map, as there are constantly changing road repairs and detours and it can be general mayhem. Upon arrival into the park, simply follow park signs.

Several massive parking lots sit at the **Visitor Center Complex** (Map p76; park headquarters 928-638-7888; www.nps.gov; Grand Canyon Village; 8am-5pm; Village, Kaibab/Rim, Tusayan, Mar 1-Sep 30), but it is easier and more pleasant to first try to find a spot in one the smaller lots by El Tovar (p85) (look behind Verkamp's too), Bright Angel Lodge (p84) or Yavapai Point and Geology Museum (p76). If you do drive into the Village and can't find parking near the rim, park at the Backcountry Information Center (p90), Shrine of the Ages (p87) or Market Plaza (p86).

Cars are not allowed on the road to the South Kaibab Trailhead and Yaki Point and, from March through November, cars are not allowed on Hermit Rd.

There is a **garage** (928-638-2631; S Entrance Rd, Grand Canyon Village; 8am-noon & 1-5pm; Village) with emergency repair and tow services. The **Desert View Chevron Service Station** (Desert View Dr, Desert View; 9am-5pm Mar-Oct, 24hr for credit-card service) is the only gas station on the South Rim, but gas stations in Tusayan are about 7 miles south of Grand Canyon Village.

LUGGAGE TRANSPORT

You can arrange for a mule to transport your duffel (p82) from the South Rim to/from Phantom Ranch, on the canyon bottom.

SHUTTLE

Free shuttle buses ply three routes along the South Rim. During the hour before sunrise and after sunset, shuttles run every half-hour or so and from early morning until sunset they run every 15 minutes. There is no shuttle service along most of the 25-mile Desert View Dr from Grand Canyon Village east to Desert View.

Park shuttles do not stop at every stop in each direction; for example, the west-bound Hermits Rest shuttle stops at 10 bus stops, whereas the east-bound shuttle stops at only five. The park map shows color-coded shuttle-routes.

Hermits Rest Route Shuttle Bus (Red) (www.nps.gov/grca/planyourvisit/hermit-red-route.htm; 1hr before sunrise to 1hr after sunset Mar-Nov) March 1 to November 30.

Hikers' Express Bus (www.nps.gov/grca/planyourvisit/hiker-express-shuttle.htm; Grand Canyon Village; departs 5am, 6am & 7am May & Sep, 4am, 5am & 6am Jun-Aug, 6am, 7am & 8am Apr & Oct, 8am & 9am Dec-Feb, 7am, 8am & 9am Mar & Nov) Year-round.

Kaibab/Rim Route Shuttle Bus (Orange) (www.nps.gov/grca/planyourvisit/kaibab-orange-route.htm; Grand Canyon Village; 1hr before sunrise to 1hr after sunrise, seasonal variation) Year-round.

Tusayan Route Shuttle Bus (Purple) (www.nps.gov/grca/planyourvisit/tusayan-route-purple.htm; 8am-9:30pm Mar-Sep) March 1 to September 30.

Village Route Shuttle Bus (Blue) (www.nps.gov/grca/planyourvisit/village-blue-route.htm; Grand Canyon Village; 1hr before sunrise to 1hr after sunset, seasonal variation) Year-round.

TAXI

Grand Canyon South Rim Taxi Service (928-638-2822; Tusayan & Grand Canyon South Rim; 24hr) Offers taxi service to and from Tusayan and within the park.

Around South Rim

Includes ➡

Best Places to Eat

➡ Joël Robuchon (p129)

➡ Proper Meats + Provisions (p107)

➡ Indian Gardens Cafe & Market (p117)

Best Places to Stay

➡ Cosmopolitan (p127)

➡ Motel Dubeau (p105)

➡ Havasu Campground (p110)

➡ Skylofts (p128)

➡ Briar Patch Inn (p116)

Why Go?

Carved into the stunning landscape of the Southwest, Grand Canyon has more than its own unique splendor to offer visitors. Stretching both north and south of the canyon is the Kaibab National Forest, and to the west of the park's South Rim are the Hualapai and Havasupai Reservations that encompass thousands of acres of desert and rim-to-river Canyon lands. Further west, where the Colorado River has been reined in by the massive engineering feat that is Hoover Dam, Lake Mead is a popular recreation area for desert dwellers thirsting for fishing, houseboating and water sports. Bordering the national park to the east, and spanning mile-upon-mile of the rim-to-rim drive, is the Navajo Reservation.

The gateway towns leading to the South Rim are destinations in their own right: Las Vegas for its slick excess and cardinal sins, Flagstaff for its cool, outdoorsy feel, Sedona for day-hiking and its red-rock landscape, and Williams for its small-town, Route 66 atmosphere.

Road Distances (miles)

	South Rim	Williams	Flagstaff	Sedona	North Rim
Williams	60				
Flagstaff	80	35			
Sedona	115	60	30		
North Rim	210	240	205	235	
Las Vegas	275	215	250	275	265

Note: distances are approximate

Kaibab National Forest (South Rim)

Divided by the Grand Canyon into two distinct ecosystems, this 1.6-million-acre forest offers a peaceful escape from the park madness. Thick stands of ponderosa dominate the higher elevations, while piñon and juniper create a fragrant backdrop further down. Sightings of elk, mule, deer, turkeys, coyotes (and even mountain lions and black bears) are all possible.

Kaibab offers several great mountain-biking trails, unlimited camping, hiking and cross-country skiing. Its Tusayan Ranger Station (p95), just outside the park's South Entrance, has maps and details. One of the best and most popular rides is the 16-mile **Arizona Trail** (www.aztrail.org), which stretches from Grandview Lookout Tower to Tusayan.

The main road through the forest is Hwy 64/180, which connects Williams and Flagstaff with the canyon.

Sights & Activities

Grandview Lookout Tower VIEWPOINT

Built by the Civilian Conservation Corps in 1936 as a fire tower, the 80ft Grandview Lookout Tower offers great views of the region for those willing and able to climb all those stairs. From Grand Canyon National Park's Desert View Dr, turn at the sign for 'Arizona Trail' between Miles 252 and 253, about 2 miles east of Grandview Point. You can hike or bike 1.3 miles on a dirt road to the lookout.

Apache Stables HORSEBACK RIDING

(Map p80; 928-638-2891; www.apachestables.com; Moqui Dr/Forest Service Rd 328; 1-/2-hr ride $53/93; vary seasonally) Trail rides (and sometimes wagon rides) through the forest, with no canyon views but plenty of serenity. You can also take a one-hour evening pony trek to a campfire and return by wagon or go both ways by wagon. The stables are about 1 mile north of Tusayan on Moqui Dr (Forest Service Rd 328) off Hwy 64/180.

You'll need to bring your own food (think hot dogs and marshmallows) and drinks.

Tusayan

928 / POP 580 / ELEV 6612FT

The little town of Tusayan, situated 1 mile south of Grand Canyon National Park's South Entrance along Hwy 64, is basically a half-mile strip of hotels and restaurants. The National Geographic Visitor Center & IMAX Theater is a good place to regroup – and buy your park tickets – before arriving at the South Entrance. In summer, to avoid traffic jams and parking hassles inside the park, you can catch the Tusayan shuttle from here into the park.

Sights

National Geographic Visitor Center & IMAX Theater MUSEUM

(928-638-2468; www.explorethecanyon.com; 450 Hwy 64; IMAX adult/child $13/10; visitor center 8am-10pm Mar-Oct, 10am-8pm Nov-Feb, theater 8:30am-8:30pm Mar-Nov, 9:30am-6:30pm Dec-Feb; Tusayan) Hourly, on the half-hour, the IMAX

HIKING IN KAIBAB NATIONAL FOREST

There are literally hundreds of miles of hiking trails to explore in Kaibab National Forest, and dogs are allowed off-leash as long as they don't bother anyone. Mountain biking is also possible after the snowmelt, roughly between April and November. A popular, moderate ride is along the **Tusayan Bike Trail**, actually an old logging road. The trailhead is 0.3 miles north of Tusayan on the west side of Hwy 64/180 (Fire Rd 605). It's 16 miles from the trailhead to the Grandview Lookout Tower, an 80ft-high fire tower with fabulous views. If you don't want to ride all that way, three interconnected loops offer round-trips of 3, 8 and 9 miles. The trailhead of the Tusayan Bike Trail and the Grandview Lookout Tower are also access points for cycling on the Arizona Trail (www.aztrail.org), which connects the two points.

From the lookout you can hike or ride part or all of the still-evolving Arizona Trail, a 24-mile one-way ride to the south boundary of the Tusayan Ranger District. This is an excellent and relatively easy ride. The northern segment of the trail unfolds beneath ponderosa pines and gambel oaks; further south, the trail passes piñon-juniper stands, sage and grasslands. Bring plenty of water, as there are no dependable sources along the trail. Ask at the ranger station about other hikes.

REGIONAL SHUTTLE SERVICES

The Trans Canyon Shuttle (p235) runs twice-daily between the North and South Rims from mid-May through November 30.

Arizona Shuttle (Map p104; 928-350-8466; www.arizonashuttle.com) runs regular routes between the Amtrak station (and other points in Flagstaff) and the Grand Canyon South Rim, Williams, Sedona and Phoenix's Sky Harbor International Airport, departing multiple times throughout the day. To the Grand Canyon from Flagstaff, it's $40 per person, one way; to Phoenix, it's $49.

theater here screens a terrific 34-minute film called *Grand Canyon – The Hidden Secrets*. This recommended film plunges you into the history and geology of the canyon through the eyes of ancient American Indians, John Wesley Powell and a soaring eagle, and is a safer, cheaper alternative to a canyon flyover.

Sleeping

Camping

Ten-X Campground CAMPGROUND $

(Map p80; information 928-638-2443, reservations 877-444-6777; www.recreation.gov; Hwy 64; RV & tent sites $10; May-Sep) Woodsy and peaceful, this USFS campground, 2 miles south of Tusayan, has 70 sites and can fill up early in the summer. You'll find large sites, picnic tables, fire rings and barbecue grills (the campground host sells firewood), cold water and toilets, but no showers. Fifteen sites are reservable up to six months in advance; the rest are first-come, first-served. No hookups.

Grand Canyon Camper Village CAMPGROUND $

(928-638-2887; www.grandcanyoncampervillage.com; 549 Camper Village Lane; tent/RV site from $31/51;) This private campground isn't the loveliest in this photogenic corner of the world, but it is convenient and reliable. There are a ton of sites, pay showers and the campground is only 1 mile south of Grand Canyon National Park on Hwy 64. Reservations are not accepted for tent sites; there are full hookups.

Lodging

A handful of chain and independent motels offer clean and friendly accommodations, but don't expect anything memorable. Folks stay here because it's conveniently located a few miles from Grand Canyon, and that's it – location, location, location.

Tusayan motel prices vary wildly between peak and low-season. Your $250-per-night room may go for $90 at other times of the year.

7 Mile Lodge MOTEL $

(928-638-2291; www.7milelodge.com; 208 Hwy 64; r $109; 9am-10pm;) Friendly and basic motel accommodations that don't take reservations; rooms here are usually filled by early afternoon in the summer.

Best Western Grand Canyon Squire Inn HOTEL $$

(928-638-2681; www.grandcanyonsquire.com; 74 Hwy 64; d/ste $209/430; ; Tusayan) Spread over three buildings, this swanky modern hotel offers 318 rooms ranging from standard doubles in a two-story 1973 annex (sans elevator) to a spacious interior and rooms in the main hotel (with elevator). Amenities include the most upscale dining in town, a bowling alley, pool tables, game room, coin laundry and seasonal outdoor pool.

Red Feather Lodge MOTEL $$

(928-638-2414; www.redfeatherlodge.com; 300 Hwy 64; d/ste $220/280;) The Red Feather Lodge offers rooms in two buildings, as well as laundry facilities and an outdoor pool. Built in 1997, the three-story hotel features elevators and interior doors; the older two-story motor lodge (c 1964) has outside entrances and stairs. Pets are $25 per stay.

Grand Hotel HOTEL $$$

(front desk 928-638-3333, reservations 303-265-7000; www.grandcanyongrandhotel.com; 149 Hwy 64; r from $260; ; Tusayan) The giant stone fireplace, antler light fixtures and nightly live cowboy-and-country music in the lounge give this hotel's public spaces a distinct Western vibe. The rooms, however, are basic chain-hotel style. This is reflected in the huge reductions you can expect outside peak season.

Eating & Drinking

Considering the number of tourists that pass through Tusayan annually, the village manages to retain a sort of old-fashioned, roadside-hub pace. There's an OK variety of eateries to choose from, but as of the time of research no one has established a notable culinary presence.

A sports bar and steakhouse/saloon are about all Tusayan offers by way of nightlife.

RP's Stage Stop CAFE $
(☎928-638-3115; www.rpsstagestop.com; 400 Hwy 64; breakfast under $6, lunch $7; ⏰6:30am-6pm; 📶👪) The only place in Tusayan to grab an espresso and pick up a sack lunch ($10.50); it also offers wi-fi.

Plaza Bonita MEXICAN $$
(☎928-638-8900; www.myplazabonitatusayan.com; 352 Hwy 64; mains $17-21; ⏰7am-11pm) Part of a (small) chain it may be, but this colorful spot serves up thoroughly satisfying plates of Mexican food, with burritos, enchiladas and combo platters all hitting the mark. Mole and carnitas are here, too, for the more adventurous.

Coronado Room AMERICAN $$$
(☎928-638-2681; www.grandcanyonsquire.com; 74 Hwy 64, Best Western Grand Canyon Squire Inn; mains $30-36; ⏰5-10pm; 📶👪) This restaurant at the Best Western Grand Canyon Squire Inn serves the most upscale cuisine in town, offering bison, elk and boar as well as salmon and steak.

Information

The National Geographic Visitor Center & IMAX Theater (p93) sells park entrance permits, arranges tours and is an excellent resource for all things Grand Canyon. Permits are also available at the Grand Canyon Trading Post, next to McDonalds, Red Feather Lodge, Best Western Grand Canyon Squire Inn, RP's Stage Shop and Canyon Plaza Resort.

Tusayan Ranger Station (Map p80; ☎928-638-2443; www.fs.usda.gov/kaibab; 176 Lincoln Log Loop) offers trail maps and directions.

Getting There & Around

Arizona Shuttle (☎928-350-8466; www.arizonashuttle.com) can get you from Flagstaff to Tusayan, via Williams, for $32 one way. You'll most likely have to drive yourself here, however, via Hwy 64 from Williams, or Hwy 180 and 64 from Flagstaff.

You can walk to most places along the highway through Tusayan. The free Tusayan Route Shuttle (p236) loops between Tusayan and Grand Canyon Visitor Center on the canyon rim from mid-May to early September.

Commercial flights do not fly into **Grand Canyon National Park Airport** (Map p80; ☎928-638-2446; www.azdot.gov/about/GrandCanyonAirport; 871 Liberator Dr); it services scenic flights and tours.

Williams

☎928 / POP 3122 / ELEV 6780FT

A pretty slow spot by day, Williams comes to life in the evening when the Grand Canyon Railway train returns with passengers from the South Rim…and then closes down again on the early side. It's a friendly town, with history up its sleeve, and an openness to Grand Canyon tourists. Route 66 passes through the main historic district as a one-way street headed east; Railroad Ave parallels the tracks and Route 66, and heads one-way west.

Williams is 35 miles west of Flagstaff on I-40 and 55 miles south of the park on Hwy 64.

Sights & Activities

Ask at the visitor center (p99) or at the ranger station (p99) for maps and information on hiking and biking in the surrounding Kaibab, Coconino and Prescott national forests. You can also cycle to the canyon on the historic Grand Canyon Railway.

Bearizona ZOO
(☎928-635-2289; www.bearizona.com; 1500 E Route 66; adult/child 4-12yr $22/11; ⏰8am-6pm Jun-Aug, reduced hrs rest of yr; 🅿👪) The ostensible main attraction here is the wildlife park – where visitors drive themselves slowly along a road that winds through 160 acres inhabited by roaming gray wolves, bison, bighorn sheep and black bears – but the real draw is the small zoo dubbed Fort Bearizona. Here, under ponderosa shade, you can see tiny baby bears sidle up the trees and playful otter brothers slide and bob through the water, plus porcupines, badgers and a handful of other small animals indigenous to the area.

Grand Canyon Deer Farm ZOO
(☎928-635-4073; www.deerfarm.com; 6769 E Deer Farm Rd; adult/child 3-13 yr/under 3 yr $14/8/free; ⏰9am-6pm Mar 16-Oct 15, 10am-5pm rest of yr; 👪) Blanketed in wood chips, a trail leads through an open area where the deer roam free and gather eagerly around visitors whose outstretched hands are full

DISPERSED CAMPING

Across the forest's three ranger districts – Tusayan, Williams and North Kaibab – there's free backcountry camping, also called dispersed camping. The forest also holds six developed campgrounds, including Ten-X Campground.

of tasty pellets. A smaller pen is home to goats (quite the loud-mouthed personalities here, mischievously reaching to munch on food, shirts, strollers, whatever). Just $3 buys enough deer food to keep kids busy for awhile. Among the more exotic animals in residence are marmosets and wallabies, while the resident parrot chats sassily.

It's 8 miles east of Williams, off I-40's exit 171.

Grand Canyon Railway RAIL

(☎reservations 303-843-8724; www.thetrain.com; 233 N Grand Canyon Bvd, Railway Depot; round-trip adult/child from $67/32; ⌚departs 9:30am) Following a 9am Wild West show by the tracks, this historic train departs for its 2¼-hour ride to the South Rim. If you're only visiting the rim for the day, this is a fun and hassle-free way to travel. Once there, you can explore by foot, shuttle or tour bus, and arrive back in Williams at 5:45pm.

Route 66 Zipline ADVENTURE SPORTS

(☎928-635-5358; www.ziplineroute66.com; 200 North Grand Canyon Bvd; $12-15; ⌚hrs vary Mar-Dec & select days Jan & Feb) Only 1400ft as a round-trip, this kitschy Route 66–inspired ride zips over the parking lot in downtown Williams. More like a carnival attraction than a zipline, it can be a very fun distraction on a lazy Williams summer evening.

Sleeping

Camping

Dogtown Lake, Kaibab Lake and White Horse Lake are three pleasant USFS campgrounds near Williams that offer seasonal camping without hookups. Swimming isn't allowed in any of the lakes. Contact the Visitor Center (p99) or the Williams Ranger Station (p99) for information.

Kaibab Lake Campground CAMPGROUND $

(☎928-635-5600, reservations 877-444-6777; www.recreation.gov; tent & RV sites $24-40; ⌚Apr–mid-Sep; 🐾) Kaibab Lake Campground has large campsites in ponderosa shade with fire rings and picnic tables. It sits 4 miles northeast of Williams; take exit 165 off I-40 and go north 2 miles on Hwy 64. Offers both reservable and first-come, first-served sites.

Circle Pines KOA CAMPGROUND $

(☎928-635-2626, reservations 800-562-9379; www.koa.com/campgrounds/williams; 1000 Circle Pines Rd; powered tent & RV site from $40, cabin from $75; ⌚mid-Mar–Oct; 📶🏊🐾) Amid 27 acres of ponderosa pine forest, a half-mile north of I-40 (take exit 167), Circle Pines offers plenty of activities for children and adults alike, including bikes, a pool, sauna and even mini golf.

Dogtown Lake Campground CAMPGROUND $

(☎928-635-5600, reservations 877-444-6777; www.recreation.gov; FR 140; tent & RV sites $24; ⌚May-Sep) There are 50 single and four double sites at this wooded USFS campground 6 miles southeast of Williams in the Kaibab National Forest. Most sites can be booked in advance. There are pit toilets, and no RV hookups. Turn south on 4th St for 3.5 miles to FR 140 and follow the signs.

White Horse Lake Campground CAMPGROUND $

(☎928-635-5600, reservations 877-444-6777; www.recreation.gov; FR 109; tent & RV sites $24; ⌚May-Sep; 🐾) Nineteen miles southeast of Williams, this 90-unit campground offers a hiking trail and fishing, but no RV hookups. From town, drive 9 miles on 4th St, turn left on FR 110 then left again onto FR 109, after another 7 miles. Reservations accepted.

VALLE

About 25 miles south of the park, middle-of-nowhere-feeling Valle marks the intersection of Hwy 64 to Williams and Hwy 180 to Flagstaff. There isn't much to it apart from a couple of curiosities, as well as a gas station and minimart. The only reason to stay in Valle is its proximity to the park.

There are rooms at the **Grand Canyon Inn & Motel** (☎928-635-9203; www.grandcanyoninn.com; 317 S Hwy 64; d $150; ❄📶🏊). This family-run motel offers standard rooms and a restaurant; the less expensive rooms in the motel section across the highway from the lobby are a bit nicer, with Southwestern flair, but they are smaller and don't have refrigerators or telephones. **Flintstones Bedrock City** (☎928-635-2600; www.bedrockaz.com; 101 S Hwy 180, junction with Hwy 64; adult $5, child under 5yr free; ⌚6am-sunset May-Oct, from 7am Nov-Apr; 👪), a kitschy 1972 roadside attraction, offers tent sites ($18) and RV hookups ($25).

Lodging

Grand Canyon Hotel HOTEL $

(928-635-1419; www.thegrandcanyonhotel.com; 145 W Route 66; dm/r from $33/89; Mar-Nov;) This rambling European-style hotel first received guests in 1891. Perched on the corner of Route 66 and S 2nd St downtown, the welcoming hotel struts its quirky stuff with themed rooms (giraffe room, anyone?) and eclectic decor. Overnight options include a hostel-style dorm, rooms with shared baths, en suite rooms and units in a separate carriage house ($145).

Canyon Country Inn MOTEL $

(928-635-2349; www.thecanyoncountryinn.com; 422 W Rte 66; r $93;) Rooms at this small family-run motel are a step up from typical motel rooms and give you more of a B&B feel. The country-style decor includes frilly curtains, floral bedspreads and a teddy bear on the bed.

Canyon Motel & RV Park MOTEL $

(928-635-9371; www.thecanyonmotel.com; 1900 E Rodeo Rd; tent/RV sites from $31/44, cottages/cabooses from $90/180;) Stone cottages (c 1940s) and rooms in two 1929 railroad cabooses and a former Grand Canyon Railway coach-car offer a quirky alternative to a standard motel. Kids will especially love the cozy caboose rooms, with bunks and modern conveniences; the larger one can include up to six guests, while five people can fit into the smaller one.

Lodge on Route 66 MOTEL $$

(928-635-4534; www.thelodgeonroute66.com; 200 E Route 66; r/ste $140/240;) This smart drive-up motel embraces its Route 66 and Southwest heritage with low-key style, carved vigas and loads of handsome charm. Rooms feature sturdy dark-wood furniture, wrought-iron accents and sumptuous linens. Most suites have kitchenettes, and there's a pleasant sitting area outside each room.

Grand Canyon Railway Hotel HOTEL $$

(928-635-4010; www.thetrain.com/lodging/the-grand-canyon-railway-hotel; 235 N Grand Canyon Blvd; r/ste $180/240;) This sprawling 297-room hotel caters primarily to Grand Canyon Railway passengers. An elegant lobby with chandelier, stone fireplace and plush leather chairs are designed to take travelers back to the romance of train travel, but rooms are the basic upscale roadside hotel variety. It's spacious, comfortable and centrally located, with a glass-enclosed indoor pool.

SUPPLY STOP

Swing by the **Safeway** (pharmacy 928-635-0500; 637 W Route 66; 5am-midnight), just southwest of the tourist hub on old Route 66, for groceries and supplies before heading up to Grand Canyon. Inside there's a pharmacy and a Starbucks, William's best bet for a strong cup of brew.

Best Western Plus Inn MOTEL $$

(928-635-4400; www.bestwesternwilliams.com; 2600 Route 66; d from $246; P) At this pleasant chain motel, the Kachina Lounge and Western View Steakhouse give you alternatives to frowsting in your room.

Red Garter Inn B&B $$

(928-635-1484; www.redgarter.com; 137 W Railroad Ave; d from $160;) Up until the 1940s, gambling and girls were the draw at this 1897 bordello-turned-B&B across from the tracks. Nowadays the place trades on its historic charm and reputation for hauntings. Of the four restored rooms, the suite was once reserved for the house's 'best gals,' who would lean out the window to flag down customers.

Trappers Rendezvous B&B $$$

(928-635-1002; www.trappersrendezvous.com; 1019 Airport Rd; r/ste from $190/500) Handsome Western-style cabins sit in a half-circle here, with barbecue grills and a fire pit. Despite being a stone's throw from the highway and only a few minutes' drive from downtown Williams, it's a peaceful spot and an excellent choice. A friendly low-key breakfast is served family-style, and there's a prairie dog colony just beyond the cabins.

Eating & Drinking

Williams boasts some lovely old-fashioned diners, alongside a smattering of more cosmopolitan food offerings.

Dara Thai Cafe THAI $

(928-635-2201; 145 W Route 66, Suite C; mains $10-14; 11am-2pm & 5-9pm Mon-Sat;) An unassuming spot tucked down a quiet side street, this is your only option for a lighter alternative to meat-heavy menus elsewhere in town. Despite its address, look for the front door along S 2nd St.

Pine Country Restaurant AMERICAN $

(928-635-9718; www.pinecountryrestaurant.com; 107 N Grand Canyon Blvd; breakfast $7-9,

HISTORIC ROUTE 66

Arizona claims bragging rights for having the longest remaining continuous stretch of Route 66, running east to west from Seligman to Topock. When the Mother Road re-routed here in 1933, roadside businesses thrived, but once the I-40 bypass was completed in 1978, this snake of a road through the desert scrub almost died away. Angel Delgadillo, a local barber, spearheaded the successful effort to designate the road an Historic Highway in 1987, and in 2005 it was listed on the National Register of Historic Places.

Getting off I-40 for part of a long road trip can be a beautiful alternative to simply blowing through this part of the country, but the tiny pockets of businesses that dot the dusty surrounds along the way are more a constructed kitschy tourist trinket than a preserved stretch of something real. There's a melancholy echo here, with the iconic romance of Route 66 boiled down to Little Debbie pastries, Route 66 mugs, T-shirts and keyrings, and vintage gas pumps.

Nineteen miles west of Williams and just off I-40 is **Ash Fork**, founded in 1882 when the Atlantic and Pacific Railroad established a stop here. These days its claim to fame is as the 'Flagstone Capital of the World,' as smooth vermilion slabs of Coconino sandstone are quarried in the area. You can stay for the night at **Ash Fork Inn** (928-637-2514; www.ashforkinn.us; 859 W Route 66; d from $57; P) and poke around the free **Ash Fork Route 66 Museum** (928-637-0204; www.facebook.com/AshForkHistoricalSociety; 901 W Route 66; 9am-3pm Mon-Fri) FREE.

From Ash Fork, the Mother Road hugs I-40 for 24 miles to **Seligman**. Juan Delgadillo once reigned supreme as an infamous prankster at his famous **Delgadillo's Snow Cap Drive-In** (928-422-3291; http://delgadillossnowcap.t2-food.com; 301 East Chino; mains $5-6.50; 10am-6pm Mar-Nov), and you can still line up for shakes and cheeseburgers. Along both sides of Seligman's stretch of Route 66 are the historic buildings that have survived over the years, as well as cafes, restaurants and souvenir shops where they lay the kitsch on thick. One of Seligman's handful of clean, basic budget motels is the nondescript **Historic Route 66 Motel** (928-422-3204; 22750 Route 66; r from $50;).

Getting back on the westward highway, the road veers north from I-40 through mile upon mile of rolling hills and canyon country towards tiny **Peach Springs** and **Grand Canyon Caverns & Inn** (928-422-3223; www.gccaverns.com; Mile 115, Rte 66; tour adult/child from $16/11; 9am-5pm May-Sep, call for off-season hrs), where you can escape the desert heat in the cool subterranean caverns 21 stories below ground, via elevator. Stay the night at the cavern inn (double $100) or the very quiet underground suite ($900) within the caverns. The caverns and the modern and recommended **Hualapai Lodge** (928-769-2230; www.grandcanyonwest.com/hualapai-lodge-and-route-66.htm; 900 Route 66; r from $150;) in Peach Springs are the closest accommodations to Hualapai Hilltop – the windswept trailhead for the 10-mile hike down to **Havasu Canyon** (camping reservations 928-448-2180, lodge reservations 928-448-2111; www.theofficialhavasupaitribe.com; Havasupai Reservation; camping per person $140, lodge $175) on the Havasupai Reservation. Both motels arrange day and overnight trips into the canyon, offering various combinations of helicopter, mule and hiking to get down and back up.

Moving westward, you'll come to teeny **Hackberry**, whose 1934 **Hackberry General Store** (928-769-2605; www.hackberrygeneralstore.com; 11255 E Route 66; 9am-6pm Apr-Oct, 10am-5pm Nov-Mar; P) lures passersby with its eccentrically decorated gas station, vintage cars in faded disrepair and rusted-out ironwork. It's run by a Route 66 memorialist and makes the best spot on this stretch to stop for a cold drink and souvenirs.

For more information on the history of this old highway, as well as details on annual events, check out the Historic Route 66 Association of Arizona (www.azrt66.com).

lunch & dinner $11-19; 7am-9pm) There's a wide variety of offerings at this wholesome diner, from pork chops to taco salad, to keep everyone happy. And the prices are right. If nothing else, swing by for a slice of one of their 50 varieties of pie, made fresh in-house daily, and an Annie Oakley (that's Williams-talk for cappucino) at the GiddyUp 'n' Go Coffee Bar.

Grand Canyon Coffee & Café DINER $
(Anna's; ☎928-635-4907; www.grandcanyoncoffeeandcafe.com; 137 W Railroad Ave; breakfast $7-9, mains $8-10; ⏲6am-3pm Sun-Thu, to 7pm Fri & Sat) Inside the Red Garter Inn, this cafe slings classic breakfasts, sandwiches and a smattering of Mexican and Asian dishes. The canyon burrito includes scrambled eggs and pork green chile, and there's a lovely brick patio. You may stumble in to find locals tuning their fiddles over afternoon coffee.

Station 66 Italian Bistro ITALIAN $$
(☎928-635-5329; www.kennellyfamilyconcepts.com; 144 W Route 66; mains $10-24; ⏲11am-10pm) Housed in an old Route 66 gas station, with live music in the sidewalk cafe and rooftop dining. Wood-fire-pizza toppings include fresh mozzarella, artichoke and prosciutto, and the $22 Butcher's Board appetizer is big enough for a meal. Station 66 serves locally produced wine and beer.

Rod's Steak House STEAK $$
(☎928-635-2671; www.rods-steakhouse.com; 301 E Route 66; mains $17-23; ⏲11am-9:30pm Mon-Sat) The cow-shaped sign and menus spell things out – if you want steak and potatoes, this has been the place to come since 1946. A dark and old-school Route 66 classic with iceberg wedge salad and prime rib.

Cruisers Café 66 AMERICAN $$
(☎928-635-2445; www.cruisers66.com; 233 W Route 66; mains $15-25; ⏲8am-10pm; 👪) Decorated with vintage gas pumps and old-fashioned Coke ads, this former Route 66 gas station is a fun place for kids. Expect barbecue fare such as burgers, spicy wings, pulled-pork sandwiches and mesquite-grilled ribs (cooked on the outdoor patio).

Grand Canyon Winery BAR
(☎855-598-0999; www.thegrandcanyonwinery.com; 138 W Route 66; ⏲noon-10pm Mon-Sat, to 9pm Sun) Grand Canyon Winery has excellent wines, produced with local grapes, and craft beer from its sister Historic Brewing Co, served by the mason glass or hefty portioned flight. It's a friendly low-key spot, with a handful of stools along the tiny bar and a few tables.

World Famous Sultana Bar BAR
(☎928-635-2021; 301 W Route 66; ⏲10am-2am, shorter hrs in winter) A slightly daunting local hangout, this 100-year-old bar is pretty darn cool, especially if you like the sort of place that's kitted out with deer skulls, stuffed mountain lions and crusty locals. It was a speakeasy during Prohibition. No food, and no doors on the male toilet stalls.

ℹ Information

North Country HealthCare (☎928-635-4441; www.northcountryhealthcare.org/locations/williams; 301 S 7th St; ⏲urgent care 8am-8pm)

Police Station (☎928-635-4421, emergency 911; 501 W Route 66)

Post Office (☎928-635-4572; 120 S 1st St; ⏲8:30am-3.30pm Mon-Fri)

Visitor Center (☎928-635-4061; www.experiencewilliams.com; 200 W Railroad Ave; ⏲8am-5pm summer) Inside the 1901 train depot, with a small but interesting museum on Williams' history, and a bookstore selling titles on the Grand Canyon, Kaibab National Forest and other areas of interest. You can purchase Grand Canyon entrance passes here.

Williams Ranger Station (☎928-635-5600; www.fs.usda.gov/kaibab; 742 S Clover Rd; ⏲8am-4:30pm Mon-Fri) Maps and details for hiking, biking, fishing and camping in the surrounding national forest. It sits just off I-40, west of downtown.

ℹ Getting There & Around

Williams is 35 miles west of Flagstaff on I-40 and 55 miles south of Grand Canyon National Park, via Hwy 64. **Amtrak** (☎800-872-7245; www.amtrak.com/stations/wma; 233 N Grand Canyon Blvd) has trains stopping at the Grand Canyon Railway Depot. **Arizona Shuttle** (☎928-350-8466; www.arizonashuttle.com) offers three daily shuttles between Flagstaff and the Grand Canyon's South Rim (per person $32) and between Williams and the Grand Canyon (per person $24).

Flagstaff

☎928 / POP 71,460 / ELEV 7000FT

Flagstaff's laid-back charms are many, from a pedestrian-friendly historic downtown crammed with eclectic vernacular architecture and vintage neon, to hiking and skiing in the country's largest ponderosa pine forest. And the locals are a happy, athletic bunch, skewing more toward granola than gunslinger: buskers play bluegrass on street corners while cycling culture flourishes. Northern Arizona University (NAU) gives Flag its college-town flavor, while its railroad history still figures firmly in the town's identity. Throw in a healthy appreciation for craft beer, freshly roasted coffee beans and an all-around good time and you have the makings of the perfect northern Arizonan escape.

Flagstaff

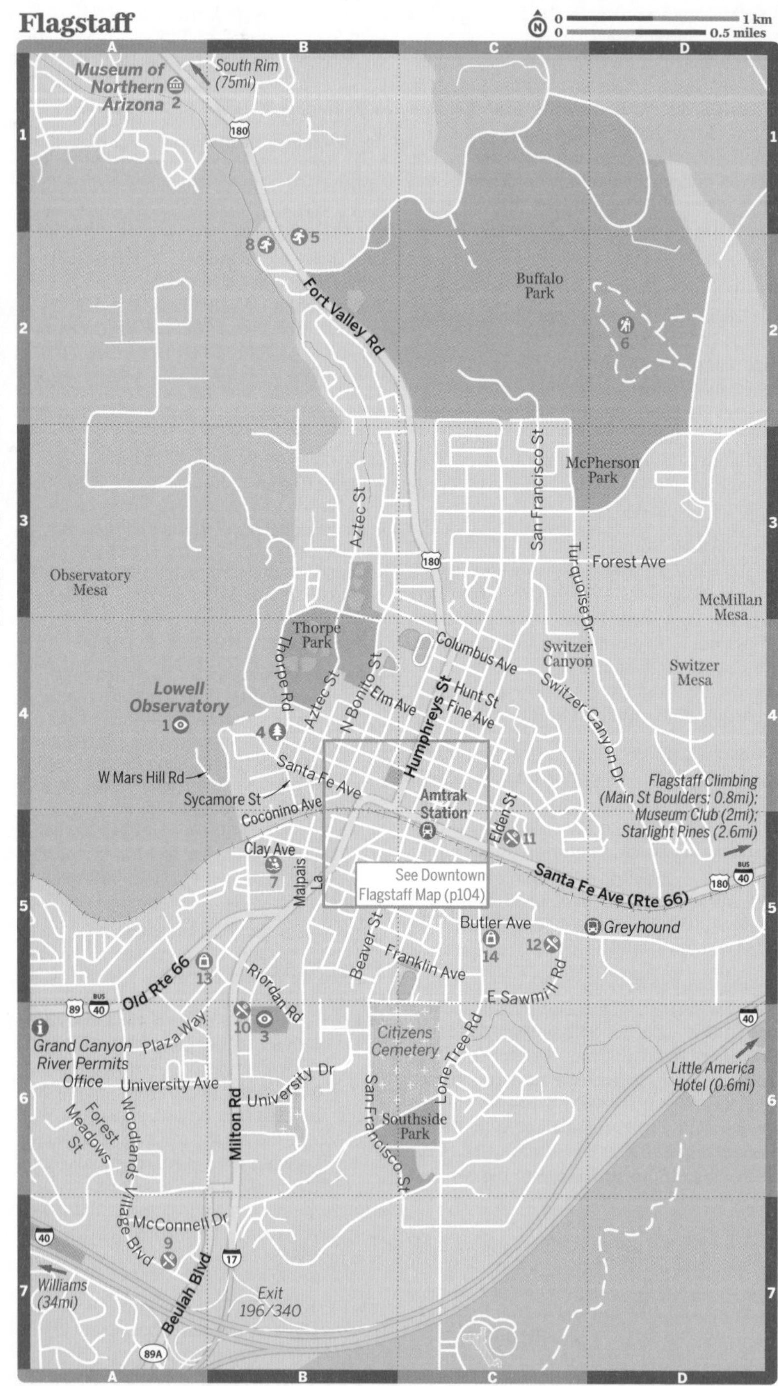

Museum of Northern Arizona
South Rim (75mi)
Fort Valley Rd
Buffalo Park
McPherson Park
Aztec St
San Francisco St
Forest Ave
Turquoise Dr
Observatory Mesa
McMillan Mesa
Thorpe Park
Thorpe Rd
Columbus Ave
Switzer Canyon
Switzer Mesa
Lowell Observatory
Aztec St
N Bonito St
Elm Ave
Humphreys St
Hunt St
Fine Ave
Switzer Canyon Dr
W Mars Hill Rd
Santa Fe Ave
Sycamore St
Coconino Ave
Amtrak Station
Elden St
Flagstaff Climbing (Main St Boulders; 0.8mi); Museum Club (2mi); Starlight Pines (2.6mi)
Clay Ave
Malpais La
See Downtown Flagstaff Map (p104)
Santa Fe Ave (Rte 66)
Butler Ave
Greyhound
Beaver St
Franklin Ave
Old Rte 66
Riordan Rd
E Sawmill Rd
Grand Canyon River Permits Office
Plaza Way
Citizens Cemetery
Lone Tree Rd
Little America Hotel (0.6mi)
University Ave
University Dr
Forest Meadows St
Woodlands Village Blvd
Milton Rd
San Francisco St
Southside Park
McConnell Dr
Beulah Blvd
Williams (34mi)
Exit 196/340

Flagstaff

Top Sights

Sights

Activities, Courses & Tours

Eating

Shopping

From downtown, I-17 heads south toward Phoenix; a few miles south of town, Hwy Alt 89 (89A) splits off and parallels I-17 as a scenic and winding road through Oak Creek Canyon 28 miles to Sedona. Hwy 180 north leads to Grand Canyon's South Entrance, and Hwy 89 beelines north to Cameron to meet Hwy 64, leading westward to the recommended East Entrance.

Sights

★Museum of Northern Arizona MUSEUM

(Map p100; ☎928-774-5213; www.musnaz.org; 3101 N Fort Valley Rd; adult/senior/child 10-17yr $12/10/8; ⏲10am-5pm Mon-Sat, noon-5pm Sun; 👪) Housed in an attractive Craftsman-style stone building amid a pine grove, this small but excellent museum spotlights local American Indian archaeology, history and culture, as well as geology, biology and the arts. Intriguing permanent collections are augmented by exhibitions on subjects such as John James Audubon's paintings of North American mammals. On the way to the Grand Canyon it makes a wonderful introduction to the human and natural history of the region.

★Lowell Observatory OBSERVATORY

(Map p100; ☎928-233-3212; www.lowell.edu; 1400 W Mars Hill Rd; adult/senior/child 5-17yr $15/14/8; ⏲10am-10pm Mon-Sat, to 5pm Sun; 👪) Sitting atop a hill just west of downtown, this national historic landmark – famous for the first sighting of Pluto, in 1930 – was built by Percival Lowell in 1894. Weather permitting, visitors can stargaze through on-site telescopes, including the famed 1896 Clark Telescope, the impetus behind the now-accepted theory of an expanding universe. Kids will love the paved Pluto Walk, which meanders through a scale model of our solar system.

Riordan Mansion State Historic Park HISTORIC SITE

(Map p100; ☎928-779-4395; https://azstateparks.com/riordan-mansion; 409 W Riordan Rd; tour adult/child 7-13yr $10/5; ⏲9:30am-5pm May-Oct, 10:30am-5pm Thu-Mon Nov-Apr) Having made a fortune from their Arizona Lumber Company, brothers Michael and Timothy Riordan built this sprawling duplex in 1904. The Craftsman-style design was the brainchild of architect Charles Whittlesey, who also designed El Tovar in Grand Canyon Village. The exterior features hand-split wooden shingles, log-slab siding and rustic stone. Filled with Edison, Stickley, Tiffany and Steinway furniture, the interior is a shrine to arts and crafts.

Arboretum GARDENS

(☎928-774-1442; www.thearb.org; 4001 S Woody Mountain Rd; adult/child $10/5; ⏲9am-5pm Wed-Mon Apr 15-Oct) This 200-acre arboretum is a lovely spot to take a break and rejuvenate your spirits. Two short trails hug a meadow and wind beneath ponderosa pines, passing a herb garden, native plants and wildflowers, and a longer loop makes an easy amble through the woods. There are also tours, summer concerts and soirees, and even wine and theater in the woods. Follow Woody Mountain Rd 3.8 miles south from Route 66 – it's unpaved, but feasible for most cars.

Activities

Flagstaff is full of active citizens, so there's no shortage of outdoor stores and places to buy or rent camping, cycling and skiing equipment.

For details on hiking and swimming in Oak Creek Canyon, about a half-hour south of Flagstaff, see Sedona (p112).

Hiking & Biking

Scores of hiking and mountain-biking trails are easily accessed in and around Flagstaff. Fifty-six miles of trails crisscross the city as

WORTH A TRIP

FLAGSTAFF NATIONAL MONUMENTS

Three small but excellent national monuments highlighting the interconnected volcanic and Native American history of the region sit within a roughly 10-mile radius of Flagstaff.

Covered by a single $25 entrance fee (valid for seven days), both Sunset Crater Volcano and Wupatki lie along Park Loop Rd 545, a well-marked 36-mile loop that heads east off Hwy 89 about 12 miles north of Flagstaff on the way to the North Rim. Walnut Canyon ($10) sits 8 miles east of Flagstaff, just off I-40.

Each site offers an interpretive visitor center, pleasant picnic grounds, ranger talks and guided walks (summer only).

Sunset Crater Volcano National Monument (928-526-0502; www.nps.gov/sucr; Park Loop Rd 545; car/motorcycle/bicycle or pedestrian $25/20/15; visitor center 9am-5pm, park 24hr) Around AD 1064 a volcano erupted on this spot, spewing ash across 800 sq miles, spawning the Kana-A lava flow and forcing farmers to vacate lands tilled for 400 years. Now the 8029ft Sunset Crater is quiet, and mile-long trails wind through the Bonito lava flow (formed c 1180), and up Lenox Crater (7024ft). More ambitious hikers and bikers can ascend O'Leary Peak (8965ft; 8 miles round-trip), or there's a gentle, 0.3-mile, wheelchair-accessible loop overlooking the petrified flow.

Wupatki National Monument (928-679-2365; www.nps.gov/wupa; Park Loop Rd 545; car/motorcycle/bicycle or pedestrian $25/20/15; visitor center 9am-5pm, trails sunrise-sunset; P) The first eruptions of Sunset Crater (AD 1040–1100) enriched the surrounding soil, luring the ancestors of today's Hopi, Zuni and Navajo to the rich agriculture land. By AD 1180 it was home to roughly 100 people, and 2000 more peppered the immediate area. By 1250, however, their pueblos stood abandoned. About 2700 of these structures lie within Wupatki National Monument, though only a few are open to the public. Entry is also valid for nearby Sunset Crater Volcano National Monument.

Walnut Canyon (928-526-3367; www.nps.gov/waca; I-40 exit 204; adult/child under 16yr $10/free; 8am-5pm Jun-Oct, 9am-5pm Nov-May, trails close 1hr earlier; P) The Sinagua cliff dwellings at Walnut Canyon are set in the nearly vertical walls of a small limestone butte amid this stunning forested canyon. The mile-long Island Trail steeply descends 185ft (more than 200 stairs), passing 25 rooms built under the natural overhangs of the curvaceous butte. A shorter, wheelchair-accessible Rim Trail affords several views of the cliff dwelling from across the canyon.

part of the **Flagstaff Urban Trail System**; maps are available online (www.flagstaff.az.gov/futs) or at the Visitor Center (p109).

Stop by the USFS Flagstaff Ranger Station (p109) for information about trails in the surrounding national forest or check www.fs.fed.us. The steep 3-mile hike (one way) up 9299ft **Mt Elden** leads to a lookout at the top of the peak's tower. If it's locked when you get there, knock and if someone is there, you may be able to climb the stairs to the lookout.

Arizona Snowbowl offers several trails, including the strenuous 9.5-mile round-trip hike up 12,633ft **Humphreys Peak**, the highest point in Arizona; wear decent boots as sections of the trail cross crumbly volcanic rock. In summer you can ride the **chairlift** (928-779-1951; www.snowbowl.ski; 9300 N Snowbowl Rd; adult $19, senior & child 6-12yr $15; 10am-4pm Fri-Sun late May–mid-Oct) to 11,500ft, where you can hike, attend ranger talks and take in the desert and mountain views. Children under eight ride for free.

Visit the super-friendly gearheads at **Absolute Bikes** (Map p104; 928-779-5969; www.absolutebikes.net; 202 E Rte 66; bike rentals per day from $39; 9am-7pm Mon-Fri, to 6pm Sat, 10am-4pm Sun Apr-Nov, shorter hr Dec-Mar) for the inside track on the local mountain-biking scene.

Kachina Trail HIKING

(Snowbowl Rd) A gentle 5-mile one-way hike through ponderosa forest and meadows offering lovely views. The trail begins at 9500ft and descends 700ft.

Humphreys Peak HIKING

(www.fs.usda.gov/recarea/coconino; Snowbowl Rd) The state's highest mountain (12,633ft) is a reasonably straightforward, though strenuous, hike in summer. The trail, which begins north of the Arizona Snowbowl parking lot, winds through forest, eventually coming out above the beautifully barren tree line. It's a little over 4.75 miles one way; allow six to eight hours for the round-trip.

Arizona Trail Walnut Canyon Rim CYCLING
(www.aztrail.org) Passage No 31 of the Arizona Trail (18 miles from Marshall Lake to the I-40) winds through pine and oak, along a tributary of Walnut Canyon. From Flagstaff, take Country Club Rd (exit 201) from I-40 and head south. Turn left at the Old Walnut Canyon Rd (FR 303); the trailhead is 4 miles along, on the south side of FR303.

All-Star Grand Canyon Tours HIKING
(928-814-8887; www.allstargrandcanyontours.com; 2420 N 3rd, Suite D; day hike per person incl lunch beginner/advanced $250/300) This well-regarded outfit runs private tours, backpacking treks and day hikes to the Canyon, with pick-ups in Flagstaff, Sedona, Las Vegas and Phoenix. The sightseeing trips are good for the less mobile, while longer treks (up to four nights) require a decent standard of fitness.

Buffalo Park HIKING
(Map p100; 2400 N Gemini Rd) This easily accessible and mostly flat 215-acre park holds a 2-mile trail winding around a lovely open expanse of grassland, dipping into the ponderosa and offering beautiful views of the San Francisco Peaks. Several exercise stops (stretch, hang, balance) pepper the wide dirt path, and it's popular with joggers, dog-walkers and families. Bicycles allowed.

Skiing

Flagstaff sees an annual average of 108in of snow. Go to Peace Surplus (p109) for ski rental.

Arizona Snowbowl SKIING
(928-779-1951; www.snowbowl.ski; 9300 N Snowbowl Rd; adult/child ski pass $79/44, summer scenic chair $19/15; 9am-4pm Nov-Apr, 10am-4pm Jun-Aug;) About 14 miles north of downtown Flagstaff, Arizona Snowbowl is small but lofty, with eight lifts that service 40 ski runs between 9200ft and 11,500ft. The ski season normally runs from November to April.

Flagstaff Nordic Center SKIING
(928-220-0550; www.arizonanordicvillage.com; 16848 Hwy 180; weekend/weekday trail pass $20/12; 9am-4pm Dec-Mar) Fifteen miles north of Flagstaff, the Nordic Center offers 25 miles of groomed trails for cross-country skiing, as well as lessons and rentals (skis are $20 on weekends). It also has snowshoe and multi-use trails, and nearby you can ski – no permit required – across Forest Service land. The parking lot is at Mile 232 on Hwy 180.

Other Activities

Flagstaff Climbing (Downtown Crag) CLIMBING
(Map p104; 928-556-9909; www.flagstaffclimbing.com; 205 S San Francisco St; day pass $16; 10am-10pm Mon-Fri, noon-8pm Sat & Sun) Flagstaff Climbing provides 7000 sq ft of indoor climbing walls, and offers indoor and outdoor classes, camps, guided trips and information on local climbing routes. There is also a second location (928-699-4246; 1519 Main St; noon-10pm Mon-Fri, to 8pm Sat & Sun), with a smaller climbing gym.

Hitchin' Post Stables HORSEBACK RIDING
(928-774-1719; www.historichitchinpoststables.com; 4848 Lake Mary Rd; 1-/2-hr ride $55/100;) Hitchin' Post Stables has trail, wagon

FLAGSTAFF & WILLIAMS FOR KIDS

- Feed the fawns at Grand Canyon Deer Farm (p95).
- Picnic and play at Thorpe Park (Map p100; 191 N Thorpe Rd;).
- Browse books in the children's section of the library (p109).
- Ride the scenic chairlift at Arizona Snowbowl (p103).
- Hike through lava flows at Sunset Crater Volcano National Monument (p102).
- Board the Grand Canyon Railway (p96) to the South Rim.
- Check out the playful otters and baby bears at Bearizona (p95).
- Pick up a gelato at the Sweet Shoppe (Map p104; 928-213-9000; www.facebook.com/sweetshoppecandy; 15 E Aspen Ave; 10am-8pm Sun-Thu, to 10pm Fri & Sat).
- Glide along the kitschy Rt 66 Zipline (p96) in downtown Williams.
- Pull up a chair in Heritage Square (Map p104; E Aspen Ave) and catch a family-friendly flick on a summer weekend.

Downtown Flagstaff

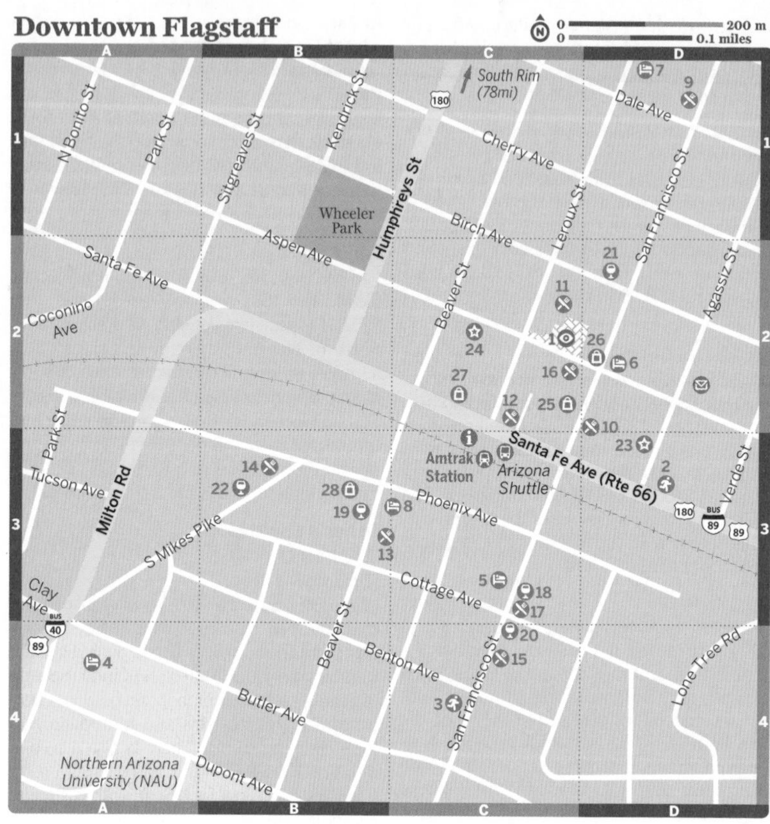

Downtown Flagstaff

Sights

1 Heritage Square C2

Activities, Courses & Tours

2 Absolute Bikes D3
3 Flagstaff Climbing (Downtown Crag) .. C4

Sleeping

4 Drury Inn & Suites A4
5 Grand Canyon International Hostel C3
6 Hotel Monte Vista D2
7 Inn at 410 ..... D1
8 Motel Dubeau C3

Eating

9 Brix Restaurant & Wine Bar D1
10 Criollo Latin Kitchen D2
11 Diablo Burger C2
12 Karma Sushi Bar C2
13 Macy's B3
14 Pizzicletta B3
15 Proper Meats + Provisions C4
16 Sweet Shoppe Candy Store C2
17 Tourist Home All Day Cafe C3

Drinking & Nightlife

18 Annex Cocktail Lounge C3
19 Beaver Street Brewery B3
20 Historic Brewing Co Barrel & Bottle House C4
21 Hops on Birch D2
Monte Vista Cocktail Lounge ..... (see 6)
22 Mother Road Brewing Company B3

Entertainment

23 Green Room D3
24 Orpheum Theater C2

Shopping

25 Aspen Sports C2
26 Babbitt's Backcountry Outfitters D2
27 Peace Surplus C2
The Artists' Gallery ..... (see 25)
28 Zani B3

and sleigh rides through the ponderosa of Coconino National Forest and through Walnut Canyon.

Sleeping

Camping

Free dispersed camping (p95) is permitted in the Coconino National Forest surrounding Flagstaff. There are also campgrounds in Oak Creek Canyon to the south of town and Sunset Crater to the north.

Flagstaff KOA CAMPGROUND $

(928-526-9926,reservations800-562-3524;www.flagstaffkoa.com; 5803 N Hwy 89; tent or RV site from $35, cabins & tipis from $60;) This big ponderosa-shaded campground lies a mile north of I-40 off exit 201, 5 miles northeast of downtown Flagstaff. A path leads from the campground to trails at Mt Elden, and it's family friendly, with banana-bike rentals, summer barrel-train rides, weekend movies and a splash park. The four one-room cabins sleep four, but bedding isn't supplied.

Bonito Campground CAMPGROUND $

(928-526-0866; www.fs.usda.gov/recmain/coconino; Loop Rd; tent & RV sites $24; May-Oct) Across from the Sunset Crater Volcano National Monument Visitor Center, the USFS-run Bonito Campground provides 44 sites with running water and restrooms but no showers or hookups. There's a 14-day limit on stays and no reservations are taken.

Little Elden Springs Horse Camp CAMPGROUND $

(928-526-0866, reservation 518-885-3639; www.recreation.gov; Elden Springs Rd; sites $22; late Mar-late Sep) In the Coconino National Forest just outside of Flagstaff, Little Elden Springs Horse Camp is a campground designated only for people with horses. It offers 15 horse-friendly campsites with hitching posts but no corrals. From here, riders can access more than 30 miles of equestrian trails through the pines, ranging from easy to the challenging Heart Trail.

Lodging

If you want to walk home after visiting Flagstaff's microbreweries and its top restaurants, choose a hotel downtown. If you just want a place to crash before heading to the Grand Canyon, chain motels and hotels line S Milton Rd, Beulah Blvd and W Forest Meadows St, clustering around exit 195 off I-40.

Unlike in southern Arizona, summer is high season here.

★ **Motel Dubeau** HOSTEL $

(Map p104; 928-774-6731; www.modubeau.com; 19 W Phoenix Ave; dm/r from $27/70;) Built in 1929 as Flagstaff's first motel, this independent hostel offers friendly service and clean, well-run accommodations. The private rooms are similar to basic but handsome hotel rooms, with refrigerators, cable TV and private bathrooms. On-site Nomads serves beer, wine and light snacks. There are also kitchen and laundry facilities.

Grand Canyon International Hostel HOSTEL $

(Map p104; 928-779-9421; www.grandcanyonhostel.com; 19 S San Francisco St; dm/r from $27/68;) Housed in a historic building with hardwood floors and Southwestern decor, this bright, homey and immaculate hostel offers eight private rooms and dorms with a four-person maximum. There's also a kitchen and laundry, plus complimentary coffee, pastries and instant oatmeal.

★ **Hotel Monte Vista** HISTORIC HOTEL $$

(Map p104; 928-779-6971; www.hotelmontevista.com; 100 N San Francisco St; r/ste from $75/145;) A huge, old-fashioned neon sign towers over this 1926 landmark hotel, hinting at what's inside: feather lampshades, vintage furniture, bold colors and eclectic decor. Rooms are named for the movie stars who stayed here, including the 'Humphrey Bogart,' with dramatic black walls, yellow ceiling and gold-satin bedding. Several resident ghosts supposedly make regular appearances.

Inn at 410 B&B $$

(Map p104; 928-774-0088; www.inn410.com; 410 N Leroux St; r from $185;) This fully renovated 1894 house offers 10 spacious,

DISC GOLF

As you might expect from an outdoorsy college town, disc golf (much like golf, but played with Frisbees and also known as Frisbee golf) is quite popular. There are four 18-hole courses in the Flagstaff area – our favorite is Snowbowl (p103), where you can while away a high desert afternoon on the quiet slopes of the ski basin. Buy discs and get details on all four courses at downtown's Aspen Sports (p109).

beautifully decorated and themed bedrooms, each with a fridge and bathroom, and many with four-poster beds and delightful views. A short stroll from downtown, the inn has a shady orchard-garden and a cozy dining room, where a full gourmet breakfast and afternoon snacks are served.

Little America Hotel HOTEL $$
(928-779-7900; http://flagstaff.littleamerica.com; 2515 E Butler Ave; d from $169;) When you reach the Sinclair truck stop just off I-40, don't drive away thinking you have the wrong place. A little further down the side driveway behind an unassuming exterior and hugging 500 acres of ponderosa forest you'll find this sprawling two-story hotel. Little America has spacious French Provincial–styled rooms, upscale bedding with goose-down pillows and large retro-tiled bathrooms.

Drury Inn & Suites HOTEL $$
(Map p104; 928-773-4900; www.druryhotels.com/locations/flagstaff-az; 300 S Milton Rd; r $170-200, ste $215-225; P) A fitness center, indoor pool, laundry and stylish rooms with microwaves and refrigerators distinguish this ecofriendly chain hotel, set on the Northern Arizona University campus and within walking distance of Flagstaff's historic downtown. Breakfast is included, as is a '5:30 Kickback' with beer, wine and a hearty spread of appetizers.

Comfi Cottages COTTAGE $$
(928-774-0731; www.comficottages.com; cottages from $150;) All but one of the these well-kept bungalows are within a mile of Flagstaff's historic district. Most were built in the 1920s and have a comfortable homey feel, with wood floors, Craftsman-style kitchens, board games and little lawns. The friendly owners have lived in Flagstaff for many years, and they're a wonderful source of tourist information.

Starlight Pines B&B $$
(928-527-1912; www.starlightpinesbb.com; 3380 E Lockett Rd; r from $169;) Low-key and friendly Starlight Pines is located in a Victorian-style home and offers four spacious, homey rooms, each with Tiffany-style lamps, antique claw-foot tubs and other lovely touches. The Lily Room makes great use of Mt Elden views, with a telescope on its private balcony.

Eating

Flagstaff's college population and general dedication to living well translates into one of the best dining scenes in the state. Self-caterers can try Bashas', a good local chain supermarket with a respectable selection of organic foods. For healthy food, there's Whole Foods Market.

★ **Tourist Home All Day Cafe** CAFE $
(Map p104; 928-779-2811; www.touristhomecafe.com; 52 S San Francisco St; mains $10-14; 6am-8pm;) Housed in a beautifully renovated 1926 house that was originally home to Basque sheepherder immigrants, this upscale market cafe serves up the best breakfast in a town full of excellent morning victuals. Try the Hash Bowl: eggs any style served on breakfast potatoes and accompanied by chorizo, spiced beets and a cilantro pesto.

PICNIC SUPPLIES

Pick up a loaf of rustic bread and fill a cooler with house-cured meats, locally sourced cheese and homemade pastries for a rimside picnic. Regardless of picnic plans, eating options at the park veer towards food court or high-end, so a cooler of goodies in the room is a good idea.

Whole Foods (Map p100; 928-774-5747; www.wholefoodsmarket.com/stores/flagstaff; 320 S Cambridge Lane; 7am-9pm;) Focus on organic and a large selection of ready-made fare.

Bashas' (Map p100; 928-774-3882; www.bashas.com; 2700 S Woodlands Village Blvd; 6am-11pm) Local chain grocery; there's a second location at Humphrey St.

Proper Meats + Provisions (p107) Upscale sandwiches, salami and grass-fed meat.

Tourist Home All Day Cafe (p106) Side salads, gourmet condiments and quirky drinks.

Simply Delicious Cafe Daily Fare (Map p100; 928-774-2855; www.simplydeliciousflagstaff.com; 408 E Rte 66; mains $8-15; 11am-4pm Mon-Sat) Sandwiches and salads.

Proper Meats + Provisions DELI $
(Map p104; ☎928-774-9001; www.propermeats.com; 110 S San Francisco St; sandwiches $10-13; ⏰10am-7pm) Come here for house-made salami and pancetta, local grass-fed beef for the barbecue and other meat-lovers' delights. There's also wine, an eclectic selection of non-alcoholic drinks, cheese and fresh-baked rustic bread. And don't miss the sensational sandwiches – perhaps the perennially popular seven-day pastrami with Aleppo pepper and cactus cream cheese, or the Vietnamese *banh mi* with confit pork shoulder.

Macy's CAFE $
(Map p104; ☎928-774-2243; www.macyscoffee.net; 14 S Beaver St; breakfast/lunch $6/7; ⏰6am-6pm;) The delicious coffee at this Flagstaff institution – house-roasted in the original, handsome, fire-engine-red roaster in the corner – has kept local students and caffeine devotees buzzing since the 1980s. The vegetarian menu includes many vegan choices, along with traditional cafe grub like pastries, steamed eggs, waffles, yogurt and granola, salads and veggie sandwiches.

Pizzicletta PIZZA $
(Map p104; ☎928-774-3242; www.pizzicletta.com; 203 W Phoenix Ave; pizzas $12-16; ⏰5-9pm Sun-Thu, to 10pm Fri & Sat) Tiny Pizzicletta, where the excellent thin-crusted wood-fired pizzas are loaded with gourmet toppings like arugula and aged prosciutto, is housed in a sliver of a white-brick building. Inside there's an open kitchen, one long table with iron chairs, Edison bulbs and industrial surrounds.

Karma Sushi Bar JAPANESE $
(Map p104; ☎928-774-6100; www.karmaflagstaff.com; 6 E Rte 66; mains $11-13, sushi $5-11; ⏰11am-10pm Sun-Wed, to 11pm Thu-Sat) A slick sushi bar with low lights and black lacquer, Karma is known for its tasty, reasonably priced rolls – try the Lucy, a signature concoction of salmon, avocado and roasted red pepper, with 10% of its proceeds donated to animal shelters. And the ramen is right on point, too.

Diablo Burger BURGERS $
(Map p104; ☎928-774-3274; www.diabloburger.com; 120 N Leroux St; mains $11-14; ⏰11am-9pm Sun-Wed, to 10pm Thu-Sat;) This locally focused gourmet-burger joint slings hefty burgers on English-muffin buns and delicious Herbes de Provence seasoned fries. The cheddar-topped Blake gives a nod to New Mexico with Hatch-chile mayo and roasted green chiles. The place is tiny, so come early or sit outside and people-watch. Beer and wine are also served.

★**Criollo Latin Kitchen** FUSION $$
(Map p104; ☎928-774-0541; www.criollolatinkitchen.com; 16 N San Francisco St; mains $17-20; ⏰11am-9pm Mon-Fri, from 9am Sat & Sun) Sister to Brix Restaurant & Wine Bar and Proper Meats + Provisions, this on-trend Latin-fusion restaurant gives similar encouragement to local producers, sourcing ingredients from Arizona wherever possible. Set up your day with the Haitian brunch of slow-roasted pork with over-easy eggs, pinto beans and Ti-Malice hot sauce, or come back at happy hour (3pm to 6pm Monday to Friday) for fish tacos and $4 margaritas.

★**Coppa Cafe** CAFE $$$
(Map p100; ☎928-637-6813; www.coppacafe.net; 1300 S Milton Rd; lunch & brunch $11-15, mains $28-31; ⏰3-9pm Wed-Fri, 11am-3pm & 5-9pm Sat, 10am-3pm Sun;) This friendly, art-strewn bistro with egg-yolk-yellow walls. offers ingredients foraged from nearby woods (and further afield in Arizona) in dishes such as slow-roasted top loin with wildflower butter, or clay-baked duck's egg with a 'risotto' of Sonoran wheat and wild herbs.

Brix Restaurant & Wine Bar INTERNATIONAL $$$
(Map p104; ☎928-213-1021; www.brixflagstaff.com; 413 N San Francisco St; mains $30-32; ⏰5-9pm Tue-Thu & Sun, to 10pm Fri & Sat;) Brix offers seasonal, locally sourced and generally top-notch fare in a handsome room with exposed brick walls and an intimate copper bar. Sister business Proper Meats + Provisions, on S San Francisco St, supplies charcuterie, free-range pork and other fundamentals of lip-smacking dishes that include cavatelli with Calabrese sausage, kale and preserved lemon. The wine list is well curated, and reservations are recommended.

Drinking

For details about festivals and music programs, call the Visitor Center (p109) or check www.flagstaff365.com. On Friday and Saturday nights in summer, people gather on blankets for free music and family movies at Heritage Sq. The fun starts at 5pm.

On Thursdays pick up a free copy of *Flagstaff Live!* (www.azdailysun.com/flaglive_new) for current shows and happenings around town.

ALE TRAIL

Craft-beer fans can follow the Flagstaff-Grand Canyon Ale Trail (www.flagstaffaletrail.com) to sample microbrews at downtown breweries and a bar or two. Buy a trail passport at the Visitor Center or one of the breweries listed on the website.

★Annex Cocktail Lounge COCKTAIL BAR
(Tinderbox Kitchen; Map p104; ☎928-226-8400; www.annexcocktaillounge.com; 34 S San Francisco St; ⏲3-11pm Mon-Wed, from 2pm Thu-Sun, to midnight Fri & Sat) This slinky cocktail bar mixes up great originals and classics: the Moscow Mule with mint and cucumber might just be the best cocktail in Flagstaff. The outdoor patio, actually a handball court built by Basque immigrants in 1926, attracts a low-key local crowd. Annexed to the wonderful **Tinderbox Kitchen** (5pm to 10pm) it also does poutine and other top-notch drinking food.

★Museum Club BAR
(☎928-440-5214; www.facebook.com/themuseumclub; 3404 E Rte 66; ⏲3pm-2am Sun-Thu, from noon Fri & Sat) This honky-tonk roadhouse on Route 66 has been kicking up its heels since 1936. Inside what looks like a huge log cabin you'll find a large wooden dance floor, animal mounts and a sumptuous elixir-filled mahogany bar. The origins of the name? In 1931 it housed a taxidermy museum.

Hops on Birch PUB
(Map p104; ☎928-440-5380; www.hopsonbirch.com; 22 E Birch Ave; ⏲noon-1:30am Sun-Thu, to 2am Fri & Sat; 🐾) Simple and handsome, Hops on Birch has 34 rotating beers on tap, live music five nights a week and a friendly local-crowd vibe. In classic Flagstaff style, dogs are as welcome as humans.

Beaver Street Brewery BREWERY
(Map p104; ☎928-779-0079; www.beaverstreetbrewery.com; 11 S Beaver St; ⏲11am-10pm Sun-Thu, to midnight Fri & Sat; 👪) Families, river guides, ski bums and businesspeople – everybody is here or on the way. The menu is typical brewpub fare, with pizzas, burgers and salads whipped up in the open kitchen. Relax with a season brew on the small outdoor terrace, or head to the cozy old-fashioned-feeling Brews & Cues (21 years and older) for a round of pool.

Historic Brewing Co Barrel & Bottle House MICROBREWERY
(Map p104; ☎928-774-0454; www.historicbrewingcompany.com; 110 S San Francisco St; ⏲11am-11pm Mon-Thu, to midnight Fri & Sat, 11am-10pm Sun; 📶) The taproom for the Historic Brewing Co, Flagstaff's local microwbrew, has 26 craft-beer taps, wine flights and bottles produced by the local Grand Canyon Winery. There's also a massive wall-refrigerator lined with a dizzying selection of beer by the bottle or can.

Mother Road Brewing Company BREWERY
(Map p104; ☎928-774-9139; www.motherroadbeer.com; 7 S Mikes Pike; ⏲2-9pm Tue & Wed, 2-10pm Thu, noon-10pm Fri & Sat, noon-9pm Sun; 🐾) Chill out with a hoppy Tower Station IPA and a wood-fired pizza from nearby Pizzicletta (p107) at this popular, stripped-back taproom beside the old Route 66. There are usually 10 beers on tap (growlers are available for takeout) while board games, toys and a relaxing patio add to the kid- and dog-friendly bonhomie.

Monte Vista Cocktail Lounge BAR
(Map p104; ☎928-779-6971; www.hotelmontevista.com; 100 N San Francisco St, Hotel Monte Vista; ⏲1pm-2am) With a prime corner spot in downtown Flagstaff, complete with broad windows for people-watching, this former speakeasy in the historic Hotel Monte Vista (p105) has a pressed-tin ceiling, pool table, live music three nights a week, plus a Sunday quiz, karaoke and all-day 'happy hour' on Mondays.

☆ Entertainment

For a complete listing of Flagstaff's many festivals, outdoor music concerts and special events, including the monthly **First Friday ArtWalk**, go to www.flagstaff365.com.

Orpheum Theater THEATER
(Map p104; ☎928-556-1580; www.orpheumflagstaff.com; 15 W Aspen Ave; tickets from $10) A grand old-style movie house from 1911, the Orpheum Theater is now a fine-looking music venue – complete with balcony, seating, bar and lounge – that hosts top regional and national bands and the occasional movie night. It has seen some troubles (heavy snowfall collapsed the roof in 1915, and it closed between 1999 and 2002), but has come back better than ever.

Green Room LIVE MUSIC
(Map p104; www.flagstaffgreenroom.com; 15 N Aggasiz St; ⏲5pm-2am Mon-Thu, 3pm-2am Fri-Sun) Grungy, cavernous and welcoming, the

Green Room is Flag's best place to catch indie, punk, electronic and other acts. There are plenty of DJ nights too (reggae and electro are popular), some of which are free.

Shopping

The hands-down best place in the area for Native American jewelry is the gift shop inside the Museum of Northern Arizona (p101).

The Artists' Gallery ARTS & CRAFTS
(Map p104; 928-773-0958; www.flagstaffartists-gallery.com; 17 N San Francisco St; 9:30am-7pm Mon-Sat, to 6pm Sun) This art co-op, locally owned and operated since 1992, carries the work of over 30 northern Arizona artists, including two-dimensional art, jewelry, ceramics and glasswork.

Zani GIFTS & SOUVENIRS
(Map p104; 928-774-9409; www.zanigifts.com; 107 W Phoenix Ave; 10am-6pm Mon-Sat, to 5pm Sun) Zani carries beautiful handmade paper, locally made jewelry of silver or fused glass, stamped leather goods and Asian-inspired gifts and homewares.

Outdoor Equipment

Flagstaff is a good place to get last-minute advice and gear before your Grand Canyon backpacking adventure. These locally owned outdoor shops sit in the heart of downtown Flagstaff.

Babbitt's Backcountry Outfitters SPORTS & OUTDOORS
(Map p104; 928-774-4775; www.babbittsback-country.com; 12 E Aspen Ave; 8am-8pm Mon-Sat, 10am-6pm Sun) Named for a pair of rancher brothers who arrived from Ohio in 1886, Babbitt's rents backpacks, tents, boots, poles, snowshoes and other outdoor gear, and sells books and USGS maps.

Peace Surplus SPORTS & OUTDOORS
(Map p104; 928-779-4521; www.peacesurplus.com; 14 W Rte 66; 8am-9pm Mon-Fri, 8am-8pm Sat, 8am-6pm Sun) Sells and rents a huge array of outdoor clothing and equipment, including downhill and cross-country skis and snowboards.

Aspen Sports SPORTS & OUTDOORS
(Map p104; 928-779-1935; www.aspensportsflag-staff.com; 15 N San Francisco St; 9am-8pm Mon-Thu, to 9pm Fri & Sat, 10am-6pm Sun) Head here for gear that's oriented toward climbing and backpacking; no rentals.

Information

Visitor Center (Map p104; 928-213-2951; www.flagstaffarizona.org; 1 E Rte 66; 8am-5pm Mon-Sat, 9am-4pm Sun) Located inside the Amtrak station, the visitor center has a great Flagstaff Discovery map and tons of information on things to do.

USFS Flagstaff Ranger Station (928-526-0866; www.fs.usda.gov/main/coconino; 5075 N Hwy 89; 8am-4pm Mon-Fri) Provides information on the Mt Elden, Humphreys Peak and O'Leary Peak areas north of Flagstaff.

Flagstaff Medical Center (928-779-3366; www.nahealth.com; 1200 N Beaver St; emergency 24hr) One of the nearest hospitals to the Grand Canyon South Rim.

Flagstaff City-Coconino County Public Library (928-779-7670; www.flagstaffpub-liclibrary.org; 300 W Aspen Ave; 10am-9pm Mon-Thu, to 7pm Fri, to 6pm Sat, to 2pm Sun;) Free internet and wi-fi.

Police Station (emergency 911, general information 928-779-3646; 911 E Sawmill Rd; emergency 24hr)

Post Office (Map p104; 928-779-2371; 104 N Agassiz St; 10am-4pm Mon-Fri, 9am-1pm Sat)

Getting There & Away

The best way to get to Flagstaff by air is to fly into Phoenix's Sky Harbor International Airport (p235), a hub for both major and budget airlines. From here drive the easy two-hour straight shot north to Flagstaff.

Approaching Flagstaff from the east, I-40 parallels Old Route 66. Their paths diverge at Enterprise Rd: I-40 veers southwest, while Old Route 66 curls northwest, hugging the railroad tracks, and is the main drag through the historic downtown. Northern Arizona University (NAU) sits between downtown and I-40. From downtown, I-17 heads south toward Phoenix, splitting off at Hwy 89A (also known as Alt 89), a spectacularly scenic road through Oak Creek Canyon to Sedona. Hwy 180 is the most direct route northwest to Tusayan and the South Rim (80 miles), while Hwy 89 beelines north to Cameron (59 miles), where it meets Hwy 64 heading west to the canyon's East Entrance.

Greyhound (Map p100; 800-231-2222, 928-774-4573; www.greyhound.com; 880 E Butler Ave; 10am-5:30am) stops in Flagstaff en route to/from Albuquerque, Las Vegas, Los Angeles and Phoenix. Arizona Shuttle (p94) has shuttles that run between Flagstaff, Grand Canyon National Park, Williams, Sedona and Phoenix's Sky Harbor International Airport.

Operated by **Amtrak** (928-774-8679, 800-872-7245; www.amtrak.com; 1 E Rte 66; 24hr), the *Southwest Chief* stops at Flagstaff on its daily run between Chicago and Los Angeles.

The regional Flagstaff Pulliam Airport (p235) is 4 miles south of town off I-17; American Airlines, the only commercial airline to Flagstaff, offers several daily flights from Phoenix Sky Harbor International Airport (p23).

The regional shuttle service is another option.

Getting Around

Mountain Line Transit (928-779-6624; www.mountainline.az.gov; one way adult/child $1.25/0.60) has several fixed bus routes daily; pick up a user-friendly map at the visitor center. Buses are equipped with ramps for passengers in wheelchairs.

If you need a taxi, call **Sun Taxi** (928-779-1111; www.suntaxi andtours.com). Several major car-rental agencies operate from the airport and downtown.

Havasupai Reservation

The blue-green waterfalls of Havasu Canyon are among the Grand Canyon region's greatest treasures. Tucked in a hidden valley, the five stunning, spring-fed waterfalls – and their inviting azure swimming holes – sit in the heart of the 185,000-acre Havasupai Reservation. Parts of the canyon floor, as well as the rock underneath the waterfalls and pools, are made up of limestone deposited by flowing water. Known as travertine, these limestone deposits give the famous blue-green water its otherworldly hue.

The Havasupai Reservation lies south of the Colorado River and west of Grand Canyon National Park's South Rim – a three- to four-hour drive. Supai, the only village within the reservation – and indeed the entire Grand Canyon – is situated 8 miles below the rim. From Hualapai Hilltop, a well-maintained trail leads to **Supai**, the waterfalls and the Colorado River.

Liquor, recreational drugs, pets and nude swimming are not allowed, nor are trail bikes allowed below Hualapai Hilltop.

For detailed information on traveling into Havasu Canyon, see www.theofficialhavasupaitribe.com.

Sights

About a mile beyond Supai are the newly formed (and unofficially named) **New Navajo Falls** and **Rock Falls** and their blue pools below. These new falls developed above the original Navajo Falls, which were lost after a major flash flood in 2008 rerouted the water. After crossing two bridges, you will reach beautiful **Havasu Falls**; this waterfall drops 100ft into a sparkling blue pool surrounded by cottonwoods and is a popular swimming hole. Havasu Campground sits a quarter-mile beyond Havasu Falls. Just beyond the campground, the trail passes **Mooney Falls**, which tumble 200ft down into another blue-green swimming hole.

To get to the swimming hole, you must climb through two tunnels and descend a very steep trail – chains provide welcome handholds, but this trail is not for the faint of heart. Carefully pick your way down, keeping in mind that these falls were named for prospector DW James Mooney, who fell to his death here.

After a picnic and a swim, continue about 2 miles to Beaver Falls. The Colorado River is 5 miles beyond. It's generally recommended that you don't attempt to hike to the river and, in fact, the reservation actively discourages this.

Sleeping

The falls lie 10 miles below the rim; reservations for an overnight stay at either Havasupai Lodge in Supai or at the nearby campground are required, and must be made in advance. Do not try to hike down and back in one day – not only is day hiking not allowed, it is dangerous and doesn't allow enough time to see the waterfalls.

Entry requires payment of a $140.56 fee for two days and one night camping per person (or $90 per person in addition to lodging fee).

★ **Havasu Campground** CAMPGROUND $

(928-448-2121; www.havasupaireservations.com;Havasu Canyon; per person 1/2/3 nights $141/171/202; Feb-Nov) Two miles past Supai, the campground stretches 0.75 miles along Havasu Creek between Havasu and Mooney Falls. Sites have picnic tables and the campground features several composting toilets and spring water (treat before drinking).

Fires are not permitted but gas stoves are allowed. Reservations required, but sites are first-come, first-served.

Havasupai Lodge LODGE $$

(928-448-2111, 928-448-2201; www.theofficialhavasupaitribe.com; Supai; r for up to 4 people $175;) The only lodging in Supai offers bare-bone white-walled motel rooms, each

VISITING THE WATERFALLS OF HAVASU CANYON

Far from any hub of tourist services and inaccessible by car, a visit to **Havasu Canyon** (camping reservations 928-448-2180, lodge reservations 928-448-2111; www.theofficialhavasupaitribe.com; camping per person $140, lodge $175) requires a bit of planning and determination. Note that just because it's isolated, it doesn't mean you'll be alone – thousands upon thousands of visitors find their way to Havasu Canyon every year.

First off, don't let place names confuse you: **Hualapai Hilltop**, the access point for Havasu Canyon, is on the Havasupai Indian Reservation, *not* the Hualapai Reservation, as one might think. The Hualapai Reservation (p118), several long and dusty hours west, is home to Grand Canyon West and the glass skywalk.

From Grand Canyon South Rim it is a four-hour drive to the middle-of-nowhere-feeling Hualapai Hilltop parking lot. From Hualapai Hilltop, you must hike, ride a horse or fly in a helicopter the 8 miles down into the canyon to the Havasupai village of **Supai**. Supai, the only village within the Grand Canyon and basically just one packed dirt 'road', is the most remote village in the lower 48 states.

Finally, from the village, it's about a 1-mile hike to the first of five waterfalls in Havasu Canyon. The trail to see all five of them involves scrambling, steep inclines, ropes and chain footholds. The descent to the pools below Mooney, in particular, can be treacherous. Before heading down to Supai for the night, you must have reservations at either Havasu Campground or Havasupai Lodge. If you camp without a reservation, you will be charged double. Consider spending the night before your descent at the recommended Hualapai Lodge (p98), a modern motel that serves as the primary tourist desk for canyon sojourns to both the Hualapai and the Havasupai reservations. Or otherwise the roadside motel Grand Canyon Caverns & Inn (p98) in tiny Peach Springs, 67 miles from Hualapai Hilltop.

Despite its popularity, the trail from Supai to Havasu Falls can be tough hiking through unpredictable desert conditions. Use caution when swimming, as there are dangerous currents. Bring plenty of water, and check weather conditions in the region. Flash floods can sweep through the canyon with no warning, even on a beautiful sunny day. The Havasupai Tribe does not allow day trips to Supai or Havasu Falls.

Visit www.theofficialhavasupaitribe.com for details on guided tours, reservations and updated conditions.

with two double beds and private showers. Reservations are accepted by phone only, but this is a good fallback if camping permits are impossible to secure. Note: staying at the lodge requires an additional entrance fee of $90 per person.

Eating

In Supai, the **Supai Cafe** (928-448-2981; Supai; mains $9-13; 8am-5pm) serves breakfast, lunch and dinner daily; **Sinyella Store** (928-448-2343; Supai; 7am-5:30pm) sells good homemade tamales, plus basic groceries, as does the **Havasupai Trading Post** (928-448-2951; Supai; 8am-5pm).

Information

Entrance to the Havasupai Reservation is $90 per person (included with camping permit). Contact the **Tourist Office** (Camping Office; 928-448-2180; 160 Main St, Supai; 6am-6pm May-Oct, 9am-3pm Nov-Apr) for all information, including options for guided tours, updated conditions, camping reservations, and horse and mule arrangements.

Getting There & Around

Seven miles east of Peach Springs on historic Route 66, a signed turnoff leads to the 62-mile paved road ending at Hualapai Hilltop.

Here you'll find the parking area, stables and the trailhead into the canyon – but no services.

HORSE & MULE

Allegations of abuse, undernourishment and overloading of pack animals continue to plague horse and mule operations to Havasupai. Although water troughs were installed at the top of the trail in 2018 and tribal leadership has promised to address ongoing issues, you're better off hauling your own gear – and so is the

TRAVEL SMART

Don't be lulled into complacency by the idyllic surrounds of Havasu Canyon. Like anywhere else, the Havasupai Reservation suffers from poverty, drug abuse and crime, and the campground is not patrolled by night. In 2007, the canyon made headlines after the stabbing murder of tourist Tomomi Hanamure on her hike from the lodge to the falls. In 2017 the FBI apprehended a man who allegedly assaulted a number of female tourists over a 15-year period by luring them with promises of a traditional sweat lodge ceremony. Do not travel alone, do not travel with valuables and avoid travel after dark.

animal. Simply pack light and take it on your own back.

If you have physical limitations, you can ride a horse (one way to the Supai Lodge $250) or arrange for your pack to be hauled in ($132). Horses and mules depart from Hualapai Hilltop. Call the Supai Lodge or Havasu Campground (wherever you'll be staying) to arrange a ride and set a time.

TOURS

Several companies offer multi-day guided hiking and camping tours. Some combine helicopter and horseback travel in their itineraries. Packages start at $400 plus associated reservation entrance fees.

Sedona

928 / POP 10,400 / ELEV 4500FT

Nestled amid striking red sandstone formations at the south end of the 16-mile Oak Creek Canyon, Sedona attracts spiritual seekers, artists and healers, as well as day-trippers from Phoenix trying to escape the oppressive heat. Many New Age types believe that this area is the center of vortexes (not 'vortices' here in Sedona) that radiate the earth's power, and you'll find all sorts of alternative medicines and practices on display. More tangibly, the surrounding canyons offer outstanding hiking, biking, swimming and camping.

The town itself bustles with art galleries and expensive gourmet restaurants. In summer the traffic and the crowds can be heavy. Regionally, **Oak Creek Canyon** begins north of Uptown Sedona; the Village of Oak Creek, however, is south of the city.

Sedona is divided into three distinct districts. The roundabout at the intersection of Hwys Alt 89 (89A) and 179, referred to locally as the 'Y', leads to each district. Directly northeast of the Y is **Uptown Sedona**, the pedestrian and tourist center and a hub for souvenir shopping. From here, Hwy 89A continues north to Midley Bridge and through Oak Creek Canyon to Flagstaff. Turning south at the Y on Hwy 179 leads a half-mile to **Tlaquepaque Village**, with many of the town's galleries and a bit less tourist bustle and mayhem.

West of the Y is **West Sedona**, where Hwy 89A heads past Airport Rd and a few miles of strip malls and chain hotels to some of Sedona's best spots. These include Dry Creek Rd (Boynton Canyon), Red Rock Loop Rd (with Red Rock State Park and Red Rock Crossing) and Page Springs Rd (to the winery).

A **Red Rock Pass** (per day/week/year $5/15/20) is required to park anywhere in the surrounding national forest and several cultural sites. You can buy one at the visitor centers, various local businesses and hotels, and at some trailheads.

Endless roundabouts on Hwy 179 and stoplights on Hwy 89A through West Sedona make driving through town tricky and frustrating.

Sights

★Red Rock Crossing/ Crescent Moon Picnic Site PARK

(Red Rock Crossing Rd; day-use per vehicle $10, cash only;) Famous for its splendid views of Cathedral Rock, this picnic area is a lovely place to while away an afternoon, and can be a great alternative when Slide Rock State Park is too busy. Splash in Oak Creek, swim in its deep swimming holes and relax on the wide, flat, red slabs that dot the water. It also provides access to Templeton, Baldwin and Cathedral Rock hiking trails.

Red Rock Crossing is 7 miles southwest of town, on the same road as Red Rock State Park. To get here, head west on Hwy 89A to FR 216 (Upper Red Rock Loop Rd), turn south, drive 1.5 miles and follow the signs. If the parking lot is full, turn around and park at the pullout where Red Rock Crossing Rd intersects Chavez Ranch Rd.

★Red Rock State Park PARK

(928-282-6907; www.azstateparks.com/redrock; 4050 Red Rock Loop Rd; adult/child/under 6 yrs $7/4/free; 8am-5pm, visitor center 9am-4:30pm;) Not to be confused with Slide Rock State Park, this 286-acre park includes an environmental education center, picnic areas and 5 miles of well-marked, interconnecting trails in a riparian environment amid gorgeous red-rock country. Trails range from flat creekside saunters to moderate climbs to scenic ridges. Ranger-led activities include nature and bird walks. Swimming in the creek is prohibited. It's 9 miles west of downtown Sedona off Hwy 89A, on the eastern edge of the 15-mile Lime Kiln Trail.

Chapel of the Holy Cross CHURCH
(☎928-282-4069; www.chapeloftheholycross.com; 780 Chapel Rd; ⏲9am-5pm) FREE Situated between spectacular, statuesque natural stone columns 3 miles south of Sedona, this 1956 Roman Catholic chapel soars from the rock like a slice of the land itself. Creator Marguerite Brunswig Staude followed the tradition of Frank Lloyd Wright – its wall of glass and the perch it occupies offer a dramatic perspective on the landscape, and the architecture is stunning.

Though there are no traditional services, the church offers a 'Taize prayer service' on Mondays at 5pm.

Honanki Heritage Site ARCHAEOLOGICAL SITE
(www.fs.usda.gov/recarea/coconino; FR 525; Red Rock Pass $5; ⏲9:30am-3pm) Honanki is an impressive vestige of the Sinaguan culture responsible for the construction of this pueblo, as well as **Montezuma Castle** (☎928-567-3322; www.nps.gov/moca; Montezuma Castle Rd, Camp Verde; combination pass with Tuzigoot National Monument adult/child $10/free; ⏲8am-5pm; P), **Tuzigoot** (☎928-634-5564; www.nps.gov/tuzi; ⏲8am-5pm; P) and other sites in the years between AD 1000 and 1400. This site includes significant cliff dwellings and petroglyphs, and was subsequently inhabited by Yavapai and Apache people.

Palatki Heritage Site ARCHAEOLOGICAL SITE
(☎reservations 928-282-3854; www.fs.usda.gov/recarea/coconino; FR 795; Red Rock Pass $5; ⏲9:30am-3pm) FREE Thousand-year-old Sinagua cliff dwellings and rock art are good-enough reasons to brave the seven or so miles of dirt road leading to this enchantingly located archaeological site on the edge of the wilderness. There's a small visitor center and three easy trails suitable for strollers, but not wheelchairs. Parties taking the trail up to the dwellings themselves are limited to 10 at a time; phone to reserve in advance.

Activities

★**Pink Jeep Tours** DRIVING
(☎928-282-5000; www.pinkadventuretours.com/sedona-tours; 204 N Hwy 89A; ⏲office 6:45am-8pm;) It seems like this veteran of Sedona's tour industry has 4WDs everywhere, buzzing around like pink flies. But once you join a tour, laughing and bumping around, you'll see why they're so popular. Pink runs 15 thrilling, bone-rattling off-road and adventure tours around Sedona, with most lasting from about two hours (adult/child from $59/54) to four hours (from $155/140).

★**Slide Rock State Park** SWIMMING
(☎928-282-3034; www.azstateparks.com/slide-rock/; 6871 N Hwy 89A, Oak Creek Canyon; per car Mon-Thu $20, Fri-Sun $30, Oct-Feb $10; ⏲8am-7pm May-Aug, shorter hr rest of yr;) One of Sedona's most popular and most crowded destinations, this state park 7 miles north of town features an 80ft sandstone chute that whisks swimmers through Oak Creek. Short trails ramble past old cabins, farming equipment and an apple orchard, but the park's biggest draw is the set of wonderful natural rock slides.

Hi Line Trail MOUNTAIN BIKING
(Hwy 179, off Yavapai Vista parking lot) This black-diamond single-track mountain-bike trail runs along the ridge to a great view of Cathedral Rock. It also makes a beautiful hike; 3 miles one way.

Northern Light Balloon Expeditions BALLOONING
(☎928-282-2274; www.northernlightballoon.com; per person $225) Spend about one hour floating above red-rock country at sunrise then enjoy a champagne picnic back on solid ground. Northern Light can pick you up at your Sedona hotel 30 minutes before sunrise.

Huckaby Trail HIKING
(Schnebly Hill Rd, Coconino NF; parking Red Rock Pass $5) Just north of town on Hwy 89, from

VORTEXES

Several vortexes (swirling energy centers where the earth's power is said to be strongly felt) are located in Sedona's Red Rock Mountains. The best-known are **Bell Rock**, **Cathedral Rock**, **Airport Mesa** (Airport Rd) and Boynton Canyon (p117).

Sedona

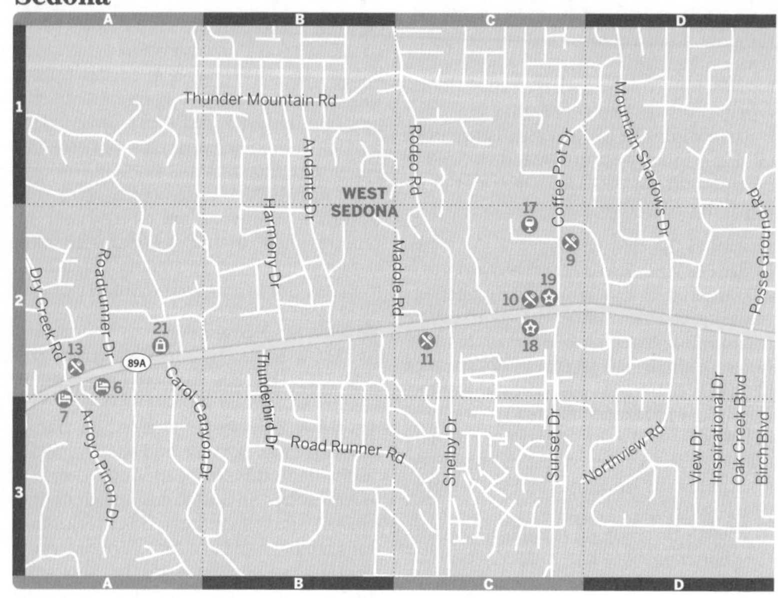

the signed trailhead a few miles up from the roundabout on Schnebley Rd to Midgley Bridge, this trail cuts across the desert scrub, along a ridge with panoramic views of Sedona, and down to Oak Creek. It's a great one-way hike if you can arrange pick-up at Midgley Bridge.

Sleeping

Sedona is rich with beautiful B&Bs, creekside cabins and full-service resorts. Rates at chain motels range from $100 to $150, reasonable by Sedona standards. Apart from these options and some beautiful but ferociously contested campsites, chichi Sedona doesn't have many choices for the budget traveler.

Camping

Dispersed camping in Red Rock Canyon is limited to designated camping corridors only; the best for red-rock views are along FR 525 in Boynton Canyon. Head west on Hwy 89A, 3 miles past Lower Red Rock Loop Rd to FR 525; dispersed camping is allowed from 2 miles north of Hwy 89A to Boynton Pass Rd.

The USFS runs campgrounds along Hwy Alt 89 in Oak Creek Canyon between Sedona and Flagstaff. All are nestled in the woods just off the road and along the Oak Creek. Reservations are accepted for a limited number of sites at each campground; otherwise, it's first-come, first-served. All three campgrounds provide drinking water, but only Cave Springs has coin-operated showers

Cave Springs CAMPGROUND **$**

(☎ reservations 518-885-3639; www.fs.usda.gov/coconino; 11345 Hwy 89A; camping $22; ⏲ 24 Mar-early Nov) Situated 11.5 miles north of Sedona, the extremely popular Cave Springs has 82 campsites with drinking water and coin-operated showers ($4). Twenty-one of the sites can be pre-booked, but you'll need to be early, and lucky.

Lo Lo Mai Springs Outdoor Resort CAMPGROUND **$**

(☎ 928-634-4700; www.lolomai.com; 11505 E Lo Lo Mai Rd, Cornville; RV & tent sites from $42, cabins from $80; 📶 🏊) A pretty, clean and friendly spot west of Sedona, with a swimming pool, easy access to swimming and splashing in Oak Creek, and a honor-code DVD library. It gets busy on weekends, but quiets down during the week. Cabins have toilets but no shower; bring your own linens. Take Hwy 89A for 7 miles southwest of Sedona and turn left onto Page Springs Rd.

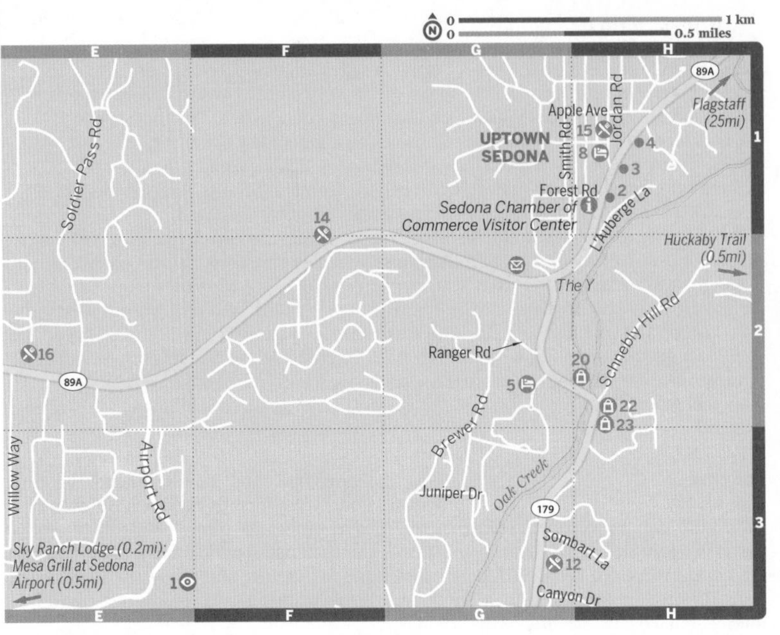

Sedona

Sights
1 Airport Mesa ... E3

Activities, Courses & Tours
2 Pink Jeep Tours ... H1
3 Red Rock Magic Trolley ... H1
4 Sedona Trolley ... H1

Sleeping
5 El Portal ... G2
6 Lantern Light Inn ... A2
7 Sedona Real Inn & Suites ... A3
8 Star Motel ... H1

Eating
9 Bashas' ... C2
10 Coffee Pot Restaurant ... C2
11 Dahl & DiLuca Ristorante ... C2
12 Elote Cafe ... G3
13 Local Juicery ... A2
14 Mariposa ... F1
15 Sedona Memories ... H1
16 Whole Foods ... E2

Drinking & Nightlife
17 Oak Creek Brewing Company ... C2

Entertainment
18 Harkins Theatres Sedona 6 ... C2
19 Mary D Fisher Theatre ... C2

Shopping
20 Center for the New Age ... H2
21 Crystal Magic ... A2
22 Garland's Navajo Rugs ... H2
23 Hike House ... H2

Manzanita CAMPGROUND $
(reservations 518-885-3639; www.fs.usda.gov/coconino; 5900 Hwy 89A; campsites $22) Manzanita has 18 campsites with drinking water, and is located 6 miles north of Sedona. Eleven of the sites are bookable, but you need to be early (and lucky) to bag one.

Pine Flat CAMPGROUND $
(reservations 518-885-3639; www.fs.usda.gov/coconino; 12240 Hwy 89A; camping $22; Apr to Oct;) Located 12.5 miles north of Sedona, Pine Flat has drinking water and 56 campsites, 18 of which can be pre-booked (by early birds with luck on their side).

GUIDED TOURS

Sedona's scenery is the backdrop for many a rugged adventure, and numerous tour operators stand by to take you into the heart of it. Bumpy off-road 4WD tours are popular, but it can be confusing distinguishing one company from the next. One thing to check is backcountry accessibility, as the companies have permits for different routes and sites. If there's a specific rock formation or region you'd like to explore, be sure to ask. Some companies expect a minimum of four participants and charge more per person for smaller groups. Many offer discounted tour prices if you reserve online.

Two trolley companies, both with offices in Uptown, provide narrated tours of Sedona. The **Sedona Trolley** (928-282-4211; www.sedonatrolley.com; 276 N Hwy 89A, Suite B; adult/child $15/10; departs hourly 9am-5pm) runs two different 55-minute tours. Tour A stops at Tlaquepaque Village and the Chapel of the Holy Cross and Tour B heads west to Boynton and Long Canyons. The **Red Rock Magic Trolley** (928-821-6706; www.redrockmagictrolley.com; 252 N Hwy 89A; adult $15-25, child $10-12) offers tours from 55 to 85 minutes, one heading to Boynton Canyon, one to the Chapel of the Holy Cross and another to Bell Rock.

Lodging

Star Motel MOTEL $

(928-282-3641; www.starmotelsedona.com; 295 Jordan Rd; r from $130;) This 10-room 1950s-era motel in Uptown is one of Sedona's best deals. Rooms are simple, with a few artsy touches, but what we like most is the hospitality. Plus the beds are comfortable, the showers strong and the refrigerators handy for chilling those sunset beers. Shops, eateries and the visitor center are just outside your door.

Sedona Real Inn & Suites MOTEL $$

(928-212-1414; www.sedonareal.com; 95 Arroyo Pinon Dr; d/ste from $160/180;) Set just off the strip in a quiet spot, this is a good bet for reasonably priced, conveniently located modern motel accommodation in Sedona. There's a free breakfast buffet, fitness center and a small park for kids (and fur kids) to run off excess energy.

Sky Ranch Lodge MOTEL $$

(928-282-6400; www.skyranchlodge.com; 1105 Airport Rd; d from $198;) At the top of winding Airport Rd, Sky Ranch boasts spectacular views of the town and surrounding red-rock country. It's a quiet respite from Sedona's peak-season hubbub, with spacious motel rooms scattered among six landscaped acres. It's free from fancy frills, with a pleasantly low-key wine bar off the lobby.

Cozy Cactus B&B $$

(928-284-0082; www.cozycactus.com; 80 Canyon Circle Dr, Village of Oak Creek; d from $210;) This five-room B&B, run by Carrie and Mark, works well for adventure-loving types – the Southwest-style house bumps up against Agave Trail, and is just around the bend from cyclist-friendly Bell Rock Pathway. Post-adventuring, get comfy beside the firepit on the back patio, perfect for wildlife-watching and stargazing, and enjoy the three-course breakfast that awaits you the next morning.

★ **Briar Patch Inn** CABIN $$$

(928-282-2342; www.briarpatchinn.com; 3190 N Hwy 89A; cabins from $285;) Nestled in nine wooded and grassy acres above Oak Creek, this bucolic and peaceful B&B hideaway offers 19 handsome cabins with Southwestern decor and American Indian art. All include patios and kitchens, many have fireplaces and several sit just above the gurgling waters.

★ **Enchantment Resort** RESORT $$$

(928-282-2900; www.enchantmentresort.com; 525 Boynton Canyon Rd; r/studio from $349/449;) Chic, exclusive and tucked into beautiful Boynton Canyon, this country-club-style resort lives up to its name. Stylish, spacious rooms with private patios and big views sprawl across the expansive grounds. Guests can hike in the canyon, splash in the pool, play tennis or golf, or utterly unwind in Mii Amo Spa. The daily resort fee is $34.

El Portal B&B $$$

(928-203-9405; www.elportalsedona.com; 95 Portal Lane; d from $279;) This discreet little inn is a beautiful blend of Southwestern and Craftsman style. It's a pocket of relaxed luxury tucked away in a corner across from the galleries and restaurants of Tlaquepaque, and marvelously removed from the chaos of Sedona's tourist-heavy downtown. The look is rustic but sophisticated, incorporating reclaimed wood, Navajo rugs, river rock and thick adobe walls.

Junipine Resort LODGE **$$$**
(928-852-4589; www.junipine.com; 8351 N Hwy 89A; r from $250;) In Oak Creek Canyon 8 miles north of Sedona, this resort offers lovely, spacious one- and two-bedroom 'creekhouses.' All have kitchens, living/dining rooms, wood-burning stoves and decks. Some have lofts, and the largest are 1400 sq ft. The Table on-site restaurant serves lunch and dinner Wednesday through Sunday and breakfast on weekends. Discounts are offered on 30-day advance bookings.

Lantern Light Inn INN **$$$**
(928-282-3419; www.lanternlightinn.com; 3085 W Hwy 89A; r from $254;) Kris and Ed, the lovely couple running this small inn in West Sedona, will put you right at ease. The antique-filled rooms range from small and cozy, overlooking the back deck and garden, to the huge guesthouse out back, and all feel comfortably overstuffed.

Orchard Canyon on Oak Creek CABIN **$$$**
(928-282-3343; www.enjoyorchardcanyon.com; 8067 Hwy 89A; cabins from $285; closed for arrivals Sun;) Set back from Oak Creek on 10 secluded and verdant acres with broad lawns, woods and an apple orchard, this friendly lodge 8 miles north of Sedona offers deliciously cozy Western log cabins, many with fireplaces. Rates include a full hot breakfast, 4pm tea and a four-course dinner (worth visiting for even if you're not staying).

Eating & Drinking

Sedona's restaurants are clustered around Uptown and strung along Hwys 89A and 179. Pick up groceries and picnic ingredients at **Whole Foods** (928-282-6311; www.wholefoodsmarket.com/stores/sedona; 1420 W Hwy 89A; 8am-9pm Mon-Sat, to 8pm Sun;) or **Bashas'** (928-282-5351; www.bashas.com; 160 Coffee Pot Dr; 6am-11pm).

★**Indian Gardens Cafe & Market** CAFE **$**
(928-282-7702; www.indiangardens.com; 3951 N Hwy 89A; breakfast $8-9, lunch $9-11; 7:30am-5pm

DAY-HIKING & MOUNTAIN-BIKING IN SEDONA

Hiking and mountain-biking trails crisscross the red-rock country surrounding Sedona and the woods and meadows of green **Oak Creek Canyon**. The free and very helpful *Recreation Guide to Your National Forest* is available online from the US Forest Service (www.fs.usda.gov/main/coconino) and at visitor centers and ranger stations. It describes hiking and biking trails for all skill levels and includes a summary of scenic drives. One deservedly popular hiking trail in Oak Creek Canyon is the 3.4-mile one-way **West Fork Trail** (928-527-3600; www.fs.usda.gov/recarea/coconino; Hwy 89A, Oak Creek Canyon; day-use per vehicle/bicycle $10/2; 9am-7pm), which follows the creek – the canyon walls rise more than 200ft in places. Wander up as far as you want, splash around at the numerous creek crossings and turn back when you've had enough. A sign notes the trail's official end. The trailhead lies about 3 miles north of Slide Rock, in the Call of the Canyon Recreation Area.

Rent bikes and buy coffee at **Bike & Bean** (928-284-0210; www.bike-bean.com; 30 Bell Rock Plaza, Village of Oak Creek; bike rental per hr/day from $19/49; 8am-5pm), not far from the bike-friendly **Bell Rock Pathway**.

Oak Creek holds several good swimming holes. If Slide Rock is too crowded, check out **Grasshopper Point** (Hwy 89A, Coconino NF; vehicle/pedestrian $8/2; 8am-dusk) a few miles south. Southwest of Sedona you can splash around and enjoy splendid views of Cathedral Rock at Red Rock Crossing/Crescent Moon Picnic Site (p112).

For an easy hike that leads almost immediately to gorgeous views, check out Airport Mesa (p113). From Hwy 89A, follow Airport Dr about half a mile up the side of the mesa to a small parking turnout on your left. From here, the short **Sedona View Trail** leads to an awe-inspiring view of Courthouse Butte and, after a brief scramble, a sweeping 360-degree panorama of the city and its flanking red rocks. This is one of Sedona's vortex sites. If you can, start this hike before 8:30am, when the parking lot starts to fill up. The Sedona View Trail links onto the longer **Airport Loop Trail**.

Another stunningly beautiful place to hike is through the red rock of **Boynton Canyon** (Dry Creek Rd, Coconino NF; parking Red Rock Pass $5), where some have reported experiencing the antics of energetic spirits (who may not necessarily want them trekking through)!

For additional details see www.redrockcountry.org.

Mon-Thu, to 6pm Fri-Sun; P) Grab a tasty breakfast sandwich here before heading north to the West Fork Trail or stop by for lunch (until 4pm each day). Coffee and craft beer are also available, and there's a lovely back garden to enjoy the fruits of your foraging.

Sedona Memories DELI $

(☎928-282-0032; 321 Jordan Rd; sandwiches $8.50; ⏰10am-2pm Mon-Fri) This tiny local spot assembles gigantic sandwiches on slabs of homemade bread. A great choice for a picnic, as they pack 'em tight to-go, so there's less mess. You can also nosh on their quiet porch. Cash only.

Local Juicery HEALTH FOOD $

(☎928-282-8932; www.localjuicery.com; 3150 Hwy 89A; mains $11-12; ⏰8am-5pm Mon-Sun; ✎) This contemporary fast-food spot in West Sedo-

HUALAPAI RESERVATION: GRAND CANYON WEST & THE GLASS SKYWALK

Bordering many miles of the Colorado River between Hoover Dam and Grand Canyon National Park, the roughly 1-million-acre Hualapai Reservation is home to Grand Canyon West, also known as the **West Rim** (☎888-868-9378, 928-769-2636; www.grandcanyonwest.com; Hualapai Reservation; per person $44-81; ⏰7am-7pm Apr-Sep, 8am-5pm Oct-Mar). This canyon-viewing alternative to the national park lies completely within the confines of the reservation and includes the much-hyped glass **Skywalk** (☎928-769-2636; www.grandcanyonwest.com; West Rim, Hualapai Reservation; per person $82; ⏰7am-7pm Apr-Oct, 8am-5pm Nov-Mar), a slender see-through glass horseshoe that juts 70ft into the canyon. Note that Grand Canyon West sits at an elevation of 4825ft, some 2000ft lower than the South Rim and 3000ft lower than the North Rim, so the views here are far less dramatic.

Driving to Grand Canyon West from the South Rim is a four-hour delight through some of the most eerily beautiful desert landscape in the region. Endless expanse of dusty flat leads to horizon-hugging mountains, and the road winds mile after Seussian mile through a spectacular 900-year-old Joshua Tree forest. Upon arrival, however, the magic falls apart.

All visitors must check in at the visitor center, a massive windowless white tent with tour desks, souvenirs and busloads of people piling through. From here purchase either a **Hualapai Legacy Package** ($49) or the **Legacy Gold Package** ($82); both include the hop-on, hop-off shuttle loop to the three overlooks (Guano Point, Hualapai Ranch and Eagle Point), but the Legacy Gold adds access to the glass skywalk at Eagle Point. The only access to the overlooks is via shuttle, and there are no hiking trails at Grand Canyon West.

As well as serving as the overlook shuttle hub, the visitor center functions as Grand Canyon West's airport. Helicopters whirl in and out all day long, transporting folk down to the river for **scenic flights** and 20-minute **smooth-water pontoon rides** on the Colorado.

The **Hualapai Ranch**, a minute's drive from the visitor center, is the only overnight accommodation. Billed as Western-styled rim-side cabins, they offer basic housing with one window and no canyon views. From guest check-in at the trailer, it's a short drive past dumpsters and rubble piles to the cabins. There is no compelling reason to stay here.

The Hualapai Nation also offers white-water day trips along the Colorado River. These trips, however, do not depart from Grand Canyon West. They leave from the modern and friendly chain-hotel-style Hualapai Lodge (p98) in tiny Peach Springs, a two-hour drive southeast from the West Rim, and a two-hour drive southwest from Grand Canyon Village. It includes a 22-mile drive along unpaved Diamond Creek Rd, the only road within the Grand Canyon.

At the end of Diamond Creek Rd is the first-come, first-served **Diamond Creek Campground** (☎928-769-2636; campsites incl entrance fee $27), offering 10 tent sites along the Colorado River. Popular with multi-day river trips, the campground has minimal shade and no drinking water, and the road here is not recommended without a 4WD vehicle. Call the lodge for road conditions.

For details and all reservations, contact **Hualapai Tourism** (☎928-769-2636; www.grandcanyonwest.com; 900 Route 66, Hualapai Lodge; ⏰variable). Note that Grand Canyon West is particularly popular as a day-trip from Las Vegas and several operators offer scenic flights, and Jeep, Hummer and bus tours; go to www.lasvegas.com/tours/grand-canyon for a listing. From Vegas, it's a two-hour drive.

na offers salads, smoothies and tantalizing veggie and fruit cold-pressed juices to cure what ails you. Try the Super Human (with blueberries, bee pollen and almond butter) or Strong & Radiant (spirulina, maca powder and strawberries). You'll feel healthier just walking in here.

Coffee Pot Restaurant BREAKFAST $

(☎928-282-6626; www.coffeepotsedona.com; 2050 W Hwy 89A; breakfast $8-9, lunch $9-10; ⏰6am-2pm; 👪) A go-to breakfast and lunch joint since the 1950s, the Pot is nothing fancy but gets the refueling job done, with massive plates of reasonably priced fare and a huge selection. There are a bewildering 101 types of omelet, including what may be the world's only peanut butter, jelly and banana special.

Mesa Grill AMERICAN $$

(☎928-282-2400; www.mesagrillsedona.com; 1185 Airport Rd; mains $13-22; ⏰7am-9pm; 📶🐾) Yes, it's a bit odd to choose to eat at an airport, on a patio next to airplanes, but 'airport' is a misnomer – it's really more of a landing strip for scenic flights. Mesa does interesting Southwestern fare, such as gulf shrimp with crispy pork belly and cheesy grits, offered in contemporary surrounds.

★**Elote Cafe** MEXICAN $$$

(☎928-203-0105; www.elotecafe.com; Arabella Hotel, 771 Hwy 179; mains $22-29; ⏰5-10pm Tue-Sat) Come here for some of the best, most authentic Mexican food in the region. Elote Cafe serves unusual and traditional dishes you won't find elsewhere, like the namesake *elote* (fire-roasted corn with spicy mayo, lime and cotija cheese) or smoked chicken in guajillo chiles. Reservations are not accepted and the line can be off-putting: come early, bring a book, order a margarita.

Dahl & DiLuca Ristorante ITALIAN $$$

(☎928-282-5219; www.dahlanddiluca.com; 2321 Hwy 89A; mains $27-38; ⏰5-10pm) Though this lovely Italian place fits perfectly into the groove and color scheme of Sedona, at the same time it feels like the kind of place you'd find in a small Italian seaside town. It's a bustling, welcoming spot serving excellent, authentic Italian food. Try the pork chop and asparagus from the grill or the four-cheese ravioli in truffle cream.

Mariposa LATIN AMERICAN $$$

(☎928-862-4444; www.mariposasedona.com; 700 W Hwy 89A; mains $30-38; ⏰11:30am-2:30pm & 4-9pm Sun-Thu, to 10pm Fri & Sat) Stunning mountain views and divine (if steeply priced) Latin-inspired food from the grill are the hallmarks of this upmarket eatery from local celebrity chef Lisa Dahl. You don't need to drop $125 on the prime rib eye – the poke of sushi-grade yellowfin tuna or the skirt steak with chimichurri and black beans deliver just as much pleasure.

WORTH A TRIP

PAGE SPRINGS CELLARS

A beautiful spot above Oak Creek, 10 miles northeast of Cottonwood, friendly **Page Springs Cellars** (☎928-639-3004; http://pagespringscellars.com; 1500 Page Springs Rd, Cornville; tours from $19; ⏰11am-7pm Sun-Wed, to 9pm Thu-Sat) offers winery tours, tastings and delicious picnic-basket meals. Tours (with tasting; $34) run at noon, 2pm and 4pm Friday to Sunday. It can get busy on weekends, although it's a lovely drive here and the wine is excellent. Happy hour is from 3pm to 6pm Tuesday to Thursday.

Known for its Pinot Noir, Mourvedre, Syrah and Grenache, Page Springs runs a popular tasting room where you can order duck rillettes or shrimp pintxos to accompany your wine flight; $25 gets you a flight of their premium drops.

Oak Creek Brewing Company BREWERY

(☎928-204-1300; www.oakcreekbrew.com; 2050 Yavapai Dr; ⏰noon-10pm Sun-Thu, to midnight Fri & Sat) In West Sedona, this spare brewery and taproom has a bit of indoor seating and a patio, and there's live music most weekends.

☆ Entertainment

For Hollywood blockbusters, head to **Harkins Theatres Sedona 6** (☎928-282-2221; www.harkins.com/locations/sedona-6; 2081 Hwy 89A).

Mary D Fisher Theatre CINEMA

(☎928-282-1177; www.facebook.com/marydfishertheatre; 2030 Hwy 89A) A Sedona International Film Festival venue in February, this movie theater also screens documentaries and art-house films year-round.

🛍 Shopping

Shopping is a big draw in Sedona, and visitors will find everything from expensive boutiques to T-shirt stores. Uptown along Hwy 89A is the place to go souvenir hunting.

For New Age shops, try **Crystal Magic** (928-282-1622; www.crystalmagic.com; 2978 Hwy 89A; 9am-9pm Mon-Sat, to 8pm Sun) or **Center for the New Age** (928-282-7220; www.sedonanewagestore.com; 341 Hwy 179; 8:30am-8pm).

Hike House SPORTS & OUTDOORS

(928-282-5820; www.thehikehouse.com; 431 Hwy 179, Suite B-1; 9am-6pm Mon-Sat, to 5pm Sun) This forward-thinking hiking store offers an 'energy cafe,' online resources such as a trail finder and 'Grand Canyon Planning Station,' gear and maps. You'll also find experienced staff who have tackled all of Sedona's trails and are happy to pass on their knowledge.

Garland's Navajo Rugs ARTS & CRAFTS

(928-282-4070; www.garlandsrugs.com; 411 Hwy 179; 10am-5pm) Founded in 1976, this Sedona institution offers the area's best selection of rugs, and sells other American Indian crafts, both current and vintage. It's an interesting store to visit, displaying naturally dyed yarns with their botanical sources of color, as well as descriptions of how many hours it takes to create a handwoven rug.

Information

Several Sedona visitor centers sell Red Rock passes and provide hiking, cycling and recreation information for Oak Creek Canyon and red-rock country. In addition, most hotels offer concierge service for booking Sedona and Grand Canyon tours and scenic flights.

Red Rock Country Visitor Center (928-203-2900; www.fs.usda.gov/coconino; 8375 Hwy 179; 9am-4:30pm) Get a Red Rock Pass here, as well as hiking guides, maps and local national forest information.

Sedona Chamber of Commerce Visitor Center (928-282-7722; www.visitsedona.com; 331 Forest Rd; 8:30am-5pm) Located in the pedestrian center of Uptown Sedona; pick up free maps and buy a Red Rock Pass.

Oak Creek Visitor Center (928-203-2900; www.fs.usda.gov/coconino; Hwy 89A, Indian Gardens; 9am-4pm Apr-Oct)

Police Station (emergency 911, non-emergency 928-282-3100; 100 Roadrunner Dr)

Post Office (928-282-3511; 190 W Hwy 89A; 9am-4:30pm Mon-Fri, 9am-1pm Sat)

Sedona Public Library (928-282-7714; www.sedonalibrary.org; 3250 White Bear Rd; 10am-6pm Mon, Tue & Thu, to 8pm Wed, to 5pm Fri & Sat;) Has wi-fi and computer terminals for internet access.

Verde Valley Medical Center (928-634-2251, emergency 911; https://nahealth.com; 3700 W Hwy 89A; 24hr emergency) On Hwy 89A, west of Uptown Sedona.

Getting There & Away

While scenic flights depart from Sedona, the closest commercial airports are Phoenix (p235; two hours' drive) or Flagstaff (30 minutes' drive).

Ace Xpress (928-649-2720; www.acex-shuttle.com; one way/round-trip adult $68/109, child $35/55; office hours 7am-8pm Mon-Fri, from 8am Sat & Sun) and **Arizona Shuttle** (928-350-8466; www.arizonashuttle.com; 959 S Camino Real, Cottonwood; one way adult/child $55/28) run shuttle services between Sedona and Phoenix's Sky Harbor International Airport.

Amtrak (800-872-7245; www.amtrak.com/stations/flg) and **Greyhound** (800-231-2222; www.greyhound.com) both stop in nearby Flagstaff and onward travel can be arranged through Arizona Shuttle.

Getting Around

Barlow Jeep Rentals (928-282-8700; www.barlows.us; 3009 W Hwy 89A; half-/1-/3-day Jeep rental $250/350/576; 8am-6pm) is great for rough-road exploring. Free maps and trail information are provided. **Bob's Taxi** (982-282-1234; www.bobstaxisedona.com) is a good local operator, while rental cars are available at **Enterprise** (928-282-2052; www.enterprise.com; 2090 W Hwy 89A; per day from $50; 8am-5:30pm Mon-Fri, 9am-2pm Sat).

Cameron

A tiny, windswept community 32 miles east of the Grand Canyon's East Entrance and 54 miles north of Flagstaff, Cameron sits on the western edge of the Navajo Reservation. There's not much to it; in fact, the town basically comprises just the **Cameron Trading Post** (928-679-2231; www.camerontradingpost.com; 466 Hwy 89; 6am-9:30pm, shorter hours in winter) and the attached motel and restaurant. In the early 1900s Hopis and Navajos came to the trading post to barter wool, blankets and livestock for flour, sugar and other goods. Today visitors can browse a large selection of quality American Indian crafts, including Navajo rugs, basketry, jewelry and pottery, and plenty of kitschy knickknacks.

If you're driving to the North Rim and need a place to stay en route or if rooms in the park are booked, this is a great option. It also makes a good lunch spot if you're driving rim-to-rim.

Sleeping & Eating

Grand Canyon Hotel MOTEL $$
(☎800-338-7385; www.camerontradingpost.com/motel.html; Hwy 89, Cameron; r/ste $129/169; P ❄ 📶) Attached to the historic Cameron Trading Post, this motel offers spacious rooms with hand-carved furniture and a Southwestern motif spread out in three two-story, adobe-style buildings. The nicest is the Hopi, set around a lovely, lush garden with fountains and benches. Ask for a room with a garden view or a view of the Little Colorado River Gorge.

Cameron Trading Post Dining Room AMERICAN INDIAN $
(☎928-679-2231; www.camerontradingpost.com; 466 Hwy 89, Cameron; breakfast $9-11, lunch $10-13, dinner $12-24; ⏰6am-9:30pm, shorter hrs in winter) A good place to try the Navajo taco (Indian frybread topped with whole beans, ground beef, green chile and cheese), the Cameron Trading Post Dining Room also does steak, fried chicken and other staples.

Lake Mead & Hoover Dam

The **Lake Mead National Recreation Area** (☎info desk 702-293-8906, visitor center 702-293-8990; www.nps.gov/lake; Lakeshore Scenic Dr; 7-day entry per vehicle $10; ⏰24hr; 👪) encompasses 110-mile-long Lake Mead, 67-mile-long Lake Mohave, many miles of bone-dry desert around the lakes, and the 726ft art-deco-style Hoover Dam. Quiet **Boulder City** is the central town for tourist services in and around Lake Mead.

At the height of the Depression, thousands of men and their families migrated here to build the dam. They worked in excruciating conditions, dangling hundreds of feet above the canyon in 120°F (49°C) desert heat. Hundreds lost their lives. Today, standing on its edge offers a dramatic perspective on both the dam itself and the startling drop in Lake Mead water levels, evidenced by the swaths of white bathtub rings on the canyon sides.

Guided tours begin at **Lake Mead Visitor Center** (Alan Bible Visitor Center; ☎702-293-8990; www.nps.gov/lake; Lakeshore Scenic Dr, off US Hwy 93; ⏰9am-4:30pm) with a video of original construction footage. An elevator takes visitors 50 stories below to view the dam's massive generators, which could each power a city of 100,000 people. Children under eight years of age are not permitted on the more extensive dam tour (first-come, first-served) that visits the dam passageways. The 3.7-mile **Historic Railroad Trail** connects the visitor center to the parking area, passing through five tunnels each 25ft in diameter and offering panoramic views of Lake Mead.

Inside the Boulder Dam Hotel, the **Boulder City/Hoover Dam Museum** (☎702-294-1988; www.bcmha.org; 1305 Arizona St; ⏰10am-5pm; 👪) FREE is worth popping into for exhibits focusing on the tough living conditions endured by the people who came to build the dam. A 20-minute film features historic footage of the project.

Despite falling water levels, the lake remains a popular place to explore by boat. Call 702-451-2992 for speedboat, pontoon and watersport equipment rental; for **houseboat rental**, contact **Callville Bay Resort and Marina** (☎480-998-7199; www.callvillebay.com; 100 Callville Bay Rd, Overton; houseboat per day from $700). To kayak Lake Mead or the Colorado River, talk to **Desert Adventures** (☎702-293-5026; www.kayaklasvegas.com; 1647

BOOTLEG CANYON

With 35 miles of single-track cross-country and downhill trails, dramatic rocky desert landscape and panoramic views of Lake Mead and beyond, popular **Bootleg Canyon Mountain Bike Park** is a mountain-biking mecca. It can be unbearably hot in the summer, so come prepared with plenty of water and consider early morning or night rides. In the grand spirit of Vegas-style living, it's open 24/7.

Bootleg Canyon is on the northwest side of Boulder City. Take Veterans Memorial Dr off Hwy 93, and turn north on Yucca St. For tours, bicycle rental and detailed information on this and other area trails, head to **All Mountain Cyclery** (☎702-453-2453; www.allmountaincyclery.com; 1601 Nevada Hwy; mountain-bike rentals per day from $40, half-/full-day tours from $180; ⏰11am-6pm Mon, 10am-6pm Tue-Fri, 9am-6pm Sat, 9am-4pm Sun). On weekends they offer a shuttle service to the top of the canyon ($5 per run, $30 per day) so you can ride down again and again and again. There's also a **zipline** (☎702-293-6885; www.flightlinezbootleg.com; 1644 Nevada Hwy; 3hr tour $159; ⏰8am-5pm) and hiking trails.

Nevada Hwy; full-day Colorado River kayak $195; 9am-6pm Apr-Oct, 10am-4pm Nov-Mar). They also rent camping equipment, offer guided smooth-water kayak tours down the Colorado River's 30-mile Black Canyon (www.lcrwatertrailalliance.com/black-canyon-water-trail), and lead hiking and cycling trips to Grand Canyon, Zion and Bryce.

Sleeping & Eating

Boulder Dam Hotel HISTORIC HOTEL $

(702-293-3510; www.boulderdamhotel.com; 1305 Arizona St; r from $85;) For a peaceful night's sleep worlds away from the madding crowds and neon of Vegas, head to this gracious Dutch Colonial–style hotel (listed on the National Register of Historic Places), which has welcomed illustrious guests since 1933. Relax with a cocktail at the art-deco jazz lounge on-site.

Milo's Cellar AMERICAN $

(702-293-9540; www.milosbouldercity.com; 534 Nevada Hwy; mains $9-14; 11am-9pm) The unassuming Milo's Cellar just down the street from the Boulder Dam Hotel makes a relaxing spot for tasty sandwiches, salads, soups, gourmet cheese plates and wine flights. There's sidewalk seating and a small wine shop.

Las Vegas

POP 594,294 / ELEV 2000FT

Las Vegas remains the ultimate escape. Where else can you party in ancient Rome, get hitched at midnight, wake up in Egypt and brunch beneath the Eiffel Tower? Double down with the high rollers, browse couture or tacky souvenirs, sip a neon 3ft-high margarita or a frozen vodka martini from a bar made of ice – it's all here for the taking.

Ever notice that there are no clocks inside casinos? Vegas exists outside time, a sequence of never-ending buffets, ever-flowing drinks and adrenaline-fueled gaming tables. In this never-ending desert dreamscape of boom and bust, once-famous signs collect dust in a neon boneyard while the clang of construction echoes over the Strip. After the alarming hiccup of the 2008 recession, the city is once more back on track, attracting well over 40 million visitors per year and bursting with schemes to lure even more in future.

Then again, park travelers using Las Vegas as a jumping-off point may be more interested in the cheap flights and proximity to the great outdoors. Red Rock Canyon is just a fat-tire hop away, and even the Grand Canyon's South Rim is a doable day trip from the Strip.

Sights

Vegas' sights are primarily concentrated along the 4.2-mile stretch of Las Vegas Blvd anchored by Mandalay Bay to the south (at Russell Rd) and the Stratosphere to the north (at Sahara Ave) and in the Downtown area around the intersection of Las Vegas Blvd (N Las Vegas Blvd at this point) and Fremont St. Note that while the street has the same name, there's an additional 2 miles between Downtown and the northern end of the Strip, with not much of interest in-between. It might look close if you decide to walk between the two, but you'll probably find yourself cursing in the desert heat if you do so. Ride-shares, the Monorail and Deuce bus services are by far the easiest ways to get around this spaced-out (in more ways than one) city.

The Strip

★**Aria** LANDMARK

(CityCenter; www.aria.com; 3780 S Las Vegas Blvd; P) We've seen this symbiotic relationship before (think giant hotel anchored by a mall 'concept'), but the way that this futuristic-feeling complex places a small galaxy of hypermodern, chichi hotels in orbit around the glitzy Shops at Crystals (p132) is a first. The uber-upscale spread includes the subdued, stylish **Vdara** (702-590-2111; www.vdara.com), the hush-hush opulent Mandarin Oriental (p128) and the dramatic architectural showpiece Aria, whose sophisticated casino provides a fitting backdrop to its many drop-dead-gorgeous restaurants.

★**Welcome to Las Vegas Sign** LANDMARK

(5200 S Las Vegas Blvd; 24hr;) FREE In a city famous for neon signs, one reigns supreme: the 'Welcome to Fabulous Las Vegas Nevada' sign, facing north and straddling Las Vegas Blvd just south of Mandalay Bay, the unofficial beginning of the Strip. Designed by Betty Willis at the end of the 'Fabulous Fifties,' this Googie-style sign is a classic photo op and a reminder of Vegas' past. Only southbound traffic can enter the parking lot, greeted by its flip-side reminder to 'Drive Carefully' and 'Come Back Soon.'

LAS VEGAS CASINOS

The Strip

Mandalay Bay (702-632-7700; www.mandalaybay.com; 3950 S Las Vegas Blvd; 24hr; P) Home to Shark Reef Aquarium, a walk-through aquarium with thousands of tropical fish and a shallow pool where you can pet pint-sized sharks.

Bellagio (702-693-7111; www.bellagio.com; 3600 S Las Vegas Blvd; 24hr; P) Airy and decadent, with elaborate gardens and the Gallery of Fine Art; don't miss the fountain show out front.

Cosmopolitan (702-698-7000; www.cosmopolitanlasvegas.com; 3708 S Las Vegas Blvd; 24hr; P) Elegant and hip.

Caesars Palace (866-227-5938; www.caesars.com/caesars-palace; 3570 S Las Vegas Blvd; 24hr; P) Out front are the same spritzing fountains that daredevil Evil Knievel made famous when he jumped them on a motorcycle on December 31, 1967 (and ended up with a shattered pelvis and a fractured skull).

Stratosphere (702-380-7777; www.stratospherehotel.com; 2000 S Las Vegas Blvd; tower adult/child $20/10, all-day pass incl unlimited thrill rides $40; casino 24hr, tower & thrill rides 10am-1am Sun-Thu, to 2am Fri & Sat, weather permitting; P) Vegas' best 360-degree panoramas, more than 100 stories tall, boasts the country's highest thrill rides.

Venetian (702-414-1000; www.venetian.com; 3355 S Las Vegas Blvd; 24hr; P) Gondola rides, Canyon Ranch Spa and Madame Tussauds interactive Vegas-centric wax museum.

Wynn & Encore Casinos (702-770-7000; www.wynnlasvegas.com; 3131 S Las Vegas Blvd; 24hr; P) Lavish, sprawling, gorgeous.

Aria (702-590-7111; www.aria.com; 3730 S Las Vegas Blvd, CityCenter; 24hr; P) Contemporary resort with a deluxe, design-savvy casino surrounded by tempting restaurants.

New York–New York (800-689-1797; www.newyorknewyork.com; 3790 S Las Vegas Blvd; 24hr; P) Statue of Liberty, the Brooklyn Bridge and, wrapped around the hotel's flashy facade, the Big Apple roller coaster, with cars resembling NYC taxicabs.

Paris Las Vegas (877-796-2096; www.caesars.com/paris-las-vegas; 3655 S Las Vegas Blvd; 24hr; P) Mini-version of the French capital, including a 34-story Hotel de Ville replica and replicas of famous facades from the Paris Opera House and the Louvre.

Luxor (702-262-4000; www.luxor.com; 3900 S Las Vegas Blvd; 24hr; P) Iconic Pyramid-shaped casino with a mildly themed Egyptian interior.

Mirage (702-791-7111; www.mirage.com; 3400 S Las Vegas Blvd; 24hr; P) Rainforest atrium and 20,000-gallon saltwater aquarium.

Treasure Island (TI; 702-894-7111; www.treasureisland.com; 3300 S Las Vegas Blvd; 24hr) Traces of the original swashbuckling skull-and-crossbones theme linger.

Circus Circus (702-734-0410; www.circuscircus.com; 2880 S Las Vegas Blvd; 24hr; P) Trapeze artists, high-wire workers, jugglers and unicyclists perform excellent free circus acts above the casino floor.

Planet Hollywood (702-785-5555; www.caesars.com/planet-hollywood; 3667 S Las Vegas Blvd; 24hr; P) Glamorous, modern, flashy, features shows by top headliners.

Downtown & Off-Strip

Hard Rock (702-693-5000; www.hardrockhotel.com; 4455 Paradise Rd; 24hr; 108) Original rock 'n' roll casino houses an impressive collection of rock-star memorabilia. It's just east of the Strip at Planet Hollywood, on Harmon.

Golden Nugget (702-385-7111; www.goldennugget.com; 129 Fremont St E; 24hr; P ; Deuce, SDX) Downtown classic, with an outdoor pool featuring a three-story waterslide through a 200,000-gallon shark tank.

Las Vegas Strip

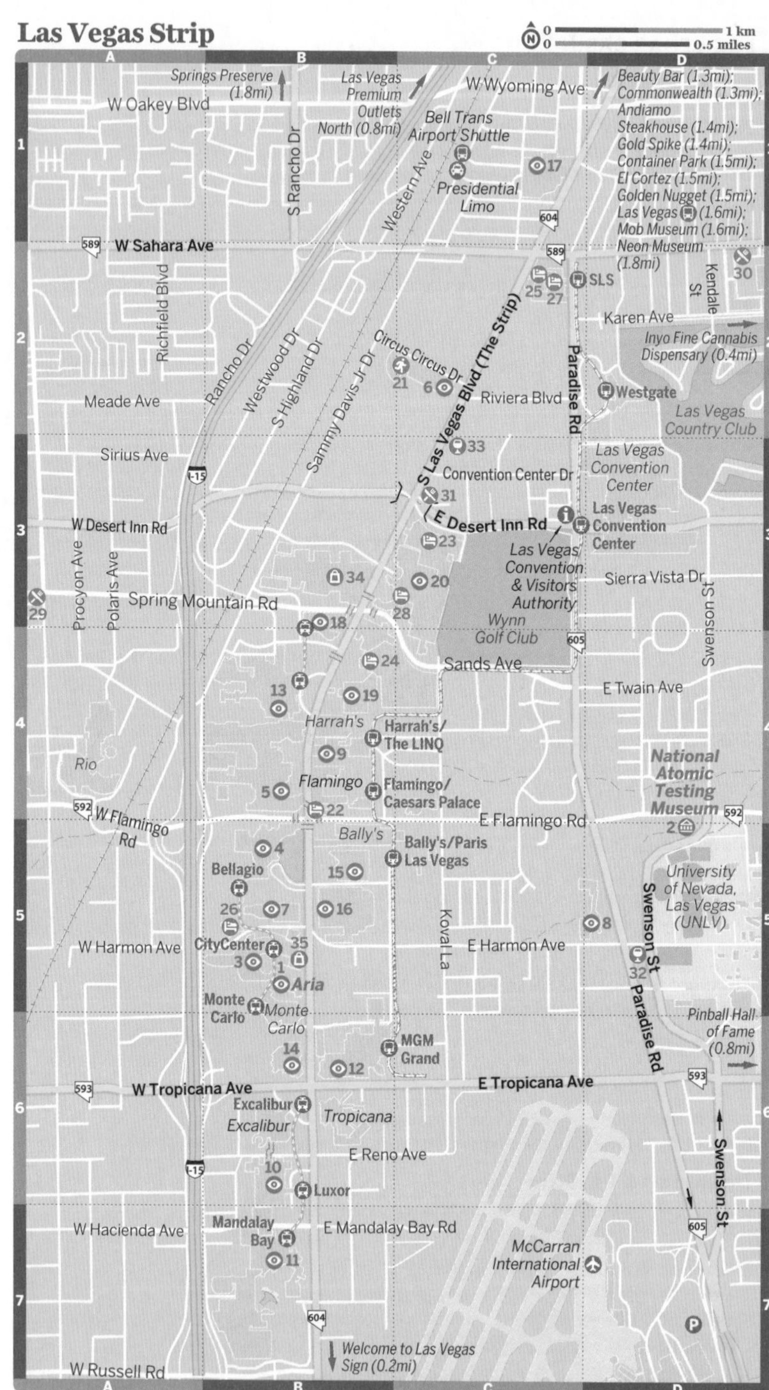

Downtown & Off-Strip

★ Neon Museum – Neon Boneyard MUSEUM

(☎702-387-6366; www.neonmuseum.org; 770 N Las Vegas Blvd; 1hr tour adult/child $28/24; ⏰tours daily, schedules vary; 🚌113) This nonprofit project is doing what almost no one else does: saving Las Vegas' history. Book ahead for a fascinating guided walking tour of the 'Neon Boneyard,' where irreplaceable vintage neon signs – Las Vegas' original art form – spend their retirement. Start exploring at the visitor center inside the salvaged La Concha Motel lobby, a mid-century modern icon designed by African American architect Paul Revere Williams. Tours are usually given throughout the day, but are most spectacular at night.

Pinball Hall of Fame MUSEUM

(☎702-597-2627; www.pinballmuseum.org; 1610 E Tropicana Ave; per game 25¢-$1; ⏰11am-11pm Sun-Thu, to midnight Fri & Sat; 👪; 🚌201) You may have more fun at this no-frills arcade than playing slot machines back on the Strip. Tim Arnold shares his collection of 200-plus vintage pinball and video games with the public. Take time to read the handwritten curatorial cards explaining the unusual history behind these restored machines.

Las Vegas Strip

Top Sights
1 Aria B5
2 National Atomic Testing Museum D5

Sights
3 Aria B5
4 Bellagio B5
5 Caesars Palace B4
6 Circus Circus C2
7 Cosmopolitan B5
8 Hard Rock D5
9 LINQ Casino B4
10 Luxor B6
11 Mandalay Bay B7
Mandalay Bay Beach .... (see 11)
12 MGM Grand B6
13 Mirage B4
14 New York–New York B6
15 Paris Las Vegas B5
16 Planet Hollywood B5
17 Stratosphere C1
18 Treasure Island B3
19 Venetian B4
20 Wynn & Encore Casinos C3

Activities, Courses & Tours
21 Adventuredome C2
Qua Baths & Spa .... (see 5)
Sahra Spa & Hammam .... (see 7)
SkyJump .... (see 17)
Spa at Encore .... (see 23)
Stratosphere Thrill Rides .... (see 17)

Sleeping
Aria Las Vegas Resort .... (see 3)
Aria Sky Suites & Villas .... (see 3)
Bellagio .... (see 4)
Cosmopolitan .... (see 7)
22 Cromwell Las Vegas B4
Delano .... (see 11)
23 Encore C3
Four Seasons Hotel .... (see 11)
Mandalay Bay .... (see 11)
Mandarin Oriental .... (see 1)
NOBU Hotel .... (see 5)
24 Palazzo B4
Skylofts .... (see 12)
25 SLS C2
26 Vdara B5
Venetian .... (see 19)
Villas at the Mirage .... (see 13)
27 W Las Vegas C2
28 Wynn C3

Eating
Eiffel Tower Restaurant .... (see 15)
Giada .... (see 22)
Guy Fieri's Vegas Kitchen & Bar .... (see 9)
29 Hot n Juicy Crawfish A3
Joël Robuchon .... (see 12)
30 Lotus of Siam D2
Morimoto .... (see 12)
Peppermill .... (see 33)
Restaurant Guy Savoy .... (see 5)
31 Tacos El Gordo C3
Twist by Pierre Gagnaire .... (see 1)
Umami Burger .... (see 25)

Drinking & Nightlife
32 Double Down Saloon D5
Drai's Beachclub & Nightclub .... (see 22)
33 Fireside Lounge C3
Hakkasan .... (see 12)
Jewel .... (see 3)
Marquee .... (see 7)
XS .... (see 23)

Entertainment
Aces of Comedy .... (see 13)
Le Rêve the Dream .... (see 28)
Michael Jackson ONE .... (see 11)
O .... (see 4)

Shopping
34 Fashion Show B3
35 Shops at Crystals B5

Mob Museum MUSEUM

(☎702-229-2734; www.themobmuseum.org; 300 Stewart Ave; adult/child $27/17; ⏲9am-9pm; P; 🚌Deuce) It's hard to say what's more impressive: the museum's physical location in a historic federal courthouse where mobsters sat for federal hearings in 1950–51, the fact that the board of directors is headed up by a former FBI special agent, or the thoughtfully curated exhibits telling the story of organized crime in America. In addition to hands-on FBI equipment and mob-related artifacts, the museum boasts a series of multimedia exhibits featuring interviews with real-life Tony Sopranos.

★**National Atomic Testing Museum** MUSEUM

(☎702-794-5151; www.nationalatomictestingmuseum.org; 755 Flamingo Rd E, Desert Research Institute; adult/child $22/16; ⏲10am-5pm Mon-Sat, noon-5pm Sun; 🚌202) Fascinating multimedia exhibits focus on science, technology and the social history of the 'Atomic Age,' which lasted from WWII until atmospheric bomb testing was driven underground in 1961 and a worldwide ban on nuclear testing was declared in 1992. View footage of atomic testing and examine southern Nevada's nuclear past, present and future, from Native American ways of life to the environmental legacy of atomic testing. Don't miss the ticket booth (how could you?); it's a Nevada Test Site guard-station replica.

RED ROCK CANYON NATIONAL CONSERVATION AREA

The dramatic vistas of **Red Rock Canyon National Conservation Area** (☎702-515-5350; www.redrockcanyonlv.org; 1000 Scenic Loop Dr; car/bicycle $15/5; ⏲scenic loop 6am-8pm Apr-Sep, to 7pm Mar & Oct, to 5pm Nov-Feb; 👪) are revered by Las Vegas locals and adored by visitors from around the world. Formed by extreme tectonic forces, it's thought the canyon, whose 3000ft red rock escarpment rises sharply from the valley floor, was formed around 65 million years ago. A 13-mile, one-way scenic loop drive offers mesmerizing vistas of the canyon's most striking features. Hiking trails and rock-climbing routes radiate from roadside parking areas.

The canyon is about 13 miles from the central Strip and just 3 miles from Summerlin.

★**Springs Preserve** NATURE RESERVE

(☎702-822-7700; www.springspreserve.org; 333 S Valley View Blvd; adult/child $19/11; ⏲9am-5pm; 👪; 🚌104) 🍃 On the site of the natural springs (which ran dry in 1962) that fed *las vegas* ('the meadows'), where southern Paiutes and Spanish Trail traders camped, and later Mormon missionaries and Western pioneers settled the valley, this educational complex is an incredible trip through historical, cultural and biological time. The touchstone is the **Desert Living Center**, demonstrating sustainable architectural design and everyday eco-conscious living.

Container Park CULTURAL CENTER

(☎702-359-9982; www.downtowncontainerpark.com; 707 Fremont St; ⏲11am-9pm, food & drink to 11pm Sun-Thu, to 1am Fri & Sat) An incubator for up-and-coming fashion designers and local artisans, the edgy Container Park stacks pop-up shops on top of one another. Wander along the sidewalks and catwalks while searching out handmade jewelry, contemporary art and clothing at a dozen or so specialty boutiques, eateries and art installations. When the sun sets, the container bars come to life and host regular themed events and movie nights. It's adults only (21-plus) after 9pm.

Activities

★**Stratosphere Thrill Rides** AMUSEMENT PARK

(☎702-380-7777; www.stratospherehotel.com/ThrillRides; Stratosphere; elevator adult $20, incl 3 thrill rides $35, all-day pass $40; ⏲10am-1am Sun-Thu, to 2am Fri & Sat; 🚝Sahara) The world's highest thrill rides await, a whopping 110 stories above the Strip. Big Shot straps riders into completely exposed seats that zip up the tower's pinnacle, while Insanity spins riders out over the tower's edge. X-Scream leaves you hanging 27ft over the edge, 866ft above ground. For a real adrenaline rush, save your dough for **SkyJump** (☎702-380-7777; www.skyjumplasvegas.com; per jump $120; ⏲10am-1am Sun-Thu, to 2am Fri & Sat).

Adventuredome AMUSEMENT PARK

(☎702-794-3939; www.adventuredome.com; Circus Circus; day pass over/under 48in tall $33/19; ⏲10am-midnight, varies seasonally; 👪) Enclosed by over 8000 pink-glass panes, Circus Circus' (p123) indoor amusement park is packed with thrills. Must-rides include the double-loop, double-corkscrew Canyon Blaster and the gravity-defying El Loco that packs a whopping -1.5 Gs of vertical acceleration. Older kids get a rock-climbing wall, bungee-jumping area, mini golf and 4D special-effect 'ridefilms.' Clowns perform free shows throughout the day.

Spas

Sahra Spa & Hammam SPA
(☎702-698-7171; www.cosmopolitanlasvegas.com/spa; Cosmopolitan; day pass spa $45-75; ⌚7am-8pm) The Cosmopolitan's (p123) spa specializes in extravagant rituals and 'transformations' inspired by Middle Eastern traditions of bathing and detoxification – just the ticket after a wild night of clubbing. Rent the heated-stone hammam for just yourself or with a few friends, followed by a clay wrap scented with cardamom, a full-body scrub or a rub-down massage. Book appointments in advance.

Qua Baths & Spa SPA
(☎866-782-0655; www.caesars.com/caesars-palace; Caesars Palace; fitness center day pass $25, incl spa facilities $50; ⌚6am-8pm) Qua evokes the ancient Roman rituals of indulgent bathing. Try a signature 'bath liqueur,' a personalized potion of herbs and oils poured into your own private tub. The women's side includes a tea lounge, a herbal steam room and an Arctic ice room where artificial snow falls. On the men's side, there's a barber spa and big-screen sports TVs.

Spa at Encore SPA
(☎702-770-3900; www.wynnlasvegas.com/Amenities/Spas/EncoreSpa; Encore; spa day pass guest/non-guest $40/75; ⌚7am-8pm) Newer than the spa at Wynn (p123), Encore's luxurious spa is splurge-worthy. Stroll down exotic, tranquil passageways lined with flickering Middle Eastern lamps and golden Buddha statues, then sink into hot or cold plunge pools under glowing Swarovski crystal chandeliers or recline on a heated chaise longue before trying a Thai oil fusion massage or the Moroccan mud wrap.

Sleeping

With over 150,000 hotel rooms and consistently high occupancy rates, prices in Vegas fluctuate constantly. Sometimes the best deals are found in advance; other times, at the last minute. As a general rule, if you find a good price on a place you love, nab it. Decent rooms Downtown start from as low as $29, while the swankiest digs on the Strip can fetch upwards of $10,000 per night!

The Strip

★ **W Las Vegas** BOUTIQUE HOTEL $
(☎702-761-8700; www.wlasvegas.com; 2535 S Las Vegas Blvd; r from $107; P❄📶≋🐾) At the time of writing, the new W Las Vegas, occupying what was one of two towers belonging to sister property **SLS** (☎702-761-7000; www.slslasvegas.com; 2535 S Las Vegas Blvd; d from $102; P❄📶≋), was the hottest ticket on the north Strip, offering excellent rates for a stylish brand-new product by this exciting world-recognized brand. If you like design and a cooler crowd, head north and hang here.

Mandalay Bay CASINO HOTEL $
(☎702-632-7700; www.mandalaybay.com; 3950 S Las Vegas Blvd; r weekday/weekend from $107/127; P❄@📶≋) Anchoring the south Strip, upscale Mandalay Bay's (p123) same-named hotel has a cache of classy rooms worthy of your attention in their own right, not to mention the exclusive **Four Seasons Hotel** (☎702-632-5000; www.fourseasons.com/lasvegas; r weekday/weekend from $229/289; P❄@📶≋) and boutique **Delano** (☎702-632-7888; www.delanolasvegas.com; r/ste from $69/129; P❄@📶≋🐾) within its bounds. Plus there's a diverse range of noteworthy attractions and amenities, not least of which is **Mandalay Bay Beach** (☎702-632-4760; www.mandalaybay.com/en/amenities/beach.html; ⌚pool 8am-7pm, Moorea Beach Club from 10am; 👪).

Cromwell Las Vegas BOUTIQUE HOTEL $
(☎702-777-3777; www.caesars.com/cromwell; 3595 S Las Vegas Blvd; r/ste from $89/427; P❄📶≋🐾) If you're 20- to 30-something, can hold your own with the cool kids, or you're just effortlessly stylish whatever your demographic, there are a few good reasons to choose Cromwell, the best being its location and frequently excellent rates on sassy, entry-level rooms. The others? You've got your sites set on partying at **Drai's** (☎702-777-3800; www.draisgroup.com/las-vegas/; nightclub cover $20-50; ⌚nightclub 10:30pm-4am Thu-Sun, beach club 11am-6pm Fri-Sun) or dining downstairs at **Giada** (☎855-442-3271; www.caesars.com/cromwell; mains $24-60; ⌚5pm-10:30pm, brunch 9am-3pm Fri-Sun).

Cosmopolitan CASINO HOTEL $$
(☎702-698-7000; www.cosmopolitanlasvegas.com; 3708 S Las Vegas Blvd; r/ste from $120/250; P❄@📶≋🐾; 🚌Deuce) With at least eight distinctively different and equally stylish

room types to choose from, Cosmo's digs are the hippest on the Strip. Ranging from oversized to decadent, about 2200 of its 2900 or so rooms have balconies (all but the entry-level category), many sport sunken Japanese tubs and all feature plush furnishings and design quirks you'll delight in uncovering.

★Aria Las Vegas Resort CASINO HOTEL **$$**
(☎702-590-7111; www.aria.com; 3730 S Las Vegas Blvd, CityCenter; r weekday/weekend from $139/199; P❄@🛜≋) Aria's (p123) sleek resort hotel has no theme, unlike the Strip's other megaproperties. Instead, its 4000-plus deluxe rooms (520 sq ft) and 560 tower suites (920-plus sq ft) are all about soothing design, spaciousness and luxury, and every room has a corner view. If you've cash to burn, Aria Sky Suites & Villas (p128), a hotel-within-a-hotel, might be for you.

NOBU Hotel HOTEL **$$**
(☎800-727-4923; www.caesars.com/nobu-caesars-palace; 3570 S Las Vegas Blvd, Caesars Palace; d from $149) This exclusive boutique hotel within Caesars Palace (p123) is one for lovers of Japanese design from the traditional to the modern. Rooms are in high demand and suites are often the domain of celebrities.

Palazzo CASINO HOTEL **$$**
(☎702-607-7777; www.palazzo.com; 3325 S Las Vegas Blvd; ste weekday/weekend from $201/231; P❄@🛜≋) Looking more like rival Bellagio (p123) than its older sister and neighbor the **Venetian** (☎702-414-1000; www.venetian.com; 3355 S Las Vegas Blvd; ste weekday/weekend from $169/299; P❄@🛜≋), from which it couldn't be more different outside, room sizes and appointments within Palazzo are on par with, if not practically identical to the Venetian's. Enormous suites come with the Venetian's signature sunken living rooms and Roman tubs, while Prestige Suites enjoy VIP check-in with complimentary champagne.

★Skylofts HOTEL **$$$**
(☎877-646-5638; www.skyloftsmgmgrand.com; MGM Grand; ste from $988; P❄@🛜≋) Glamorous, one-of-a-kind apartments designed by innovative architect Tony Chi have loft bedrooms and two-story windows. They're also outfitted with almost every imaginable indulgence, from spa tubs and steamy 'immersion' showers to gourmet kitchens and top-flight entertainment centers. A 24-hour butler and personal concierge are included, of course.

Mandarin Oriental HOTEL **$$$**
(☎702-590-8888; www.mandarinoriental.com; 3752 S Las Vegas Blvd, CityCenter; r/ste from $219/349; ❄🛜≋) Part of the Aria (p122) complex, luscious oriental flavors meet the latest technology in Mandarin Oriental's 392 slick, state-of-the-art yet effortlessly elegant guest rooms and suites, undoubtedly some of the finest to be found on a Strip dripping with gold and shimmering with shiny things. Add a high ratio of courteous, attentive staff to each guest and you're on a winning streak.

Villas at the Mirage VILLA **$$$**
(☎800-637-0295; www2.mgmresorts.com/mirage/villas; Mirage; villas from $2500; P❄🛜≋🐾) Formerly the domain of 'whales' – the highest echelon of casino hotshot who'd be enticed to the property with complimentary stays – these secluded, unique self-contained oases with private pools were completely renovated by Mirage, which decided to reintroduce them into the paid luxury and celebrity market. If you can afford one, you probably know about this hush-hush release already.

Aria Sky Suites & Villas BOUTIQUE HOTEL **$$$**
(☎702-590-7111; www.aria.com; Aria; ste/villa from $340/3000) A cut above the rest, Aria's (p123) Sky Suites & Villas go the extra mile in terms of service levels and standard inclusions. Being a 'Sky' guest buys you status (assuming you don't have it already), access to the exclusive Sky Pool and Sky-only lounges, off-the-charts amenities, table reservations at **Jewel** (☎702-590-8000; www.jewelnightclub.com; Aria; cover female/male from $20/30; ⏰10:30am-4am Fri, Sat & Mon) nightclub, private chauffeurs and butler service (villas only).

★Bellagio CASINO HOTEL **$$$**
(☎702-693-7111; www.bellagio.com; 3600 S Las Vegas Blvd; r weekday/weekend from $179/249; P❄@🛜≋🐾) When it opened in 1998, Bellagio was the world's most expensive hotel. Aging gracefully, it remains one of America's finest. Its sumptuous oversized guest rooms fuse classic style with modern amenities and feature palettes of platinum, indigo and muted white-gold, or rusty autumnal oranges with subtle splashes of *matcha* green. Cashmere throws, mood lighting and automatic drapes complete the picture.

Encore CASINO HOTEL $$$
(☎702-770-7100; www.wynnlasvegas.com; 3131 S Las Vegas Blvd; r/ste from $199/259; P ❄ ☎ ≋) Choose from Resort or Tower rooms at Steve Wynn's youngest and arguably most stylish property, whose curvaceous form is an almost perfect inversion of Wynn's, three years its senior. Encore's equally lavish guest rooms, although bearing similar elements, are furnished in an altogether more contemporary style: three years is a long time in the world of high fashion and design.

Downtown & Off-Strip

Many off-Strip casino hotels offer free guest shuttles to/from the Strip.

★ **El Cortez** CASINO HOTEL $
(☎702-385-5200; www.elcortezhotelcasino.com; 600 Freemont St E; r weekday/weekend from $45/85; P ❄ @ ☎) A wide range of rooms with all kinds of vibes are available at this fun, retro property close to all the action on Fremont St. Rooms are in the 1980s tower addition to the heritage-listed 1941 El Cortez casino and the modern, flashier El Cortez Suites, across the street. Rates offered are generally great value, though don't expect the earth.

Red Rock Casino Resort & Spa CASINO HOTEL $
(☎702-797-7777; www.redrock.sclv.com; 11011 Charleston Blvd; d from $79; P ❄ ☎ ≋) Located 6 miles east of the **Red Rock Canyon Visitor Center** (☎702-515-5350; www.redrockcanyonlv.org; ⊙8am-4:30pm; 👪) and a world away from the Strip, this luxe resort boasts dining, services and entertainment on par with the city's top casinos. Centered on a sumptuous pool, a wide range of gorgeous rooms, suites and villas, all with great views, awaits. Worth considering if you prefer nature over neon.

Eating

The Strip has been studded with celebrity chefs for years. All-you-can-eat buffets and $10 steaks still exist, but today's high-rolling visitors demand ever more sophisticated dining experiences, with meals designed – although not personally prepared – by famous taste-makers. Flash enough cash and you can taste the same cuisine served at revered restaurants from NYC to Paris to Shanghai.

The Strip

★ **Tacos El Gordo** MEXICAN $
(☎702-982-5420; www.tacoselgordobc.com; 3049 S Las Vegas Blvd; small plates $3-12; ⊙10am-2am Sun-Thu, to 4am Fri & Sat; P 🖉 👪; 🚌Deuce, SDX) This Tijuana-style taco shop from SoCal is just the ticket when it's way late, you've got almost no money left and you're desperately craving carne asada (beef) or *adobada* (chile-marinated pork) tacos in hot, handmade tortillas. Adventurous eaters order the authentic *sesos* (beef brains), *cabeza* (roasted cow's head) or tripe (intestines) variations.

★ **Umami Burger** BURGERS $
(☎702-761-7614; www.umamiburger.com; SLS, 2535 S Las Vegas Blvd; burgers $12-15; ⊙10am-10pm Sat & Sun, from 1pm Mon & Fri; P) The SLS (p127) burger offering is one of the best on the Strip, with its outdoor beer garden, extensive craft-beer selection and juicy boutique burgers made by the chain that won *GQ* magazine's prestigious 'burger of the year' crown.

Guy Fieri's Vegas Kitchen & Bar AMERICAN $$
(☎702-794-3139; www.caesars.com/linq; LINQ Casino, 3535 S Las Vegas Blvd; ; mains $19-35; ⊙9am-midnight) *Diners, Drive-ins and Dives* celebrity chef Guy Fieri has opened his first restaurant on the Strip at LINQ Casino, dishing out an eclectic menu of his own design, inspired by so many years journeying America's back roads for the best and fairest down-home cooking.

★ **Joël Robuchon** FRENCH $$$
(☎702-891-7925; www.mgmgrand.com/en/restaurants.html; MGM Grand, 3799 S Las Vegas Blvd; tasting menus $120-425; ⊙5:30-10pm) The acclaimed 'Chef of the Century' leads the pack in the French culinary invasion of the Strip. Adjacent to the MGM Grand's high-rollers' gaming area, Robuchon's plush dining rooms, done up in leather and velvet, feel like a dinner party at a 1930s Paris mansion. Complex seasonal tasting menus promise the meal of a lifetime – and they often deliver.

★ **Morimoto** FUSION $$$
(☎702-891-3001; www.mgmgrand.com/en/restaurants.html; MGM Grand; mains $24-75; ⊙5-10pm Sun-Thu, to 10:30 Fri & Sat) Iron Chef Masaharu Morimoto's latest Vegas incarnation is in his eponymous showcase restaurant, which

pays homage to his Japanese roots and the cuisine of this city that has propelled him to legend status around the world. Dining here is an experience in every possible way and, we think, worth every penny.

★ Twist by Pierre Gagnaire FRENCH **$$$**
(☎ 702-590-8888; www.mandarinoriental.com/las-vegas; Mandarin Oriental, CityCenter; mains $67-76, tasting menus $170-295; ⏲ 6-10pm Tue-Thu, to 10:30pm Fri & Sat) If romantic Twist's sparkling nighttime Strip views don't make you gasp, the modern French cuisine by this three-star Michelin chef just might. Seasonal tasting menus may include squid-ink *gnocchetti* topped with carrot gelée or langoustine with grapefruit fondue, finished off with bubble-gum ice-cream with marshmallow and green-tea crumbles. Reservations essential; dress code is business casual.

Eiffel Tower Restaurant FRENCH **$$$**
(☎ 702-948-6937; www.eiffeltowerrestaurant.com; Paris Las Vegas; mains lunch $18-32, dinner $32-89, tasting menu with/without wine pairings $205/125; ⏲ 11:30am-10:30pm Mon-Fri, from 10am Sat & Sun) At this haute eatery midway up its namesake tower, the Francophile wine list is vast, the chocolate soufflé is unforgettable and views of the Strip and Bellagio's fountains are breathtaking. Contemporary renditions of French classics are generally well executed. Lunch is your best bet, but it's more popular to come for sunset. Reservations essential.

Restaurant Guy Savoy FRENCH **$$$**
(☎ 702-731-7286; www.caesars.com/caesars-palace; Caesars Palace; mains $80-110, tasting menus $120-350; ⏲ 5:30-9:30pm Wed-Sun) With Strip-view picture windows, this exclusive dining room is the only US restaurant by three-star Michelin chef Guy Savoy. Both the culinary concepts and the prices reach heavenly heights. If you just want a small taste, perhaps of artichoke black-truffle soup or crispy-skinned sea bass, sit in the Cognac Lounge for drinks and nibbles. Dinner reservations are essential.

Downtown & Off-Strip

Get off the Strip for more reasonable prices.

★ Lotus of Siam THAI **$$**
(☎ 702-735-3033; www.lotusofsiamlv.com; 953 E Sahara Ave; mains $9-30; ⏲ 11am-2:30pm Mon-Fri, 5:30-10pm daily; ✎; 🚌 SDX) Saipin Chutima's authentic northern Thai cooking has won almost as many awards as her distinguished European and New World wine cellar. Critics have suggested this might be America's best Thai restaurant and we're sure it's up there with the best. Although the strip-mall hole-in-the-wall may not look like much, foodies flock here. Reservations essential.

Echo & Rig STEAK **$$**
(☎ 702-489-3525; www.echoandrig.com; 440 S Rampart Blvd; lunch $10-13, dinner $21-36; ⏲ 11am-11pm Mon-Fri, from 9am Sat & Sun; P ❄) Check out this restaurant's homepage to get a sense of this classy, original joint (pun intended). Sourcing the freshest cuts from its eponymous butcher, the idea is that customers will stop by the butcher and try it at home, once these talented folk have inspired them.

Hot n Juicy Crawfish SEAFOOD **$$**
(☎ 702-891-8889; www.hotnjuicycrawfish.com; 4810 Spring Mountain Rd; baskets $12-20; ⏲ noon-10pm Sun-Thu, to 11pm Fri & Sat; P ✎ 👪) The name says it all: spicy, hot and juicy crawfish served by the pound or in baskets and a wide range of other seafood treats. Ridiculously popular.

★ Andiamo Steakhouse STEAK **$$$**
(☎ 702-388-2220; www.thed.com/dining/andiamo-steakhouse/; 301 Fremont St E, The D; mains $24-79; ⏲ 5-11pm; 🚌 Deuce, SDX) Of all the old-school steakhouses inside Downtown's carpet joints, the current front-runner is Joe Vicari's Andiamo Steakhouse. Upstairs from the casino, richly upholstered half-moon booths and impeccably polite waiters set the tone for a classic Italian steakhouse feast of surf-and-turf platters and housemade pasta, followed by a rolling dessert cart. Extensive Californian and European wine list. Reservations recommended.

Drinking & Nightlife

You don't need us to tell you that Las Vegas is party central – the Strip is ground zero for some of the country's hottest clubs and most happening bars, where you never know who you'll be rubbing shoulders with. What you might not know is that Downtown's Fremont East Entertainment District is the go-to place for Vegas' coolest non-mainstream haunts.

The Strip

★ Hakkasan CLUB
(☎ 702-891-3838; www.hakkasanlv.com; MGM Grand; cover $20-75; ⏲ 10:30pm-4am Thu-Sun) At this lavish Asian-inspired nightclub, international jet-set DJs such as Tiësto and Steve Aoki rule the jam-packed main dance floor

bordered by VIP booths and floor-to-ceiling LED screens. More offbeat sounds spin in the intimate Ling Ling Club, revealing leather sofas and backlit amber glass. Bouncers enforce the dress code: upscale nightlife attire (no athletic wear, collared shirts required for men).

Marquee CLUB

(☎702-333-9000; www.marqueelasvegas.com; Cosmopolitan; ⏲10:30pm-5am Mon, Fri & Sat) The Cosmopolitan's (p123) glam nightclub cashes in on its multimillion-dollar sound system and a happening dance floor surrounded by towering LED screens displaying light projections that complement EDM tracks hand-picked by famous DJs. From late spring through early fall, Marquee's megapopular daytime pool club heads outside to a lively party deck overlooking the Strip, with VIP cabanas and bungalows.

Fireside Lounge LOUNGE

(☎702-735-7635; www.peppermilllasvegas.com; 2985 S Las Vegas Blvd, Peppermill; ⏲24hr; 🚌Deuce) Don't be blinded by the outlandishly bright neon outside. The Strip's most spellbinding retro hideaway awaits at the pint-sized **Peppermill** (☎702-735-4177; www.peppermilllasvegas.com; ⏲24hr) casino. Courting couples adore the sunken fire pit, fake tropical foliage and 64oz goblet-sized 'Scorpion' cocktails served by waiters in black evening gowns.

★XS CLUB

(☎702-770-0097; www.xslasvegas.com; Encore; cover $20-30; ⏲10:30pm-4am Fri-Sun) XS is the hottest nightclub in Vegas – at least for now. Its extravagantly gold-drenched decor and over-the-top design mean you'll be waiting in line for cocktails at a bar towered over by ultra-curvaceous, larger-than-life golden statues of female torsos. Famous electronica DJs make the dance floor writhe, while high rollers opt for VIP bottle service at private poolside cabanas.

Double Down Saloon BAR

(☎702-791-5775; www.doubledownsaloon.com; 4640 Paradise Rd; ⏲24hr; 🚌108) This dark, psychedelic gin joint appeals to the lunatic fringe. It never closes, there's never a cover charge, the house drink is called 'ass juice' and it claims to be the birthplace of the bacon martini. When live bands aren't terrorizing the crowd, the jukebox vibrates with New Orleans jazz, British punk, Chicago blues and surf-guitar king Dick Dale.

Downtown & Off-Strip

★Beauty Bar BAR

(☎702-598-3757; www.beautybarlv.com; 517 Fremont St E; cover free-$10; ⏲9pm-4am; 🚌Deuce) Swill a cocktail or just chill with the cool kids inside the salvaged innards of a 1950s New Jersey beauty salon. DJs and live bands rotate nightly, spinning everything from tiki lounge tunes, disco and '80s hits to punk, metal, glam and indie rock. Check the website for special events such as 'Karate Karaoke.' There's often no cover charge.

Commonwealth BAR

(☎702-445-6400; www.commonwealthlv.com; 525 Fremont St E; ⏲7pm-late Tue-Sat; 🚌Deuce) It might be a little too cool for school but, whoa, that Prohibition-era interior is worth a look: plush booths, softly glowing chandeliers, Victorian-era bric-a-brac and a saloon bar. Imbibe your old-fashioned cocktails on the rooftop patio overlooking the Fremont East scene. They say there's a secret cocktail bar within the bar, but you didn't hear that from us.

Gold Spike BAR

(☎702-476-1082; www.goldspike.com; 217 N Las Vegas Blvd; ⏲24hr) Gold Spike, with its playroom, living room and backyard, is many things: bar, nightclub, performance space, work space; sometime host of roller derbies, discos, live bands or dance parties; or just somewhere to soak up the sun with a relaxed crew and escape mainstream Vegas.

☆ Entertainment

That sensory overload of blindingly bright neon lights means you've finally landed on Las Vegas Blvd. The infamous Strip has the lion's share of gigantic casino hotels, all flashily competing to lure you (and your wallet) inside, with larger-than-life production shows, celebrity-filled nightclubs and burlesque cabarets. Head off-Strip to find jukebox dive bars, arty cocktail lounges, strip clubs and more.

★O THEATER

(☎702-693-8866; www.cirquedusoleil.com/o; Bellagio; tickets $99-212; ⏲7pm & 9:30pm Wed-Sun) Phonetically speaking, it's the French word for water *(eau)*. With a lithe international cast performing in, on and above water, Cirque du Soleil's *O* tells the tale of theater through the ages. It's a spectacular feat of imagination and engineering, and you'll pay dearly to see it – it's one of the Strip's few shows that rarely sells discounted tickets.

Le Rêve the Dream THEATER

(☎702-770-9966; http://boxoffice.wynnlasvegas.com; Wynn; tickets $115-175; ⏲shows 7pm & 9:30pm Fri-Tue) Underwater acrobatic feats by scuba-certified performers are the centerpiece of this intimate 'aqua-in-the-round' theater, which holds a one-million-gallon swimming pool. Critics call it a less-inspiring version of Cirque's *O*, while devoted fans find the romantic underwater tango, thrilling high dives and visually spectacular adventures to be superior. Beware: the cheapest seats are in the 'splash zone.'

Michael Jackson ONE THEATER

(☎702-632-7580; www.cirquedusoleil.com/michael-jackson-one; Mandalay Bay; tickets from $69; ⏲7pm & 9:30pm Thu-Mon) Cirque du Soleil's musical tribute to the King of Pop blasts onto Mandalay Bay's (p123) stage with showstopping dancers and lissome acrobats and aerialists all moving to a soundtrack of MJ's hits, moonwalking all the way back to his break-out platinum album *Thriller*. No children under five years old allowed.

★**Aces of Comedy** COMEDY

(☎702-792-7777; www.mirage.com; Mirage; tickets $40-100; ⏲schedules vary, box office 10am-10pm Thu-Mon, to 8pm Tue & Wed) You'd be hard pressed to find a better A-list collection of famous stand-up comedians than this year-round series of appearances at the Mirage (p123), which delivers the likes of Jay Leno, David Spade and Tim Allen to the Strip. Buy tickets in advance online or by phone, or go in person to the Mirage's **Cirque du Soleil** (☎877-924-7783; www.cirquedusoleil.com/las-vegas) box office.

Shopping

Surprisingly, Vegas has evolved into a sophisticated shopping destination. International purveyors of haute couture on the Strip cater to cashed-up clientele, whether it's catwalk fashions fresh off the runways, diamond jewels once worn by royalty or sports cars. But Sin City is still the kind of place where porn-star-worthy bling, Elvis wigs and other tacky souvenirs fly off the shelves.

★**Shops at Crystals** MALL

(www.simon.com/mall/the-shops-at-crystals; 3720 S Las Vegas Blvd, CityCenter; ⏲10am-11pm Mon-Thu, to midnight Fri-Sun) Design-conscious Crystals is the most striking shopping center on the Strip. Win big at blackjack? Waltz inside Christian Dior, Dolce & Gabbana, Prada, Hermès, Harry Winston, Paul Smith or Stella McCartney showrooms at Aria's shrine (p122) to haute couture. For sexy couples with unlimited cash to burn, Kiki de Montparnasse is a one-stop shop for lingerie and bedroom toys.

Las Vegas Premium Outlets North MALL

(☎702-474-7500; www.premiumoutlets.com/vegas-north; 875 S Grand Central Pkwy; ⏲9am-9pm Mon-Sat, to 8pm Sun; 👪; 🚌SDX) Vegas' biggest-ticket outlet mall features 120 mostly high-end names such as Armani, Brooks Brothers, Diane von Furstenberg, Kate Spade, Michael Kors and Theory, alongside casual brands such as Banana Republic and Diesel.

Inyo Fine Cannabis Dispensary DISPENSARY

(☎702-707-8888; www.inyolasvegas.com; 2520 Maryland Pkwy #2; ⏲9am-10pm Mon-Thu, to 11pm Fri & Sat, 9am-6pm Sun) One of the first medical marijuana dispensaries in Las Vegas is all set for the burgeoning legal recreational market.

Information

Most casino hotels charge a fee of up to $15 per 24 hours for internet access (sometimes only wired access is available). Free wi-fi hot spots are more common off-Strip. Cheap internet cafes hide inside souvenir shops on the Strip and along Maryland Pkwy opposite the UNLV campus.

The **Las Vegas Convention & Visitors Authority** (LVCVA; ☎702-892-7575; www.lasvegas.com; 3150 Paradise Rd; ⏲8am-5pm Mon-Fri; 🚝Las Vegas Convention Center) hotline provides up-to-date information about shows, attractions, activities and more; staff may help with finding last-minute accommodations.

Check out www.vegas.com for additional tourist resources and bookings.

Sunrise Hospital & Medical Center (☎702-731-8000; www.sunrisehospital.com; 3186 S Maryland Pkwy; ⏲24hr) Specialized children's trauma services available at a 24-hour emergency room.

University Medical Center (UMC; ☎702-383-2000; www.umcsn.com; 1800 W Charleston Blvd; ⏲24hr) Southern Nevada's most advanced trauma center has a 24-hour ER.

Getting There & Away

AIR

McCarran International Airport (p235) is one of the USA's 10 busiest airports. Taxis to Strip hotels average $15 to $20 (cash only, plus tip);

superslow airport shuttle buses charge half as much. **Airport shuttles** (☎435-652-1100; www.stgeorgeexpress.com; 805 S Bluff St; 1-way Las Vegas $19-38) also run to/from St George, Utah.

BUS

Greyhound (☎214-849-8100; www.greyhound.com) Runs long-distance buses connecting Las Vegas with Reno ($81, 9½ hours) and Salt Lake City (from $48, eight hours), as well as regular discounted services to/from Los Angeles (from $11, five to eight hours). Book in advance for the cheapest fares.

Las Vegas Bus Station (☎702-384-9561; www.greyhound.com; 200 S Main St; ⏲24hr; 🚌SDX) Located off Fremont St in the old Las Vegas Station, a short walk from Downtown casino hotels and the Deuce and SDX express bus lines south to the Strip.

CAR & MOTORCYCLE

The main roads into and out of Las Vegas are the I-15 Fwy and Hwy 95. Hwy 93 connects downtown with Hoover Dam. I-215 goes by McCarran International Airport (p235). Freeway traffic often crawls along, particularly during morning and afternoon rush hours and on weekend nights, especially near the Strip (Las Vegas Blvd).

When traffic is snarled on I-15 and Las Vegas Blvd, stick to surface routes, such as Paradise Rd, east of the Strip; Frank Sinatra Dr and Industrial Rd, west of the Strip; and the Desert Inn Rd super-arterial, which flies east–west across the Strip and I-15. Tune into KXNT (100.5FM/840AM) for traffic and weather updates.

ℹ Getting Around

BUS

RTC (Regional Transportation Commission of Southern Nevada; ☎702-228-7433; www.rtcsnv.com/transit; 2/24/72hr bus pass $6/8/20, child under 5yr free) buses operate from 5am to 2am daily, with popular Strip and downtown routes running 24/7 every 15 to 20 minutes. Double-decker Deuce buses to/from downtown stop every block or two along the Strip. Quicker SDX express buses stop outside some Strip casino hotels and at the **Fashion Show** (☎702-369-8382; www.thefashionshow.com; 3200 S Las Vegas Blvd; ⏲10am-9pm Mon-Sat, 11am-7pm Sun; 👪), the city's convention center and a few off-Strip shopping malls. Have exact change or bills ready when boarding or buy a pass before boarding from ticket vending machines at bus stops.

Many off-Strip casino hotels offer limited shuttle buses to/from the Strip, usually reserved for hotel guests (sometimes free, but a surcharge may apply).

MONORAIL

The **Las Vegas Monorail** (☎702-699-8299; www.lvmonorail.com; single ride $5, 24/72hr pass $13/29; ⏲7am-midnight Mon, to 2am Tue-Thu, to 3am Fri-Sun) links some Strip casino resorts, zipping between MGM Grand, Bally's/Paris, Flamingo/Caesars, Harrah's/LINQ, Las Vegas Convention Center, Westgate and SLS/W. Although service is frequent (every four to 12 minutes), stations are only on the east side of the Strip, set back from Las Vegas Blvd at the rear of the casinos served. On the plus side, air-conditioned trains are stroller- and wheelchair-friendly, and it takes just 13 minutes to travel the entire route.

SHUTTLE

Many off-Strip casino hotels offer limited free shuttle buses to and from the Strip, although some are reserved for hotel guests. Conveniently, free public shuttles connect the Rio with a couple of its sister casino-hotel properties on the Strip – Harrah's and Bally's/Paris Las Vegas – usually every 30 minutes from 10am until 1am daily.

Bell Trans Airport Shuttle (☎800-274-7433; www.airportshuttlelasvegas.com; 1900 S Industrial Rd) is a reliable paid shuttle service.

TAXI & LIMOUSINE

It's illegal to hail a cab on the street. Instead taxi stands are found at almost every casino hotel and shopping mall. By law, the maximum number of passengers is five. All companies must have at least one wheelchair-accessible van, but you'll usually have to call ahead and then wait.

Vegas is surprisingly compact, so taxis can be reasonable on a per-trip basis. A lift from one end of the Strip to the other, or from mid-Strip to downtown, costs at least $20, depending on traffic. Tip the driver 10% to 15%, rounded up to the nearest dollar. Not all taxis accept credit cards (cash only) so ask when getting in.

For special occasions or stepping out in style, some parties will hire a limousine. Popular companies include **Presidential Limo** (☎702-438-5466; www.presidentiallimolv.com; 2000 S Industrial Rd; ⏲24hr). Hourly rates start at around $45 for a town car and go up to $125 for a 14-passenger Super Stretch Hummer H2 Limo with a complimentary champagne bar.

A good resource can be found at www.vegas.com/transportation/las-vegas-taxis.

TRAM

Free air-conditioned trams that anyone can ride shuttle between some Strip casino hotels. One connects the Bellagio, CityCenter and Park MGM. Another links Treasure Island and the Mirage. A third zips between Excalibur, Luxor and Mandalay Bay. Trams run all day and into the evening, usually stopping from late-night until the early morning hours.

North Rim

928 / ELEV 8000FT

Includes ➡

Best Viewpoints

- Cape Royal (p151)
- Bright Angel Point (p151)
- Point Sublime (p151)

Best Hikes

- Thunder River Trail (p148)
- Widforss Trail (p138)
- North Kaibab Trail (p146)
- Cape Royal Trail (p144)

Why Go?

The North Rim is Grand Canyon plus. Here, the elevation is a little higher, the temperatures are a little cooler, the trails are a little steeper and the views...yeah, they're a little bigger. Since it gets more rain and snow, erosion has chewed deeper into the North Rim, creating mazes of side canyons while leaving sky islands and temples towering above the Colorado River.

As the crow flies, its only 11 miles from the South Rim's Bright Angel Lodge to North Rim's Grand Canyon Lodge, but it'll take you at least five hours to drive – or two days by foot (if you're extremely fit). There are no major travel routes or large cities nearby, meaning fewer visitors – and more solitude. With a single historic lodge, one campground and a general store all linked by forested trails, the North Rim has a distinctive summer-camp vibe that encourages you to linger just a little bit longer.

When to Go

North Rim

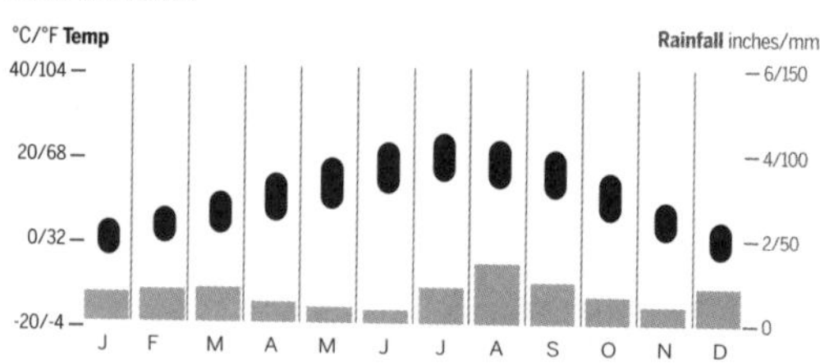

May Opening month is rife with meadow wildflowers and blooming cliff rose.

Jul The North Rim's higher altitude offers relief from the canyon's summer sizzle.

Sep–Oct Long autumn sunsets and golden aspen leaves make for epic photography

Entrances

The **North Rim Entrance Gate** (www.nps.gov/grca; Hwy 67; ⏲May 15-Nov), 31 miles south of Jacob Lake, does not accept cash; only credit and debit cards or a check. The entrance is open 24 hours a day, but if nobody is on duty, you should pay at the self-serve station behind the visitor center. A pass is valid for seven days no matter where you pay – the South Rim does accept cash.

DON'T MISS

If you think the views from Grand Canyon Lodge (p151) are nice, wait until you see the canyon from Point Imperial and Cape Royal. These are two of several drives you'll want to make time for when visiting the North Rim. Wear your hiking boots – many of the overlooks are connected to easy (and family-friendly) trails – and pack a picnic, as you won't find many services after pulling away from the North Rim General Store (p152). At an altitude of 8819ft, the aptly named Point Imperial is a popular day-trip destination, the highest lookout on either rim, and a prime spot to watch cloud shadows moving across the canyon below. The second essential drive takes you to the spectacular Cape Royal (p151) lookout. Stop for lunch at one of the picturesque picnic spots along the way, and don't miss the once-in-a-lifetime photo-op at the striking natural arch known as **Angels Window** (www.nps.gov/grca; Cape Royal).

When You Arrive

➡ Upon entry, you'll receive a map and a copy of *The Guide*, a National Park Service (NPS) newspaper with information on ranger programs, hikes and park services.

➡ Do not lose your entrance receipt, as you'll need it if you intend on leaving and re-entering the park. If you have an annual pass, senior pass, or access pass, display it from your rearview mirror using the hangtag provided.

➡ The road dead-ends at Grand Canyon Lodge. At the lodge entrance you'll find the North Rim Visitor Center (p153) as well as a cafeteria, a saloon and coffee shop, and various other amenities.

Practical Tip

Grand Canyon National Park no longer sells disposable plastic water bottles. Bring your own reusable container and fill it up at one of the water stations on the North Rim: at the North Kaibab Trailhead, at the North Rim Visitor Center (adjacent to the restrooms), and at the North Rim Backcountry Office. The backcountry water station stays open year-round.

PLANNING TIPS

Park accommodations are limited to Grand Canyon Lodge and the campground. All facilities at the Grand Canyon North Rim are closed mid-October through mid-May.

Fast Facts

➡ Rim trail length: 25 miles

➡ Highest point: Point Imperial at 8819ft

➡ Elevation change from rim to Colorado River: 5850ft

Reservations

➡ Book your cabin one year ahead at Grand Canyon Lodge (p152) as rooms are limited.

➡ North Rim Campground (p152) takes reservations up to six months in advance and stays open through late October. Hiker/cyclist sites are usually available without reservation.

Resources

National Park Service (www.nps.gov/grca) Best resource for current information, including backcountry permits, lodging and tours.

Grand Canyon Lodge North Rim (www.grandcanyonforever.com) Lodging and dining on the North Rim, plus mule rides.

Kaibab National Forest (www.fs.usda.gov/kaibab)

Lonely Planet (www.lonelyplanet.com/usa/southwest/north-rim)

North Rim

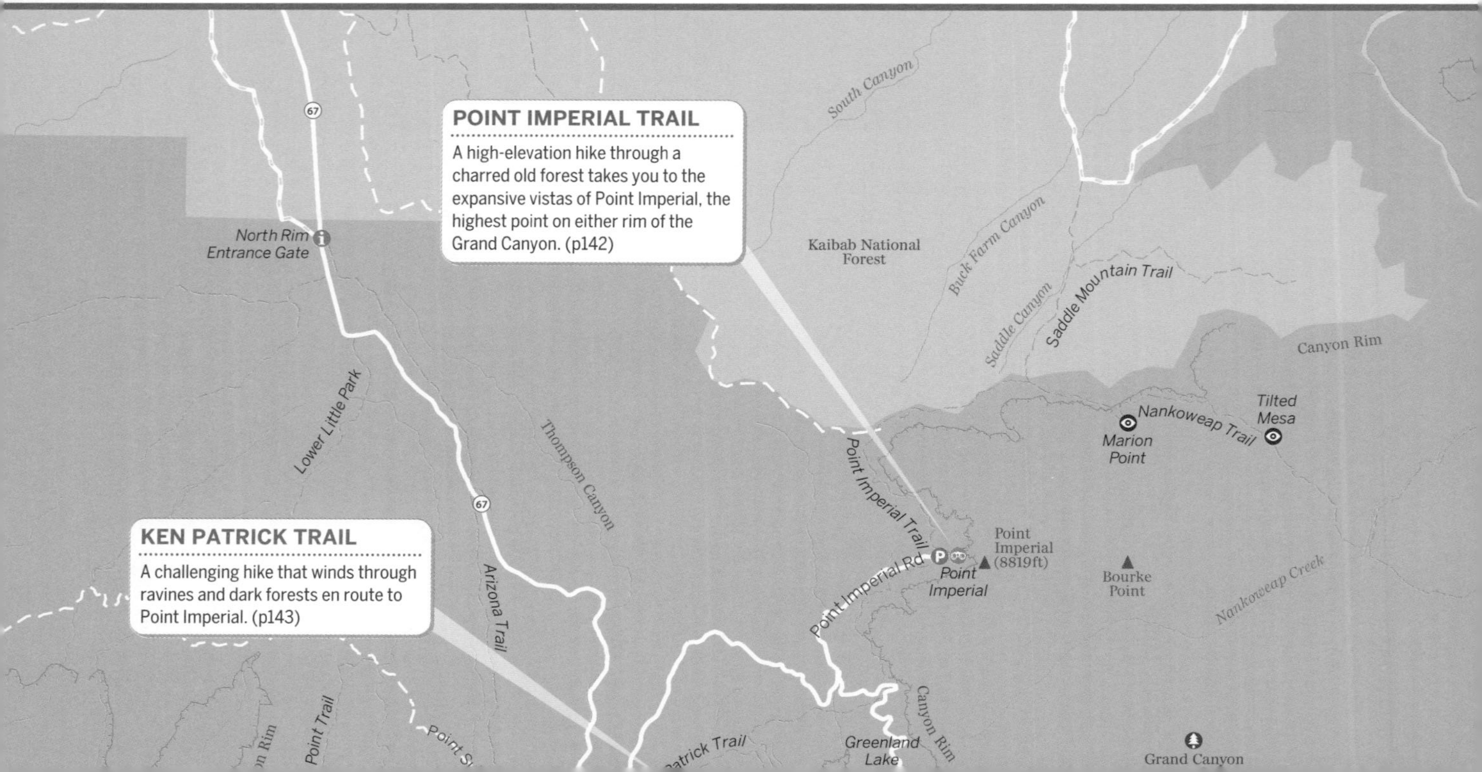
0
0
10 km
5 miles
POINT IMPERIAL TRAIL
A high-elevation hike through a charred old forest takes you to the expansive vistas of Point Imperial, the highest point on either rim of the Grand Canyon. (p142)
KEN PATRICK TRAIL
A challenging hike that winds through ravines and dark forests en route to Point Imperial. (p143)
67
North Rim
Entrance Gate
Lower Little Park
Thompson Canyon
Arizona Trail
South Canyon
Kaibab National
Forest
Buck Farm Canyon
Saddle Canyon
Saddle Mountain Trail
Canyon Rim
Tilted
Mesa
Nankoweap Trail
Marion
Point
Point Imperial Trail
Point Imperial Rd
Point
Imperial
Point
Imperial
(8819ft)
Bourke
Point
Nankoweap Creek
Greenland
Lake
Grand Canyon
Point Trail

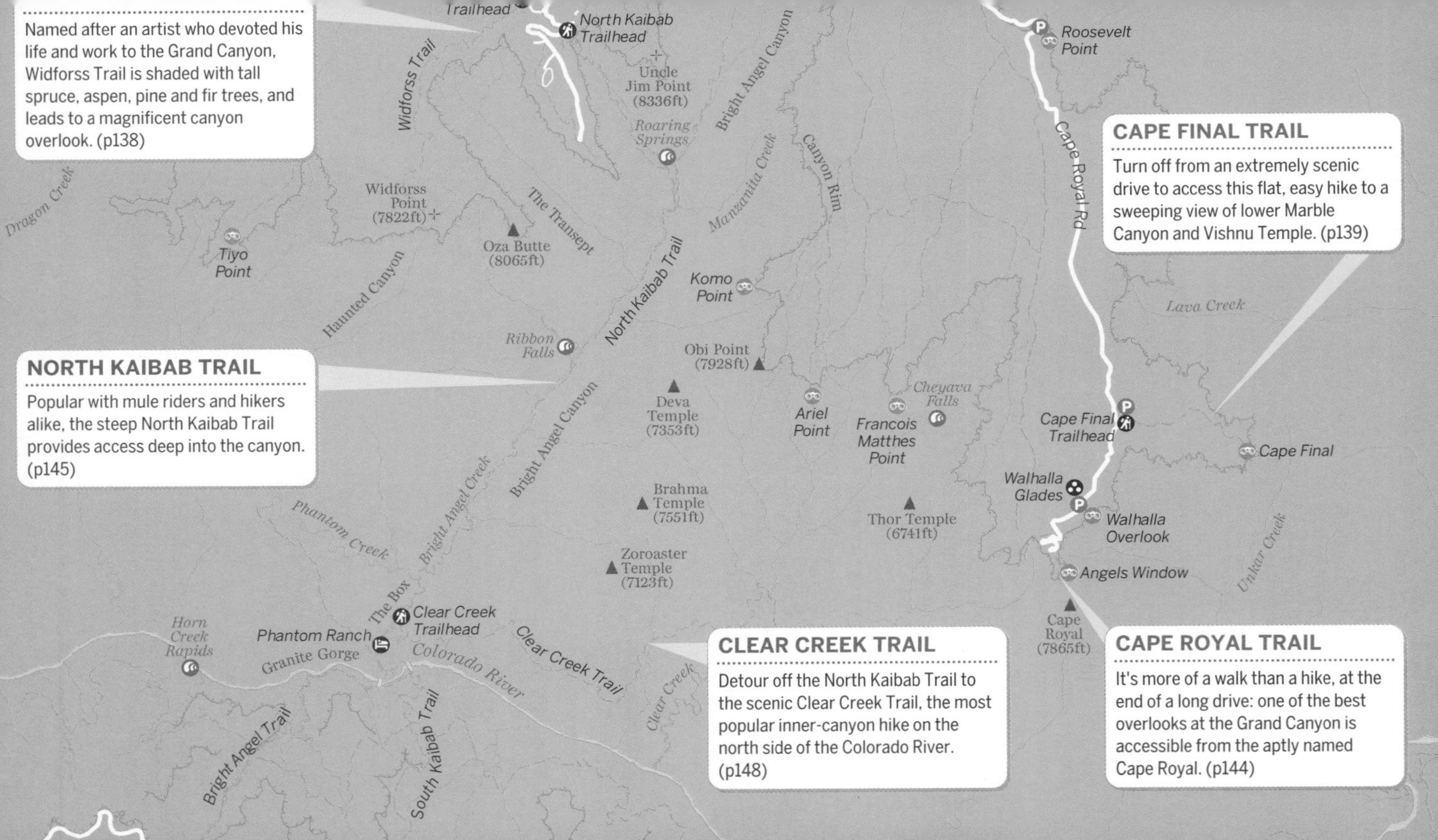
Named after an artist who devoted his life and work to the Grand Canyon, Widforss Trail is shaded with tall spruce, aspen, pine and fir trees, and leads to a magnificent canyon overlook. (p138)
NORTH KAIBAB TRAIL
Popular with mule riders and hikers alike, the steep North Kaibab Trail provides access deep into the canyon. (p145)
CAPE FINAL TRAIL
Turn off from an extremely scenic drive to access this flat, easy hike to a sweeping view of lower Marble Canyon and Vishnu Temple. (p139)
CLEAR CREEK TRAIL
Detour off the North Kaibab Trail to the scenic Clear Creek Trail, the most popular inner-canyon hike on the north side of the Colorado River. (p148)
CAPE ROYAL TRAIL
It's more of a walk than a hike, at the end of a long drive: one of the best overlooks at the Grand Canyon is accessible from the aptly named Cape Royal. (p144)
Trailhead
North Kaibab Trailhead
Widforss Trail
Uncle Jim Point (8336ft)
Bright Angel Canyon
Roaring Springs
Roosevelt Point
Cape Royal Rd
Dragon Creek
Widforss Point (7822ft)
The Transept
Manzanita Creek
Canyon Rim
Tiyo Point
Oza Butte (8065ft)
North Kaibab Trail
Komo Point
Haunted Canyon
Lava Creek
Ribbon Falls
Obi Point (7928ft)
Deva Temple (7353ft)
Ariel Point
Francois Matthes Point
Cheyava Falls
Cape Final Trailhead
Cape Final
Bright Angel Canyon
Walhalla Glades
Brahma Temple (7551ft)
Thor Temple (6741ft)
Walhalla Overlook
Phantom Creek
Bright Angel Creek
Zoroaster Temple (7123ft)
Angels Window
Unkar Creek
The Box
Clear Creek Trailhead
Horn Creek Rapids
Phantom Ranch
Granite Gorge
Colorado River
Clear Creek Trail
Cape Royal (7865ft)
Clear Creek
Bright Angel Trail
South Kaibab Trail

DAY HIKES

From Grand Canyon Lodge or the North Rim Campground, you'll have to drive to access most trails: some trailheads are a few miles down the road, others require an hour or more in the car. Most of the rim trails provide excellent day-hiking opportunities, while tackling the first few miles of any of the inner-canyon routes can be rewarding – if exhausting. The only maintained rim-to-river trail from the North Rim is the North Kaibab, a steep 14-mile haul to the river that's often busy with mule riders. Day hikers will find multiple turnaround spots, plus restrooms and drinking water midway down. Do not attempt to hike to the Colorado River and back in one day.

In addition to the official trails, a number of old, unmarked, unmaintained and closed fire roads off Cape Royal Rd lead several miles to rarely visited Komo Point, Ariel Point and Francois Matthes Point. They don't have the sweeping views of the North Rim's standard overlooks, but they promise solitude. Ask at the visitor center for current conditions and details.

Bright Angel Point

Duration 30 minutes round-trip

Distance 0.5 miles round-trip

Difficulty Easy

Start/Finish Grand Canyon Lodge

Transportation Car

Summary More a walk than a hike, this paved trail wraps up, down and out along a narrow finger of an overlook that dangles between The Transept and Roaring Springs Canyon.

A short, paved, undulating walk to a spectacular viewpoint at the end of the knife-edge ridge dividing The Transept and Roaring Springs Canyon, this is one of the few trails on the North Rim where you feel like you're walking along a precipice, with the canyon dropping off from either side of the trail.

The trail begins on the left side of the sun porch, or you can start at a second trailhead at the log shelter in the parking area by the visitor center. While it is paved and relatively easy, the few steep hills, a handful of rocky spots and the narrow path make this dangerous for strollers and prohibitive to wheelchairs. A few rock benches offer pleasant spots to rest along the way.

Anyone with a fear of heights should think twice before lacing up their walking shoes – there aren't always guard rails, and a misplaced step could be disastrous.

Widforss Trail

Duration Six hours round-trip

Distance 10 miles round-trip

Difficulty Moderate

Start/Finish Widforss Trailhead, Point Sublime Rd

Transportation Car

Summary A moderate hike through woods and meadows with peeping canyon views leads to a spectacular canyon overlook.

Meandering through shady forests of mixed conifer, old growth ponderosa pine and quaking aspen punctuated by carpets of lupine, the Widforss Trail rolls past the head of The Transept and out to Widforss Point. Although it's a relatively popular day hike, people disperse quickly, and you likely won't see more than a few other explorers.

To reach the trailhead, turn onto the dirt road just south of the Cape Royal Rd turnoff, continuing a mile to the Widforss Trail parking area. After a 15-minute climb, The Transept comes into view. For the next 2 miles, enjoy wide views of the canyon to one side and meadows and woods to the other. Halfway into the hike, the trail veers away from the rim and dips into gullies of lupines and ferns. The canyon doesn't come into view again until the end. Stops along the self-guided trail (brochures are often available at the trailhead, but get one at the visitor center just in case) end at mile 2.5, and many turn around here for a shorter option. Though any given hill is slight, the rolling terrain adds up, and you'll climb and descend about 1100ft over the course of the full 10-mile round trip. Bring plenty of water.

The trail is named for Gunnar Widforss, an early-20th-century artist who painted many of America's national parks. He spent his final years living at the Grand Canyon and is buried on the South Rim.

Cliff Springs Trail

Duration One hour round-trip

Distance 1 mile round-trip

Difficulty Easy–moderate

North Rim – Day Hikes

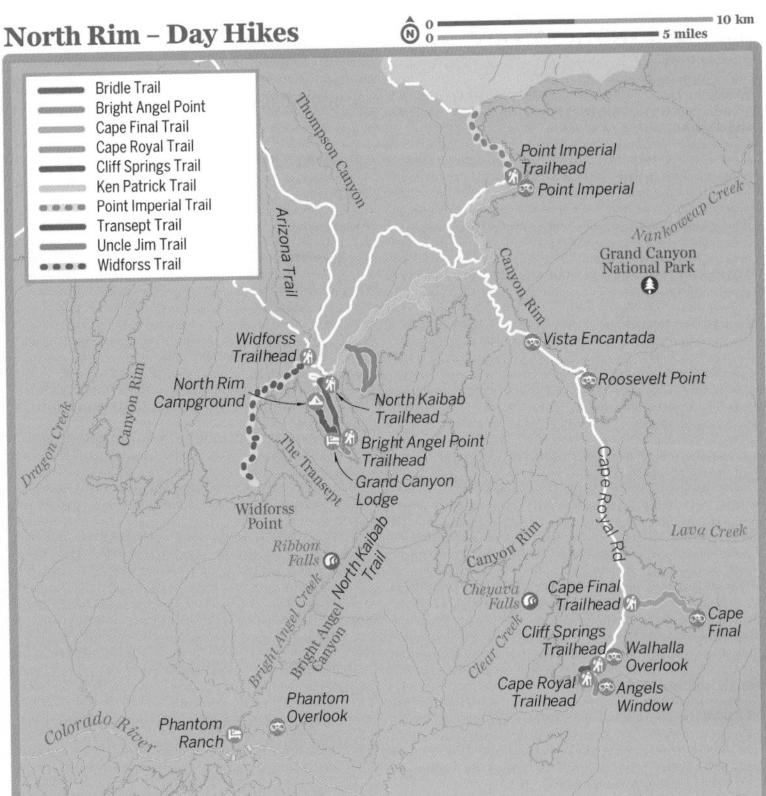

Start/Finish Cliff Springs Trailhead, Cape Royal Rd

Transportation Car

Summary Take this short leg-stretcher down to a fern-covered seep under a long rock ledge that almost hums with the energy of prehistoric occupation.

From the road, the trail immediately heads downhill, over loose rock and through the wood to an Ancestral Puebloan stone granary likely once used to store corn, beans and squash. From there, it continues to a short, rocky descent into the ravine hugging the wall of a narrow side canyon before it passes under a rocky overhang to Cliff Spring.

The spring itself is a tiny trickle emerging from the ground, forming a large puddle fringed with ferns and verdant thistle. A huge, flat rock, cooled by steady breezes, invites you to sit a while and contemplate this hidden grotto. The scenery here is strikingly different from other North Rim trails: you're intimately tucked away inside the canyon rather than standing high above it.

Look for the trailhead directly across the road from a small pullout on a curve 0.3 miles from Cape Royal. Do not drink from the spring: the water may be contaminated.

Cape Final Trail

Duration Two hours round-trip

Distance 4 miles round-trip

Difficulty Easy

Start/Finish Cape Final Trailhead, Cape Royal Rd

Transportation Car

Summary Forested walk to jutting rock over the canyon, with spectacular views of the canyon and the Painted Desert.

HIKING IN THE NORTH RIM *Elevation change is not exact

NAME	START LOCATION	DESCRIPTION
Rim Trails		
Bridle Trail (p143)	Grand Canyon Lodge	Flat, utilitarian trail provides access between lodge, campground and North Kaibab trailhead
Bright Angel Point (p138)	Grand Canyon Lodge	Short, paved hike to a narrow peninsula with canyon views
Cape Royal Trail (p144)	Cape Royal Rd	Paved, wheelchair-accessible walk out to viewpoint
Cape Final Trail (p139)	Cape Royal Rd	Flat, forest hike along Kaibab Plateau to Marble Canyon overlook
Cliff Springs Trail (p138)	Cape Royal Rd	Perfect for kids, this short trail passes ancient ruins and ends at a verdant spring
Ken Patrick Trail (p143)	North Kaibab Trailhead parking lot	Point-to-point wooded trail opening up to spectacular views at Point Imperial
Point Imperial Trail (p142)	Point Imperial	Short rim trail through old burn; views of eastern canyon
Transept Trail (p142)	Grand Canyon Lodge	Enjoyable amble along path rimming the canyon, ends at campground
Uncle Jim Trail (p143)	North Kaibab Trailhead parking lot	A loop atop the Kaibab Plateau, with views of Roaring Springs Canyon
Widforss Trail (p138)	signed turnoff 2.7 miles north of Grand Canyon Lodge	Lovely forested walk with some of the finest canyon views on the North Rim
North Kaibab Trail (p145)		
To Coconino Overlook	North Kaibab Trailhead	Views of Roaring Springs and Bright Angel Canyon at the end of this short hike
To Supai Tunnel	North Kaibab Trailhead	Steep, spectacular hike to red sandstone tunnel with sweeping views of inner canyon
To Redwall Bridge	North Kaibab Trailhead	Challenging descent along switchbacks leads to Redwall Bridge
To Roaring Springs	North Kaibab Trailhead	A favorite for strong hikers, featuring pools in a green oasis on the otherwise-hot trail
To Cottonwood Campground	North Kaibab Trailhead	Last 2 miles of this trail traces Bright Angel Creek to the campground
To Bright Angel Campground	From Cottonwood Campground	Relatively flat hiking through the inner gorge past Ribbon Falls
Other Trails		
Clear Creek Trail (p148)	North Kaibab Trail, 0.3 miles north of Phantom Ranch	Off the North Kaibab, the most popular inner-canyon hike on the Colorado's north side
Nankoweap Trail (p146)	Forest Service Saddle Mountain Trail	Steep, scary goat path to one of the larger inner-canyon drainage systems
North Bass Trail (p147)	Swamp Point	Difficult trail requiring route-finding to historic Bass camp on Shinumo Creek
South Canyon Route (p144)	House Rock Valley off Fire Road 632	Ledgy inner-canyon scramble to the Colorado River
Thunder River Trail (p147)	Indian Hollow	Hot desert descent to springs, waterfalls and river

  *Drinking Water*   *Restrooms*  *Ranger Station Nearby*  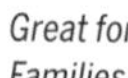 *Great for Families*  *Wildlife-Watching*

DIFFICULTY	DURATION	ROUND-TRIP DISTANCE	ELEVATION CHANGE*	FEATURES	FACILITIES
easy	1hr (one way)	2 miles (one way)	200ft		
easy	30min	0.5 mile	150ft		
easy	1hr	0.8 miles	30ft		
easy	2.5hr	4.2 miles	850ft		
easy-moderate	1hr	1 mile	400ft		
moderate-difficult	6-7hr (one way)	10 miles (one way)	1800ft		
easy	3hr	5.4 miles	300ft		
easy	1hr (one way)	2 miles (one way)	250ft		
easy-moderate	3hr	5 miles	600ft		
moderate	6hr	10 miles	1100ft		
easy- moderate	1hr	1.5 miles	800ft		
moderate-difficult	3-4hr	3.5 miles	1400ft		
difficult	4-5hr	5.2 miles	2200ft		
difficult	7-8hr	9.4 miles	3300ft		
difficult	4½hr (one way)	6.8 miles (one way)	4170ft		
moderate	5hr (one way)	7.4 miles (one way)	1600ft		
moderate-difficult	10hr	16.8 miles	4400ft		
very difficult	2 days (one way)	14 miles (one way)	7000ft		
very difficult	10hr (one way)	13.5 miles (one way)	7300ft		
very difficult	8hr	13 miles	5500ft		
very difficult	12hr (one way)	12.6 miles (one way)	5000ft		

Views

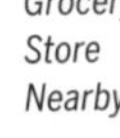
Grocery Store Nearby

Restaurant / Snack Shop Nearby

Waterfall

Backcountry campsite

OFF THE BEATEN TRACK

HIDDEN SPOTS ON THE NORTH RIM

You're already getting away from it all by just being on the North Rim, but a few easily accessible hideaways can complete your escape.

➡ **Uncle Jim's Cave**, once used as a ranger residence, lies in the rocks on the north side of **Harvey Meadow** on the way to the Widforss trailhead – easy to get to and free of crowds. The meadow and cave make a pleasant spot to hang out, particularly for children.

➡ The **Moon Room** below the sun porch of Grand Canyon Lodge is an overlooked cool and quiet rimside refuge.

➡ On the road to Cape Royal, few folks bother stopping at **Greenland Lake**, which is a peaceful place for a picnic, especially at the old salt cabin over the hill just beyond.

➡ Unmaintained forest roads heading toward Point Sublime (p155) lead to miles of exploration and endless backcountry overlooks. Ask at the visitor center for details, and secure a permit if you plan on primitive camping.

Hikes are usually about the journey, not the destination. Not this one: it's all about the destination. The approach through an open ponderosa forest is not unpleasant per se, it's just a lot the same and almost completely flat. It rewards your patience, however, with an insider view of the massive Unkar Canyon system framed by Juno and Juniper Temples.

After an initial, moderate, 10-minute incline of about 200ft, the trail levels off. About 1.5 miles in, a short side trail veers left to an overlook – take a few minutes to rehydrate before returning to the main trail. There is one more view before the trail narrows, turns rocky and descends 100ft over half a mile as the ponderosa give way to piñon, sagebrush and cliffrose. Your first prize-winning photo op: a flat, rocky triangle roughly 25ft by 25ft that juts over the canyon. Hike five more minutes through cactus and scramble up some boulders to Cape Final. Look for the imposing **Vishnu Temple** directly south, and note the Little Colorado River just beyond Juno Temple slicing through the Painted Desert toward the confluence.

The ease of this hike makes it great for children, but it's a frighteningly dangerous overlook and there are no guardrails.

Transept Trail

Duration 45 minutes one way

Distance 1.5 miles one way

Difficulty Easy

Start Grand Canyon Lodge

Finish North Rim Campground

Transportation Car

Summary A rocky dirt path with moderate inclines following the rim above The Transept, connecting Grand Canyon Lodge to the campground.

From the bottom of the steps off the Grand Canyon Lodge sun porch, follow the trail along the rim to the right. The walk is especially nice in the evening as the sun sets across The Transept, a dramatically sheer defile running perpendicular to Bright Angel Canyon like the transept of a cross-shaped church. The trail eventually backs away from the edge and becomes relatively level – more a walk through the woods than a hike. Watch for the small ancient Puebloan site and several viewpoints before reaching the rim-view tent sites of the campground. The general store is just beyond.

Point Imperial Trail

Duration Two hours round-trip

Distance 4 miles round-trip

Difficulty Easy

Start/Finish Point Imperial Trailhead

Transportation Car

Summary Embark on a hot walk through recent burns with – predictably – spectacular views of Nankoweap drainage, Marble Canyon and the Painted Desert beyond.

From the Point Imperial parking lot this trail heads north and west along the rim, veers through areas initially burned by a 2000 fire and re-burned in the 2016 Fuller Fire. It technically ends at the park's northern border, but connects to Forest Service trails that lead back into the park on the rugged backcountry Nankoweap Trail (p146) – a tempting route for expert canyon backpackers. Expect to see a haunting landscape of blackened remains of burnt forest mixed with tender regrowth and emerging meadows, and keep an eye out for the white-tailed Kaibab squirrel and mule deer. Though this quiet trail rolls gently along the rim, the high elevation can make it seem more difficult. Unlike other trails on the North Rim, it doesn't lead to a spectacular overlook and doesn't form a loop. You'll need to retrace your steps to return to the Point Imperial parking lot.

Ken Patrick Trail

Duration Six hours one way

Distance 10 miles one way

Difficulty Moderate–difficult

Start North Kaibab Trail parking area

Finish Point Imperial

Transportation Car

Summary Offering rim and forest views, the full trail ascends and descends numerous ravines as it winds from the North Kaibab Trail to Point Imperial.

While the entire route is enjoyable for different reasons, you'll get the most bang for your buck along the 3-mile section between Point Imperial and Cape Royal hugging the rim high above Nankoweap drainage.

From Point Imperial it's a rolling downhill to the road which can be challenging for some on the return. It passes through sections of remnant forest and an old burn, which, while sunny, does open up panoramic views of Marble Canyon, the Little Colorado River gorge, the Painted Desert, and the San Francisco Peaks far to the south. Allow four hours for this round-trip journey.

At the other end, the trail starts from the North Kaibab trailhead with a gentle climb into the woods and winds through gambel oak, ponderosa pine, white fir and aspen woodland. Views are intermittent, offering quick glimpses of Roaring Springs Canyon. The first mile of the trail sees a lot of mule traffic, and it shows: it's a soft sandy path moistened by urine. Thankfully, after a mile the riders split off on the Uncle Jim Trail, while the Ken Patrick veers to the left at an unsigned junction (look for the lollipop turnaround lined with logs). Beyond this, the trail grows increasingly serene – at times faint but still discernible – as it dips in and out of forest, crossing eroded ravines with a few difficult uphill stretches.

The trail is named for a former Grand Canyon ranger later gunned down as he was tracking poachers at Point Reyes National Sea Shore – the first National Park Service ranger to be killed in the line of duty.

Uncle Jim Trail

Duration Three hours round-trip

Distance 5 miles round-trip

Difficulty Easy–moderate

Start/Finish North Kaibab Trail parking area

Transportation Car

Summary Wooded loop to a canyon overlook.

This dusty mule-trodden lollipop loop – named for a hunting advocate and forest-service warden who shot hundreds of mountain lions on the North Rim to protect resident deer – shares the Ken Patrick trailhead but diverges to vista points above Bright Angel Canyon.

After diverging from the Ken Patrick Trail it's about 0.5 miles up and down to the 2-mile loop. We recommend taking it clockwise as the overlooks build in intensity until the final point near the hitching posts and pit toilet. The commanding view of the North Kaibab switchbacks makes you appreciate that trail even more, while Roaring Springs, the Walhalla Plateau and the South Rim are all a feast for the eyeballs.

That being said, the trail alternates between old junky forest left too long without a fire, and the hot scrubby consequence of that fire eventually arriving with a vengeance, and it sees heavy mule use through its entire length. Not the North Rim's best.

Bridle Trail

Duration 40 minutes one way

Distance 1.2 miles one way

Difficulty Easy

Start Grand Canyon Lodge

Finish North Kaibab Trailhead

Transportation Car

Summary Hard-packed, utilitarian trail and the only one in the park that allows dogs and bicycles.

The uninspiring Bridle Trail offers visitors a means of walking from the lodge to the campground, and on to the North Kaibab Trailhead. It hugs the road for 1 mile to the

WORTH A TRIP

TUWEEP & TOROWEAP POINT

Sometimes you need to put the world back into perspective – to experience what it feels like to be absolutely insignificant, completely alone and incredibly alive. Welcome to **Tuweep** (www.nps.gov/grca/planyourvisit/tuweep.htm). Not only does it have what is quite possibly the most dramatic overlook in the Grand Canyon, it's located where the Middle of Nowhere goes when it needs to get away from it all.

And while the **Toroweap Overlook** (sunrise-30min past sunset) – a dizzying, near-vertical 3000ft above the river – certainly gets the heart pounding, there's an even bigger thrill that comes from being wholly immersed in the raw desert landscape. There's no visitor center, no grocery stores, no gas stations, no phone service, no water, and not even much of a road. It's just you and the canyon – and it won't even notice your existence.

Half the fun of Tuweep is getting here. The most reliable route leaves Hwy 389 8 miles west of Fredonia and 82 miles north of Grand Canyon Lodge. Turn south on county road 109 (it's signed) and begin the 62 miles of dirt road that alternates from monotonous to bone-jarring to sandy to completely washed out. High-clearance 4WD vehicles are required, and the sharp limestone rocks are notorious for shredding tires. Locals commonly carry two full-sized spare tires, assorted patches and a heavy duty pump. Fully expect to spend the night somewhere you are not expecting.

Know that your GPS lies to you, and will probably break anyway, so be sure to pick up the *Arizona Strip Visitor Map* from the Bureau of Land Management.

Around 46 miles from the highway, look for Mt Trumbull Rd. Take a 5-mile detour to the west to a small parking lot and a 0.5-mile walk to **Nampaweap Petroglyphs** carved into the lava rock. Back on route, the Tuweep Ranger Station should be about 55 miles from the highway. The campground – by permit only, get in advance from the Backcountry Information Center (p153) – is another 5.4 miles, and the overlook is a mile beyond that.

Aside from the dramatic scenery, Tuweep provides balcony seats for the boat rodeo of Lava Falls Rapid: often described as the exclamation point at the end of the Grand Canyon. From this distance vantage point, you may even hear the cheers and screams as people successfully navigate – or not – the roiling waters and cheese-grater rocks.

A few trails near the campground make for fine day trips. Strike out on the Tuckup Trail for excellent esplanade exploration, but know that you likely won't cover the full 60 miles. A more manageable 1.5-mile Saddle Horse Loop Trail leaves the campground across from site no 5 for additional river views.

campground before climbing a bit up through the woods to the North Kaibab parking area.

Cape Royal Trail

Duration 45 minutes round-trip

Distance 1 mile round-trip (with Angels Window)

Difficulty Easy

Start/Finish Cape Royal Trailhead

Transportation Car

Summary A paved, wheelchair-accessible trail out to the park's most encompassing viewpoint.

Take a stroll out to the North Rim's most southern viewpoint located at the great westward bend of the Colorado River. The 0.4-mile paved, wheelchair-accessible, somewhat-shaded **trail** (www.nps.gov/grca; Cape Royal Rd) is lined with interpretive signs about local plants and animals, and takes in several fine viewpoints.

Halfway to Cape Royal Point, detour out to Angels Window, a natural arch in the Kaibab Limestone with plummeting views into Unkar Creek Drainage. Hold on to your hat as you look for the baby window nearby just to the south.

South Canyon Route

Duration Eight hours round-trip

Distance 13 miles round-trip

Difficulty Very Difficult

Start/Finish Fire Road 632 via Buffalo Ranch Road, Inner Canyon

Transportation Car

Summary Not so much a trail, this expert

route-finding fiesta on the northeast end of the park descends to the dramatic Redwall narrows of Marble Canyon, the Colorado River, lush Vasey's Paradise and historic Stanton's Cave.

You start at the top of the Kaibab limestone, the same layer that makes up the North Rim – only it's 3300ft lower here due to the East Kaibab Monocline dramatically jutting up to the west. From the parking area, the trail descends a chute toward the canyon floor requiring some scrambling, navigating a few tight switchbacks and a little bit of down-climbing, leaving you no doubt what you're up against.

Once you achieve the bottom, it's a brushy boulder-hopping good time to a pair of pour-overs that are best skirted by following the rock cairns on the south side of the drainage. The final Redwall narrows are dramatic and inviting, but stick to the goat path on the north side of the canyon which routes you up and over through the Supai to a break in the Redwall above the Colorado River. Just downriver, explorers found 4000-year-old split-twig figurines in the now-closed Stanton's Cave, and just beyond, the riparian oasis of Vasey's Paradise is home to an endangered species of snail.

The trailhead is 85 miles from Grand Canyon Lodge via Hwy 67 and 89A. Turn south off Hwy 89A at mile marker 559.5 on Buffalo Ranch Road through House Rock Valley; from here it's 20 miles of rough washboard dirt driving suitable for most vehicles if they go slow. After 18 miles, turn left onto Fire Road 632 for about 2 miles to a small signed parking area.

OVERNIGHT HIKES

The Grand Canyon offers some of the most challenging backpacking in the world, and the North Rim trails are among the most difficult routes in the park. With the sole exception of the North Kaibab, trails are unmaintained and seldom traveled – making them true wilderness experiences. If you're an expert backpacker with prior canyon experience, the North Rim should be on the top of your bucket list.

North Kaibab Trail

Duration Nine hours down, 12 hours up

Distance 14.2 miles one way

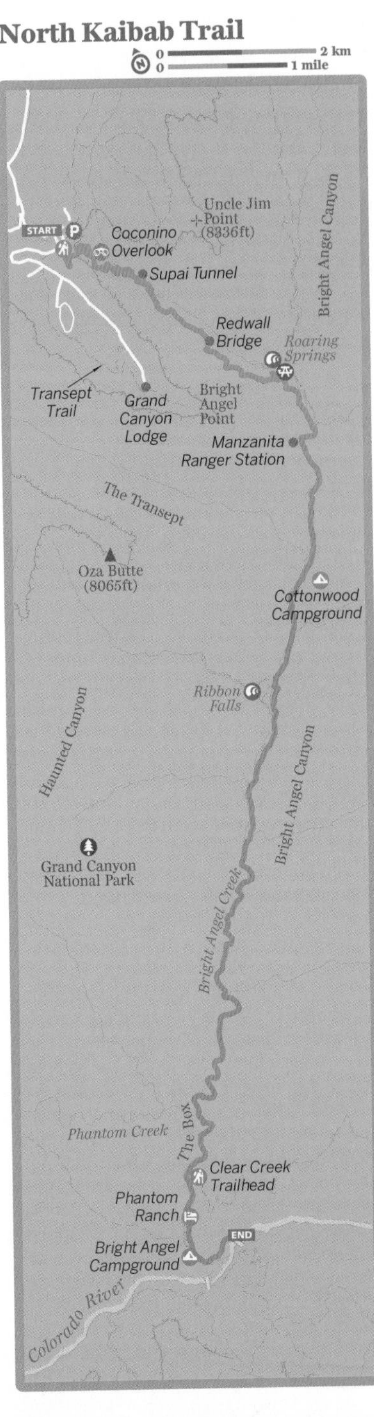

Difficulty Difficult

Start North Kaibab Trailhead

Finish Colorado River

Transportation Car/Shuttle

Summary The North Rim's most accessible inner-canyon trail features strenuous switchbacks, raging waterfalls, a campground fringed with cottonwood and long creekside stretches. It takes a few days to complete – depending on how you pace it – but the first few miles also make for popular day hikes for those wanting a peek inside the canyon.

The sandy trail begins at 8241ft, under the shade of pines, but is less than pleasant as hikers share the first 2 miles with mules who keep the trail disturbingly muddy – even during a drought. Accept this for what it is, and soldier on; the trail quickly breaks from the trees and the vistas will distract you from the mule muck.

At **Coconino Overlook** (0.7 miles, 7450ft), a flat ledge offers clear views of Bright Angel Canyon and Roaring Springs. Around 45 minutes later, **Supai Tunnel** (1.7 miles, 6840ft) – blasted through the rock in the 1930s – is just beyond a tree-shaded glen with seasonal drinking water and and pit toilets. On the other side of the tunnel, views open to an intimidating set of switchbacks beside a knuckle-biting drop-off. It's a tough descent to **Redwall Bridge** (2.6 miles, 6040ft), built in 1966 when more than 14in of rain fell over 36 hours and washed away huge sections of the North Kaibab Trail. Once you cross the bridge, the trail thins, hugging the canyon wall to the right and hovering above sheer drops to the left.

The next major stop (and ideal turnaround for a long day hike) is the cascading waterfall of **Roaring Springs** (4.7 miles, 4960ft) itself. There are picnic tables at the day-use area and plenty of cool pools to soak your feet. Seasonal water is available both at Roaring Springs and another mile down the trail at Manzanita Ranger Station where New York City-born Grand Canyon artist Bruce Aiken (www.bruceaiken.com) lived and worked here as the pump operator from 1973 until his retirement in 2006. Park rangers occasionally stay here, but don't count on their presence.

From Manzanita, the trail follows the small and inviting Bright Angel Creek to **Cottonwood Campground** (6.8 miles, 4080ft). Here, tall cottonwoods offer a shaded spot to relax along the creek – a welcome oasis while both descending and ascending. There are pit toilets, a phone, a ranger station and an emergency medical facility.

From the campground, the trail levels off considerably. The steepest grind is over, and it's a gentle downhill walk along Bright Angel Creek to the Colorado River, but it's mostly through the black vishnu schist of the inner gorge which can be mind-numbingly hot during midday. If things are getting toasty, wait for the evening at the mystical Ribbon Falls (8.3 miles, 3720ft) surrounded by fern, columbine and monkeyflower. It's a short 0.3-mile spur across the bridge and up a side canyon to the west.

Below Ribbon Falls, the trail enters The Box, a narrow passage between 2000ft walls that seems to kill any breeze that tries to enter. It's a slog, but mostly flat walking to Phantom Ranch and **Bright Angel Campground** (14 miles, 2480ft) and, a few minutes later, the Colorado River (2400ft).

Nankoweap Trail

Duration 1½ days down, 2 days up

Distance 14 miles one way

Difficulty Very difficult

Start Saddle Mountain Trail

Finish Colorado River

Transportation Car

Summary The reward for this epic, exhausting and miserable undertaking: ancient granaries high above the Colorado frame one of the canyon's most sublime river views.

The fact that this is the hardest named trail in the park cannot be overemphasized. John Wesley Powell improved an old Native American route to study geology in the 1880s, and little has changed since. Expect a grueling, waterless trek that, at times, narrows down to about a foot wide where a single misstep can have deadly consequences.

The route is slow-going, and most backpackers overnight on Marion Point or Tilted Mesa – the only flat spots available – both going and returning. Start at either end of the Saddle Mountain trail (the north trailhead means tackling a 3.5-mile 500ft ascent, while the west trailhead gives you a 3-mile 1000ft descent) which connects to the Nankoweap trail at the park boundary. The route hugs the edge of the canyon as it traverses along the Supai group with narrow sections not suitable for anyone overweight or afraid of heights. After about 2 miles it reaches Marion Point, a great micro-campsite and excellent turnaround point for day hikers. Stash water here for your return trip.

From Marion Point to Tilted Mesa, the trail continues traversing for a few miles more before descending the ridge between Little Nankoweap and Nankoweap Drainages via a pair of 8ft down-climbs through sandstone cliffs. From there, the exposure lessens, but the trail steepens and the tread loosens as you descend rapidly to Nankoweap Creek, your first source of water. It's then 3 miles of ankle-twisting wash-bed walking to the Nankoweap Delta, the Colorado River, and – if you're lucky – a river trip willing to share their cold beer. Stay awhile: the endless side canyons of Nankoweap can entertain desert explorers for days. Plan on two long days for the hike out.

Do not attempt this trail unless you are extremely fit, and have completed several other overnight inner-canyon trips without major mishap.

North Bass Trail

Duration 10 hours down, 18 hours up

Distance 13.5 miles one way

Difficulty Very difficult

Start Swamp Point

End Colorado River

Transportation Car

Summary The route is relentlessly steep, overgrown and challenging to navigate, but rewards with rushing Shinumo Creek and hidden sections of polished canyon narrows.

One of the more difficult routes in the park, the historic North Bass Trail was constructed in 1901 by miner and tour-operator William Wallace Bass to continue his South Bass Trail which brought tourists to his camp.

The North Bass Trail starts at Swamp Point, immediately dropping 1 mile to Muav Saddle and a historic ranger cabin. From there it's about 2.6 miles to a natural bridge hiding on the east side of the canyon. This is also a natural turnaround for day hikers – you've got 2500ft of climbing back to your car.

The trail then skirts along the top of the Redwall on the right side of White Creek for another mile before dropping sharply back down to the drainage. Follow the the wash for about 2 miles, bypassing any obstacles via cairned goat paths to the right until you reach the top of the Tapeats narrows. Here the trail veers out of the creek bed to the right, executing a long and hot traverse before dropping down to gushing Shinumo Creek 10 miles from the trailhead. There are decent camps here, and the Tapeats narrows of White Creek are begging to be explored – from both the top and the bottom.

After reaching Shinumo Creek it's another 1.7 mile brushy hike to Bass' old camp, and 1.5 miles more – over a steep, hot saddle left of the creek – to gain the Colorado River. Many hikers bail on the river bid, and instead are content to play in the narrows downstream of Bass Camp.

This is a remote and little-used route, as evidenced by the time we left our knife at an obvious lunch spot next to the trail, only to recover it a year later.

BACKCOUNTRY PERMITS

Backcountry permits ($10 per permit, plus $8 per camper below the rim and $8 per group above the rim per night) are required for overnight hiking, overnight camping at rim sites beyond North Rim Campground, and camping below the rim. Apply for permits by mail on the 20th of the month six months prior to your trip date. For example, for an overnight trip in June, apply January 20 through February 1. See www.nps.gov/grca/planyourvisit/backcountry-permit.htm for details.

A handful of last-minute walk-up permits for the inner corridor (North and South Kaibab Trails, Bright Angel Trail) may be available at the North Rim Backcountry Information Center (p153); check the morning before your first availability and expect to be put on a waiting list.

Thunder River Trail

Duration 1½ days down, 2 days up

Distance 10.2 to Deer Creek Falls or 11.4 to Lower Tapeats Camp

Difficulty Very difficult

Start Indian Hollow or Monument Point

End Colorado River

Transportation Car

Summary The crown jewel of North Rim backpacking is a hot, miserable trail connecting an embarrassment of waterfalls, swimming holes and slot canyons. By combining Thunder River and Tapeats Creek trails with a 3-mile scramble along the Colorado River to Deer Creek, you create an epic adventure that highlights everything we love about the Grand Canyon.

Thunder River Trail officially starts at Indian Hollow, but most hikers opt to descend the Bill Hall Trail, shaving 2.5 miles off the trip. From the Bill Hall junction it's 3 miles of relatively flat walking through the barren and beautiful slickrock Esplanade marked by cairns. Turn around here for an excellent day hike, or else the trail then drops abruptly through the Supai and Redwall formations, losing 1300ft in a mile to Surprise Valley. If you thought you were hot before, 'surprise!': this stretch is the devil's frying pan.

Here, routes diverge. Either head east to Thunder River, or west to Deer Creek. We prefer east, crossing 1.2 miles of flat, shadeless misery to drop another grueling 1300ft in a mile. Only this time, you get to stop at Thunder River Spring, which gushes an awesome amount of water out of the Redwall. The water flows through an extensive cave system in the Redwall, accessible with proper equipment and nerves of steel.

After reaching the riparian jungle of Tapeats Creek, there's a camp downstream, and another near the Colorado River 2.2 miles beyond. An unofficial goat path connects Tapeats Creek with Deer Creek via the river – a 3-mile scramble that will take a few hours and involves lining packs (bring rope) and full-on climbing. Expect to see a river trip or two (or three) docked at Deer Creek, as this is one of the iconic stops in the Grand Canyon, and for good reason: Deer Creek falls bursts out of a sensuous slot canyon to violently plunge 180ft to a swimming hole below.

There's a campground and toilets 1 mile up the Deer Creek Trail from the river (the narrows are off limits) and from there it's a grueling 2.2 miles back to Surprise Valley, the Thunder River Trail, and the slog back home

Clear Creek Trail

Duration Five hours one way

Distance 8.4 miles one way

Difficulty Moderate–difficult

Driving Tour Cape Royal

START INTERSECTION OF HWY 67 & CAPE ROYAL RD
END CAPE ROYAL
LENGTH 25 MILES; FOUR HOURS

Start heading east down Cape Royal Rd at the intersection with Hwy 67, approximately 3 miles north of Grand Canyon Lodge. You're in a mixed conifer forest, typical of the Rocky Mountains with healthy stands of Englemann spruce and Douglas fir. As you pass through the 1 **alpine meadows**, you'll notice they're fringed by quaking aspen with shimmering bright-green leaves. Aspen are the advance soldiers of a conquering forest. They occupy meadows providing shade for the sensitive conifer seedlings that will eventually overgrow them and kill them.

If you walk to the south side of the meadow at the second opening, 1.5 miles from the Hwy 67, you may be able to see the faint scars of the old road that accessed the original tourist trail down to the Colorado River via Bright Angel canyon. The 2 **Woolley Trail** was named after visionary entrepreneur Edwin Woolley who saw the automobile as the key to a thriving tourism industry on the North Rim.

Shortly beyond, you enter the scar of an intense 3 **forest fire** that cleared much of this region in the year 2000. After decades of fire suppression, accumulated dead wood meant that when fire eventually came through this area, it burned hot and complete. After such an intense burn, the process of regeneration is slow.

At mile 5.5, pass the headwaters of the 4 **Bright Angel Canyon** and turn left toward Imperial Point, ascending through the devastating scar of the 5 **Fuller Burn** which reburned the already burnt forest in 2016. At 6 **Point Imperial** (p152) – the park's highest viewpoint – stretch your legs on the 7 **Ken Patrick Trail** (p143), or simply sit and watch the white-throated swifts dive-bomb canyon-rim insects at breakneck speed. Down below is Nankoweap Canyon which was once home to a thriving community of Puebloan farmers.

Retrace the drive back to Cape Royal Rd and continue south, looking for the small

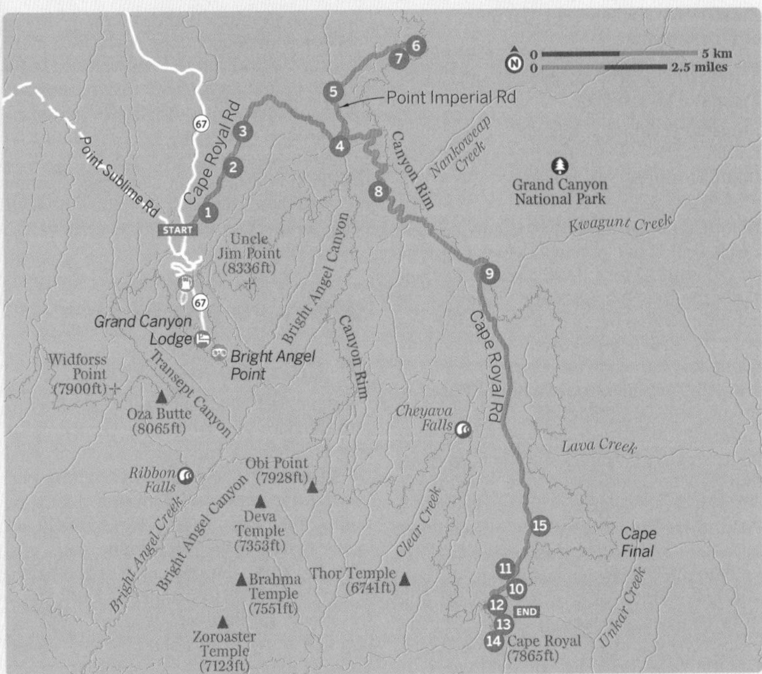

pull-off for 8 **Greenland Lake**. The lake was originally a sink hole, improved by early ranchers to provide water for livestock. Now it is fenced off to protect it from marauding herds of non-native bison.

The drive winds along the edge of the plateau past a few overlooks, the most notable of which is now named 9 **Roosevelt Point** in honor of former president and conservationist Theodore Roosevelt, who said of the Grand Canyon: 'Leave it as it is, you cannot improve on it.' Somewhat fitting, just east of here is the site of the proposed multi-billion-dollar tourist trap that won't be installed at the confluence with the Little Colorado River – for now.

As you continue south, the road dives back into the forest. Notice around mile 20 what a healthy ponderosa pine forest is supposed to look like: regular fire keeps undergrowth and deadfall at a minimum. When the road regains the rim at mile 24 you'll be at 10 **Walhalla Overlook**. Take a moment to look over the rim at Unkar Delta along the Colorado River before walking back to 11 **Walhalla Glades Pueblo** (p151). As the population outgrew the farming capacity of the delta, groups of early puebloans began spending summers up here growing crops throughout the plateau.

At the bend in the road at mile 24.5 you'll want to pull off and take the quick trip down to 12 **Cliff Springs** (p139). It's a short (but steep) jaunt into the upper reaches of a side canyon complete with an ancient stone granery and shaded seep. The intimate view here is unlike most others in that you're inside a small corner of the canyon rather than trying to capture the whole thing in a single photograph.

The road continues south for another half-mile, climbing up a sharp switchback to the unpaved parking lot. Picnic tables at the south end make for a fine lunch spot, and there's even a few benches hidden off to the side ready for the next wedding. Follow the paved trail 0.2 miles to the 13 **Angels Window** spur (worth a trip if you're not afraid of heights) and 0.4 miles to 14 **Cape Royal** (p151), one of the most expansive viewpoints in the park. Despite the crowds, people tend to use hushed tones while talking – overcome by the reverence this awesome place demands.

Return the way you came, stopping by the 15 **Cape Final Trail** (p142) if you're itching for a longer hike.

Start North Kaibab Trail, 0.3 miles north of Phantom Ranch

Finish Clear Creek

Transportation Foot

Summary This side hike off the North Kaibab offers spectacular views and backcountry camping.

Well-maintained and easy to follow, the Clear Creek Trail is one of few inner-canyon trails on the north side of the Colorado River and easily the most popular. The views into the gorge and across the canyon are massive, and even the first few miles pay big dividends; hiking an hour or two and turning around is a worthy day hike from Phantom Ranch or Bright Angel Campground.

Built in 1935, Clear Creek Trail was originally created for mules so visitors to Phantom Ranch could access a side canyon and do some trout fishing in the stocked creek. Pick up the trail 0.3 miles north of Phantom Ranch. Heading east off the North Kaibab, the trail switchbacks up to the base of Sumner Butte, and in just under 1 mile stone benches at Phantom Overlook offer a pleasant rest and view of Phantom Ranch. The trail levels for a bit and offers views of the river before ascending to the Tonto Platform. It then meanders along the contours and canyon folds, passing beneath Zoroaster and Brahma Temples on the left, before dropping to the dry stream bed. You need to hike the drainage about 100ft down to the cottonwood-fringed backcountry campground alongside tiny Clear Creek. You can spend the night with a backcountry permit, or retrace your steps to Phantom Ranch.

Several rough trails follow the creek's tributaries from the campground, and the 6-mile scramble down the wash and through the inner gorge to (almost) the Colorado River is highly recommended. The northeast fork of Clear Creek leads up to Cheyava Falls, but it only flows in the spring after heavy snowfall, and it's 10 miles round-trip from Clear Creek.

Note that because most of the trail lies on the south-facing slope, it bears the brunt of the sun. It is unspeakably hot during the summer, and there's no shade or water anywhere. Bring plenty of water and get an early start.

OTHER ACTIVITIES

Cross-Country Skiing

Once the first heavy snowfall closes Hwy 67 into the park (as early as late October or as late as January), you can cross-country ski the 44 miles to the rim. A backcountry permit ($10) is required for an overnight stay; request the permit at least two weeks in advance if you want to receive it by mail.

In the park, you can camp at the campground (no water; pit toilets); check www.nps.gov/grca/planyourvisit/backcountry-permit.htm for details about at-large camping areas. You can ski any of the rim trails, though none are groomed. For more information call the Backcountry Information Center – South Rim (p232) between 1pm and 5pm. The closest ski rental is in Flagstaff.

Mule Rides

For those unable to hike, or interested in experiencing a slice of Grand Canyon history, the North Rim mule rides offer low-commitment forays down the dusty trail. A one-hour trip takes riders along the first mile of the Uncle Jim Trail, while different three-hour options

SCENIC DRIVES

Exploring the North Rim by vehicle involves driving miles of slow, twisty roads through dense stands of evergreens and aspen to get to the most spectacular overlooks. The only other paved road, besides Hwy 67, splits off 3 miles north of Grand Canyon Lodge, heading east to Point Imperial, Cape Royal, and a number of side hikes, overlooks and historic sites.

The dirt roads to Point Sublime (p151; an appropriately named 270-degree overlook; 34 miles round-trip) and Toroweap /Tuweep (p144; a sheer-drop view of the Colorado River 3000ft below; 122 miles round-trip) are rough enough to require high-clearance 4WD vehicles. While they certainly offer amazing views, they require navigating treacherous roads and if your goal is absolute solitude, you might be disappointed.

At the meadow near North Kaibab Lodge (5 miles north of park entrance gate) forest roads 22 and 611 split off in opposite directions connecting you to hundreds of miles of washboard routes connecting various high-plateau springs, valleys and viewpoints. Take a Forest Service travel map.

either stay above the rim or descend North Kaibab Trail to the Supai Tunnel.

See **Canyon Trail Rides** (Map p151; ☎435-679-8665; www.canyonrides.com; 1/3hr mule ride $45/90; ⏰7:30am, 8:30am or 12:30pm mid-May–mid-Oct) for details and bookings.

SIGHTS

★Cape Royal VIEWPOINT
(www.nps.gov/grca) Strategically located on the southernmost tip of the North Rim high above the great westward turn of the Colorado River, Cape Royal takes in almost every major part of the Grand Canyon with thousand-mile views. Imposing Wotan's Throne fills the foreground to the southwest, while solitary Vishnu Temple to the south evokes a sacred shrine from a distant land.

★Grand Canyon Lodge HISTORIC BUILDING
(Map p151) Enter the front door of the lodge and see...the Grand Canyon, somehow looking even larger framed by the massive windows of the sunroom. Built in 1937 out of Kaibab limestone, the lodge features spacious rimside dining rooms and porches lined with Adirondack chairs. A National Historic Landmark and an architectural delight, the lodge's natural materials blend unobtrusively into the landscape – especially since it was rebuilt further back from the rim after the original burned down in the 1930s.

Point Sublime VIEWPOINT
(www.nps.gov/grca) Not at all superlative, Point Sublime is exactly that – made more so by the difficult access and limited camping (only two sites, reserve at the Backcountry Information Center, see p153). Sheer on all sides, this driveable fin of rock feels like it could crumble into the canyon at any moment.

Bright Angel Point VIEWPOINT
(Map p151; www.nps.gov/grca) An easily accessible overlook that gives unfettered views down into Bright Angel Canyon: a maze of mesas, buttes, spires and side canyons. The South Rim lodges are 11 miles across the canyon as the crow flies – look for the switchbacks of the Bright Angel Trail scaling the opposite valley – and the distant San Francisco Peaks towering over Flagstaff define the horizon.

Walhalla Glades Pueblo RUINS
(www.nps.gov/grca/planyourvisit/brochures.htm; Cape Royal Rd) Around 900 years ago, as the

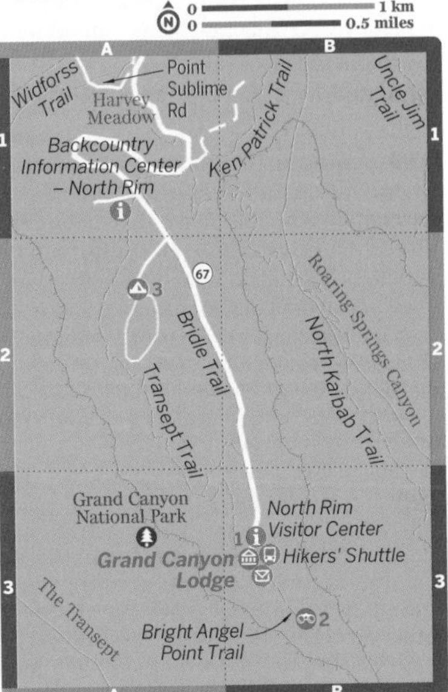

North Rim Visitor Area

growth of the village on Unkar delta outpaced its farming output, a group of Ancestral Puebloans established a summer residence up here on the rim – likely migrating up to plant as the snow melted and returning to the canyon bottom at summer's end. It's a tiny site with only the remains of foundations to look at, but it's still worth pausing here to imagine life in this challenging land.

Point Imperial VIEWPOINT
(www.nps.gov/grca) The highest viewpoint in Grand Canyon National Park (8819ft) takes in the entirety of Marble Canyon as it cuts northeastward into the Painted Desert beneath the imposing Vermillion Cliffs. Directly below, Nankoweap drainage seems impossible to access, but once housed a bustling community of ancient Puebloan farmers. The prominent pinnacle to the southwest is Mount Hayden.

SLEEPING

Accommodations on the North Rim are limited to one lodge and one campground. If these two options are fully booked, try snagging a cabin at the Kaibab Lodge (p159), or a site at the nearby DeMotte Campground (p228), both north of the park.

There's also free dispersed camping in the surrounding Kaibab National Forest (p93). Otherwise, you'll find more options another 60 miles north in Kanab, UT.

North Rim Campground CAMPGROUND $
(Map p151; 877-444-6777, late arrival and cancellations 928-638-7814; www.recreation.gov; tent sites $18, RV sites $18-25; by reservation May 15–Oct 15, first-come, first-served Oct 16-31;) Operated by the NPS, this campground, 1.5 miles north of the Grand Canyon Lodge, offers shaded sites on level ground among the pondorosas. Sites 11, 14, 15, 16 and 18 have canyon views...and cost $25 – but site 10 is pretty sweet too.

You can – and should – make reservations online up to six months in advance. Walk-up sites available for hikers and bikers only. There's water, a store, a snack bar, coin-operated showers and laundry facilities, but no hookups.

Cottonwood Campground CAMPGROUND $
(928-638-7888; www.nps.gov/grca/planyourvisit/campsite-information.htm; permit $10 plus $8 per night.) Around 7 miles down the North Kaibab Trail, this backcountry campground has 12 group sites accommodating six to 11 people. It's a beautiful spot, with seasonal drinking water, pit toilets and a phone, but not all campsites are shaded. A backcountry permit is required.

Grand Canyon Lodge HISTORIC HOTEL $$
(Map p151; advance reservations 877-386-4383, same-day reservations 928-638-2611; www.grandcanyonforever.com; r/cabins from $141/155; May 15–Oct 15) Guest rooms are not in the lodge (p151) itself; most are in log cabins nearby. Four of the Western Cabins have the only canyon views to speak of, and that's where you want to be if you can justify the $22 surcharge. Book them at least a year in advance.

EATING & DRINKING

Food options are limited to the Grand Canyon Lodge dining room, takeout from Deli in the Pines, or the paltry offerings at the General Store. Bring your own groceries and plan on picnics or cookouts at several of the rim's vehicle-accessible viewpoints.

North Rim General Store SUPERMARKET $
(Map p151; 928-638-2611; www.nps.gov/grca; 7am-8pm mid-May–mid-Oct;) Fill up water bottles and pick up basic groceries, camping supplies, beer and wine at the General Store, adjacent to the North Rim Campground and just over a mile from the Grand Canyon Lodge. This is also the wi-fi hot spot on the North Rim, such as it is.

Deli in the Pines CAFETERIA $
(Map p151; 928-638-2611; www.grandcanyonforever.com; lunch & dinner $6-15; 10:30am-9pm mid-May–mid-Oct) The name is misleading: this isn't a deli, but a small cafeteria; and it's not in the pines, it's attached to Grand Canyon Lodge. But putting that aside, it serves takeaway salads and sandwiches to pack for a hike or picnic as well as pizza, soft-serve ice cream, and a handful of daily specials like chili and pulled pork.

Grand Canyon Lodge Dining Room AMERICAN $$
(Map p151; May-Oct 928-638-8560, Nov-Apr 928-645-6865; www.grandcanyonforever.com; breakfast $8-11, lunch $10-15, dinner $18-33; 6:30-10am, 11:30am-2:30pm & 4:30-9:30pm May 15–Oct 15;) While the solid dinner menu includes buffalo steak, western trout and several vegetarian options, don't expect great culinary memories – the view is the thing. Lunch is just OK, and the breakfast buffet is entirely forgettable; order something prepared. Although seats beside the window are wonderful, views from the dining room are so huge it really doesn't matter where you sit.

Coffee Shop & Rough Rider Saloon COFFEE, BAR

(Map p151; ☎928-638-2611; www.grandcanyonforever.com; Grand Canyon Lodge; ⏰5:30-10:30am & 11:30am-10:30pm) If you're up for an early-morning hike, stop for coffee and a breakfast burrito at the Coffee Shop – a space that morphs back into a saloon by noon, serving beer, wine and mixed drinks, snacks and pizza. Teddy Roosevelt memorabilia lines the walls (and inspires the cocktails), honoring his role in the history of the park.

This is the only bar in the lodge, so if you want to enjoy a cocktail on the sun porch or in your room, pick it up here.

SHOPPING

Gift Shop GIFTS & SOUVENIRS

(Map p151; ⏰8am-9pm May 15-Oct 15) Pick up books, Native American jewelry, maps – and warmer clothing, if need be – at this well-stocked shop next to the Coffee Shop & Rough Rider Saloon.

Information

INTERNET ACCESS

If you came here to surf the net, you're missing the point entirely. But, if you need it, the General Store (p152) offers free, spotty, and frustratingly slow wi-fi. In the Grand Canyon Lodge sunroom, some cell phones can get high-speed data from across the canyon.

MEDICAL SERVICES

There is no clinic on the North Rim. The nearest medical facilities are in Kanab, UT or Page, UT. For emergencies, dial 911.

MONEY

ATMs can be found in the North Rim General Store and the Coffee Shop & Rough Rider Saloon.

Note: the North Rim entrance gate (p135) only accepts credit or debit cards and checks. No cash.

POST

Post Office (Map p151; ⏰8am-noon & 1-5pm Mon-Fri May 15-Oct 15) Offers outgoing post and parcel services from a window next to the Coffee Shop & Rough Rider Saloon.

TOURIST INFORMATION

Backcountry Information Center – North Rim (Map p151; ☎928-638-7875; www.nps.gov/grca; Administrative Bldg; ⏰8am-noon & 1-5pm May 15-Oct 15) Backcountry permits for overnight camping on and below the rim, at Tuweep Campground, or camping anytime between November 1 and May 14.

North Rim Visitor Center (Map p151; ☎928-638-7888; www.nps.gov/grca; ⏰8am-6pm May 15-Oct 15) Beside Grand Canyon Lodge, this is the place to get information on the park, and the starting point for ranger-led nature walks.

Kaibab National Forest Visitor Center (Jacob Lake) Go here for the skinny on dispersed camping and viewpoints outside the park.

Getting There & Away

The only access road to the Grand Canyon North Rim is Hwy 67, which closes with the first snowfall and reopens in spring after the snowmelt (exact dates vary).

Although only 11 miles from the South Rim as the crow flies, it's a grueling 215-mile, four- to five-hour drive on winding desert roads between here and Grand Canyon Village. You can drive yourself or take the Trans-Canyon Shuttle (p235). Reserve at least two weeks in advance.

Although trails do connect the two rims, the three-day route should not be attempted by anyone except experienced canyon hikers in excellent physical condition.

Getting Around

SHUTTLE

The complimentary (tips appreciated) **Hikers' Shuttle** (Map p151) takes early birds from Grand Canyon Lodge to the North Kaibab Trailhead between 3am and 6:30am. Sign up 24 hours in advance at the lodge's front desk. Note that there's no service from North Kaibab Trailhead back to the lodge, but it's only a couple of miles down the road.

CAR & MOTORCYCLE

Expect narrow winding roads with slow traffic. Parking is usually available near Grand Canyon Lodge and most trailheads, though the North Kaibab lot tends to fill early morning.

The **Service Station** (⏰8am-5pm, 24hr pay at the pump, May 15-Nov) near North Rim Campground sells gas 24 hours with a credit card and has prices typically cheaper than outside the park. There is no garage or towing service in the park. North Rim Country Store (p159), 5 miles north of the park entrance, has gas and can patch flat tires. The closest full-service garage and 24-hour towing is located in Kanab, 80 miles north of Grand Canyon Lodge.

MICHELEVACCHIANO/GETTY IMAGES ©

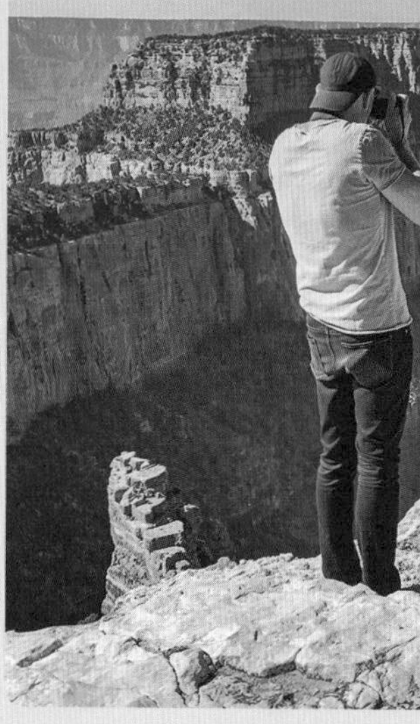

1. Walhalla Glades Pueblo (p151)
Around 900 years ago a group of Ancestral Puebloans established a summer residence here.

2. Cape Royal Point (p144)
The North Rim's most encompassing viewpoint is on a paved and wheelchair-accessible trail.

3. Thunder River Spring (p147)
Your reward after a long, hot and difficult hike up Thunder River Trail is this spring gushing from the Redwall.

4. Grand Canyon Lodge (p151)
Settle into a rimside Adirondack chair for a sunset glass of wine.

ARPAD BENEDEK/GETTY IMAGES ©

FOTOS593/SHUTTERSTOCK ©

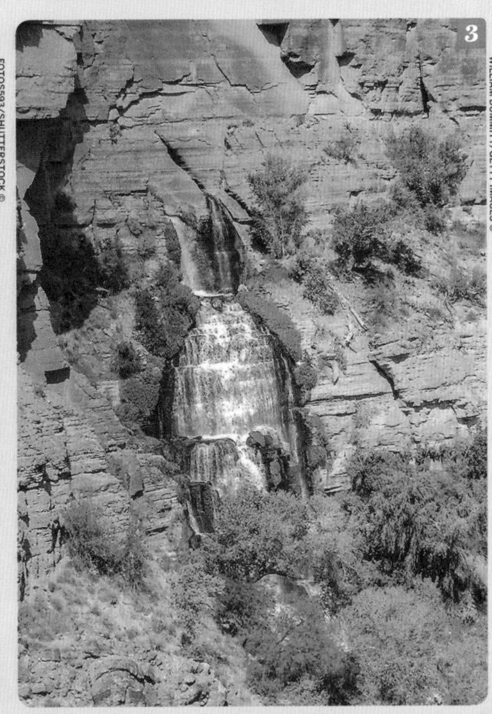

3

WILLIAM DUMMITT/GETTY IMAGES ©

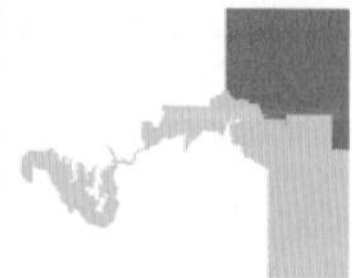

Around North Rim

Includes ➡

Best Activities

- ➡ Coyote Buttes North (p172)
- ➡ Dreamland Safari (p161)
- ➡ Wire Pass to Buckskin Gulch Hike (p173)
- ➡ Arizona Trail: Park Boundary Trailhead to Crystal Spring (p157)

Best Places to Stay

- ➡ Canyons Lodge (p161)
- ➡ Cliff Dwellers Lodge & Restaurant (p171)
- ➡ Lees Ferry Campground (p171)
- ➡ Canyons Boutique Hotel (p162)

Why Go?

The North Rim sits on the southern edge of the spectacular 1010-sq-mile North Kaibab Plateau, refreshingly cool and green at 8000ft and surrounded below by red-rock scenery, miles of trails and vast expanses of desert wilderness. You can easily spend a week exploring the dramatic diversity of the region, boating on Lake Powell one day, hiking a slot canyon the next and biking through the aspen and meadows of the Kaibab another. Combine a visit to the North Rim with Zion and Bryce National Parks (see Lonely Planet's *Zion & Bryce Canyon National Parks*), both within a few hours north of the park.

Road Distances (miles)

	North Rim	North Rim Entrance Gate	Kanab	Page	Vermilion Cliffs
North Rim Entrance Gate	15				
Kanab	80	70			
Page	125	110	75		
Vermilion Cliffs	85	75	80	75	
Fredonia	75	60	7	80	70

Note: Distances are approximate

Kaibab National Forest (North Rim)

928 / ELEVATION 3100FT TO 9000FT

Hwy Alt 89 (also known as 89A) winds 5000ft up from the burning canyons of the Paria Canyon–Vermilion Cliffs Wilderness, past the Kaibab National Forest boundary and through the eerie black-timbered remains of a 2001 forest fire, to the outpost of **Jacob Lake**. Nearly everyone heading up to the canyon stops here, piling out of dusty vehicles to breathe in the mountain air, shop for canyon souvenirs, grab a cookie or an extra-thick milkshake – the Jacob Lake Inn (p160) is famous for both. They then continue south on Hwy 67 through the meadows, rolling hills, aspen and ponderosa pine of the Kaibab National Forest on their way to the North Rim.

On the 30 miles between Jacob Lake and the park entrance, dirt forest-service roads on either side lure curious travelers, offering yellow canopies in the fall, wildflowers in the summer and miles of opportunities for hiking, biking, snowmobiling and cross-country skiing. While most folk simply pass through on their way to the rim, the Kaibab is an idyllic setting in its own right and a worthwhile stop for a couple of days.

Sights & Activities

The 68,340-acre **Kanab Creek Wilderness**, comprised of classic canyon-land formations cut by Kanab Creek, lies in the southwestern corner of the Kaibab and abuts the western edge of the Kaibab Plateau. Here you'll find many desert trails for experienced hikers; the 21.5-mile **Snake Gulch** rewards hikers with loads of incredible petroglyphs. On the southeast corner, abutting the eastern edge of the Kaibab Plateau, is the **Saddle Mountain Wilderness**. Stop by the Kaibab Plateau Visitor Center (p159) in Jacob Lake for maps and information on the network of hiking trails throughout the region. In the winter, you can cross-country ski or snowmobile throughout the Kaibab. The Jacob Lake Inn is open year-round, but the 44-mile road from Jacob Lake to the North Rim Lodge (which is closed from mid-October through mid-May) is not plowed and there are no services north of Jacob Lake.

Dirt roads veer off Hwy 67 in both directions to overlooks on the edge of the plateau. The drives are lovely, particularly in the fall when the aspen turn or in late summer when wildflowers and tall grass burst out of the meadows, but they are long and bumpy. Even in a 4WD, be prepared to drive at a snail's pace in some spots. Consider tackling the roads to Fire Point, Crazy Jug, Indian Hollow and the recommended Jumpup Point overlooks, all of which make nice backcountry camping sites. The five overlooks connected by Rainbow Rim Trail may see a few more people, but they have the advantage of excellent hiking and mountain biking from each point.

While they're certainly beautiful, don't expect classic canyon vistas at any of the Kaibab's overlooks; for that, head to the park itself.

Marble Viewpoint VIEWPOINT

(Forest Road 219) A favorite of the many Kaibab National Forest overlooks, this viewpoint makes a hauntingly spectacular picnic or camping spot. From bald 1-acre hilltop – covered with Indian paintbrush and hiding Coconino sandstone fossils – views extend over the eastern edge of the canyon to the paper-flat expanse beyond. This is not a quintessential Grand Canyon overlook that you'll see on postcards; you're looking down to where the Colorado first cuts into the rocks at Lees Ferry.

From Hwy 67 head east on Forest Rd 610 and follow the signs. The point is about 18 miles from the highway, and the road seems to end at a less-impressive overlook; take the narrow road through the woods to the right about 300ft to Marble Viewpoint proper. Dispersed campsites are scattered along the treeline back from the overlook itself.

Arizona Trail: Park Boundary Trailhead to Crystal Spring HIKING

(www.aztrail.org) This narrow meander through wide meadows bordered by aspen and ponderosa is a hidden gem of the North Kaibab. There are no big views or cliffs, but plenty of room to run and scramble. Keep your eye out for fossils in the rocks along the trail.

Perfect for families, this hike can be shortened considerably by hiking 2.3 miles to **Sourdough Wells** and turning around, or lengthen it by hiking an added 1.5 miles to East Rim View (p159).

Rainbow Rim Trail MOUNTAIN BIKING

The 22-mile Rainbow Rim Trail connects **Parissawampitts**, **Fence**, **Locust**, **North Timp** and **Timp Points**, each a finger of the Kaibab Plateau that sticks out over the Grand Canyon. Although the actual viewpoints are fleeting, the ride itself is beautiful – meandering through meadows and forest

Kaibab National Forest (North Rim)

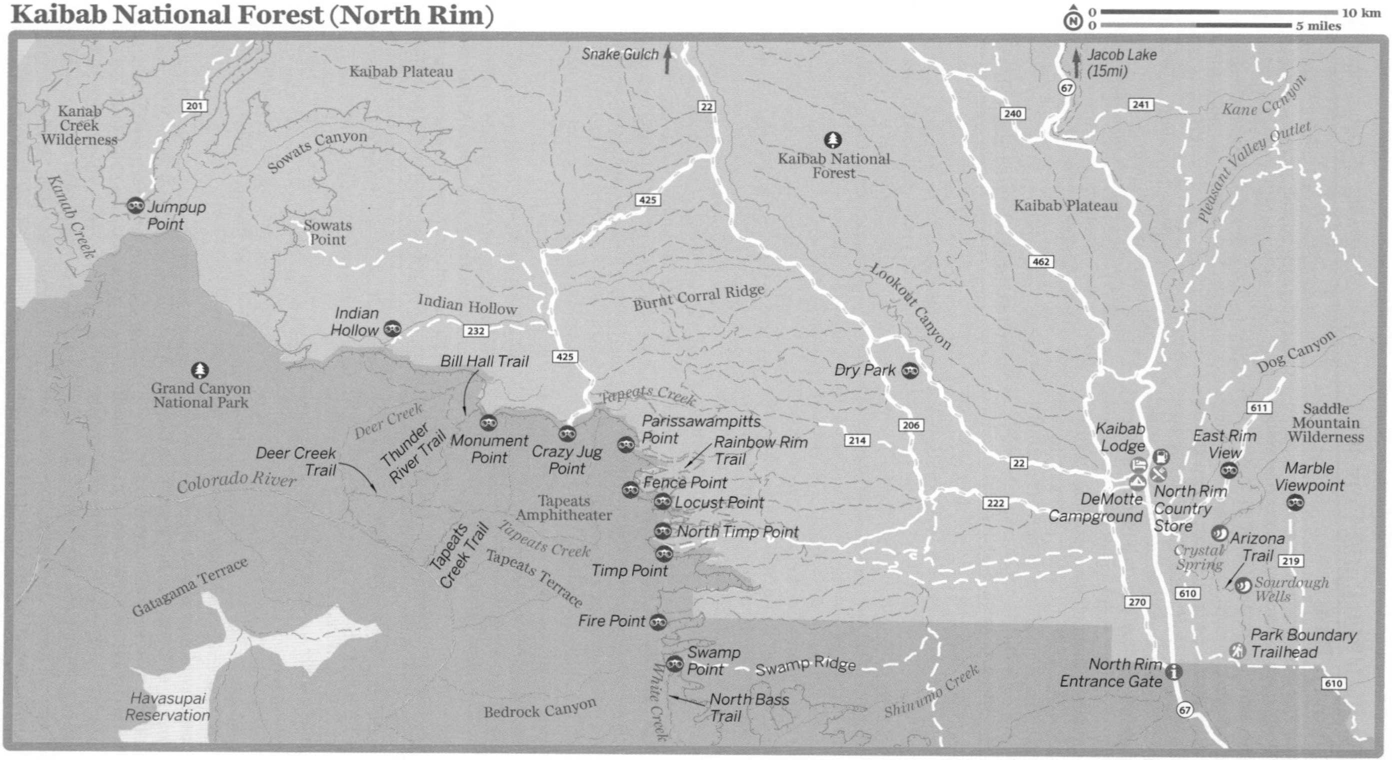

0 — 10 km
0 — 5 miles

Snake Gulch
Jacob Lake (15mi)
67
Kaibab Plateau
201
Kanab Creek Wilderness
Kanab Creek
Sowats Canyon
Jumpup Point
Sowats Point
22
425
Kaibab National Forest
240
241
Kane Canyon
Pleasant Valley Outlet
Kaibab Plateau
462
Lookout Canyon
Burnt Corral Ridge
Indian Hollow
Indian Hollow
232
425
Bill Hall Trail
Dry Park
Dog Canyon
Grand Canyon National Park
Deer Creek
Tapeats Creek
Parissawampitts Point
Rainbow Rim Trail
214
206
611
Saddle Mountain Wilderness
Kaibab Lodge
East Rim View
Marble Viewpoint
Deer Creek Trail
Thunder River Trail
Monument Point
Crazy Jug Point
22
Colorado River
Fence Point
Locust Point
222
DeMotte Campground
North Rim Country Store
Tapeats Amphitheater
North Timp Point
Arizona Trail
Crystal Spring
219
Tapeats Creek Trail
Tapeats Creek
Timp Point
Sourdough Wells
Gatagama Terrace
Tapeats Terrace
270
610
Fire Point
Park Boundary Trailhead
Swamp Point
Swamp Ridge
North Rim Entrance Gate
610
Havasupai Reservation
Bedrock Canyon
White Creek
North Bass Trail
Shinumo Creek
67

between each overlook, with no particularly challenging technical sections and no single climb more than 250ft.

East Rim View HIKING

(FR 611) With views east into the Saddle Mountain Wilderness, Marble Canyon and the Vermilion Cliffs, this easily accessible overlook (elevation 8810ft) is suitable for strollers and wheelchairs. In fact, it's so easy to reach, it's amazing there aren't more people out here. East Rim doesn't offer the inviting views, picnic and camping opportunities of Marble View, but it's a beautiful spot. From the overlook you can hike the East Rim Trail 1.5 miles down, and connect to longer hikes.

Sleeping & Eating

Free dispersed camping is allowed in the national forest provided you refrain from camping in meadows, within a quarter-mile of the highway or any surface water, or within a half mile of any developed campground.

Kaibab Lodge Camper Village CAMPGROUND $

(summer 928-643-7804, winter 928-635-5251; www.kaibabcampervillage.com; Jacob Lake; tent/RV site $20/40, cabins $50-105; mid-May–mid-Oct) Open during the Grand Canyon North Rim's annual season (May 15 to October 15), this pine-shaded campground a mile south of Jacob Lake has more than 100 bookable sites for tents and RVs. There are also one- and two-person cabins; you need to bring your own bedding for the economy ones.

DeMotte Campground CAMPGROUND $

(877-444-6777, visitor center 928-643-7298; www.recreation.gov; off Hwy 67; campsites $20; May 15-Oct 15;) Near Kaibab Lodge (on Hwy 67, about 6 miles north of the park entrance, in Kaibab National Forest) DeMotte Campground's 38 primitive sites are perched on the edge of a meadow teeming with wildlife. Too bad the sites are crammed so close together. Half of them are first-come, first-served; none have hookups. It usually fills up between noon and 3pm.

Kaibab Lodge LODGE $

(928-638-2389; www.kaibablodge.com; Hwy 67; cabins from $106; May 15–Oct 15;) Located about 6 miles north of the Grand Canyon North Rim entrance, surrounded by meadows and ponderosa and aspen forest, Kaibab Lodge is a simple place where grazing deer generate the biggest excitement. There's a lot of variability in the rooms, however, and maintenance doesn't seem high on the list of priorities. Snag a newer Aspen cabin if available.

OFF THE BEATEN TRACK

HISTORIC FIRE LOOKOUTS

In addition to various hikes, the region has a unique historic feature: three steel towers, all on the National Register of Historic Places, and still used as fire lookouts. Built in 1934, the towers in Big Springs and Jacob Lake stand 100ft tall, while the one in Dry Park, built in 1944, is 120ft tall. You can drive out to any of them and climb up and up and up for great views of the national forest and the Arizona Strip beyond, but be warned that they sway in any kind of wind – not for the faint of heart. Though the lookout rooms at the top are locked, someone staffs them May through October and they'll usually let you in. The easiest to reach is the Jacob Lake tower, as it's on Hwy 67 about 1 mile south of Jacob Lake Inn.

North Rim Country Store MARKET $

(928-638-2383; www.northrimcountrystore.com; Hwy 67; 6:30am-7pm May 15–Oct) This small and friendly store, coffee truck and gas station north of the park entrance sells a limited selection of groceries, wine and beer. There are also camping supplies, ice and souvenirs. The gas is typically more expensive than in the park, but its tire-repair shop – the only one around – stays plenty busy.

Information

The Kaibab Lodge, North Rim Country Store and DeMotte Campground, the only facilities between Jacob Lake and Grand Canyon Lodge, cluster together 18 miles north of the North Rim and 26 miles south of Jacob Lake. Jacob Lake itself is nothing more than a lodge and restaurant, visitor center, campground and gas station.

The US Forest Service **Kaibab Plateau Visitor Center** (928-643-7298; www.fs.usda.gov/kaibab; cnr Hwys 89A & 67; 8am-5pm May 15-Oct 15) features a small museum and bookstore, and has maps on the region's many trails and forest roads.

Getting There & Around

Hwy 89A is the only road in and out of Jacob Lake. **Jacob Lake Inn Chevron** (928-643-7232; www.jacoblake.com; cnr Hwys 89A & 67; 7:30am-8pm, credit-card sales 24hr) services flat tires and can do basic mechanical work, but the closest towing services are in Fredonia and Kanab.

Kanab

435 / POPULATION 4500 / ELEVATION 4925FT

Vast expanses of rugged desert surround the remote outpost of Kanab. Look familiar? Hundreds of Western movies were shot here. Founded by Mormon pioneers in 1874, Kanab was put on the map by John Wayne and other gun-slingin' celebs in the 1940s and '50s. Just about every resident had something to do with the movies from the 1930s to the '70s. You can still see a couple of movie sets in the area and hear old-timers talk about their roles.

Kanab sits at a major crossroads: Grand Staircase–Escalante National Monument (GSENM) is 20 miles away, Zion 40 miles, Bryce Canyon 80 miles, Grand Canyon's North Rim 81 miles and Lake Powell 74 miles. It makes a good base for exploring the southern side of GSENM and Paria Canyon–Vermilion Cliffs formations such as the Wave (p172).

Coral Pink Sand Dunes State Park (435-648-2800; www.stateparks.utah.gov/parks/coral-pink/; Sand Dunes Rd; day use/camping $8/20; day-use dawn-dusk, visitor center 9am-9pm Mar-Oct, 9am-4pm Nov-Feb) is a big rompin' playground to the northwest.

DON'T MISS

JACOB LAKE INN

Traveling to or from the Grand Canyon's North Rim, it's hard to miss the pull-off for this high-elevation roadside inn, 44 miles north of the national-park entrance. It's one of the only places to stop for gasoline, restrooms and snacks – but not just any snacks. **Jacob Lake Inn** (928-643-7232; www.jacoblake.com; cnr Hwys 89A & 67; cabins/r from $96/128; 6:30am-9pm mid-May–mid-Oct, 8am-8pm mid-Oct–mid-May; P) is rightly famous for its fantastic freshly baked cookies and extra-thick milkshakes. It's also a good place to stock up on snacks for the next day's hike, like dried fruit and almonds. Take the time to look around the gift shop containing wares inspired or created by local tribes: if you happen to be passing through in the evening, you might even catch a quick lecture by a naturalist or a member of one of the region's native tribes.

Sights & Activities

The Kane County Office of Tourism (p164) has an exhibit of area-made movie posters and knowledge about sites.

★ Best Friends Animal Sanctuary WILDLIFE RESERVE

(435-644-2001; www.bestfriends.org; 5001 Angel Canyon Rd, Hwy 89; 8am-5pm;) FREE Kanab's most famous attraction is outside of town. Surrounded by more than 33,000 mostly private acres of red-rock desert 5.5 miles north of Kanab, Best Friends is the largest no-kill animal rescue center in the country. The center shows films and gives facility tours four times a day; call ahead for times and reservations. The 1½-hour tours let you meet some of the more than 1700 horses, pigs, dogs, cats, birds and other critters on-site.

Pipe Spring National Monument NATIONAL PARK

(928-643-7105; www.nps.gov/pisp; 406 N Pipe Spring Rd; adult/child $10/free; 8am-5pm May-Aug, 8:30am-4:30pm Sep-Apr) A vital source of water for desert flora and fauna, the Ancestral Puebloan people, the Paiute Indians, and for the Mormons who followed them into this stark, stunning country, Pipe Springs is now a monument to pioneer history. Visitors can experience the Old West amid cabins and corrals, an orchard, ponds and a garden. There's a museum with regular guided tours throughout the day and, in summer, rangers and costumed volunteers reenact various pioneer tasks.

Little Hollywood Land Museum MUSUEM

(435-689-0706; www.littlehollywoodmuseum.org; 297 W Center St; 7:30am-11pm Apr-Oct, 10am-5pm Nov-Mar) FREE Wander through a bunkhouse, saloon and other buildings used in Western movies filmed locally, including *The Outlaw Josey Wales,* and learn some tricks of the trade (such as low doorways to make movie stars seem taller). This classic roadside attraction sells all the Western duds and doodads you could care to round up.

Kanab Heritage Museum MUSEUM

(435-644-3966; www.kanabheritagemuseum.com; 13 S 100 E; 9am-7pm Mon-Fri, from 1pm Sat May-Oct) FREE For a glimpse into the region's popular history, this small museum is worth a stop. While the few pieces of memorabilia aren't particularly riveting, it's fun to browse the 30-plus spiral-bound notebooks filled with movie newspapers, magazine articles, written histories and photographs.

Squaw Trail HIKING

Accessed just north of Jacob Hamblin Park at the end of 100 East, this short but steep 800ft scramble leads to spectacular views of Kanab and the surrounding desert wilderness. It's about a mile to the city overview; you can continue another 0.5 miles to the top, with 360-degree views, or retrace your steps.

Allen's Outfitters HORSEBACK RIDING

(435-689-1660; Jacob Lake; 2hr/half-day/full-day trail ride $75/100/130) Offers multi-hour, half-day, full-day and custom-designed overnight or multiday horseback rides through the woods and to overlooks. Children must be at least five years old. Reservations are not required for short rides – just stop by the corrals just south of Jacob Lake Lodge.

Tours

★ **Dreamland Safari** TOURS

(435-644-5506; www.dreamlandtours.net; 4350 E Mountain View Dr; 3hr slot-canyon tour $90) Hikes with naturalist tour guides to gorgeous backcountry sites and slot canyons reached by 4WD. It also offers nature photography and multiday backpacking trips.

Terry's Camera TOURS

(435-644-5981; 19 W Center St; vary) Open when it's open, this little ye-olde camera store can organize bespoke photography tours of the area. Phone ahead.

Windows of the West Hummer Tours ADVENTURE

(888-687-3006; www.wowhummertours.com; 208 S 300 E; tours from $99) Personalized backcountry excursions (two hours to a full day) to slot canyons, petroglyphs and spectacular red-rock country.

Festivals & Events

Western Legends Roundup FILM

(435-644-3444; www.westernlegendsroundup.com; Aug) The town lives for the annual Western Legends Roundup in late August. There are concerts, gunfights, cowboy poetry, dances, quilt shows, a film festival and more. Take a bus tour to all the film sites.

Sleeping

Kanab has a great selection of B&Bs and lodgings. For a full listing see www.visitsouthernutah.com.

Be aware that the town serves as overflow accommodation not only for the North Rim but for Zion and Bryce National Parks to the north, and during the high season of summer it can be surprisingly difficult to find a room.

Hitch'n Post Campground CAMPGROUND $

(435-644-2142; www.hitchnpostrvpark.com; 196 E 300 S; tent/RV sites with hookups $23/35, camping cabins $45-50;) Friendly 17-site campground near the town center; has laundry and showers.

★ **Canyons Lodge** MOTEL $$

(435-644-3069; www.canyonslodge.com; 236 N 300 W; r from $169;) A renovated motel with an art-house Western feel. There's a warm welcome, free cruiser bikes and good traveler assistance. In summer, guests enjoy twice-weekly live music and wine and cheese by the fire pit. Rooms feature original artwork and whimsical touches. Recycles soaps and containers.

Purple Sage Inn B&B $$

(435-644-5377; www.purplesageinn.com; 54 S Main St; r $135-165;) A former Mormon polygamist's home, this later became a hotel, where Western author Zane Grey stayed. Now it's a B&B with exquisite antique details. Zane's namesake room – with its quilt-covered wood bed, sitting room and balcony access – is our favorite.

WORTH A TRIP

ANGEL CANYON

During Kanab's Hollywood heyday, Angel Canyon became the site of scores of movies and TV shows, including *The Lone Ranger*, Disney's *The Apple Dumpling Gang* and *The Outlaw Josey Wales*. A dirt and gravel road winds up and down through Best Friends Animal Sanctuary, offering quintessential red-rock scenery and desert views. Just across from the sanctuary's Welcome Center, a dirt path veers east about 0.5 miles down to Kanab Creek, a shallow, clear creek that's excellent for dogs and kids. A mile further, just beyond the horse corral on the left, is **Angels Landing**. This small natural amphitheater borders a grassy field and makes a perfect picnic spot. To get to Angel Canyon, look for the signs for Best Friends Animal Sanctuary, 5 miles northwest of Kanab on Hwy 89; the road loops 5 miles and reconnects with Hwy 89.

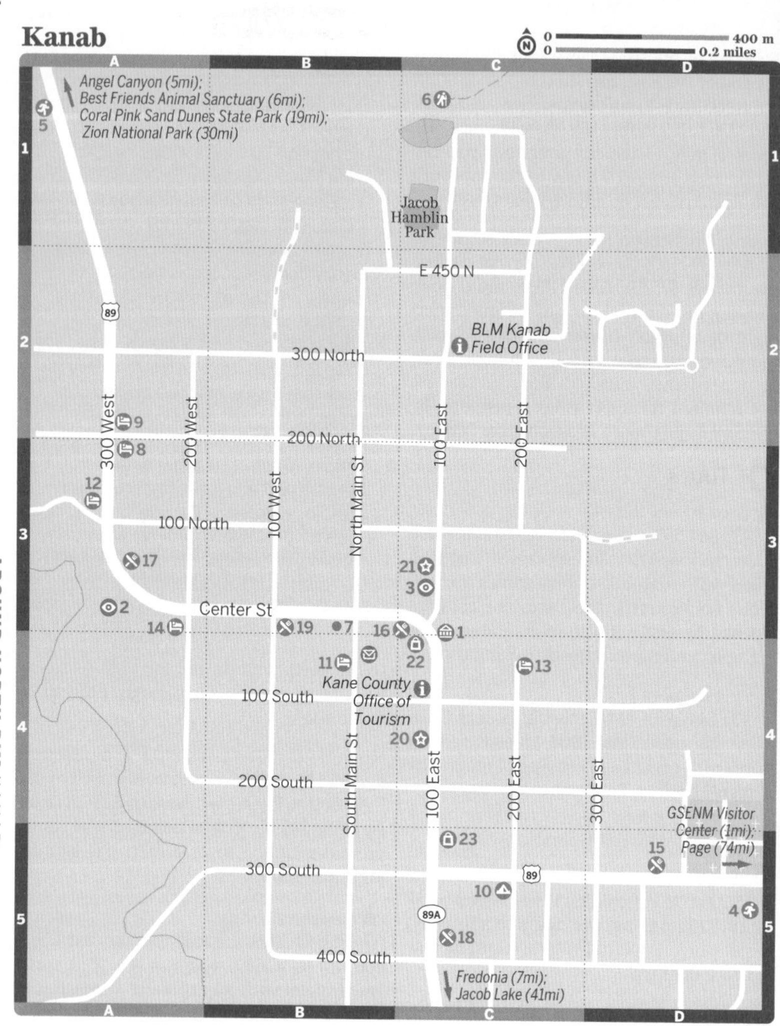

Canyons Boutique Hotel BOUTIQUE HOTEL **$$**
(☎435-644-8660; www.canyonshotel.com; 190 N 300 W; r/ste from $159/239;) From the architecture to appointments, this inn is a modern-day remake of period Victoriana. Ethan Allen furnishings, gas fireplaces and jetted tubs grace every room, but it all looks a little stiff in these parts. Look for the on-site restaurant.

Quail Park Lodge MOTEL **$$**
(☎435-215-1447; www.quailparklodge.com; 125 N 300 W; r from $149;) With Schwinn cruiser bicycles and a postage-stamp-size pool, retro pervades all 13 rooms at this refurbished 1963 motel with surprisingly plush rooms. Mod cons include free phone calls, microwaves, minirefrigerators and complimentary gourmet coffee.

Savage Point B&B B&B **$$**
(☎435-644-2799; www.savagepointbedbreakfast.com; 53 S 200 E; ste $125;) Bunk at a cozy home filled with winsome pets and hosts. Laurel and Russell, a guide and ranger, are helpful with hiking tips. Guests have a separate entrance. There's a Finnish sauna and cold pool in the garden area, pick-your-own fruit and fresh farm eggs for breakfast.

Kanab

Sights
1 Kanab Heritage Museum.......C3
2 Little Hollywood Land Museum.......A3
3 Parry Lodge.......C3

Activities, Courses & Tours
4 Allen's Outfitters.......D5
5 Grand Canyon Expeditions.......A1
6 Squaw Trail.......C1
7 Terry's Camera.......B3

Sleeping
8 Canyons Boutique Hotel.......A3
9 Canyons Lodge.......A2
10 Hitch'n Post Campground.......C5
Parry Lodge.......(see 3)
11 Purple Sage Inn.......B4
12 Quail Park Lodge.......A3
13 Savage Point B&B.......C4
14 The Flagstone Boutique Inn & Suites.......A3

Eating
15 Escobar's.......D5
16 Houston's Trail's End Restaurant.......C3
17 Kanab Creek Bakery.......A3
18 Luo's Cafe.......C5
Peekaboo Kitchen.......(see 14)
19 Rocking V Cafe.......B3
Sego Restaurant.......(see 8)

Entertainment
20 Crescent Moon Theater.......C4
21 Old Barn Playhouse.......C3

Shopping
22 Denny's Wigwam.......C4
23 Willow Canyon Outdoor Co.......C5

The Flagstone Boutique Inn & Suites MOTEL $$
(435-644-2020; www.theflagstoneinn.com; 223 W Center St; r from $159;) A fully refurbished upscale motel. All rooms have full kitchens and accessories to enjoy a cup of coffee. Forget your idea of dusty old motels: there are king beds, flat-screen TVs and sleek style here.

Eating

An oasis in a food desert, Kanab's dining scene offers impressive creativity for such a tiny town.

★**Kanab Creek Bakery** BAKERY $
(435-644-5689; www.kanabcreekbakery.com; 238 W Center St; mains $6-16; 6:30am-5pm Tue-Sun) For fancy-pants pastries and gourmet breakfasts, this is your first (and only) stop. Croissants, *boules* (tiny pieces of chocolate-covered truffle), baguettes and rye bread are baked daily. Try the Jerusalem *shakshuka*, a cast-iron skillet of eggs in a rich pepper sauce. For lunch there's roast chicken and paella baked in the wood-fired oven.

Escobar's MEXICAN $
(435-644-3739; 373 E 300 S; mains $7-14; 11am-9:30pm Sun-Fri) Sometimes it feels like all of Kanab is stuffed into this busy, family-run restaurant with swift service and XL portions. Start with the complimentary homemade chips and salsa then move on to a green chili burrito and a chilled mug of beer.

Peekaboo Kitchen CAFE $
(435-689-1959; www.peekabookitchen.com; 233 W Center St; mains $10-18; 7am-2:30pm Tue-Sun, 5-9pm Tue-Sat;) A godsend to green diets, this cafe goes big on vegetarian and vegan dishes, salads and beet chips. The artisan pizzas are pretty good too. Breakfast options include lattes, eggs Benedict served in artichokes, and pumpkin flapjacks. If you are bone-tired, it can also deliver.

Luo's Cafe CHINESE $
(435-644-5592; www.luoscafechinese.com; 365 S 100 E; mains $6-18; 11am-10pm Mon-Sat;) For a change. Surprisingly good Chinese food; great vegetable selection.

★**Sego Restaurant** MODERN AMERICAN $$
(435-644-5680; www.segokanab.com; 190 N 300 W; mains $14-26; 6-10pm Mon-Sat) If Kanab is aspiring to be the next Sedona, this boutique hotel-restaurant will fast-track things. Gorgeous eats range from foraged mushrooms with goat cheese to noodles with red-crab curry and a decadent flourless torte for dessert. There are also craft cocktails and local beers. Hours may be expanding. Reserve ahead: there are few tables.

Houston's Trail's End Restaurant AMERICAN $$
(435-644-2488; www.houstons.net; 32 E Center St; breakfast $5-16, mains $9-26; 11am-9pm Mon-Thu, from 7am Fri & Sat) Join the locals for chicken-fried steak and razzleberry pie – you know the food must be good if they'll frequent a place where the waiters wear cowboy boots and toy six-shooters. No alcohol.

Rocking V Cafe AMERICAN $$$
(☎435-644-8001; www.rockingvcafe.com; 97 W Center St; lunch $8-18, dinner $18-48; ⏰11:30am-10pm Thu-Mon; ✍) Fresh ingredients star in dishes like hand-cut buffalo tenderloin and chargrilled zucchini with curried quinoa. Local artwork decorating the 1892 brick storefront is as creative as the food. Off-season hours vary.

Entertainment

Crescent Moon Theater THEATER
(☎435-644-2350; www.crescentmoonkanab.com; 150 S 100 E; ⏰May-Sep) Screens movies from Wednesday to Saturday.

Old Barn Playhouse THEATER
(☎435-644-2601; www.parrylodge.com/old-barn-theater; 89 E Center St; ⏰shows 8pm Sat Jun-Aug) During summer, Parry Lodge shows free classic Western films nightly at 8pm in the barn behind the lodge. Seating ranges from overstuffed to folding wood, and the popcorn and ice cream are cheap. Movies open with two short films about the Western film industry and Kanab history.

Shopping

Western clothing and bric-a-brac are sold, along with Native American knickknacks, at shops all along Center St.

Willow Canyon Outdoor Co SPORTS & OUTDOORS
(☎435-644-8884; www.willowcanyon.com; 263 S 100 E; ⏰7:30am-8pm) It's easy to spend hours sipping espresso and perusing the eclectic books here. Before you leave, outfit yourself with field guides, camping gear, US Geological Survey maps, hiking clothes and gas for your camp stove. Off-season hours vary.

Denny's Wigwam GIFTS & SOUVENIRS
(☎435-644-2452; www.dennyswigwam.com; 78 E Center St; ⏰9am-7pm) For all kinds of cowboy gear, as well as Native American pottery, jewelry and rugs. Dress up in old-fashioned duds and get your photo taken, or pick up anything from a John Wayne mug and toilet paper to rhinestone flip-flops – this is the place for touristy shopping.

Information

Kanab has several grocery stores, ATMs, banks and services.

BLM Kanab Field Office (☎435-644-1200; www.blm.gov/office/kanab-field-office; 318 N 1 E; ⏰8am-4:30pm)

GSENM Visitor Center (☎435-644-1300; www.blm.gov/visit/kanab-visitor-center; 745 E Hwy 89, Kanab; ⏰8am-4:30pm)

Kanab City Library (☎435-644-2394; www.kanablibrary.org; 374 N Main St; ⏰10am-5pm Mon & Fri, to 7pm Tue-Thu, to 2pm Sat; 📶) Free internet and wi-fi access.

Kane County Hospital (☎435-644-5811, emergency 911; www.kchosp.net; 355 N Main St; ⏰24hr)

Kane County Office of Tourism (☎435-644-5033; www.visitsouthernutah.com; 78 S 100 E; ⏰8am-8pm Mon-Fri, 9am-6pm Sat & Sun)

Police Station (☎435-644-5854; 140 E 100 S)

Post Office (☎435-644-2760; 39 S Main St; ⏰9am-4pm Mon-Fri, to 1pm Sat)

Zion Pharmacy (☎435-644-2693; www.zionpharmacyut.com; 14 E Center St; ⏰9am-7pm Mon-Fri, to 2pm Sat)

Getting There & Around

There is no public transportation to or around Kanab.

AIR

The closest airline hubs are Las Vegas (four hours southwest) and Salt Lake City (five hours north). Flagstaff, 200 miles and almost four hours south, offers limited airline service to Phoenix.

CAR

Kanab is about a 2½-hour drive northwest of the North Rim. The only car-rental place in town is **Xpress Rent-a-Car** (☎435-644-3408; www.xpressrentalcarofkanab.com; 1530 S Hwy 89A).

Ramsey Towing and Service Garage (☎435-644-2468; www.ramsaytowandservice.com; 115 S 100 E; ⏰8am-5:30pm Mon-Fri, to 4pm Sat) offers a full-service garage with 24-hour towing service.

Southern Utah, Marble Canyon & Vermillion Cliffs

The interior of the oval formed by Hwy 89 and Alt 89, and the surrounding area, comprises the Paria Canyon–Vermilion Cliffs Wilderness, Vermilion Cliffs National Monument, the southern section of the 1.9-million-acre Grand Staircase–Escalante National Monument, the southeast corner of Glen Canyon National Recreation Area, the Navajo Indian Reservation and the northern tip of the Kaibab National Forest.

For the traveler, however, these are arbitrary distinctions. Whenever you peer out of your car window, it's all simply desert. Dry, windy, seemingly endless desert. This is a lonely, desperate kind of wilderness that lures photographers and hikers with its brilliant red and chalky-white buttes, slot canyons and multihued rock formations. While dirt roads may tempt drivers into exploring, the roads are sandy and unpredictable; with a little bit of rain, they can become impassable within minutes and slot canyons can fill with torrents of water that wash away or kill anything or anyone in their path. Do not depend on GPS navigation beyond Hwy 89 and Alt 89, as it tracks roads that are, at best, rough 4WD trails and tragically miscalculates driving times.

Between the tourist hubs of Kanab and Page, there's mile after mile after mile of emptiness. Alt 89 (Hwy 89A), the southern stretch of the oval, winds up from Lees Ferry and Marble Canyon several thousand feet and about 45 miles to Hwy 67 at Jacob Lake, 44 miles north of the North Rim, and then loops back down and north to Kanab. From Kanab, Hwy 89 passes several scenic drives, hiking trails and two visitor centers on the 74-mile stretch to Page.

Along Highway 89 from Kanab to Page

☎435 / ELEVATION 3100FT TO 6500FT

Sights & Activities

Big Water Visitor Center has a small dinosaur museum 16 miles northwest of Page, with displays on the extensive paleontology research in the area. Check out the tray of what looks like black stones – they're 200-million-year-old sharks' teeth, all found in the area.

Paria Townsite & Movie Set FILM LOCATION

(Pahreah) The movie set at Paria (pa-*ree*-uh), where many Westerns were filmed, burnt down during the 2007 Western Legends Roundup. A 5-mile dirt road leads to a picnic area and an interpretive sign that shows what the set used to look like.

Hike 1.5 miles further north to see the rudimentary remnants of Paria (aka Pahreah) ghost town and cemetery on the other side of the Paria River. Floods in the 1880s rang the death knell for the 130-strong farming community.

To get here, head 35 miles east of Kanab on Hwy 89 to the signed 5-mile dirt road (passable with a 2WD when dry).

The Toadstools LANDMARK

(Hwy 89A) This wander gives passersby a taste of the harsh Utah desert and cool rocks. The thin sand trail meanders through the scrub-brush, desert boulders and hoodoos about 1 mile to the first toadstool, a sandstone rock in the form of, you guessed it, a toadstool. Slanting, late-afternoon light is best for catching the shape and depth of the eerie features. The unmarked trailhead sits at a small parking area 1.4 miles east of the Paria Contact Station.

Cottonwood Road SCENIC DRIVE

This washboard dirt road heads through the magnificent rocky desert landscape of Grand Staircase–Escalante National Monument and Kodachrome Basin State Park. The entrance, 3 miles west of the Paria Contact Station, heads north 49 miles to Cannonville, just outside Bryce Canyon National Park, and beyond.

Johnson Canyon SCENIC DRIVE

Johnson Canyon is a popular paved scenic drive through a corner of Grand Staircase–Eslcalante National Monument. Movies have been filmed here, and 6 miles along you can see in the distance the Western set where the longtime TV classic *Bonanza* was filmed (on private land). Turn north off Hwy 89, 9 miles east of Kanab.

Paria Outpost ADVENTURE

(☎928-691-1047; www.paria.com; Mile 21, Hwy 89, Big Water; tours from $175) Friendly, flexible and knowledgeable. Offers guided horseback rides in Grand Staircase–Escalante National Monument, as well as 4WD tours and guided hikes.

Sleeping

Paria Outpost & Outfitters B&B $

(☎928-691-1047; www.paria.com; Mile 21, Hwy 89; r from $65; ❄🐾) Paria Outpost & Outfitters has spartan B&B rooms at its kicked-back lodge and campground. Sign up for a half-day 4WD tour to area slot canyons or set up a trailhead shuttle with the staff.

Information

Paria Contact Station (☎435-644-1200; www.blm.gov/visit/paria-contact-station; Mile 21, Hwy 89; ⏲8am-4:30pm mid-Mar–mid-Nov) This seasonal information center can provide important weather and road updates and is the last place to fill up on water before your backcountry exploits. It's 44 miles east of Kanab.

Big Water Visitor Center (☎435-675-3200; www.blm.gov/visit/big-water-visitor-center; 100 Upper Revolution Way; ⏲8:30am-5pm) Near Lake Powell.

Getting There & Around

The only way to get to and around the region is by car, and you'll need a 4WD for most roads beyond the highway. Paria Outpost (p165) offers a hikers' shuttle service for the area.

Page & Glen Canyon National Recreation Area

POP 7599 / ELEVATION 4300FT

An enormous lake tucked into a landlocked swath of desert? You can guess how popular it is to play in the spangly waters of **Lake Powell**. Part of the **Glen Canyon National Recreation Area** (928-608-6200; www.nps.gov/glca; 7-day pass per vehicle $25, per pedestrian or cyclist $12), the country's second-largest artificial reservoir was created by the construction of Glen Canyon Dam in 1963.

Straddling the Utah–Arizona border, the 186-mile-long lake has 1960 miles of empty shoreline set amid striking red-rock formations, sharply cut canyons and dramatic desert scenery. Lake Powell is famous for its houseboating, which appeals to families and college students alike.

The gateway to Lake Powell is the small town of Page, which sits right next to Glen Canyon Dam in the far southwest corner of the recreation area. Page was originally built to house the scores of workers who constructed the dam. Hwy 89 (called N Lake Powell Blvd in town) forms the main strip.

Sights

For one of the best views of the Glen Canyon Dam – and the Colorado River snaking away from it – head to the overview just behind the Denny's in Page. A 940ft round-trip walk down stairs and over sandstone leads to a sheltered overlook.

★Horseshoe Bend CANYON

(Hwy 89) Calling the view at Horseshoe Bend 'dramatic' is an understatement – the overlook sits on sheer cliffs that drop 1000ft to the river below, as it carves a perfect horseshoe through the Navajo sandstone. Toddlers should be kept safely away from the edge at all times, as there are no guardrails and the rim of the canyon can be treacherous. The trailhead is south of Page off Hwy 89, just past Mile 545.

Glen Canyon Dam DAM

(928-608-6072; www.glencanyonnha.org; Hwy 89; tour adult/child 7-16yr $5/2.50; tours 8am-6pm Sun-Tue & Thu, to 5pm Fri & Sat, to 4pm Wed) At 710ft tall, Glen Canyon Dam is the nation's highest concrete arch dam (the Hoover Dam, 16ft taller, is a different kind of structure). It was constructed between 1956 and 1966. From April through October, 45-minute guided tours depart from the Carl Hayden Visitor Center (p170) and descend deep inside the dam via elevators. Exhibits tell the story of the dam's construction, complete with all kinds of astounding technical facts. Three different videos spotlight various aspects of the region.

Rainbow Bridge National Monument PARK

(928-608-6200; www.nps.gov/rabr; sunrise-sunset) Rainbow Bridge is the largest natural bridge in the world, at 290ft high and 275ft wide. A sacred Navajo site, it resembles the graceful arc of a rainbow. Most visitors arrive by boat (www.lakepowell.com, adult/child $122/77), with a 1.2-mile round-trip hike. The natural monument is located on the south shore of Lake Powell, about 50 miles by water from Wahweap Marina in Arizona.

John Wesley Powell Museum MUSEUM

(928-645-9496; www.powellmuseum.org; 6 N Lake Powell Blvd; 9am-5pm Apr-Dec, 10am-3pm Jan-Mar) FREE In 1869 one-armed John Wesley Powell led the first Colorado River expedition through the Grand Canyon. This small museum displays memorabilia of early river runners, including a model of Powell's boat, with photos and illustrations of his excursions. It also has exhibits on geology, paleontology and the history of Page, and houses the regional visitor center.

Activities

Boating & Cruises

Aramark runs five of the lake's six marinas, including the often-frenetic Wahweap Marina (p170), 6 miles northwest of Page. The only other marina on the Arizona side is the much more peaceful Antelope Point Marina, on the Navajo Reservation, 8 miles east of Page. Amenities and services vary by marina; check www.lakepowell.com for specifics.

At Wahweap and Bullfrog Marinas you can rent kayaks ($50 per day), 19ft powerboats ($550), personal watercraft ($450) and other toys. Stand-up paddleboards are available at Wahweap for $90 per day. From Wahweap Marina, Aramark runs boat cruises to Rainbow Bridge National Monument. Canyon cruises and a dinner cruise are also offered.

Houseboating is also hugely popular and, with its many coves and beaches to explore, Lake Powell is perfect for kayaking. Expect wind in the spring and monsoon rains in late July and August.

Driving

The region's most immediately gratifying, dramatic backcountry drive, **Burr Trail Rd** is a comprehensive introduction to southern Utah's geology. You pass cliffs, canyons, buttes, mesas and monoliths – in colors from sandy-white to deep coral red. Sweeping curves and steep up-and-downs add to the attraction. Just past the Deer Creek trailhead look for the towering vertical red-rock slabs of Long Canyon.

Hiking & Mountain Biking

If you only have time for one activity in the region, make sure it's the 1.5-mile round-trip hike to the overlook at Horseshoe Bend, where the river wraps around a monolithic outcropping to form a perfect U.

The 10-mile **Rimview Trail**, a mix of sand, slickrock and other terrain, circumnavigates the town and offers views of the surrounding desert and Lake Powell. A popular starting point is behind Lake View School at the end of N Navajo Dr. It's open for hiking and bicycling; pick up a brochure at the John Wesley Powell Museum.

Ask at the Carl Hayden Visitor Center (p170) at the Glen Canyon Dam for information about the area's many hiking and mountain-biking trails.

Swimming

The best place to enjoy Lake Powell's cold, clear water (short of jumping off your boat) is at the **Chains**. Look for the tiny hiking trail sign just east of the dam and turn left; from the parking lot, a short walk leads to flat, smooth sandstone that juts directly into the water.

A good option for kids is the boat launch at **Antelope Point Marina**, about 8 miles east of town on Rte 22 off Hwy 98, where you can wade into the water from the small, rocky areas.

Twelve miles northwest of Page, across the Utah border, the area around **Lone Rock** offers endless shoreline access, though there's no shade. It's worth it to drive out here for the photo opportunity alone.

Tours

Lake Powell Resorts & Marinas BOATING
(Wahweap; ☎928-645-2433; www.lakepowell.com; 100 Lakeshore Dr) Popular trips include the Rainbow Bridge cruise (adult/child $122/77, seven hours), the Canyon Adventure cruise (adult/child $75/49, three hours) and the Canyon Princess Dinner Cruise (adult/child $77/33, two hours, Tuesday and Saturday only). It also does half-day trips to Navajo Tapestry and 1½-hour rides to Antelope Canyon.

Ekis' Antelope Canyon Tours TOURS
(☎928-645-9102; www.antelopecanyon.com; 22 S Lake Powell Blvd; adult/child 5-12yr from $45/35) Bookings are required for this long-term operator, which takes parties on 90-minute tours of Antelope Canyon. The 11:30am tour, when the light is generally at its most striking, is $13 more.

Ken's Tours TOURS
(☎928-606-2168; www.lowerantelope.com; guided tour adult/child $40/20; ⏲6:30am-4:30pm early Mar-early Nov, 9am-3:30pm early Nov-early Mar) The longest-running outfitter taking tours into the Antelope Lower Canyon. Like competing agencies, Ken's offers a Photographer's Tour. Reserve online or drive to the canyon's entrance and find your way to the 'walk-ins' line (and expect to wait during peak times.) Tours leave every 20 minutes until one hour before closing. Cash only.

Sleeping

You can camp anywhere along the Lake Powell shoreline for free, as long as you have a portable toilet or toilet facilities on your boat. There are several good mom-and-pop motels along the 'Avenue of Little Motels' in downtown Page.

HOUSEBOATING ON LAKE POWELL

Lake Powell is famous for its houseboating and it's a huge attraction for families and college students alike. Though the lake hosts hundreds of houseboats daily, you can explore Lake Powell's secluded inlets, bays, coves and beaches for several days without seeing many folk at all. For details and reservations contact the recommended Antelope Point Marina, which generally has more elegant boats and more personalized service, or Aramark's Wahweap Marina (p170).

DON'T MISS

ANTELOPE CANYON

Many visitors plan trips to Page just to experience the oft-photographed **Antelope Canyon**, a surreal landscape you'll have to see to believe. It's divided into two sections, Upper and Lower. The Navajo names for both sides hint at what to expect: the Upper Canyon is *Tsé bighánílíní* ('The place where water runs through rocks') and the Lower Canyon is known as *Hasdestwazi* ('Spiral rock arches').

Managed by the Lake Powell Navajo Tribal Park, the canyon can only be visited by tour. The Upper Canyon is more accessible and appropriate for small children, while the Lower Canyon involves steep staircases and is considered more beautiful. The tours are through one of several local outfitters, such as Ken's Tours (p167) or Ekis' Antelope Canyon Tours (p167). Reservations are recommended if you'd like to secure a particular tour time (noon tours receive the best light); otherwise, walk-ins are served on a first-come, first-served basis.

Lone Rock Beach CAMPGROUND $
(www.nps.gov/glca; Utah Hwy 89; sites $14; 🐾) A strikingly beautiful natural setting on the edge of Lake Powell is the home of this sprawling first-come, first-served campground. It's a popular spot with families and college revelers alike in high season – escape to the dunes or the far edges of the lot if you're looking for quiet. It's just north of the state line, 2 miles south of Big Water.

Halls Crossing Campground CAMPGROUND $
(☎435-684-7008; www.lakepowell.com/rv-camping/halls-crossing-rv-campground; Hwy 276; tent & RV sites $47; ⏲Mar-Oct; 🐾) Offers 21 pull-through spaces (with hookups) and 41 campsites with showers, grills and restrooms. Pets must be on a leash.

Ticaboo Lodge MOTEL $
(☎435-788-2110; www.ticaboo.com; Hwy 276; r $89; ⏲May-Sep;) Inland 12 miles or so from Bullfrog Marina (p169), Ticaboo Lodge is a fine money-saving sleeping alternative with a three-meal-a-day restaurant and bar attached. The big, interior-access motel rooms all have two queen beds and are quite tidy.

Best Western View of Lake Powell Hotel HOTEL $$
(☎928-645-8868; www.bestwestern.com; 716 Rimview Dr; d from $180;) Possibly the nicest Best Western you'll stay in. Perched on the edge of a hill overlooking Glen Canyon Dam, this smartly updated chain has surprisingly modern guest rooms, a swimming pool with a spectacular view, and a complimentary breakfast buffet with a yogurt bar and make-it-yourself waffles.

Lake Powell Motel MOTEL $$
(☎480-452-9895; www.lakepowellmotel.net; 750 S Navajo Dr; ste from $99, r with kitchen from $139; ⏲Apr-Oct;) Formerly Bashful Bob's, this revamped motel was originally constructed to house Glen Canyon Dam builders. Four units have kitchens and book up quickly. A fifth smaller room is typically held for walk-ups, unless specifically requested.

Defiance House Lodge HOTEL $$
(☎435-684-3000; www.lakepowell.com/lodging/defiance-house-lodge; Hwy 276, Bullfrog Marina; r $145-169; ⏲Mar-Oct; 🐾) Modern, attractive rooms and killer views characterize this hotel sitting pretty in Glen Canyon National Recreation Area's Bullfrog Marina (p169). It has modern amenities and an in-house restaurant.

Lake Powell Resort RESORT $$$
(☎928-645-2433; www.lakepowell.com/lodging/lake-powell-resort; 100 Lakeshore Dr, Wahweap; r/ste from $199/344, child under 18yr free; 🐾) This bustling resort on the shores of Lake Powell offers beautiful views and a lovely little pool perched in the rocks above the lake, but it is impersonal and frenetic. Rates for lake-view rooms with tiny patios are well worth the extra money. In the lobby you can book boat tours. Wi-fi is available in the lobby and lounge only.

Eating & Drinking

There's some decent American food (and sushi) in town, but bringing your own provisions is necessary to fill in the gaps, particularly if you are houseboating. Most restaurants stretch along Dam Plaza, a back-to-back strip mall in the Safeway parking lot at the corner of Lake Powell Blvd and Navajo Dr. For a picnic with a lake view, pick up groceries (and coffee) at Safeway and drive to the Wahweap picnic area, just past Lake Powell Resort on the road to the marina. Fast-food options and a supermarket inside

Wal-Mart are located on Rte 89 on the way into town from the turn-off for Horseshoe Bend.

Big John's Texas BBQ BARBECUE $
(☎928-645-3300; www.bigjohnstexasbbq.com; 153 S Lake Powell Blvd; mains $13-18; ⏱11am-9pm; 👪) Cheerfully occupying a partially open-air space that was once a gas station, this barbecue joint is a friendly place to feast on pulled-pork sandwiches and ribs. Pull up a seat at one of the casual picnic tables, and look for live folk and bluegrass music several evenings of the week.

Ranch House Grille DINER $
(☎928-645-1420; www.ranchhousegrille.com/page; 819 N Navajo Dr; mains $9-14; ⏱6am-3pm) There's not much ambience but the food here is good, the portions huge and the service fast. This is your best bet for breakfast. For lunch, get a bowl of the tasty pork chile verde. To get here from the Glen Canyon Dam, turn left off of N Lake Powell Blvd onto N Navajo Dr.

Canyon Crepes Café CRÊPES $
(☎928-614-4530; www.canyoncrepescafe.com; 669 Elm St, Suite 3; crêpes & mains $8-9; ⏱8am-8pm Mon-Fri, to 4pm Sat, 9:30am-2pm Sun; 📶🌶) Creative sweet and savory crêpes, plus soups, salads and free wi-fi, in a convenient location near many of Page's tour outfitters. It's just off the breezeway in the shopping complex across from Safeway.

Slackers BURGERS $
(☎928-645-5267; www.slackersqualitygrub.com; 635 Elm St; mains $6-9; ⏱10:30am-9pm Mon-Sat Apr-Sep, shorter hrs rest of year; 👪) A chalkboard menu includes excellent burgers, subs, salads and kids' meals. Count on long lunch lines, or call to order in advance. Picnic tables offer shaded outdoor strip-mall seating.

Bonkers AMERICAN $$
(☎928-645-2706; www.bonkerspageaz.com; 810 N Navajo Dr; mains $18-23; ⏱4-10pm Tue-Sat Mar-Oct) Impressive murals of local landscapes cover the walls inside this unfortunately named restaurant – open for dinner only – that serves good steaks, seafood and pasta dishes.

Latitude 37 AMERICAN $$
(☎928-645-2433; www.lakepowell.com; 100 Lakeshore Dr, Wahweap; mains $12-25; ⏱11am-9pm Fri-Sun Jun-Oct) Lake Powell Resort's floating restaurant is only open in high season, when boaters pull straight up to table-side slips. The Southwest-inspired menu includes smoked ribs and burgers, while the vistas of Castle Rock and Navajo Mountain provide an excellent cocktail-sipping backdrop.

Blue Buddha Sushi Lounge SUSHI $$
(☎648-645-0007; www.bluebuddhasushilounge.com; 644 N Navajo Dr; sushi $8-11, mains $20-29; ⏱5-9pm Tue-Sat) Darn good sushi for the desert we say, and the food and drinks at this blue-hued, ultra-cool hideaway hit the spot after a hot and dusty day of exploring. Beyond sushi, there's teppanyaki, steak and seafood.

Rainbow Room BAR
(☎928-645-2433; www.lakepowell.com; 100 Lakeshore Dr, Wahweap; ⏱5-10am Tue-Fri, from 6am Sat-Mon, 5-9pm daily) The Rainbow Room is perched above Lake Powell, with picture windows framing dramatic red-rock formations against blue water. Your best bet is to eat elsewhere and come to the bar here for a beautiful sunset drink.

ℹ Information

The Glen Canyon National Recreation Area entrance fees, good for up to seven days, are $30 per vehicle or $15 per individual entering on foot or bicycle. Boat entry is $30.

EMERGENCY

For the National Park Service 24-Hour Dispatch Center, call 800-582-4351 or 928-608-6300.

On the water, use Marine Band Channel 16.

Police Station (☎928-645-2462, emergency 911; 808 Coppermine Rd)

MARINAS

All the marinas except Antelope Point have rangers stations, and Wahweap and Bullfrog Marinas rent boats. Check the Glen Canyon National Recreation Area newspaper for additional services at each marina.

Antelope Point (☎928-645-5900; www.antelopepointlakepowell.com; 537 Marina Pkwy) Peaceful Navajo-owned marina, 8 miles northeast of Page.

Bullfrog Marina (☎435-684-3000; www.lakepowell.com; Hwy 276; 3-day houseboat rentals from $1896; ⏱9am-4pm Mar-Oct; 🐾) Rents out boats: 19ft runabouts and personal watercraft by the day, but houseboats are its big business. You can rent a 46ft boat that sleeps 12 for a minimum of three days; weekly rates are cheaper. There are also luxury options. Invest in the waterproof *Lake Powell Photomap* so you can pilot your craft to some great canyon hikes.

Dangling Rope (928-691-0206; www.lakepowellmarinas.com; 8am-6pm) Smallest marina, accessible only by boat. Forty lake-miles from Page.

Halls Crossing Marina (435-684-7000; www.lakepowellmarinas.com; Hwy 276; 8am-5pm Mar-Oct, 9am-4pm Nov-Feb;) The Halls Crossing marina has a store, boat launch, campground and a great playground for kids.

Wahweap Marina (928-645-1027; www.lakepowellmarinas.com) A frenetic place with shops, food, fuel, lodging and campgrounds. Offers boat and water-sport rentals, as well as tours. It's located 6 miles northwest of Page.

MEDICAL SERVICES

Page Hospital (928-645-2424, emergency 911; www.bannerhealth.com; 501 N Navajo Dr) Has 24-hour emergency services.

Pharmacy (928-645-5714; 650 Elm St, Safeway; 9am-8pm Mon-Fri, to 6pm Sat, 10am-4pm Sun) Inside the Safeway.

POST

Post Office (928-353-4821; 101 W Glenn St; 8am-4pm Mon-Sat)

TOURIST INFORMATION

For regional information, stop by the John Wesley Powell Museum (p166). In addition to the **Carl Hayden Visitor Center** (store 928-608-6068, tours 928-608-6072; www.nps.gov/glca; Hwy 89; 8am-6pm mid-May–mid-Sep, shorter hrs rest of yr), there is a third GCNRA Visitor Center 39 miles southwest of Page at Navajo Bridge in Marble Canyon.

You can also find information at the Big Water Visitor Center (p165) near Lake Powell.

Bullfrog Visitor Center (435-684-7423; www.nps.gov/glca; Hwy 276; 9am-5pm May-Aug) offers great general information.

USEFUL WEBSITES

Glen Canyon National Recreation Area (www.nps.gov/glca) Official website.

Lake Powell Resorts & Marinas (www.lakepowell.com) Marina lodging, boat rentals and boat tours for GCNRA.

Page Information Center (www.visitpagelakepowell.com)

Wayne's Words (www.wayneswords.com) Information on fishing in Lake Powell.

Getting There & Away

There is no longer commercial airline service to **Page Municipal Airport** (928-645-4240; www.cityofpage.org/departments/airport; 238 N 10th Ave), however, car rental is still available at the airport through **Avis** (928-645-2024; www.avis.com; 238 N 10th Ave, Page Municipal Airport; 8am-5:30pm Mon-Sat).

Getting Around

Halls Crossing Ferry (435-893-4747; www.udot.utah.gov; Hwy 276; vehicles/walk-on $25/10; 8am-7pm May-Sep) Connects to Bullfrog Marina (p169) by 30-minute ferry.

Along Highway 89A: Marble Canyon & Lees Ferry

About 14 miles past the Hwy 89/89A fork, Hwy 89A crosses the Navajo Bridge over the Colorado River at Marble Canyon. Actually, there are two bridges: one built in 1995 and a historical one from 1929. Walking across the latter, you'll enjoy fabulous views down Marble Canyon to the northeast lip of the Grand Canyon. The Navajo Bridge Interpretive Center on the west bank has info about the bridges, as well as the area's natural wonders. Keep an eye out for California condors!

Just past the bridge, a stunning 6-mile drive leads to the fly-fishing mecca of Lees Ferry. Sitting on a sweeping bend of the Colorado River, it's in the far southwestern corner of Glen Canyon National Recreation Area and a premier put-in spot for Grand Canyon rafters. Fishing here requires an Arizona fishing license, available at local fly shops and outfitters such as Marble Canyon Lodge (p172).

Sights

Historic Lees Ferry & Lonely Dell Ranch HISTORIC SITE

(928-608-6200; www.nps.gov/glca/planyourvisit/lees-ferry.htm; Glen Canyon National Recreation Area; 7-day Glen Canyon Pass per vehicle/motorcycle/person $30/25/15) Lees Ferry was the site of the region's original ferry crossing, and of Charles Spencer's 1910 effort to extract gold from the surrounding hills. Today it's the launching area for rafting trips down the Colorado through the Grand Canyon. Nearby, Lonely Dell Ranch provided for families who worked at the crossing in the 1880s and '90s. Their log cabins and a pioneer cemetery remain, as well as an idyllic orchard where visitors are welcome to pick (and eat) the fruit.

Navajo Bridge Interpretive Center MUSEUM

(928-355-2319; www.nps.gov/glca; Hwy 89A; 9am-5pm Apr-Oct; P) This center on the west bank of the Colorado River has good background information on the region and the bridge. Look up – California condors are often spotted overhead – and look

WORTH A TRIP

HOPI & NAVAJO RESERVATIONS

Many folk zoom past the Hopi and Navajo Reservations, registering them as nothing more than vast desert expanses and a few lonely souvenir huts standing windblown along the road between the North and South Rims. But for those with the time and a willingness to explore the unpolished reality of the American West, a side tour to this desolate area east of the Grand Canyon can be a highlight. Scenic rim drives offer breathtaking beauty, and you can explore the interior on guided hikes or horseback rides.

The surreal red-rock formations of **Monument Valley**, featured in hundreds of movies, advertisements, calendars and magazines, emerge magically from the flat and drab landscape 154 miles from Desert View and 246 miles from the North Rim.

Lying 208 miles east of Desert View on the New Mexico border, **Canyon de Chelly**, a many-figured canyon dotted with ancestral Puebloan ruins and etched with **pictographs**, strikes even the most jaded traveler as hauntingly memorable. Navajo families winter on the rims and move to traditional hogans (one-room structures traditionally built of earth, logs, stone and other materials, with the entrance facing east) on farms on the canyon floor in spring and summer.

The private and isolated Hopi communities of **First**, **Second** and **Third Mesas**, about two hours from Grand Canyon's Desert View, consist of 12 traditional villages perched atop 7200ft mesas. At the end of First Mesa is the tiny village of **Walpi**, the most dramatic of the Hopi enclaves; Hopi guides offer 45-minute walking tours. The **Hopi Cultural Center**, on Second Mesa, has a small museum, and artisans sell woven baskets, kachina dolls and other crafts from roadside booths. On Third Mesa, **Old Oraibi** rivals Taos, New Mexico, and Acoma, New Mexico, as the oldest continuously inhabited village on the continent. Kachina dances are often open to the public, and tribe members sometimes personally invite visitors to other ceremonies. An invitation is an honor; be sure to respect local customs.

The Hopi strictly prohibit alcohol, as well as any form of recording, including sketching. Each of these spots has one or two motels, and there are a handful of chain motels in Kayenta, 24 miles south of Monument Valley.

down, too, to possibly catch a view of rafting groups who've recently left nearby Lees Ferry on the start of their river journey through the Grand Canyon.

Activities

The calm waters of the Colorado River, deep in a canyon between the Glen Canyon Dam and Lees Ferry, offer excellent and world-renowned nymph fly-fishing thanks to regular (and controversial) stocking.

Marble Canyon Outfitters FISHING
(☎928-645-2781; www.leesferryflyfishing.com; Hwy 89A, Marble Canyon Lodge; guided fly-fishing per day from $250) This outfit takes anglers fly-fishing on the broad shallows of the Colorado River at Lees Ferry via boat, or wading in the shallows.

Lees Ferry Anglers FISHING
(☎928-355-2261; www.leesferry.com/lees-ferry-anglers; Hwy 89A, Marble Canyon, Cliff Dwellers Lodge; guided fly-fishing per day from $425; ⏲6am-9pm) For nymph fly-fishing along the Colorado River, call Lees Ferry Anglers for current conditions and to arrange a guided trip.

Sleeping & Eating

A campground and three lodges are the extent of your options. The lodges in the area have restaurants.

Lees Ferry Campground CAMPGROUND $
(☎928-608-6200; www.nps.gov/glca; Lees Ferry, Glen Canyon National Recreation Area; tent & RV sites $20) On a small hill, Lees Ferry Campground has 54 river-view sites along with drinking water and toilets, but no hookups. With views of towering red rocks and the river, it's a strikingly pretty spot to camp. Public coin showers and a laundry are available at Marble Canyon Lodge.

Cliff Dwellers Lodge & Restaurant LODGE $
(☎928-355-2261; www.cliffdwellerslodge.com; Hwy 89A, Marble Canyon; d/house from $80/250; ⏲6am-9pm; 📶) This roadside lodge, charmingly set at the base of enormous cliffs 10 miles west of Navajo Bridge, is ground zero

for fly-fishing enthusiasts and popular for its excellent restaurant with breezy porch seating. Opt for a room with knotty pine walls and a recently remodeled bathroom. The owners run on-site Lees Ferry Anglers (p171): ask about guided trips and local hikes.

Lees Ferry Lodge LODGE $
(928-355-2231; www.vermilioncliffs.com; Hwy 89A, Vermilion Cliffs; r/apt $74/125; P ❄ 🐾) Rustic, comfortable, but not actually in Lees Ferry (it's 3 miles west of Marble Canyon), this lodge has 10 rooms, plus a restaurant-bar with a huge array of international beers. The bar is the kind where you're never quite sure who's going to roar off the highway and stomp through the door – but they'll surely have an interesting story.

Marble Canyon Lodge LODGE $
(928-355-2225; www.marblecanyoncompany.com; Hwy 89, Marble Canyon; s/d/apt $79/89/180; P 🐾) The closest accommodations to Navajo Bridge (and nearby Lees Ferry) are at this friendly lodge, with 60 rooms, eight suites and apartments for up to six people. There's also a mini-market, where you can buy a fishing permit, and a basic restaurant.

Information

A post office, laundromat and pay showers are next to the gas station just west of Navajo Bridge. Don't be surprised if you can't get a cell-phone signal here – there's a wi-fi hot spot by Marble Canyon Lodge, but it wasn't working when we visited.

Getting There & Away

Marble Canyon and Lees Ferry are a 1½-hour drive northeast from the North Rim and an hour's drive southwest of Page.

Hwy 89A is the only way in, short of a helicopter or a raft on the Colorado.

House Rock Valley Road (Paria Canyon & Vermilion Cliffs National Monument)

With miles of weathered, swirling slickrock and slot-canyon systems that can be hiked for days without seeing a soul, it's no wonder that this wilderness area is such a popular destination for hearty trekkers, canyoneers and photographers. Day-hike permits cost $5 to $7 and several are very tough to get. Remember that summer is scorching; spring and fall are best – and busiest. Beware of flash floods.

Trailheads lie along House Rock Valley Rd 4.7 miles west of the Paria Contact Station (p165); it's a dirt road that may require 4WD. Inquire with rangers.

Sights & Activities

One of the Southwest's most famous geologic sights – **the Wave**, an ancient, natural rock formation - is hidden away in a protected area of the Coyote Buttes North section of the Paria Canyon-Vermilion Cliffs Wilderness Area.

As an alternative, do the 3.4-mile round-trip Wire Pass to Buckskin Gulch Hike, a popular slot-canyon day hike with self-service trailhead permits. The pass dead-ends where Buckskin Gulch narrows into some thrillingly narrow slots. Die-hard hikers may wish to continue on the Buckskin Gulch to White House Hike, a remote and beautiful 16-mile backpack through the canyon.

Coyote Buttes North HIKING
(435-688-3200; www.blm.gov/programs/recreation/permits-and-passes/lotteries-and-permit-systems/arizona/coyote-buttes; Hwy 89A, Paria Canyon-Vermilion Cliffs Wilderness Area; permit $7) The Coyote Buttes are regarded as one of the most beautiful and unique geologic environments in the US. It follows that the most coveted of hiking permits are the 20 issued per day by lottery, granting access to the trail-less expanse of slickrock leading to a spectacular natural formation known as **The Wave.** Directions are only given to the lottery winners, who embark on a magical 6.5-mile, five-hour round-trip hike within the Coyote Buttes North section of the park, among swirling, striped slickrock.

Coyote Buttes South HIKING
(www.blm.gov/programs/recreation/permits-and-passes/lotteries-and-permit-systems/arizona/coyote-buttes; Hwy 89A, Paria Canyon-Vermilion Cliffs Wilderness Area; permit $5) If you want to see related slickrock formations but are finding it hard to get a permit for Coyote Buttes North, an alternative is to explore Coyote Buttes South. Permits are in less demand and can be obtained online between four months and one day in advance at https://www.blm.gov/az/paria/index.cfm?usearea=CB.

Wire Pass to Buckskin Gulch Hike

HIKING

(www.blm.gov/visit/search-details/16450/2; day permit $6) Wire Pass (3.4-mile round-trip) is a great slot-canyon day hike within the Paria Canyon-Vermilion Cliffs Wilderness Area. Descend a sandy wash to where the gorge becomes a slot canyon, shoulder-width in places. You'll scramble down a few boulder-choked sections, and under logs jammed 50ft overhead, before reaching a wide alcove with what was likely an ancient granary ledge; look for the petroglyph panel on the far end.

Buckskin Gulch to White House Hike

HIKING

(www.blm.gov/visit/buckskin-gulch; day permit $6) This 16-mile backpack within the Paria Canyon-Vermilion Cliffs Wilderness Area starts at the Buckskin Gulch trailhead and ends at White House trailhead. It travels through one of the longest continuous slot canyons on the planet. Those overnighting must obtain a backcountry permit online in advance or from the BLM Kanab Field Office (p164).

Condor Release Site at Vermilion Cliffs

BIRDWATCHING

(www.blm.gov/az; Hwy 89A) The largest population of wild California condors anywhere calls these spectacular cliffs home, giving you your best shot at catching a glimpse of these massive birds. Coming from Vermilion Cliffs or Navajo Bridge, the site is located on Hwy 89A, on the way to Jacob Lake. Turn right on House Rock Rd – the release site is located two miles north.

Sleeping & Eating

There are campsites and a few lodges. In the backcountry, use of human-waste carryout bags is required; the Paria contact station (p165) provides them for free.

Bring your own provisions to the park. Water can be refilled at contact station.

Stateline Campground

CAMPGROUND

(House Rock Valley Rd, Kanab) FREE On the Utah/Arizona state line, this attractive, small campground is the most central for Wire Pass or North Coyote Buttes. Its four spots are first-come, first-served, with picnic tables, fire pits and pit toilets. It's 1 mile south of the Wire Pass trailhead, 9.3 miles south of Hwy 89. The clay road can be impassable when wet.

White House Campground

CAMPGROUND $

(☎435-644-4600; www.blm.gov/visit/search-details/256924/1; off Hwy 89, Paria Contact Station; tent sites $5) This primitive campground along the Paria River is frequently used as the endpoint of a Buckskin Gulch trip or the beginning of a Paria Canyon trip. The five walk-in sites have pit toilets, but no water and few trees. It's 2 miles down a dirt road behind the contact station (p165), at the White House trailhead.

Information

In-season info and permits are picked up at Paria Contact Station (p165), 44 miles east of Kanab. Rangers at the BLM Kanab Field Office (p164) are in charge of permits from November 16 through March 14.

Getting There & Around

A 4WD vehicle is preferable for accessing many trails and necessary for more remote adventures. Expect washboard surfaces, washed-out roadbeds, deep wallows of sand, and mud. Don't attempt clay surface roads when the rain turns them into a quagmire, and never attempt to cross a flash flood – it may look only a few inches deep, but that's assuming the road surface is still where it's supposed to be.

HOUSEROCK VALLEY ROAD

Providing access to a few key sights in Vermilion Cliffs National Monument, the beautiful – if bone-jarringly washboarded – drive along Houserock Road passes through piñon and juniper, hugs brilliant red sandstone cliffs and offers an excellent opportunity to get off the main drag.

Ten miles south of Hwy 89, at the Utah–Arizona state line, the road changes from Utah County Rd 700 to BLM Rd 1065. Here you will find State Line Campground and a bathroom. The road passes a condor-release site 2.9 miles before connecting with Alt 89. Look for Houserock Rd about 40 miles east of Kanab.

Colorado River

Includes ➡

Best Hikes

- ➡ Tapeats Creek to Thunder Spring (p182)
- ➡ Deer Creek (p182)
- ➡ Matkatamiba (p183)
- ➡ Elves Chasm (p182)
- ➡ Beaver Falls (p184)

Best Rafting Companies

- ➡ Arizona Raft Adventures (p179)
- ➡ OARS (p179)
- ➡ Canyon Explorations/ Expeditions (p179)
- ➡ Outdoors Unlimited (p179)
- ➡ Hatch River Expeditions (p179)

Why Go?

As one park ranger recently said, 'rafting the Colorado is absolute bliss punctuated by moments of pure terror'. Indeed, a journey down the river is a once-in-a-lifetime experience – a virtual all-access pass to the Grand Canyon, in all its wildness, peace and ancient, mighty glory. There's the rush of running world-class rapids with spectacular canyon walls towering above, and the peace of floating down sections of smooth water. Rafters have the exclusive privilege of hiking to beautiful side canyons, hidden waterfalls, petroglyphs and ruins. As you fall asleep on a sandy beach under the stars, you'll feel connected to the people who lived here long before – and inspired by the tales of intrepid explorers who ran the river when it was still uncharted. Here at the bottom of the Grand Canyon, the depth and beauty of the gorge will take your breath away.

Road Distances (miles)

	Colorado River (Silver Suspension Bridge)	South Rim Entrance	North Rim Entrance	Lees Ferry	Phantom Ranch
South Rim Entrance	15				
North Rim Entrance	25	205			
Lees Ferry	90	140	65		
Phantom Ranch	1	15	25	85	
Whitmore Wash	180	300	155	155	175

Note: Distances are approximate

Entrance & Exit Points

Though boats must ply the full course, rafters may join, leave or rejoin a river excursion at several points.

➡ Put in at Lees Ferry (river Mile 0), 15 miles below Glen Canyon Dam.

➡ Rafters can take out at Phantom Ranch (Mile 87.5) and hike up to the South Rim on the Bright Angel Trail.

➡ Rafters can also take out at Whitmore Wash (Mile 187.5), fly to the rim via helicopter and transfer to a plane bound for Las Vegas.

➡ The last take out points are at Diamond Creek (Mile 226), or Pearce Ferry (Mile 279.5) or South Cove (Mile 296.5), both on Lake Mead.

DON'T MISS

Despite their thrills, walloping river rapids aren't the only attraction on this ride. One of the great rewards of floating the river is the opportunity to hike to places that are difficult to access from the rim – like the ancient Puebloan granaries at Nankoweap, where you'll also discover gorgeous views of the river and inner gorge. Side canyons reveal cool, verdant grottos like Elves Chasm and swirling rock formations as in North Canyon. Set aside your pride and strap your personal flotation device (PFD) to your bum to bump down the warm, turquoise waters of the Little Colorado, a tributary sourced from mineral springs.

Be sure to stop for a cold lemonade and scribble a postcard at Phantom Ranch, your one brush with civilization. And don't miss the otherworldly blue-green waters of Havasu Creek.

When You Arrive

➡ Arrangements for river trips are usually made well in advance. By the time you arrive, you'll already have received plenty of information from your outfitter about the kind of trip you'll be taking, what to expect and what to pack.

➡ Generally speaking, travelers access the Colorado River through a commercial rafting trip that runs between three and 18 days, and runs part of the river from Lees Ferry to Diamond Creek.

➡ Boat options include large motorized rafts, oared rafts, paddle rafts and dories.

➡ Self-guided raft trips, or private river trips, are possible only with a permit that's available through a special weighted lottery.

PLANNING TIP

Plan as far ahead as possible: many commercial trips book out a year in advance. Spring and fall trips mean pleasantly milder temperatures, but bring warm and waterproof gear; read the recommended packing list. Many outfitters supply travelers with large waterproof bags.

Fast Facts

➡ River miles: 277

➡ Major rapids: 160

➡ River drop: 1900ft

➡ Phantom Ranch elevation: 2400ft

Private Trip Permits

Apply for a permit through the Grand Canyon River Permits Office (p239). Successful applicants are charged an automatic, nonrefundable $400 deposit to reserve a spot.

Resources

National Park Service (www.nps.gov/grca/planyourvisit/whitewater-rafting.htm)

Grand Canyon River podcasts (https://www.nps.gov/grca/learn/photosmultimedia/podcasts.htm)

Grand Canyon River Outfitters Association (www.gcroa.org)

Hualapai River Runners (www.grandcanyonwest.com) One-day motorized trips.

Colorado River

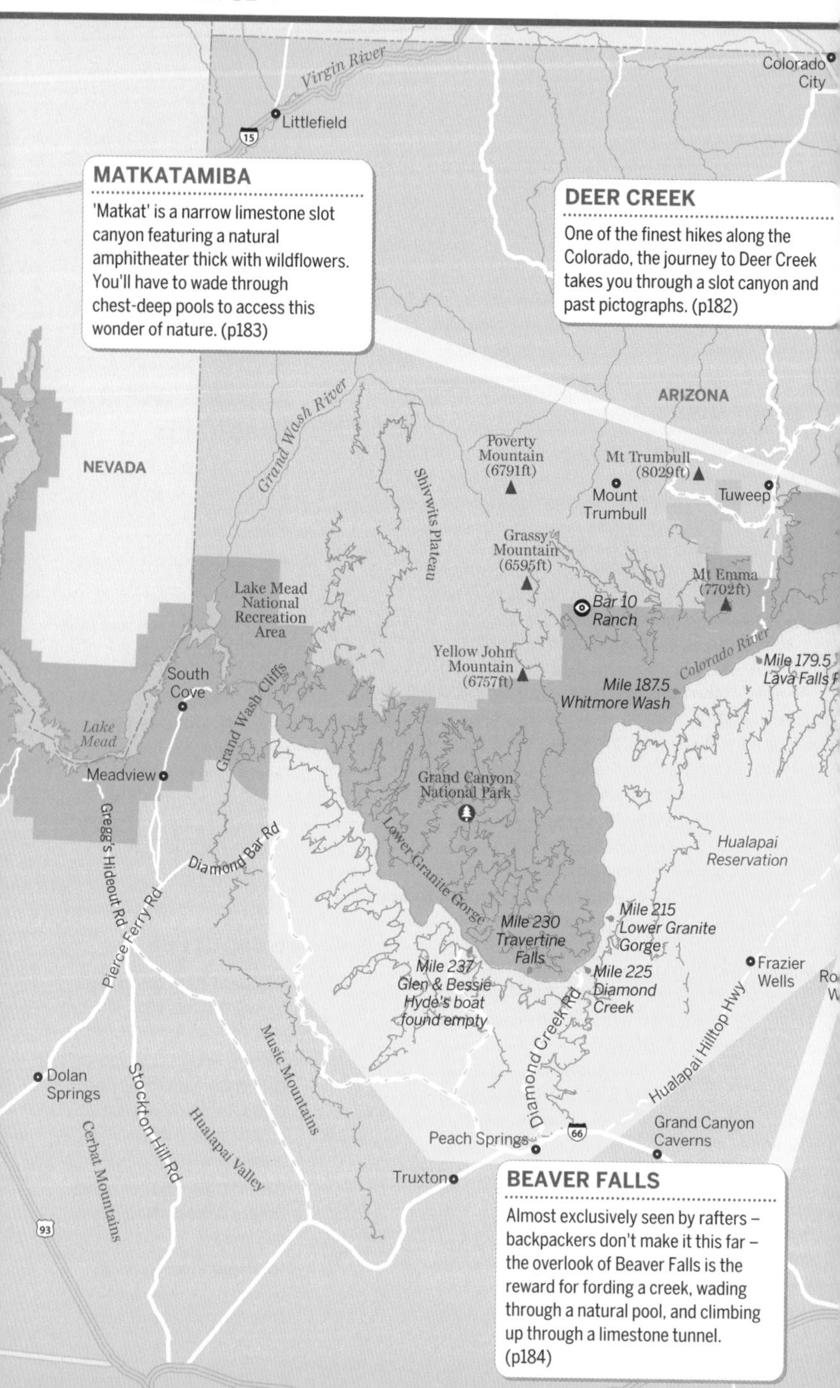

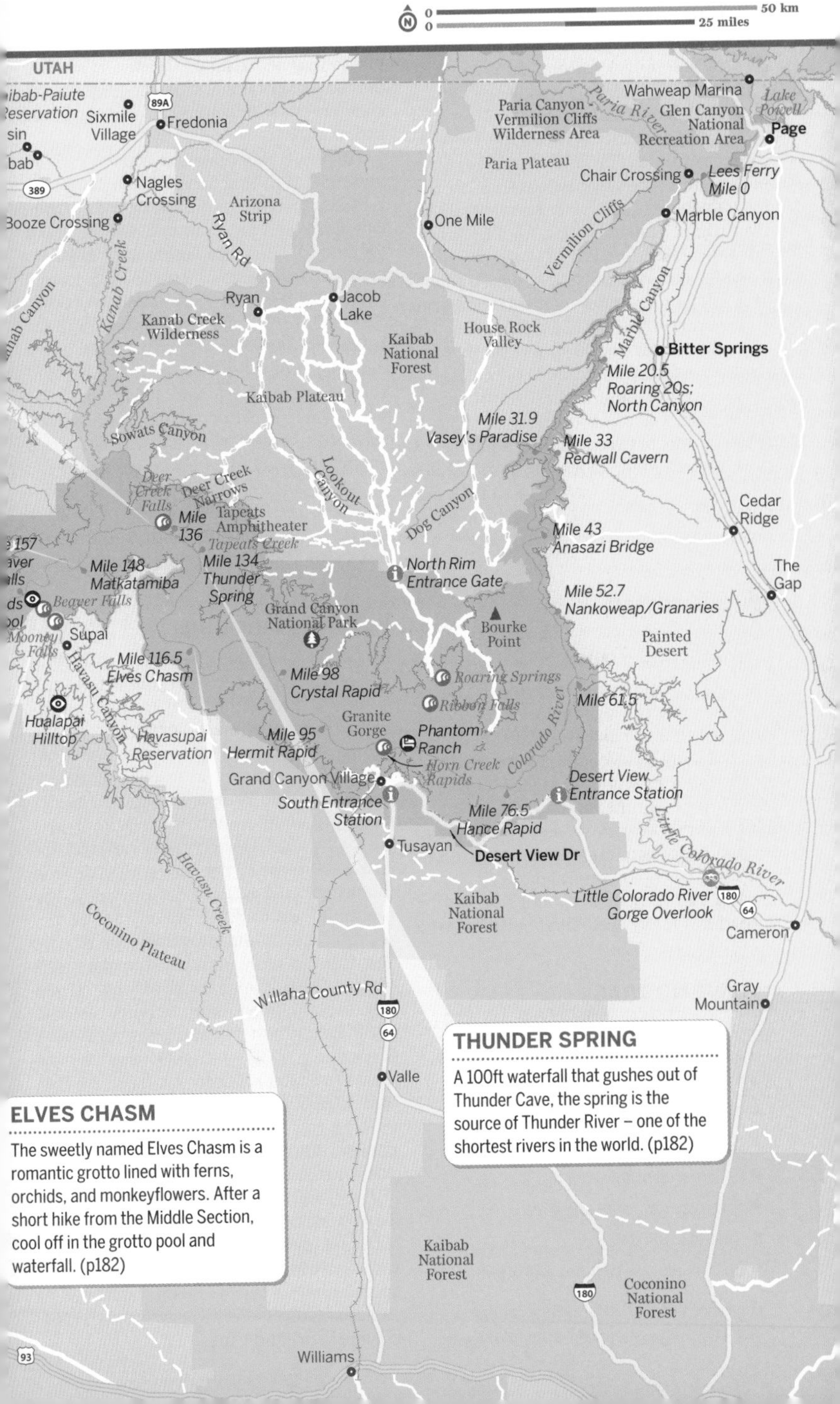

THUNDER SPRING

A 100ft waterfall that gushes out of Thunder Cave, the spring is the source of Thunder River – one of the shortest rivers in the world. (p182)

ELVES CHASM

The sweetly named Elves Chasm is a romantic grotto lined with ferns, orchids, and monkeyflowers. After a short hike from the Middle Section, cool off in the grotto pool and waterfall. (p182)

Planning

The Grand Canyon stretch of the Colorado sees 22,000 annual visitors and is run year-round, though access to some sections is limited under certain conditions. Most commercial trips operate between April and October, with June, July and August being the peak months. Park regulations stipulate that individuals may take only one recreational river trip per calendar year, whether private or commercial.

While summer draws the most traffic, it also brings more afternoon thunderstorms and searing, triple-digit temperatures. The only way to stay cool is to engage in water fights with fellow rafters and take quick dips in the face-numbing water – controlled releases from Glen Canyon Dam keep water temperatures between 48°F (9°C) and 55°F (13°C) year-round. Monsoon rains in July and August can also spawn flash floods and increased sediment that turns the water a murky reddish-brown.

RAFTING

Commercial Trips

Given two or three weeks, you can run all 277 river miles through the canyon between Lake Powell and Lake Mead. If that's more vacation than you've got, you can raft one of three shorter sections (each 100 miles or less) in four to nine days, or raft a combination of two shorter sections. Choosing to run the river via motorboat rather than raft shortens the trip by several days.

Most rafters join a commercial outing with one of many accredited outfitters who offer trips lasting from three to 21 days. Due to their popularity, tours often sell out a year in advance. However, a small percentage of cancellations do occur, so it's sometimes possible to get in on a trip at the last minute.

For those short on time, there are half- and full-day rafting trips, though not necessarily on sections within the Grand Canyon. Operating out of Diamond Creek, about four hours from the South Rim, **Hualapai River Runners** (928-769-2636, tourism office 928-769-2219; www.grandcanyonwest.com; 900 East Hwy 66, Peach Springs; 1-/2-day rafting trip $451/705; mid-Mar–Oct) offers daylong, motorized raft trips in the canyon's west end. Don't want a white-knuckle white-water experience? Wilderness River Adventures (p180) runs half-day float trips on the silky-smooth 16-mile stretch of the Colorado that flows between Glen Canyon Dam and Lees Ferry. Xanterra (p84) offers full-day trips from the South Rim that bus rafters to Page, where they connect with the float trip.

LEAVE NO TRACE

Make a minimal impact on wilderness areas by following these seven principles:

- Plan ahead and prepare.
- Travel and camp on durable surfaces.
- Dispose of waste properly.
- Leave what you find.
- Minimize campfire impacts.
- Respect wildlife.
- Be considerate of other visitors.

For more detailed information, check out www.lnt.org/learn/7-principles.

Rafting Companies

By far the most popular means of getting out on to the water is to join a tour run by one of the commercial rafting companies. There are many operators offering rafting trips, and all provide the boat, all rafting and camping gear, cooking equipment and food. Your multitalented guides wear yet another hat as chefs and prepare all meals. Oar-powered rafting trips cost $200 to $325 per day, while trips via motorboat cost $225 to $375 per day. The minimum age ranges from eight to 12, depending on the outfitter and type of trip. The trips are very popular, so make reservations six to 12 months in advance. If you feel overwhelmed with options, contact the Flagstaff-based booking agency **Rivers & Oceans** (928-440-0849; www.riversandoceans.com; 1500 E Cedar Ave, Suite 86, Flagstaff, AZ 86004; 1-/2-day rafting trip $451/795; 9am-6pm); it works with all of the companies running trips on the Colorado and doesn't charge a booking fee.

Pre- and post-trip accommodations, as well as transport to or from the trip's start/end point, may not be included in the river-trip price. Many companies offer special-interest trips for those interested in subjects as diverse as geology, botany, classical music, art and wine.

BOATS & RAFTS

➡ Most commonly used boats are 18ft neoprene rafts seating three to five passengers, with a guide rowing wooden oars. High center of gravity provides greater stability while giving the guide more power down big rapids.

➡ Dories – 17ft rigid, flat-bottomed boats – comfortably seat up to four passengers and a guide rowing a set of long wooden oars. Dory trips take one or two days longer than rafting trips.

➡ Motorized rafts are, typically, inflatable pontoons lashed together to create a 33ft craft. They seat eight to 16 passengers and two or three guides.

➡ Hard-shell kayaks are most often used on private trips, while some commercial operators provide inflatable kayaks on request.

Arizona Raft Adventures RAFTING
(☎928-526-8200; www.azraft.com; 4050 East Huntington Dr, Flagstaff, AZ 86004; 6- to 16-day raft trips $2227-4503, 8-/10-day motor trips $2840/3334) This multi-generational family-run outfit offers motor, oar and paddle (with opportunities for both paddling and floating) trips. Look online for details on photography, music, yoga and kayak 'specialty adventure' trips.

OARS RAFTING, HIKING
(☎209-736-4677; www.oars.com; 6 days from $2701, 12 days from $4948, 15 days from $5386;) One of the most respected outfitters working in the canyon, OARS boasts the best guide-to-guest ratio in the business (1:4). With inflatable rafts and dory trips, and the option of carbon offsetting your trip, OARS offers more elegance than the standard. See website for details on river running and four- to five-day rim-to-river hiking trips.

Canyon Explorations/Expeditions KAYAKING
(Map p100; ☎928-774-4559; www.canyonexplorations.com; 675 West Clay Ave, Flagstaff, AZ 86001; 7-day upper-canyon trips $2333, 14-day full-canyon trips $3985, 16-day full-canyon trips $4385; ⊙9am-4:30pm Mon-Fri) Canyon offers two styles of trip: Hybrid (involving five oar boats, one paddle boat, and two inflatable kayaks) and All Paddle (with three paddle boats and four gear rafts). It also offers a 15-day journey with the accompaniment of a string quartet led by a member of the Seattle Symphony. During the trip, the classical musicians perform in side canyons, on the beach and in camp.

Outdoors Unlimited RAFTING
(☎800-637-7238; www.outdoorsunlimited.com; 6900 Townsend Winona Rd, Flagstaff; 5-day upper-canyon oar trips from $1845, 13-day full-canyon oar trips from $4195) In business for more than four decades, Outdoors Unlimited specializes in all-paddle expeditions. As with most outfitters, some spring and fall trips stretch one or two days longer to allow more hikes and exploration along the way. To beat the crowds, ask about April and September departures.

Hatch River Expeditions RAFTING
(☎800-856-8966; www.hatchriverexpeditions.com; 5348 E Burris Lane, Flagstaff; 4-day upper-canyon motor trips $1375, 7-day full-canyon trips $3104) Repeat travelers rave about the good food and knowledgeable guides at Hatch River Expeditions, a company that's been around since 1929. For those seeking a faster trip down the river, it's a good option. In addition to partnering with Leave No Trace, Hatch is affiliated with organizations like the Whale Foundation, Girl Scouts of America and the American Cancer Society.

Arizona River Runners RAFTING
(☎602-867-4866, 800-477-7238; www.raftarizona.com; 15211 North Cave Creek Rd, Suite A, Phoenix AZ, 85032; 3-day combined ranch visit & motor trips from $1425, 13-day full-canyon oar trips from $3795) At its game since 1970, this outfit offers oar-powered and motorized trips. In addition to regular trips it has 'Hiker's Special' trips that take place over five to 15 days in the cooler temperatures of April. The company also caters to travelers with special needs, offering departures for people with disabilities.

Canyoneers RAFTING
(☎928-526-0924; www.canyoneers.com; 7195 N Hwy 89, Flagstaff, AZ 86004; 6-day upper-canyon oar trips from $2130, 7-day full-canyon motor trips from $2595; ⊙8am-5pm Mon-Fri) In operation since 1938, the family-run Canyoneers is the oldest commercial river-running outfitter in the

Grand Canyon. Choose between two options: motorized trips on pontoon rafts (convenient if you only have a few days and want to see more of the canyon) or human-powered rowing trips in inflatable rafts. Some oar-powered trips travel with the Sandra, a historic 'cataract boat' originally used in the '40s.

Grand Canyon Expeditions RAFTING
(Map p162; ☎435-644-2691, 800-544-2691; www.gcex.com; 641 N Hwy 89, Kanab, UT 84741; 8-day rafting trips $2850, 14-day dory trips $4199) Travelers rave about the gourmet meals on the river provided by Grand Canyon Expeditions, offering oar and motor trips. A popular option is the eight-day all-inclusive expedition; the outfitter also offers special trips focused on history, geology, photography and ecology. Transportation to and from Las Vegas is included (but optional) in all trips.

Colorado River & Trail Expeditions RAFTING
(☎801-261-1789; www.crateinc.com; 5058 S Commerce Dr, Salt Lake City, UT 84107; 5-day upper-canyon paddle or rowing trips $2082, 5-day motor trip $1568) Offering a range of motorized and oar-powered trips, this outfit also includes transportation to or from Las Vegas. It's a proud partner with several environmental organizations, including Leave No Trace and the Utah Society for Environmental Education.

Grand Canyon Whitewater RAFTING
(☎928-779-2979; www.grandcanyonwhitewater.com; 1000 N Humphreys St, Suite 202, Flagstaff; 6-day upper-canyon oar trips from $2200, 8-day full-canyon motor trips from $2905) The environmentally friendly Grand Canyon Whitewater offers nine trip options, including oar-powered and motorized, that run from four to 15 days. The company contributes to the Grand Canyon Fund, which supports nonprofit groups working toward conservation in the canyon.

Western River Expeditions RAFTING
(☎866-904-1160, 801-942-6669; www.westernriver.com; 7258 Racket Club Dr, Salt Lake City, UT 84212; 3-day lower-canyon trips $1435-1745, 6-/7-day upper- & middle-canyon motor trips $2750/3050) If you're starting or ending in Vegas, these three-day river trips are as convenient as it gets: the itinerary starts at the Las Vegas Marriott and includes flight out, including a helicopter ride that takes you down to the rafts.

Wilderness River Adventures RAFTING
(☎928-645-3296; www.riveradventures.com; 6-day full-canyon motor trips $2675, 12-day full-canyon oar trips $4360;) Wilderness River Adventures' hybrid trips give rafters the chance to be active and relaxed, combining hands-

PRIVATE TRIPS

The Colorado River Management Plan (CRMP) serves to protect the river and to preserve a high-quality experience for visitors, carefully regulating the number of rafts on the Colorado. There are two kinds of rafting trips on the river: the more common commercial trip, run by one of many professional river outfitters in conjunction with the National Park Service, and the less common private or non-commercial trip.

The latter, the private trip, is only available through a weighted lottery, and is usually arranged at least a year in advance. Even before you can begin working out the necessary details, from supplies to waste management to emergency options, you'll need to score a permit and at least one member of your party must have the technical rafting experience to run the Colorado. The application fee is $25. If accepted, you'll be awarded a launch date and must pay a deposit ($400 for standard trips, $200 for smaller trips.) Ninety days before the launch date, each person on the trip will pay an addition $100. All fees are non-refundable.

Visit www.nps.gov/grca/planyourvisit/weightedlottery.htm for more information on the lottery, and be sure to click over to the FAQs page.

There are no developed campsites or facilities anywhere along the Colorado. Because this is a wilderness area, where the Leave No Trace ethic applies (www.lnt.org), visitors are required to make the least impact possible by removing any waste generated and by sticking to established trails to minimize erosion. Groups on the river are self-sufficient, packing in all food and gear and packing out all waste. Rafters camp on pristine, sandy beaches, most of which are fringed with invasive (but lovely) tamarisk stands providing wisps of shade. Usually, only one group will camp on any given beach, affording everyone heaps of privacy.

on paddling one day with floating the next. Check the website: you can save hundreds of dollars on the quoted rates by choosing the 'Pay Now' option.

Tour West RAFTING
(☎801-225-0755; www.twriver.com; 3-day lower-canyon motor trips $1560, 12-day oar trips $3895) Tour West, running the river since 1969, considers its greatest asset to be its well-informed guides. Trips include transportation. In addition to camping, accommodations on the first night are included. Oar trips take out at Whitmore Wash; helicopter to rim and charter flight to Las Vegas or Marble Canyon are also included.

Orientation

The Colorado River runs 277 miles from Lees Ferry to Lake Mead, with more than 160 sets of rapids keeping things exciting. Unlike most rivers, where the rapids are rated in difficulty as Class I through V on the American white-water rating system, Colorado River rapids are rated from Class 1 through 10 (a Class 10 on the Colorado being about equal to the standard Class V; that is, a King Kong rapid). The biggest single drop (from the top to the base of the rapids) is 37ft, and nearly 20 rapids drop 15ft or more.

The Colorado is a serious river and demands respect. If you do everything your guide tells you and take responsibility for your own safety and that of others, you should have an exciting but safe trip. Be aware that the temperature of the river remains cold year-round, and hypothermia can set in quickly. Always check with your guides whether a place is far enough removed from the swift current to be safe for a dip.

Along the length of the river, the side canyons and tributaries feeding into the Colorado provide a wealth of hidden places to explore. Many of the canyon's waterfalls, slot canyons and inviting pools are difficult to reach unless you start from the river, and most can't be seen from the rim. Visits to these remote spots can be the most rewarding part of a river trek.

RAFTING ROUTES

Upper Section: Lees Ferry to Phantom Ranch

MILE 0 TO MILE 87.5

Beginning at Lees Ferry, where it cuts through the top sedimentary layer of the Moenkopi shale, the upper section of the Colorado River then passes through Marble Canyon and Granite Gorge. The walls of **Marble Canyon** rise higher and higher, quickly exposing layers of rock beneath. Once you hit Mile 20.5, you've entered the **Roaring 20s**, a series of rapids (rated up to 8) that begin with North Canyon Rapid.

At Mile 31.9 you'll see, springing forth from the wall on your right, **Vasey's Paradise**, a lush green garden nourished from the water escaping the Redwall limestone. Shortly thereafter, the wide, low mouth of the enormous **Redwall Cavern** (Mile 33) appears ahead.

Around Mile 50, the beautiful dark-green, burgundy and purple layers of Bright Angel Shale appear, as do the doorways of ancient **Puebloan granaries** (Mile 52.7) dating to AD 1100, sitting high above the water. The canyon reaches its confluence with the **Little Colorado River** at Mile 61.5.

This stretch features 28 rapids, 17 of which are rated 5 or higher. Nine rapids drop 15ft or more, including **Hance Rapid** (Mile 76.5), which boasts one of the river's largest single drops, a whopping 30ft. Near Mile 77 the appearance of pink Zoroaster granite intrusions into black Vishnu schist marks the start of **Granite Gorge**.

Side Hikes

Short hikes on the Upper Section end up in amazing little places.

North Canyon

Duration 1½ hours round-trip

Distance 2 miles round-trip

Difficulty Moderate

Start/Finish Mile 20.5, river right

Summary Hike up to a sculptural pool carved by water.

There isn't much elevation gain to this short hike, but it does entail a scramble up a wash to reach the pool. The erosion pattern above the pool has carved its sinuous curves with a design not unlike a three-dimensional topographic map or Georgia O'Keeffe painting.

Nankoweap to Granaries

Duration 1½ hours round-trip

Distance 1.5 miles round-trip

Difficulty Moderate

Start/Finish Mile 52.7, river right

Summary Steep hike that rewards the effort with an Ancestral Puebloan site and a killer view.

Though short, this steep hike takes you about 700ft above the river to the ancient Puebloan granaries built into the cliff face. The stacked-stone walls with their square openings can be seen from the river. From up on the ledge, those who aren't awed by the well-preserved archaeological site will be struck by the beautiful views downriver.

Middle Section: Phantom Ranch to Whitmore Wash

MILE 87.5 TO MILE 187.5

Rafters hike in from the South Rim to the boat beach near Phantom Ranch to raft **Middle Granite Gorge**, where Tapeats sandstone meets the Vishnu schist.

This section claims the Colorado's biggest white water, where 'Adrenaline Alley' begins with **Horn Creek Rapid** (Mile 90) and burly **Hermit Rapid** (Mile 95). It also offers the most technically challenging rapids: **Crystal Rapid** (Mile 98) and the granddaddy **Lava Falls Rapid** (Mile 179.5) with its gut-in-throat drop of 37ft. From Lava Falls Rapid, the next 80 miles downstream are a geologic marvel. Columnar basalt lines the canyon walls for thousands of vertical feet.

To leave Whitmore Wash, rafters take a helicopter to the Bar 10 Ranch (www.bar10.com), a rustic Old West–style retreat located 80 miles along a dirt road from St George, Utah.

The middle section boasts 38 rapids, 23 of which are rated 5 or higher (Crystal and Lava Falls rapids both rate 10s). Eight rapids drop between 15ft and 18ft. Operators run this stretch between May and July. Between July and September trips continue to **Diamond Creek** (Mile 226). Oar-powered rafts take seven to nine days; motorboats four to five.

Side Hikes

On the Middle Section you can float in a mossy pool or hike the world's shortest river.

Elves Chasm

Duration 20 minutes round-trip

Distance 1 mile round-trip

Difficulty Easy

Start/Finish Mile 116.5, river left

Summary Quick scramble to a pretty grotto.

Ferns, orchids and scarlet monkeyflowers drape the walls of this grotto, where a waterfall tumbles over intricate travertine formations. It takes five minutes to scramble up Royal Arch Creek from the river. Dive into the grotto's pool and swim to the base of the waterfall. Clamber up through the cave to an opening above a moss-draped rocky chute, then jump back into the pool below.

Tapeats Creek to Thunder Spring

Duration 4½ hours round-trip

Distance 5 miles round-trip

Difficulty Moderate-difficult

Start/Finish Mile 133.7, river right

Summary Hike to one of the world's shortest rivers, then connect with the Deer Creek Trail.

Thunder Spring, the roaring 100ft waterfall that gushes out of the Muav limestone at Thunder Cave, is the source of Thunder River, one of the world's shortest rivers. Over its half-mile course it plunges more than 1200ft to the confluence with Tapeats Creek.

Just before Mile 134, follow the **Thunder River Trail** upstream along cottonwood-shaded **Tapeats Creek**, crossing it twice. You'll reach the first crossing, a thigh-deep ford of rushing water, in about 45 minutes. The second crossing, an hour later, is via a fallen log.

Leaving Tapeats Creek, you'll slowly zigzag up an open slope for 30 minutes to expanding views of **Tapeats Amphitheater** and **Thunder Spring** (3400ft) – you'll hear the roar before seeing the waterfall. Enjoy a picnic in the shade at the base of the fall before retracing your steps (1400ft elevation change).

You can make this a seven-hour near-loop hike by continuing on the Thunder River Trail beyond the waterfall, traversing Surprise Valley and descending the Deer Creek Trail to the Colorado.

Deer Creek

Duration 5 hours round-trip

Distance 6 miles round-trip

Difficulty Moderate–difficult

Start/Finish Mile 136.3, river right

Summary One of the inner gorge's finest hikes, with lush waterfalls and pictographs in a curvy slot canyon.

PIONEERS OF THE COLORADO

Today, a rafting trip down the Colorado River through Grand Canyon National Park is considered a once-in-a-lifetime experience. Excellent commercial outfitters take care of all the details, but as with any adventure sport, there's risk involved – which is exactly what makes it so intriguing to consider what a similar trip might have been like for the river's earliest pioneers.

The geologist and ethnographer John Wesley Powell was one of the river's first non-native explorers, leading a small group nearly 1000 miles down the river in the summer of 1869, when Powell was just 35 years old. It's not an exaggeration to say the trip was almost disastrous – the rapids were too powerful for the group's small boats. Powell was better prepared when he returned for another river trip, this one sponsored by the Smithsonian Institution, in 1871. He wrote extensively on his observations, and his work served as the early basis for knowledge about the Grand Canyon, an area that few non-native people had seen in the late 19th century. Perhaps most eloquent were his thoughts about the ever-changing nature of the canyon's immense landscape, which, he said, couldn't be comprehended in a single glance. According to Powell, one had to experience it by wending through its maze of passageways and gullies.

Decades later, Nathaniel Galloway – today considered the father of modern whitewater rafting technique – changed the course of river running forever with the invention of his flat-bottomed upturned boat. Shallow and easier to maneuver, Galloway's boats were rowed backwards. In 1909, a financier named Julius Stone took advantage of Galloway's invention to organize the first rafting trip 'for pleasure' down the Colorado, starting in Wyoming and ending up three months later in California.

Around the same time, enterprising brothers Ellsworth and Emery Kolb were the first to film their own 101-day excursion down the river. They screened the film daily in their studio to the rapt attention of tourists.

Of course, there was tragedy, too, for the river's early runners: honeymooners Glen and Bessie Hyde vanished on the Colorado River in 1928. Bessie reportedly wanted to be the first woman to ride the river the entire way through the Grand Canyon, but she never made it: their boat was found floating upright and fully stocked the following winter, and the adventurers were never heard from again.

The ebullient Georgie White Clark took the title of first woman to row a boat through the Grand Canyon in the 1950s. And in 1955, encouraging others to share in the adventure, she began escorting tourists on 'share the expense' trips down the Colorado – making her the first professional woman outfitter, and the forerunner for the many rafting companies that run the river today.

Downstream from Granite Narrows below Mile 136, **Deer Creek Falls** tumbles into the Colorado. From this welcoming trailhead you head 500ft up a steep, bushy slope to a stunning overlook. From here the trail leads into **Deer Creek Narrows**, an impressive slot canyon where the walls bear remarkable pictographs. The narrows end in an inviting cascade. Above, lush vegetation lines the trail as it meanders along the cottonwood-shaded creek.

The trail crosses the creek and ascends open, rocky slopes to **Deer Creek Spring**, the trail's second waterfall. From here retrace your steps back to the river. Despite having to scramble up and down steep slopes over loose rocks and follow narrow, exposed trails, this hike is one of the inner canyon's best.

Matkatamiba

Duration 20 minutes round-trip

Distance 0.8 miles round-trip

Difficulty Moderate

Start/Finish Mile 148, river left

Summary Pull yourself through the narrows to get to the amphitheater at Matkatamiba.

Matkatamiba, named for a Havasupai family and nicknamed Matkat, is a very narrow Redwall limestone slot canyon that meets the Colorado at Mile 148. So, wet or dry? You must quickly decide how to spend the next 10 minutes heading up to Matkat's acoustically perfect natural **amphitheater**, lined

RUNNING THE LITTLE COLORADO

In drier seasons, the Little Colorado flows down from a mineral spring, which gives the water its tropical warmth and turquoise hue. If the water is clear, the confluence with the big Colorado creates a lovely juxtaposition of colors. While a lucky few on rafting trips get the chance to see the mini-rapids up close, any visitor to the park can view the Little Colorado River Gorge from an overlook that's located in a section of the park informally known as Grand Canyon East, on the rim-hugging road between the South Rim and Cameron, AZ; travelers driving from the South Rim to the North Rim pass right by the turnoff, about 12 miles west of Cameron between miles 285 and 286. As it's part of Navajo Nation, you'll see several traditional Native American vendors selling crafts and jewelry near the scenic overlook. There's no price to enter, but tribespeople do encourage and accept donations.

by ferns and wildflowers. On the tricky wet route, you head upstream through the creek – wading when possible, and crawling on all fours and using handholds to pull yourself over slippery boulders.

But hang on, you get wet on the dry route too, since the first 25ft of both routes start by wading through a chest-deep pool, clambering over a boulder as wide as the creek, then wading through yet another pool. Here the dry route leaves the creek and ascends 100ft of steep rock to an exposed trail that overlooks the narrow chasm. At a sculpted curve where the amphitheater emerges, the two routes merge. The wet route is too dangerous to descend, so return via the dry route.

Beaver Falls

Duration 4 hours round-trip

Distance 8 miles round-trip

Difficulty Easy–moderate

Start/Finish Mile 157, river left

Summary Explore the blue-green waters of Havasu Canyon from the riverside.

The blue-green spring-fed waters of Havasu Creek plunge over a series of four breathtaking waterfalls to the Colorado. Beaver Falls, which tumbles over travertine formations with one prominent fall, is the cascade nearest to the river. Most backpackers hike in only as far as Mooney Falls, so Beaver Falls – 2 miles further – is almost the exclusive domain of rafters.

The slot canyon near Mile 157 doesn't hint at what lies further up **Havasu Canyon**. A few minutes from the Colorado, the rock walls part to reveal wild grapevines, lush ground cover and tall cottonwoods along the level creekside trail. On this gentle hike, you'll spend about 20 minutes in water as you ford Havasu Creek, cross deep pools and wade upstream through knee-deep water. Once through the first and biggest water obstacle – the lovely, chest-deep **Big Kids Pool** – you'll emerge and climb a log staircase through a Muav limestone tunnel. The trail continues upstream to the base of a cliff near the confluence with Beaver Creek. Scramble up the cliff to reach an **overlook** of Beaver Falls. Retrace your steps, relaxing and swimming in the several pools.

Lower Section: Whitmore Wash to South Cove

MILE 187.5 TO BEYOND MILE 277

Rafters join the river at Whitmore Wash via helicopter from the North Rim. **Lower Granite Gorge**, the third and last of the canyon's sister granite gorges, starts at Mile 215, marked by the appearance of metamorphic and igneous rock. Though it features more flat water than other stretches, this section still boasts great white water, including 11 rapids, seven of which are rated 5 or higher. The two biggest drops are 16ft and 25ft. Oar-powered rafts take four to five days, motorboats three to four days.

In July and August the trip wraps up at **Diamond Creek** (Mile 226). Trips in May and June, however, continue downstream and can catch a glimpse of the water shimmering over the limestone deposits that make **Travertine Falls** (Mile 230) a petrified waterfall.

You might also muse over the unsolved mystery of Glen and Bessie Hyde's disappearance in 1928 at **Mile 237**, where their flat-bottomed boat was found peacefully floating with everything in it but the Hydes. Eventually the trip continues beyond the canyon's terminus at **Grand Wash Cliffs** to end at South Cove on Lake Mead.

Understand the Grand Canyon

Grand Canyon Today

Staring across this overwhelmingly massive landscape of rock, you might feel like humans could never affect the Grand Canyon. But consider the combined effect of six million annual visitors. This staggering number taxes water resources and brings air pollution from vehicles. It also catches the imagination of developers – sometimes with little regard for maintaining the region's pristine nature. Combine this with the relaxing of regulations regarding mining around the park, and suddenly this place looks alarmingly fragile.

Best on Film

Koyaanisqatsi (1982) Music by Philip Glass accompanies images of humanity and nature in this experimental, nonverbal film that briefly captures the shifting light of the Grand Canyon.

Into the Wild (2007) Seeker and wanderer Chris McCandless is depicted kayaking the canyon – a fictional embellishment to a wild but true tale.

Thelma & Louise (1991) This genre-defining women-on-the-run story ends at the Grand Canyon (though the final scene was actually shot near Moab).

Best in Print

The Hidden Canyon: A River Journey (John Blaustein, Edward Abbey; 1999) Blaustein's expansive photographs illustrate Abbey's scathing wit and inspiring cynicism penned during their 1977 dory trip down the Colorado River.

Over the Edge: Death in the Grand Canyon (Michael P Ghiglieri & Thomas M Myers; 2001) Morbidly fascinating survey of the many ways people have died in the canyon.

Beyond the Hundredth Meridian: John Wesley Powell and the Second Opening of the West (Wallace Stegner; 1992) A vibrant retelling of John Wesley Powell's explorations of the Grand Canyon and its broader historical contexts.

Flyovers

While tragic deaths from crashes have shrunk to a record low of one person per year, the negative effects of scenic overflights on the hikers and wildlife below remain a perennial source of contention between conservationists and tour operators. Noise pollution's effect on solitude-seeking hikers is well understood, but it's harder to quantify how the constant whomp of helicopter rotors affects resident animal species.

Although the Federal Aviation Administration limits flights over Grand Canyon National Park to narrow corridors (and only during certain times of the day) there are no such restrictions on the west end of the canyon owned by the Hualapai Tribe. There, as many as 450 helicopters a day carry sightseers from Las Vegas over a stretch of canyon known colloquially as 'Good Morning Vietnam.'

While Wilderness activists point out that the view from a helicopter is no better than from the rims, overflights remain a very popular activity.

(Non-)Native Development

Native American tribes bordering the park have long sought to capitalize on their unique locations – though not all grand plans by outside developers have had the locals' best interests at heart.

The Navajo Nation finally killed a massive tourism-development proposal in 2018 after a long and controversial battle. The $65-million plan – which included a 1.4-mile tramway to the confluence of the Colorado and Little Colorado rivers – was the brainchild of outside investors. They sought commercial rights to 420 acres on the rim while barring the Navajo from establishing 'competing businesses' along some 40,000 acres paralleling the new road to the site.

On the other hand, Grand Canyon West, further downstream, is rapidly becoming Las Vegas East. Anchored by the Grand Canyon Skywalk (a glass walkway jutting out from the rim some 2000ft above the rocks below) this tourism complex on Hualapai tribal land has angered some tribe members who consider the area sacred. However, the million visitors a year it attracts have brought much-needed economic opportunity to the tribe who fully owns and operates the attractions.

Meanwhile, the Havasupai (one of the country's smallest tribes) continue to keep things relatively low key in their slice of the canyon northwest of Tusayan. They limit visitation to their iconic falls to a manageable 300 people per day and only allow overnight guests.

Radioactive Issues

The Trump administration began trying to reverse a 20-year ban on uranium mining around the Grand Canyon in late 2017. The ban was established to safeguard fragile riparian ecosystems and protect drinking water while scientists had a chance to research the potential risks to the hydrology in this geologically complicated region.

Uranium mining started in 1950s, and the hundreds of abandoned mines in and around the canyon have already left a lasting legacy. A National Park Service warning tells hikers along the popular Hermit Trail to not drink the water from Horn Creek due to contamination by the old Orphan Mine – unless death is their only other option.

A lower court upheld the ban, but the foreign companies that own 93% of the active Grand Canyon claims hope to take the issue to the Supreme Court. Meanwhile, the Trump administration has also proposed cutting all government funding for scientific study into mining impacts on the region.

It's a Boom Town

As visitation increases steadily year after year, residents of the tiny town of Tusayan (population 600) on the south side of the park clash on how best to manage their unique position as the gateway to Grand Canyon. One proposal by an Italian developer: build 2200 new homes and millions of square feet of commercial space.

The plan has faced opposition for decades, most notably by the Havasupai Tribe, whose life-blood – the fairy-tale waterfalls that attract tourists, but also water their crops – may be threatened by the thirsty development 35 miles upstream. The US Forest Service essentially killed the expansion plan in 2016 by refusing to grant easements for utilities, but the investors haven't given up.

Now on the table: an off-the-grid community powered by wind and solar, with water trucked in by tankerload from...somewhere else.

THE GRAND CANYON IS:

1 MILE DEEP

18 MILES ACROSS AT ITS WIDEST

277 RIVER MILES LONG

LOCATED IN COCONINO COUNTY, ARIZONA

if 100 people visited where would they go?

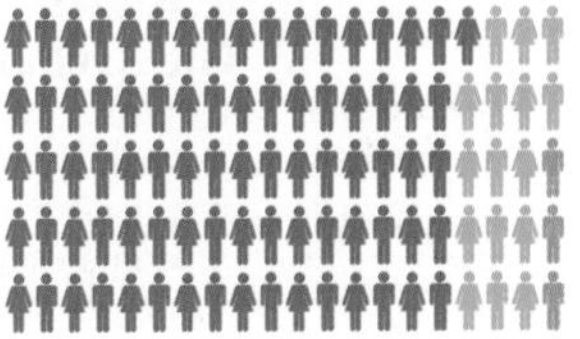

81 would go to the South Rim
16 would go to the North Rim
3 would go to the Colorado River

Seasonal Visitation

(% of visitors)

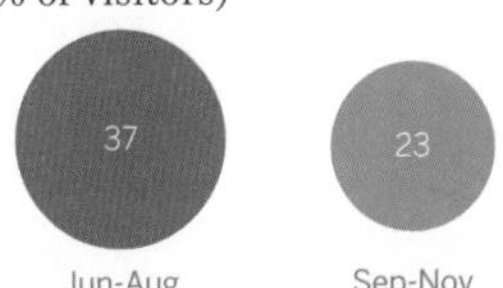

population per sq mile

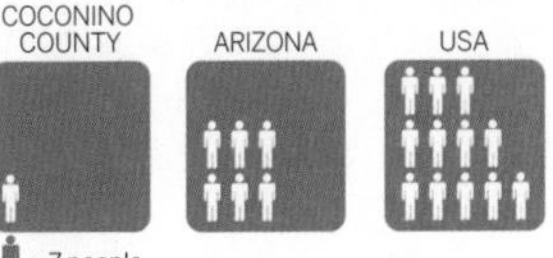

History

Well preserved in the folds of the Grand Canyon are cryptic markings, pottery shards and the stone foundations of villages that hint at millennia of human habitation. The Colorado River and its tributaries have long been key sources of life in a largely inhospitable landscape – a landscape hotly contested during the westward expansion of the US. Once explorers and prospectors began penetrating the canyon's depths, the prescient formation of the park ensured that this landscape would forever remain protected.

Ancient Cultures of the Grand Canyon

Puebloan Ruin Sites

- *Phantom Ranch*
- *Tusayan Museum & Ruin*
- *Walnut Canyon National Monument*
- *Wupatki National Monument*

The Archaic Periods

Archaeological evidence suggests that humans visited the Grand Canyon region as early as 11,500 BC toward the end of the last ice age. They were likely nomadic, following Pleistocene game animals like mammoth through a changing climate. As the environment warmed – creating expanded environmental zones and new opportunities for hunting – the descendants of the Paleo-Indians adapted and developed Archaic cultures.

The Early Archaic period, characterized by seasonal habitation, atlatl (spear-throwers), woven sandals and ground stone tools, saw an increase in population on the plateaus despite the drier climate and the loss of large Pleistocene game.

About 6000 years ago, a drought that would last on and off for almost 2000 years defined the Middle Archaic period. Conditions became even tougher, and many peoples migrated to more amenable lands. Those who stayed moved between canyons and plateaus, sometimes camping in caves and leaving evidence of their culture.

As the drought eased, about 4000 years ago (2000 BC), people returned to the region, and the population of the Southwest exploded rapidly into the 1000-year Late Archaic period.

Evidence of this era of occupation found at the Grand Canyon includes dozens of elaborate split-twig animal figurines from four different caves that show no other signs of occupation. A few of these are pierced by small twigs (and one by a cactus thorns) thought to represent arrows, and some were found in shrine-like arrangements. Archaeologists be-

TIMELINE

9500 BC

Paleo-indian hunters migrate through the Grand Canyon region in pursuit of Pleistocene megafauna, such as mammoth and giant sloth, which had begun to disappear.

7000 BC–1000 BC

Archaic peoples occupy the canyon leaving behind evidence of their existence in rock-art panels, split-twig figurines and chipped-stone tools which were probably used for hunting.

1000 BC–AD 1300

Basketmaker and ancient Puebloan cultures develop farming communities in and around the canyon, establishing complex trail systems that allowed for outside contact and trade.

lieve that nomadic groups used the caves for hunting rituals, and left these totems as offerings.

Basketmaker & Puebloan Cultures

From 500 AD to 1500 AD, Grand Canyon residents began settling down and experimenting with agriculture during the Formative Period. This more sedentary lifestyle allowed for the development of baskets, pottery and lasting dwellings.

Puebloan culture blurs with the Basketmaker culture (the canyon's earliest corn-growing people, named for the intricate coiled and watertight baskets they made), and the gradual shift from one period to the other is a result of complicated migrations and developments. Puebloan culture, as defined and explained by archaeologists, includes corn-growing cultures that inhabited the southern Colorado Plateau and the Four Corners Region. The word pueblo means 'town' and refers to the above-ground adobe or stone structures in which these people lived. Religious ceremonies took place in kivas (circular below-ground buildings reminiscent of pit houses).

Ancestral Puebloan culture is a general term that includes several distinct traditions based on pottery style, geographic location, architecture and social structure; among them are the Chacoan, Mesa Verde, Kayenta, Virgin River, Little Colorado River, Cohonina and Sinagua cultures. By about 700 AD, Basketmaker culture had been replaced by Puebloan culture.

The Tusayan Ruin, on the eastern side of the South Rim, may have been the last Puebloan community in the Grand Canyon region. Archaeological records place its construction around 1185 and show it housed about 30 people for a mere 25 years.

Agriculture & Abandonment

About 1000 years ago precipitation in the region increased slightly, and for the next 150 years, the Grand Canyon experienced a heyday of farming. Taking advantage of the subtle shift in climate, bands of ancestral Puebloans spread out, strengthened and flourished. While the canyon was by no means lush, the high water table, increased precipitation and wide alluvial terraces made it more agriculturally productive than it would be today.

ANCIENT TRAILS

Ancestral Puebloan occupants of the Grand Canyon established an intricate trail system that provided access all over the region and down to the river. Spurs in every direction linked canyon communities and facilitated trade with cultures throughout the Southwest. Remnants of some paths can be seen in seemingly impossible places, while others – improved by prospectors, early entrepreneurs or the National Park Service – are still in use.

One of the most striking of these ancient trails is a wooden pole bridge across a gap in the cliffs called Anasazi Bridge, which can be seen on river left, upstream from President Harding Rapid. Experts suspect it may have connected to a rim route via an ascent requiring highly skilled climbing.

1150–1300

Puebloan tribes abandon their settlements across the Southwest for unknown reasons that might include severe drought, hostile invasions or a combination of both.

1250

The Cerbat/Pai, ancestors of today's Hualapai and Havasupai, migrate from the Mojave Desert to the South Rim, while Southern Paiute migrate from southern Utah to the northern canyon.

1400

Dine and Navajo people arrive in the area.

1540

Spanish explorer García López de Cárdenas and his party of 12 follow Hopi guides to the South Rim of the Grand Canyon and unsuccessfully attempt to reach the river.

Split-twig figurines depicting common prey like bighorn sheep, pronghorn antelope and deer can be viewed at the Tusayan Museum & Ruin on the South Rim. Radiocarbon dating places these totems as between 2000 to 4000 years old, dating to the Late Archaic period.

Various groups of early Puebloans staked claim to the region. On the South Rim, the Cohonina inhabited the canyon west of Desert View (including Havasu Canyon and the Coconino Plateau) and mingled with the Kayenta, living seasonally in the uplands and along the river. Pottery shards and extensive building foundations found in places like Chuar and Nankoweap indicate that despite difficult access, farming communities thrived – albeit for a short time – in the inner canyon.

Then, relatively abruptly, between 1150 and 1200, Puebloans abandoned the Southwest including Grand Canyon, Chaco Canyon in northwest New Mexico, and Mesa Verde in Southern Colorado. Scientists cannot agree on why such elaborate and thriving communities would so suddenly leave their homes, but analyses of tree rings, stalagmites and lake pollen show that a severe drought descended upon the region around this time.

With decreased precipitation, corn reserves dwindled and canyon people were faced with malnutrition and starvation. Though there was no single mass exodus from the canyon, the Puebloans drifted away. Cohonina migrated toward Flagstaff; Sinagua migrated to the east, blending with the Hopi living among the mesas. The Kayenta villagers stayed a bit longer than their contemporaries to construct fort-like buildings along the South Rim. These defensive structures suggest that hostile invasions from migrating tribes may have further weakened the already vulnerable Puebloan communities and contributed to their eventual withdrawal.

Whatever the reason – drought, warfare or a combination of the two – by 1300 the Grand Canyon became merely an echo of the once-thriving agrarian past. Though the evidence suggests that they would visit periodically, Puebloans never returned permanently.

Europeans 'Discover' the Grand Canyon

Spanish conquistador García López de Cárdenas became the first European to see the Grand Canyon when Coronado sent him in 1540 to explore reports of a large river in the arid landscapes north of Cibola. After following their Native American guides for 20 days, Cárdenas and 12 men reached the South Rim.

It is not clear where Cárdenas stood when he first saw the Grand Canyon, but based on his written record historians believe it was somewhere between Moran Point and Desert View. Though Hopi guides knew of relatively easy paths into the canyon, they didn't share them, and Cárdenas' men managed to descend only about one-third of the way before turning back.

No European would return for at least 200 years, and even then it was but a sprinkling of missionaries, trappers and mountain men that trespassed across the inhospitable landscape.

1734

French cartographer Jacques-Nicolas Bellin uses the name 'Colorado' for the main stem of the river for the first time.

1848

The Treaty of Guadalupe Hidalgo ends the Mexican–American War and the US annexes Mexico's northern territory and Texas: 914,166 sq miles that include Arizona.

1858–59

First Lieutenant Joseph Christmas Ives and his expedition become the first European Americans to reach the river within the canyon; he declares the region 'altogether valueless.'

1864–69

One-third of the Hualapai population is killed during a war with the US.

Then, in 1848, the treaty of Guadalupe Hidalgo ended the Mexican-American War, and a sawmill operator in California accidentally found gold. These two unrelated events combined to have profound impact on Northern Arizona and the Southwest.

With the treaty, the US acquired Mexico's northern territory which included present-day Arizona, California, Nevada, Utah, Colorado and New Mexico. This vast land – along with the Louisiana Purchase – more than doubled the size of the US, forcing the federal government to grapple with the problem of running a country and maintaining a national identity despite great geographic and cultural distances. Meanwhile, the forty-niners rushing toward California gold, and the pioneers hoping to build homes in the new West, all needed wagon roads.

And so the US sent military men to identify and map its territory throughout the 1850s. Among the first of these was Edward Fitzgerald Beale, who led a caravan of camels – part of a short-lived army pack-animal experiment – across the desert surveying a trail that would eventually become a section of Route 66.

In 1858 First Lieutenant Joseph Christmas Ives set out on a steamship from the Gulf of California to explore the still-mysterious 'big canyon' region and seek an inland waterway. After two months of travel, he crashed into a boulder in Black Canyon (near today's Hoover Dam) well shy of the Grand Canyon. He then set out on foot with soldiers, packers, trail builders, artists, local guides, a geologist and about 150 mules. After a month, they scrambled down a side canyon north of Peach Springs and became the first European Americans to reach the river within the canyon.

Frustrated with the difficulty of the terrain and lack of water, Ives reported that the region was beautiful, but 'valueless.' He stated confidently that few (if any) explorers would find cause to venture into the canyon again.

Removal of American Indians

From the early 19th century, US military forces pushed west across the continent, protecting settlers and wresting land from American Indians, who didn't share European concepts of land ownership. With the 1848 Treaty of Guadalupe and the discovery of gold in California, non-native Americans crossed the continent in unprecedented numbers. It wasn't long before they intruded into and permanently transformed the lives and homes of American Indians who had lived in and around the Grand Canyon for centuries.

As the NPS developed Grand Canyon National Park, they evicted the Havasupai who had been living around the South Rim and Indian Garden area, with the last group leaving the inner canyon in 1928.

Hualapai

After the murder of Hualapai chief Wauba Yuman in 1866 – the result of land conflicts – Hualapai chief Sherum engaged American troops in a three-year war. The US Army destroyed their homes, crops and food

1868

After hundreds die during forced marches to New Mexico known as the Long Walk, the Navajo Reservation is established on 5500 sq miles in the heart of their ancestral lands east of the canyon.

1869

Geologist, naturalist and Civil War veteran John Wesley Powell and a crew of nine attempt to boat the Colorado River through the Grand Canyon. Six make it to the end.

1876

The Fred Harvey Company, aka the 'civilizer of the West,' is founded. Its owner plans to make the Grand Canyon a major tourist attraction by opening refined hotels with gourmet restaurants.

1880s

President Rutherford Hayes establishes the Havasupai Reservation on a mere 518 acres along Havasu Creek. President Chester Arthur establishes the Hualapai Reservation on 1 million acres of their ancestral lands.

Wupatki National Monument (p102)

supplies until the Hualapai surrendered in 1869. They were forced onto a reservation on the lower Colorado and, deprived of rations and unused to the heat of the lower elevations, many died from starvation or illness. The Hualapai escaped the reservation, only to be confined again when President Chester Arthur set aside the now one-million-acre reservation on the southern side of the Grand Canyon.

Havasupai

Though the Havasupai escaped the brutality of the Indian Wars, they too were eventually forced to give up their lands and were confined to a reservation as European Americans settled in the Grand Canyon region. In 1880 President Rutherford Hayes established 38,000 acres as the Havasupai Reservation, but two years later it was reduced to an area 5 miles wide and 12 miles long. After the park was established in 1919, their

1884

Prospector John Hance, having given up on mining yields, takes the first tourists into the canyon on his mining trails and charges them $1 for dinner and lodging.

1890

William Wallace Bass sets up a dude ranch on the South Rim and takes tourists into Havasu Canyon, befriending the Havasupai and facilitating cross-cultural exchange with the relatively isolated tribe.

1893

President Benjamin Harrison proclaims the Grand Canyon a National Forest Preserve, a designation that offers some environmental protection but still allows mining and logging.

1901

The Atchison, Topeka and Santa Fe Railway completes a spur line from Williams to the South Rim.

canyon home was increasingly disturbed by Anglo explorers, prospectors and intrepid tourists. In the early 1970s, the reservation was increased to its present-day boundaries that encompass 188,077 acres.

Paiute

US westward expansion brought disease to the Paiute people as settlers stole the best lands north of the Colorado River. By the late 1860s conflict with Anglo pioneers had become common. In the early 20th century only about 100 Kaibab Paiute lived north of the canyon in Moccasin Spring. They were moved onto a reservation in 1907. Today the Kaibab Reservation surrounds Pipe Springs National Monument, about 80 miles north of the North Rim.

Navajo

After the beloved Navajo leader Narbona was scalped in 1849, over a decade of skirmishes between the Navajo and western settlers made life miserable for everyone. In 1864, Christopher 'Kit' Carson was assigned by the New Mexico Territory government to round up the Navajo and drive them 300 miles east to Bosque Redondo near Fort Sumner. Of the 10,000 that made that trek, 200 died en route and nearly a third died at the internment camp. In 1868 the captives were allowed to return to their homeland, and the Navajo Nation was established east of the park – now the largest reservation in the US.

Anasazi, the Navajo term traditionally used to describe early Native Americans of the Southwest, translates roughly as 'Enemy Ancestors.' Because Hopi and Zuni find this term offensive, contemporary scholars refer to the Anasazi as 'Ancestral Puebloans' or 'prehistoric Puebloans.'

John Wesley Powell

Fascinated by reports about the Grand Canyon from previous explorers, John Wesley Powell cobbled together a makeshift team of volunteers, and secured private funding and government support to finance an expedition down the Colorado River. The work of this one-armed Civil War veteran and professor of geology would set the stage for the canyon's transformation from a hurdle to a destination.

In May 1869, Powell and his crew of nine launched four self-designed wooden boats, laden with thousands of pounds of scientific equipment and 10 months' worth of food, from Green River, Wyoming. They floated peacefully until one of the boats, the *No Name*, smashed into rocks at Lodore Canyon rapids – which Powell called Disaster Falls. Despite this tragic loss of supplies, they continued down the Green River, joined the Colorado River on July 17 and floated through Glen Canyon without further mishap.

The waters of the Colorado in the 'big canyon,' however, were not so kind. The crew portaged their heavy equipment around rapids and ran others. The hot sun baked their skin. Boats sprung leaks. Powell took notes on the geology and natural history as his crew scrambled over

1902

A survey crew caught in the North Rim winter weather determined that Bright Angel Canyon was the best route to the river; this later became the North Kaibab Trail.

1905

The Fred Harvey Company, in partnership with the Atchison, Topeka and Santa Fe Railway, opens El Tovar on the South Rim, designed by Mary Colter.

1906

Grand Canyon Game Preserve is set aside on the North Rim; it limits livestock grazing but also results in the hunting and eventual disappearance of indigenous wolves and mountain lions.

1907

Kaibab Paiute are moved to a reservation encompassing fewer than 200 sq miles that do not border Grand Canyon National Park and comprise a fraction of their ancestral lands.

sharp cliffs, taking measurements and examining rocks, canyons and streams. All while they subsided on meager rations of flour, coffee and dried apples. Powell called the Grand Canyon their 'granite prison.'

Arnold Berke's *Mary Colter: Architect of the Southwest* is a beautifully illustrated and well-written examination of the life and work of Mary Colter.

On August 27 the expedition came to a particularly wild rapid where three men – Bill Dunn and brothers Seneca and Oramel Howland – abandoned the journey. Whether they were simply exhausted and frightened, or fed up with Powell's gruff leadership is open for debate, but they helped line the boats down the first set of falls, then hiked up what Powell named Separation Canyon. The river runners made it through without incident; the three men were never heard from again – likely killed by Shivwits Paiute who mistook them for murderous prospectors.

Two days later, Powell and his remaining crew members exited the canyon near present-day Lake Mead. After 14 weeks on the river, they became the first humans in recorded history to have floated the length of the Colorado through what Powell christened the Grand Canyon.

Not content to rest on his laurels, Powell immediately began raising money for a second expedition, and returned to the Colorado River in 1871. This time he brought a photographer, EO Beaman (who produced about 350 images of the Grand Canyon), and artist Frederick Samuel Dellenbaugh. However, it was not until he convinced renowned painter Thomas Moran to return with him to the rim in 1873 that Powell succeed in captivating the imagination of the US and planting the idea of the canyon as a viable tourist destination.

Within a quarter of a century, through the combined forces of prospectors-turned-tourist-guides, the railroad, and the Fred Harvey Company investment in infrastructure, the Grand Canyon would become an iconic American treasure.

Thomas Moran's painting *The Grand Chasm of the Colorado*, purchased by Congress in 1874 for $10,000, hung in the National Capitol building and was influential in securing national-park status for the Grand Canyon.

Evolution of a Park

With the completion of a railroad to the South Rim in 1901, tourism at the canyon accelerated. Instead of paying $20 and enduring a teeth-rattling 12-hour stagecoach ride to Diamond Creek, visitors could pay $3.95 and reach the rim from Williams in three hours.

In 1902 brothers Ellsworth and Emery Kolb came to the canyon, and within a few years they set up a photography studio on the rim. Tourists could ride a mule into the canyon in the morning and have a photo of their journey by the next day – a feat accomplished by one of the brothers running the plates down to Indian Garden (the only water source) to process them before running them back to the rim.

Only four years after the train's arrival at the rim, the visionary Fred Harvey Company built El Tovar, an elegant hotel, and established the Mary Colter–designed Hopi House. Fred Harvey hired Hopi to live there, demon-

1908
President Teddy Roosevelt creates Grand Canyon National Monument, one of the acts for which he became known as a pioneering conservationist in the US.

1919
The Grand Canyon finally earns a national-park designation, becoming the US' 15th national park; during this year, the Grand Canyon receives 44,000 visitors.

1922
The Fred Harvey Company builds Phantom Ranch, designed by Mary Colter, along the Colorado River at the confluence of Bright Angel Creek and Phantom Creek.

1928
Newlyweds Glen and Bessie Hyde disappear on the Colorado River while attempting to raft through the Grand Canyon. Their boat is discovered intact, but the couple is never seen again.

strate their crafts, wear native costumes and perform dances for the tourists. The Grand Canyon was rapidly becoming a must-visit destination.

President Theodore Roosevelt created the Grand Canyon National Monument in 1908, and in 1919 President Woodrow Wilson upgraded it to become the 15th national park in the US. Around 40,000 people visited the park that year, but by 1956 the number surpassed one million.

The Great Depression then WWII slowed the frenzy of park development, and from 1933 to 1942, the Civilian Conservation Corps, the Public Works Administration and the Works Progress Administration touched up buildings, created trails and cleaned ditches. Fewer tourists visited during this period, giving rangers space to develop interpretive programs.

As soon as WWII ended, Americans – in love with the automobile, and eager to explore and celebrate their country – inundated the national parks. The flood prompted another flurry of construction, and from 1953

MARY COLTER'S GRAND VISION

Mary Colter's buildings blend so seamlessly into the landscape that, were it not for the throngs of people flowing in and out, you might miss seeing them entirely. Indeed, Colter's creations add to the beauty of Grand Canyon National Park because they succeed so magnificently in adding nothing at all.

One of the few female architects of her time, Colter spent four decades designing hotels, shops, restaurants and train stations for the Fred Harvey Company and the Santa Fe Railway. These two companies worked as a team to transform the American West into a tourist destination.

Colter's style follows the sensibility of the American Arts and Crafts Movement. In keeping with the nationalist spirit of the late 19th century, and reacting against industrialized society, the Arts and Crafts aesthetic (or Craftsman style) looked toward American models, rather than European traditions, for inspiration. It reveres handcrafted objects, clean and simple lines and the incorporation of indigenous materials. For an excellent example of well-preserved, classic Arts and Crafts design, stop by the Riordan Mansion (p101) in Flagstaff.

Colter spent a great deal of time researching all her works, exploring ancient Hopi villages, studying American Indian culture, and taking careful notes. The Colter buildings in Grand Canyon National Park use local materials such as Kaibab limestone and pine to blend with their surroundings. They embrace American Indian motifs, evoking woven textile and geometric design, and echoing American Indian architecture with kiva fireplaces and vigas (rafters) on the ceiling.

Through her creative inspiration, Colter solved the challenge of preserving expansive western landscapes while developing them for tourists. Her buildings, known as 'National Park Service rustic,' stand in harmony with their natural environment and served as models and inspiration for construction in other national parks throughout the country.

1936

Hoover Dam (formerly known as Boulder Dam), a feat of engineering, is built on the Colorado River west of the canyon, creating Lake Mead.

1952

Georgie White becomes the first woman to raft the full length of the Grand Canyon, then goes on to become the first woman to offer commercial rafting trips in the region.

1956

Two airplanes on eastward flights from Los Angeles collide midair over the canyon, resulting in the establishment of a national air-traffic control system.

1963

Controversial Glen Canyon Dam is built on the Colorado River upstream, flooding Glen Canyon and altering the ecosystem of the Grand Canyon.

NORTH RIM DEVELOPMENT

Safely removed from railroad access, the North Rim developed more slowly than the South Rim. The areas nearby were largely empty, inhabited only by Mormons trying to escape increasingly strict laws against polygamy.

In 1906 Teddy Roosevelt set aside much of the land as Grand Canyon Game Preserve. But while new regulations prohibited deer hunting, to boost herd numbers the reserve's first warden – James T 'Uncle Jim' Owens – oversaw the killing of hundreds upon hundreds of badgers, coyotes, wolverines, cougars and grizzly bears.

The first car arrived on the North Rim in 1909 and four years later the US Forest Service completed the 56-mile Grand Canyon Hwy to the Bright Angel Ranger Station at Harvey Meadow. Tourist facilities included tent accommodations and the North Kaibab Trail to a tourist camp at the site of present-day Phantom Ranch.

A suspension bridge connecting the North and South Kaibab trails was completed in 1928, the same year Union Pacific architect GS Underwood constructed the original Grand Canyon Lodge. It burnt down four years later, but was reconstructed in 1937.

Little has changed on the North Rim since, and it stills sees a fraction of the visitors numbers to the South Rim.

to 1968 Grand Canyon built more trails, enhanced existing trails, improved roads, and constructed Maswik, Kachina and Thunderbird Lodges. Jarring steel and concrete buildings joined the landscape-inspired architecture of Mary Colter and the rustic 'parkitecture' like El Tovar. Meanwhile, engineers fascinated with other ways concrete and steel could tame the west constructed Glen Canyon Dam between 1956 and 1963, forever altering the ecosystem of the Grand Canyon river corridor.

Proposed construction of two gigantic dams on the Colorado in the mid-1960s was quashed by public protest after the Sierra Club published full-page ads in major newspapers famously asking, 'Should we also flood the Sistine Chapel so tourists can get nearer the ceiling?'

In 1975 President Gerald Ford signed the Grand Canyon National Park Enlargement Act, doubling the size of the park by integrating it with Grand Canyon National Monument and Marble Canyon National Monument. This same act returned land to the Havasupai. The following year, the park received three million visitors. In 1979, Grand Canyon National Park was designated a Unesco World Heritage Site.

Over at the West Rim outside the park boundary, the Hualapai Nation opened Grand Canyon Skywalk in 2007 bringing a new flood of tourism and controversy concerning the sustainability of more development in this fragile environment. In 2017, visitation to the Park passed the six-million mark. As numbers continue to increase in and around the Grand Canyon, land managers struggle to balance tourism with environmental stewardship.

1979

Grand Canyon National Park is designated a Unesco World Heritage Site, recognized not only for its extraordinary beauty but also for its geologic and ecological significance.

1993

One hundred and thirty years after Joseph Christmas Ives predicted that the canyon would be 'forever left unvisited and undisturbed,' almost five million people visit Grand Canyon National Park.

2007

The Hualapai Nation opens the controversial glass Skywalk at Grand Canyon West, bringing droves of tourist traffic to the relatively remote West Rim.

2017

Annual visitation surpasses six million people.

Grand Geology

The yawning maw of the Grand Canyon is a geology book opened wide. From the rim, you can see two billion years of earth's history – accounting for nearly half of the planet's existence. Each layer is easy to identify, and each tells a story of oceans, deserts and violent mountain uplifts. Even if you don't yet know sandstone from schist, a few short minutes of study can add an entirely new depth to your visit.

The Story of the Rocks

Vishnu Schist & Zoroaster Granite

What we can see of the geologic story begins in the canyon's innermost recesses, where the Colorado River continues to carve a deep channel into progressively older rock. The bottommost layer, Vishnu schist, is dark and fine-grained, with vertical or diagonal bands that contrast with the canyon's horizontal upper layers. Down around Phantom Ranch, look for intruding bands of pinkish Zoroaster granite. Together, these are among the oldest exposed rocks on earth's surface.

Decipher the layers along the Bright Angel Trail, with the handy, light and laminated *Guide to Geology Along the Bright Angel Trail* by Dave Thayer.

The schist offers evidence that two billion years ago the canyon region lay beneath an ancient sea. For tens of millions of years, silt and clay eroded into the water from adjacent landmasses, settling to the seafloor. These sediments, along with occasional dustings of lava and ash, accumulated to a thickness of 5 miles and were later buried beneath another 10 miles of additional sediment.

Eventually, as plate tectonics brought land masses crashing together, these layers experienced extreme heat and pressure, metamorphosing into schist and gneiss as they were thrust up into mountain ranges that rose above the water.

Stromatolites

After the basement-layer mountains formed – roughly 1.7 billion years ago – the region began a northward migration from the equator while undergoing a long spell of erosion. This weathering eventually ground the mountains down to form a low coastal plain that gradually sunk back beneath the sea. This underwater shelf provided a perfect platform for marine algae, whose deposits built the Bass limestone that now sits atop the Vishnu schist. Marine fossils in the Bass limestone include such primitive life forms as the cabbage-like stromatolites created by stacked layers of cyanobacteria.

The Precambrian Era & the Great Unconformity

In the late Precambrian era (1.2 billion to 570 million years ago) the region alternated between marine and coastal environments as the ocean repeatedly advanced and retreated, each time leaving distinctive layers of sediment and structural features. Pockmarks from raindrops, cracks in drying mud and ripple marks in sand have all been preserved in one form or another, alongside countless other clues. Much of this evidence was lost as the forces of erosion scraped the land back down to Vishnu schist. The resulting gap in the geologic record is called the Great Unconformity: where older rocks abut against much newer rocks with no intervening layers. Fortunately, pockets of ancient rock that once perched atop the Vishnu schist still remain and lie exposed along the North and South Kaibab Trails, among other places.

The Paleozoic Era

The Precambrian era came to an end about 570 million years ago. The subsequent Paleozoic era (570 to 245 million years ago) spawned nearly all of the rock formations visitors see today. The Paleozoic also ushered in the dramatic transition from primitive organisms to an explosion of complex life forms that spread into every available aquatic and terrestrial niche – the beginning of life as we know it. The canyon walls contain an abundant fossil record of these ancient animals, including shells like cephalopods and brachiopods, trilobites, and the tracks of reptiles and amphibians.

The Paleozoic record is particularly well preserved in the layers cut by the Colorado, as the region has been little altered by geologic events such as earthquakes, faulting or volcanic activity. Every advance and retreat of the ancient ocean laid down a characteristic layer that documents whether it was a time of deep oceans, shallow bays, active coastline,

A ROCK PRIMER

The three main classes of rock – sedimentary, igneous and metamorphic – are each well represented in the Grand Canyon.

Sedimentary

Think of sedimentary rock as things that settled – either at the bottom of an ocean, along a lakeshore, or on a dry sandy plain. Over time these bits and pieces cemented together, forming horizontal layers that preserved clues as to how they formed. Three types of sedimentary rock are present in the canyon:

Limestone The calcium-carbonate remnants of coral and other sea creatures piling up at the bottom of deep seas, limestone softens and easily erodes when wet, resulting in the miles of caves found in the Redwall layer.

Sandstone Loosely stacked sand particles are eventually glued together by calcium carbonate, making this a very hard and durable rock. Originally deposited by sand dunes and beaches, these layers often contain fossilized tracks of terrestrial critters.

Mudstone (including shale) Flaky particles that stack so closely together there's little room for the binding cement, mudstone is often very soft and breakable. These are formed by deposits from alluvial benches and coastal wetlands.

Igneous

Igneous rock originates as molten magma, which cools either deep underground or after erupting to the surface as lava or ash. Relatively recent volcanic events formed the basalt flows and cinder cones west of Tuweep Valley, creating prominent features such as Vulcan's Throne and the infamous (to river rafters anyway) Lava Falls. Ancient magma cooling deep inside the earth after a mountain building period formed the granite that lies exposed along the inner canyon in what is appropriately known as Granite Gorge.

Metamorphic

Metamorphic rock starts out as either sedimentary or igneous, then transforms into other kinds of rock following exposure to intense heat or pressure – especially where the earth's crust buckles and folds into mountain ranges. Metamorphic rock usually remains hidden deep underground.

Two types of metamorphic rock are common in the canyon: schist and gneiss. Schist lines the inner gorge, and is derived from shale, sandstone or igneous rock. You can distinguish it by the narrow wavy bands of shiny mica flakes. The light-colored intrusions within the schist are gneiss, identified by its coarse texture and the presence of quartz and feldspar.

mudflats or elevated landscape. Geologists have learned to read these strata and to estimate climatic conditions during each episode.

The Mesozoic Period & the Kaibab Uplift

Considering the detailed Paleozoic record, it's puzzling that evidence of the following Mesozoic period (245 to 70 million years ago) is entirely absent at the canyon, even though its elaborate layers are well represented just miles away on the Colorado Plateau and in nearby Zion, Bryce and Arches National Parks. Towering over the landscape just south of the South Rim, Red Butte is a dramatic reminder of how many thousands of feet of Mesozoic sediments once covered the canyon. So what happened to all of this rock, which vanished before the river even started shaping the canyon? About 70 million years ago the same events that gave rise to the Rocky Mountains created a buckle in the earth known as the Kaibab Uplift, a broad dome that rose several thousand feet above the surrounding region. Higher and more exposed, the upper layers of this dome eroded quickly and completely.

Don't miss the daily ranger-led fossil walks on the South Rim. In just a half mile you'll discover many interesting marine fossils and have the opportunity to pick the brains of canyon experts.

Volcanism has added a few layers of rock in parts of the west canyon, where lava flows created temporary dams across the canyon or simply flowed over the rim in spectacular lava waterfalls. The stretching of earth's crust also tilted the region to the southwest, shifting drainage patterns accordingly.

But the story that interests visitors most – namely how the canyon formed – is perhaps the most perplex chapter of all. Geologists have several competing theories but few clues. One intriguing characteristic is that the canyon's eastern end is much older than the western portion, suggesting that two separate rivers carved the canyon. This fits into the oft-repeated 'stream piracy' theory that the Kaibab Uplift initially served as a barrier between two major river drainage systems. The theory assumes that the western drainage system eroded quickly into the soft sediments back-carving eastward into the uplift, eventually breaking through the barrier and 'capturing' the flow of the ancient Colorado River, which then shifted course down this newly opened route.

Alternate theories assume other river routes or different timing of the erosion, placing it either before or after the uplift. Until more evidence is uncovered, visitors will have to simply marvel at the canyon and formulate their own theories about how this mighty river cut through a giant bulge in earth's crust millions of years ago.

Reading the Layers

Kaibab Limestone

The white limestone caprock of the Kaibab Formation may be the youngest layer in the canyon, but it still pre-dates the dinosaurs. It was deposited 270 million years ago by shifting seas when the region was at the edge of the continent. Look for fossils of sponges, coral and brachiopods while you consider that this layer was once buried under Mesozoic rock up to a mile thick.

Toroweap Formation

The Toroweap Formation is the vegetated slope between the chunky Kaibab limestone above and the massive Coconino cliffs below. It was deposited 273 million years ago from a mix of intertidal buildup and coastal dunes which formed both limestone and sandstone depending on the sea level. Being softer than the layers above and below, it has eroded into a ramp.

Coconino Sandstone

The sheer cliffs of the Coconino sandstone are obvious throughout the park, and create the first major challenge for those hoping to hike to the river. In this layer are the remains of extensive coastal dunes; look for the striated cross-bedding formed when prevailing winds deposited sand in different directions. Even more fascinating are the millipede, spider and scorpion tracks preserved in the rock from the Permian Period – though no fossilized critters have been found.

The Yavapai Geology Museum on the South Rim features kid-friendly interactive exhibits explaining the geology of the canyon from various angles. Rangers give daily geology talks and walks in the afternoon.

Hermit Shale

The crumbly red Hermit shale located below the Coconino is more properly known as mudstone or siltstone. It tells the story, through fossilized mud cracks, ripple marks and the footprints of reptiles and amphibians, of a semi-arid lowland or broad coastal plain with forests and meandering rivers. The release of iron oxide through erosion forms the red color that stains the layers below it. The sloping shelf supports a distinctive band of vegetation including scrub oak, hop tree and serviceberry. In places, the soft layer has eroded completely, leaving a broad terrace of Esplanade sandstone.

Supai Group

Just below the Hermit shale are the red cliffs and ledges of the Supai Group. Though similar in composition and color, these intermingled layers consist of shale, limestone and sandstone, with each dominating different portions of the canyon. All formed under swampy coastal conditions, where shallow waters mingled with sand dunes. Deposited some 300 million years ago when amphibians first evolved, the formations preserve early footprints of these new animals. Supai cliffs can be stained red by iron oxides or black from iron or manganese.

Redwall Limestone

The canyon's most impenetrable layer, the famous Redwall towers 500ft to 800ft over the broad Tonto Platform below. Around 340 million years ago, much of North America was covered by an inland sea that deposited this layer now known for its extensive cave systems. The rock is actually light-gray limestone that has been stained red by iron oxides washed down from the Hermit shale and Supai Group above.

Muav Limestone

The cliff-forming Muav limestone can be difficult to distinguish from the Redwall, but was deposited during the Middle Cambrian period deep beneath the sea when the first primitive fishes were just appearing on the scene. This 500-million-year-old marine formation contains few fossils but features many eroded cavities and passages.

Bright Angel Shale

Perched just above the dark inner gorge, the broad, gently sloping Tonto Platform is the only consistent horizontal break in a jumble of vertical cliffs and ledges. The platform is not a formation at all but rather the absence of one, where soft greenish Bright Angel shale with purple and red layers has been largely stripped away to reveal the hard Tapeats sandstone beneath. The Bright Angel was deposited in a shallow coastal zone as sea levels were rising.

Tapeats Sandstone

The lowest (and oldest) sedimentary layer is the Tapeats sandstone formed as the rising Paleozoic seas began to inundate what is now North America. Even more interesting is what they covered: a billion years of missing geologic record. This gap was first noticed by self-taught geologist John Wesley Powell who dubbed it 'The Great Unconformity.'

TRAIL OF TIME

For an excellent primer on Grand Canyon geology, hike the Trail of Time (p75) on the South Rim between Grand Canyon Village and Yavapai Geology Museum. Each one million years is represented by 1m (3.3ft) along the way, marked by bronze signs embedded in the trail. Alongside the trail are beautiful, polished examples of stone from geologic layers deep within the canyon that correspond with the time period on the trail. Interpretive information and viewing spots dot the way, breaking up the 2km (1.3-mile) geological journey.

Inner Gorge

Some 1.7 billion years ago the intense pressure and heat from 13 miles of earth overhead metamorphosed the inner canyon layers into the Vishnu schist and Zoroaster granite you see today. The angular orientation of these rocks indicates periods of tectonic uplift and displacement. The flat transition between the inner gorge and Tapeats sandstone indicates over a billion years of erosion.

Water at Work

While geologists still aren't sure exactly how the Grand Canyon formed, one thing is certain: it had a lot to do with water. Steady flowing water; cataclysmic flood water; freezing water; subterranean water; lake water. Even the distinct lack of water in this high desert environment is key to the erosion that carved this awesome landscape.

Different rock types are affected by the forces of erosion, as evidenced by the canyon's stair-step profile. Softer sedimentary layers crumble into gentle slopes at the foot of the harder sheer cliffs, while erosion seems to have all but ceased once the river hit the extremely hard basement rocks.

At the very basic level, water absorbed into the rock can gradually dissolve minerals, weakening the matrix that binds a layer together. Eventually gravity may take over, pulling chunks of debris to the layer below. During colder months, water that finds its way down into cracks and freezes exerts a tremendous outward force (up to 30,000lb per square inch) prying blocks of rock from the canyon cliffs.

More actively, flowing streams gradually erode the side canyons of both rims, cutting back ever deeper into their headwalls. The higher-altitude North Rim catches more runoff from storms and winter snow, and because of the angle of the Colorado Plateau, North Rim moisture flows into the canyon while South Rim runoff tends to flow away. The combined effect of these factors are why the side canyons on the North Rim tend to be cut further back from the river than in the south.

Water is not always as patient or imperceptible. Monsoon thunderstorms can cause violent flash floods which have the potential to dramatically alter the landscape in minutes. The parched earth does not readily absorb the sudden onslaught of rain, but sends it rushing down canyon. A tiny trickling brook carrying grains of sand can explode into a powerful torrent tossing boulders and debris against its confining walls.

The mighty Colorado River is the most recognizable force of erosion: its strong current cuts through the soft sedimentary layers at lightning speed (geologically speaking). Now that it has reached the hard Vishnu schist, however, erosion has slowed dramatically. More recently, Glen Canyon Dam has also stopped the once-seasonal floods that scoured loose rocks and sand from the corridor, further retarding canyon growth.

Eventually, as the river cuts toward sea level, downward erosion will cease altogether, even as the canyon continues to widen. And since lateral (sideways) erosion proceeds 10 times faster, some day a few million years in the future your ancestors may be standing on the edge of Grand Valley National Park.

The steep Hermit Trail offers excellent opportunities to see various types of fossils. Near the trailhead, the Kaibab limestone holds marine fossils. About a mile down the trail, fossilized reptile tracks appear in Coconino sandstone, and not quite 2 miles down you can find fossils of ferns.

ED FREEMAN/GETTY IMAGES ©

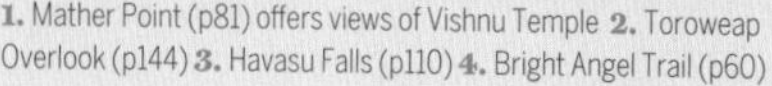

1. Mather Point (p81) offers views of Vishnu Temple **2.** Toroweap Overlook (p144) **3.** Havasu Falls (p110) **4.** Bright Angel Trail (p60)

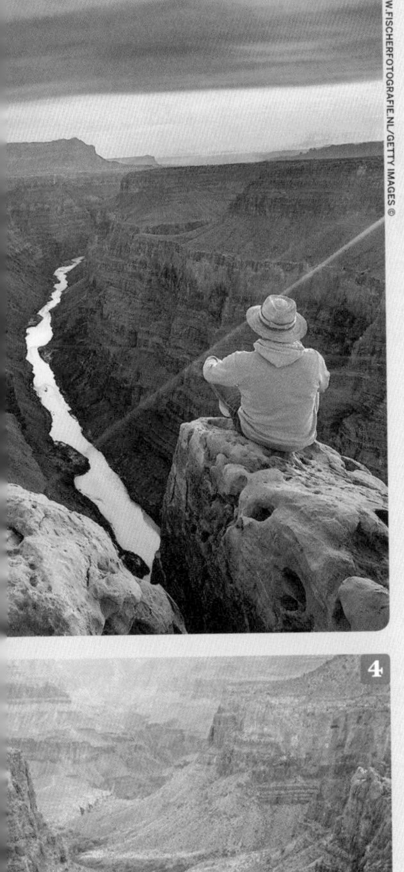

WWW.FISCHERFOTOGRAFIE.NL/GETTY IMAGES ©

Geologic Wonders

The entire national park is a geologic spectacle, but a few landmarks stand out from the rest. Even if you don't get the chance to see all of the following natural wonders in person, you may recognize them: they're prominently featured on postcards.

Bright Angel Canyon

An excellent example of how creeks follow fault lines across the landscape. Accessible from the South Rim, it's located partway down the Bright Angel Trail (p60) on the path to Phantom Ranch.

Havasu Creek

Stupendous travertine formations and beautiful waterfalls. A tributary leading into the Colorado River, Havasu Creek (p180) runs through Havasu Canyon and the village of Supai.

Toroweap Overlook

The canyon's most dramatic viewpoint (p143). It's located 3000ft above the Colorado River in a remote section of the North Rim, approximately 55 miles west of the North Rim headquarters.

Vishnu Temple

One of the canyon's most prominent temples (p142), it's visible from the South Kaibab Trail and lookout points such as Mather Point on the South Rim.

Wildlife of the Grand Canyon

The thriving communities of critters – big and small – that call the Grand Canyon home can be as fascinating as the landscape itself. All manner of life has adapted to the extremes of the park, from the cool North Rim forests to the sizzling inner gorge, and it is home to 447 bird, 91 mammal, 17 fish, and 58 reptile and amphibian species.

Large Mammals

Elk

The largest members of the deer family, elk are easily recognizable by the male's sprawling antlers, which can weigh up to 40lb (18kg). Elk were brought to the park from Yellowstone between 1913 and 1928, and being poorly adapted to the desert tend to stay close to water. Watch out for them near bottle filling stations and irrigation runoff where they can look quite at ease surrounded by humans. Don't be fooled.

Elk are the park's most dangerous animals and have injured several visitors angling for that perfect photo. Keep a distance of at least 100ft (30m) and never get between a mother and her calf. Bull elk are particularly aggressive during the fall rut when they strut their stuff and bugle at each other in impressive displays of dominance. Stay well away.

Mountain Lions

Although your likelihood of seeing the secretive mountain lion is extremely rare, there is a good chance one will see you. The Grand Canyon hosts a healthy population, and while they commonly prowl the forests along the canyon's edge in pursuit of their favorite food – mule deer – they do also roam the interior. One radio-collared female descended from the South Rim to the river, swam across, then scaled the North Rim in under eight hours. Reaching up to 8ft in length and weighing as much as 160lb, this majestic solitary animal is a formidable predator, but one that typically avoids humans.

Amateur naturalists should track down *A Field Guide to the Grand Canyon* by Stephen Whitney (also available in ebook version) or *A Naturalist's Guide to Canyon Country* by David Williams, both of which cover the region's common plants and animals.

Mule Deer

Spotting mule deer can be particularly exhilarating when you encounter one in the middle of the road at night while you're driving around a blind corner – seemingly their favorite time and place to hang out.

After their predators were systematically hunted out of the park in the early 1900s (even Teddy Roosevelt came to the canyon to bag mountain lions), mule deer experienced a massive population explosion. They are most common on the North Rim, but range throughout the park – even down to the edge of the Colorado River. Look for them around dusk grazing in herds along the forest edge.

THE MEXICAN WOLF

In 1998 an endemic Southwestern predator took its first tentative steps back to the wild. Eleven captive-bred Mexican wolves, a subspecies of the gray wolf, were released in east-central Arizona. The project aimed to reintroduce 100 wolves into a 7000-sq-mile area over 10 years. The current population stands at about 113, but you still won't see them in the Grand Canyon, and their future is suddenly in jeopardy.

The Mexican wolf traditionally ranged in 'sky islands' (high-elevation areas) as far south as central Mexico and as far north as southern Colorado. They are the smallest, most genetically distinct subspecies of gray wolf in North America. Early-20th-century campaigns to eradicate predators resulted in the wild US population of Mexican wolves going extinct by the 1950s. In 1976 they were declared an endangered species, a designation that remains in place today.

Despite the early success of the recovery program, the Trump administration approved a revised recovery plan in 2017 which scientists and conservationists warn spells disaster for the Mexican wolf. The plan will strip wolves of their protected status when the population reaches only 320 animals – well below a stable number. Further, it limits recovery efforts to south of I-40, cutting off access to critical habitat around the Grand Canyon where humans, cattle ranching and road density are low but mule deer and elk are plentiful.

Bighorn Sheep

Scan for motionless desert bighorn perched on seemingly inaccessible cliff faces or ridgelines, their distinctive curled horns making impressive silhouettes. During breeding season, males charge each other at 20mph and ram horns so loudly the sound echoes for miles between canyon walls. You can find the park's largest native animal in side canyons along the Tonto Platform beneath the South Rim, but bring binoculars as hikers seldom encounter them at close range.

Coyotes & Foxes

Wild members of the dog family include the ubiquitous coyote and its much smaller cousin, the gray fox. Both share the same grayish-brown coat, but foxes typically have a tell-tale black tip to their tail. Each has adapted to human activity, growing increasingly comfortable around roads, buildings and (of course) any unattended food. Foxes often emerge at night, when you might spy one crossing a trail or road. Look for coyote scouring meadows for tasty rodents any time of day, and listen for their haunting chorus around sunset - a cacophony of yips, cries and...taunting laughter?

Black Bears

Black bears are extremely rare in the Grand Canyon, and the occasional sighting typically makes the local news. They mostly hide in the quiet forested areas on the North Rim, though drought conditions may compel them to seek new water sources near populated areas.

Although your chances of seeing one are slim, you should still practice smart bear-safe tactics while camping. Don't leave food out (including pet food) and pack up trash. If you do spot a bear, do not approach or feed it: a fed bear is a dead bear (and you may not fare so well either).

The black bear's larger cousin and longtime member of the endangered species list - the grizzly bear - has long been absent from the Grand Canyon (as well from 96% of their ancestral homeland). Petitions for the reintroduction of these regal beasts have not gathered much momentum.

Mammals of the Grand Canyon

A total of 89 mammal species live in Grand Canyon National Park, from the solitary mountain lion to the amusing nocturnal ringtail. While some of the following species inhabit only certain sections of the park, you're likely to spot one of the following during a quiet hike on either rim.

1

1. Mule Deer

Rim forests and meadows are the favored haunts of mule deer, which commonly graze at dusk in groups of a dozen or more, moving seasonally to find water and avoid deep snows.

2. Ringtail

One of the area's most intriguing creatures is the nocturnal ringtail, which looks like a wide-eyed housecat with a raccoon's tail.

3

3. Mountain Lion

The canyon rates among the best places in North America to spot this elusive cat, reaching up to 8ft in length and weighing as much as 160lb. They gravitate to forests along the North Rim in pursuit of their favorite food, mule deer.

4

4. Bighorn Sheep

Like solemn statues, bighorn sheep often stand motionless on inaccessible cliff faces or ridgelines and are readily identified by their distinctive curled horns. Bring binoculars.

5. Fox

The coyote's much smaller cousin, the gray fox, often emerges at night, when you might spy one crossing a trail or road.

6. Chipmunk

The South Rim is the exclusive domain of the gray cliff chipmunk, an extremely vocal species that can bark an estimated 5800 times in half an hour, twitching its tail with each call.

7

7. Coyote

Wild members of the dog family include the ubiquitous coyote. You stand a good chance of seeing coyotes in the daytime, especially around meadows, where they hunt for rodents.

8. Squirrel

Living on opposite rims, Abert's and Kaibab squirrels were a single population only 20,000 years ago, then the forested climate warmed and dried, and the canyon was transformed into desert habitat.

9. Bat

You'll spot plenty of these, especially close to the Colorado River, but don't get too close: the NPS reported that several local bats tested positive for rabies in 2018.

TOM WALKER/GETTY IMAGES ©

CHARLES SCHUG/GETTY IMAGES ©

JOEL BAUCHAT GRANT/SHUTTERSTOCK ©

RAZYPH/GETTY IMAGES ©

CHASE SWIFT/GETTY IMAGES ©

BISON

Your chance of seeing the illusive House Rock bison herd on the North Rim has increased in recent years – this is not a good thing. As their population grows, so does the havoc they wreak on the landscape. The 2000lb beasts trample sensitive alpine meadows, destroy springs, pollute groundwater, disrupt archaeological sites and spread invasive plants.

The 'Cattalo' are the remnants of a failed 1900s experiment in cross-breeding American bison and cattle to create an animal that had the meat of a cow, the hide of a buffalo, and could survive in the harsh Arizona environment. For decades about 100 of these non-native transplants roamed House Rock Valley where the Game and Fish Department managed them for hunting. However, once they found their way to the forests of the Kaibab Plateau – and the protective boundary of the national park – the population exploded to 600 or more, and so did their impact.

Park managers have detailed an aggressive removal program to thin the herd to 200 animals or less. And while some people think the only acceptable number is zero, others are proposing a controversial re-introduction of more bison to House Rock Valley to maintain opportunities for hunting.

Small Mammals

Chipmunks & Squirrels

Living on opposite rims, Abert's and Kaibab squirrels are excellent examples of divergent evolution. These long-eared mammals were a single population only 20,000 years ago, thriving in the forests that covered the region after the last ice age. When the climate warmed, leaving isolated pockets of ponderosa pines at higher elevations, the squirrels – who rarely stray more than 20yd from their favorite trees – split into two distinct species. The dark-bellied, white-tailed Kaibab squirrel lives exclusively on the North Rim, and is a subspecies of the Abert's squirrel of the South Rim.

The most conspicuous members of the squirrel family, however, are speckled gray rock squirrels, which scoot fearlessly amid visitors' feet along rim trails and viewpoints, hoping for handouts (never give them handouts). True to its name, this species nearly always inhabits rocky areas.

While similar in appearance, the region's three chipmunk species do bear subtle differences. The South Rim is the domain of the gray cliff chipmunk, an extremely vocal species that can bark an estimated 5800 times in a half hour, twitching its tail with each call. This species shares the North Rim with least chipmunks and Uinta chipmunks, although cliff chipmunks stick to the rocky ledges. Least chipmunks inhabit open areas, while Uinta chipmunks live in forests and are abundant around North Rim campgrounds and picnic sites.

The last wild condor to soar over the Grand Canyon was spotted in 1924 – that is until 1996, when six adults raised in a captive breeding program were released at Vermilion Cliffs.

Ringtails

Looking like a cross between a ferret, bat, squirrel and a raccoon, the ringtail is one of the area's most intriguing creatures, and Arizona's state mammal. They were once common marauders of park campsites, but modern food-storage techniques have somewhat discouraged these nocturnal members of the raccoon family, though you'll still see them along the rims and river corridors.

Birds

Small Birds

The call of the tiny canyon wren defines the soundscape of the park: a hauntingly descending crescendo evoking a water droplet plummeting off a cliff's edge to the rocks below. It's hard to believe that the little reddish rock-dweller could produce such music. Intrepid hikers may also spot a black-throated sparrow around the sparsely vegetated Tonto Platform, or encounter the aquatic American dipper (aka water ouzel) diving under waves and surfing the eddies of inner-canyon creeks.

A harbinger of spring, the broad-tailed hummingbird zips energetically about the park from May through August, common in wildflower-filled glades on both rims. The sparrow-sized Junco hops along the forest floor in search of seeds and insects. White-throated swifts swoop and dive over scenic viewpoints at impossible speeds. Watch your head.

If you're sleeping out, keep your valuables safely stashed. Curious ringtails have been known to run off with headlamps, jewelry, food and even paperback books.

Birds of Prey

Six owl species call the park home, including the highly vocal great horned owl, which can fill the canyon walls with their echoing, booming hoots. Among the largest and most fearsome of the region's raptors, when a great horned owl moves into the neighborhood, other owls and hawks move out – or run the risk of becoming the hunted. Listen for the threatened Mexican spotted owl's four-note location call. They're most vocal during the early summer breeding months.

Golden eagles command expansive hunting territories of some 50 sq miles, and are often observed soaring high above the park in search of jackrabbits and other prey. Meanwhile, look for red-tailed hawks standing in the middle of North Rim meadows keeping an eye on ground-dwelling mammals.

Given their endangered status, peregrine falcons are surprisingly common throughout the park: over 100 nesting pairs of the world's fastest animal call Grand Canyon home. If you're lucky, you'll watch one dive-bomb another bird – its exclusive prey – at speeds up to 200mph (320km/h), breaking its meal's back in midair. Look for the falcon's long, slender wings and dark helmet pattern extending below its eyes.

Condors

The critically endangered California condor's near-miraculous return from the brink of extinction has made them poster children for Grand Canyon conservation efforts – despite their wrinkled, balding heads and a tendency to defecate on their own legs to keep themselves cool. Watching one of these massive prehistoric birds take flight over the canyon on 9ft wings is a highlight of any park visit.

After California condors soared the skies for 40,000 years, they became extinct in the wild in 1987 when the remaining birds were taken into captivity in a desperate effort to save the species. Nine years later, biologists released six captive-bred individuals at nearby Vermilion Cliffs, and the canyon experience was forever and profoundly altered. Now, more than 80 condors call the Grand Canyon region home, but their struggle is far from over.

Despite efforts by rescuers to train condors to fear humans, they have a strong affinity for large crowds. This is an evolutionary trait, as they are scavengers and use keen eyesight to look for congregations of animals – an indicator that food may be close. As a result, they often hang around popular viewpoints near Grand Canyon Lodge and in Grand Canyon Village. Do not approach or feed them, and don't be upset if a park ranger scares the birds away for their own safety.

1

JARED HOBBS/GETTY IMAGES ©

2

4

PANTHER MEDIA GMBH/ALAMY STOCK PHOTO ©

. Great Basin Rattlesnake (p213)
attlesnakes rapidly shake their namesake tails s a warning. If you hear the distinctive buzz move way quickly.

. California Condor (p209)
he critically endangered California condor, which as a 9ft wingspan, is coming back from the brink f extinction due to conservation efforts.

. Gila Monster (p212)
he rarely seen Gila monster is one of the park's nost interesting reptiles. Growing up to 2ft long is mostly placid but can lunge quickly and has a owerful (and venomous) bite.

. Dark-Eyed Junco (p209)
he sparrow-sized Junco searches the forest floor or seeds and insects.

VACLAV SEBEK/SHUTTERSTOCK ©

The most pernicious threat to condor recovery, however, is bullets – but not from being shot at. Lead ammunition found in the carcasses and gut piles left behind by hunters is toxic to scavengers. Over 70 California condors have died from lead poisoning since 1984 – a significant percentage considering only 276 birds live in the wild. Arizona Game and Fish provides free lead-free bullets for those hunting around the canyon, but has not yet followed California (home of the other main release site) which banned the use of all lead ammunition from 2019.

If you really want to freak yourself out, take a UV flashlight with you while camping. Bark scorpions hunt at night and glow an iridescent blue under ultraviolet light.

How can you tell a California condor from a common turkey vulture? First, they have a much longer wingspan, averaging about 9ft versus a turkey vulture's 6ft. Second, turkey vultures tend to rock slightly in the wind and flap more often than their smooth-soaring cousins. Finally, if you're still in doubt, look for the white-numbered GPS tags attached to the wings of most condors.

Ravens

Though common throughout the west, the ravens of the Grand Canyon have a well-deserved reputation for cunning and thievery. About the size of a red-tailed hawk, ravens are larger than crows, and tend to travel in pairs or be solitary. Backpackers often return to camp to find the black-feathered bandits have unzipped zippers or untied bags to get at food or whatever shiny objects they can fit in their piercing beaks.

Amphibians & Reptiles

Frogs & Toads

The bleating choruses you'll hear next to boulder-strewn canyon streams are likely not domestic sheep, but rather the common canyon tree frog. Gray-brown and speckled like stone, these tiny frogs dwell in damp crevices by day, emerging beside rocky pools at night. Occupying similar habitats is the aptly named red-spotted toad, whose call is more sustained and higher pitched.

Lizards

In addition to the common fence lizard you might see doing push-ups to show others how buff he is (it's a dominance thing), the Grand Canyon is home to some astounding lizards.

The banded gecko has thin, practically translucent velvety skin and prefers to hunt in the cool night. It's quick to shed its tail if grabbed, but it trades short-term safety for long-term peril as its tail is also a critical storage compartment for food and water.

What some people mistakenly call a horny toad is actually the short-horned lizard. Found on both rims and in the canyon, it employs a bizarre defense mechanism: a squirt of blood from its eyes that contains chemicals irritating to cats – its main predator.

Spend a night anywhere near water below the rim and you'll likely be treated to an incredible chorus of frogs and toads croaking en masse, a cacophony of chirps and grumps echoing off the canyon walls.

You might catch a glimpse of a chuckwalla, a relative of the iguana, in the inner canyon. The second-largest lizard in North America can reach 18in long, has loose folds of skin around its neck, and if frightened will wedge itself between rocks, gulp in air and puff up its body, thoroughly locking itself in the tight space.

Perhaps the park's most interesting reptile is the rarely seen Gila monster, found on the far western end of the park. It grows up to 2ft long and looks like an orange-and-black bumpy sausage with legs. Mostly placid, America's largest lizard can lunge quickly and has a powerful bite, often locking on to its victims. The Gila monster is venomous, and Arizona Poison Control suggests you use a strong stick to remove the animal as soon as possible – a process typically more successful if the lizard's feet can touch the ground.

Snakes

The park is home to some 22 snake species, including six resident rattlesnakes, each with a distinct color pattern. The southwestern speckled and the northern black-tailed rattlesnake are the rarest, while the other four are subspecies of the western diamondback family: the Great Basin, the Mojave, the Hopi and, the most common of all, the Grand Canyon pink – found nowhere else on earth. Rattlesnakes rapidly shake their namesake tails as a way of warning you to stay away. They would rather be left alone than waste venom, and most bites occur when people harass one or try to pick it up. If you hear the distinctive buzz, move away quickly and let it live in peace.

Of the six rattlesnake species found in the canyon, the most common is the Grand Canyon pink, a subspecies of the western diamondback that evolved to blend in amazingly well with the warm tints of the canyon's geologic layers.

Fish

The historically warm and silty water of the Colorado River was once home to eight species of fish adapted to survive in the murky environment; six of these are endemic, meaning they're not found outside the Colorado river basin.

In the years since Glen Canyon Dam turned the water clear and cool and invasive fish were introduced upstream, the native population has plummeted: only five species remain. The once-plentiful humpback chub with its pronounced fleshy bump behind its head and the razorback sucker with a sharp keel before its dorsal fin are both now endangered. Only one native fish – the speckled dace – is considered common.

Non-native brown and rainbow trout prefer the cool clear water, and can be found where side creeks like Bright Angel flow into the river. Recreational fishing in the park is allowed with a license, and there is no bag limit on invasive trout species.

Insects

Over 1400 invertebrate species inhabit the Grand Canyon ecosystem, and while most of these creepy-crawlies are content to remain hidden, there are a few worth looking for – and a few worth looking out for.

The distinctive orange-and-black monarch highlights the canyon's many butterfly species. It flutters through the park in large numbers in late summer on its multi-thousand-mile migration to Mexican wintering grounds. In its larval stage, the monarch feeds on milkweed plants, which contain noxious alkaloids. These compounds remain in the adults, providing would-be predators with a nasty reaction if they try to eat one.

The drone of the desert cicada bores into the brains of summer visitors as if it's the buzz of the sun itself, relentlessly beating down on your head. Males produce the rasping and clicking by vibrating membranes stretched over resonating sound chambers in their body. But while you'll find it difficult to escape the screech, actually finding one of these inch-long insects is another matter altogether: they are masters of camouflage – one reason they're able to sing all day yet avoid predators.

Black widow spiders hide in debris piles or between rock cracks where the distinct red hourglass on their underside may not be visible. They are typically not aggressive, and bite only when they feel threatened, but be concerned if one does. If you begin to feel nausea, difficulty breathing or other systemic symptoms, seek medical attention.

While the pincers of the diminutive bark scorpion may look menacing, it's the poison tip on their whiplike tails that do the real damage. Bark scorpions are the most venomous scorpion in North America, but typically a sting will result only in localized pain and swelling. But, again, if you experience difficulty breathing, nausea or convulsions, seek medical help.

Environmental Issues & Conservation

Sprawling across 1875 sq miles, Grand Canyon National Park protects a sizable portion of the Colorado Plateau, as well as 277 free-flowing miles of the Colorado River. The fact that millions of people visit this fragile desert landscape each year means that tourism and development have a lasting impact. Even an action as simple as walking off the trail is detrimental when multiplied many times over by a steady stream of visitors, most of whom drive to the park in private vehicles.

Damming Consequences

In 1963 Glen Canyon Dam pinched off the flow of the Colorado River and began to fill Lake Powell behind it; the impacts to the Grand Canyon were immediate, severe and lasting.

Before the dam was built, the river would warm up to 80°F (27°C) in the summer and be thick with sediment. Flows annually fluctuated between a few hundred to 100,000cfs (cubic feet per second) with at least one flood in the last 1600 years reaching 500,000cfs. These high volumes would move boulders downriver, scour out vegetation, and rebuild sandbars and beaches.

Now, the dam releases a predictable flow between 8000cfs and 25,000cfs at a near constant temperature of 46°F (8°C). Since Lake Powell acts as a settling pond, the Colorado below it is clear after dumping 380,000 tons of sediment per year into Glen Canyon.

These even, sediment-free flows constantly eat away at the beaches and sandbars along the river corridor, damaging archaeological sites and destroying the backwaters and eddies that many fish call home. Without the massive floods to scour the remaining sandbanks, highly invasive plant species like tamarisk have established strongholds along the Colorado from where they can send billions of wind-born seeds up fragile side canyons in search of sensitive riparian areas. Algal growth has skyrocketed due to sunlight penetrating the now-clear water; the algae soak up phosphorus, a critical nutrient that otherwise fuels aquatic diversity.

In 2012 the Bureau of Reclamation (who operates Glen Canyon Dam) adopted guidelines requiring annual high-flow releases if enough sediment builds up at the mouth of the Paria River 15 miles downstream. Previous experimental floods showed that pushing 200,000 metric tons of Paria silt downriver could dramatically rebuild beaches during multiday flows above 35,000cfs. Further, in 2018, new protocols reduced water levels on the weekends to expose shoreline rocks for aquatic insects to lay eggs. These insects are important food for fish, bats and other canyon critters.

However, despite the incremental successes of these releases, they are no substitute for the natural cycles of a free-flowing river, and the Grand Canyon corridor will continue to need active intervention to protect its endangered species.

Above Glen Canyon Dam (p166), Colorado River

Right Cryptobiotic soil (p216) with yucca plants, Toroweap

JOY STEIN/SHUTTERSTOCK ©

The Year the River Almost Escaped

In 1983 record snows and warmer temperatures sent runoff into Lake Powell at 210% of normal rates. This caught dam operators flat footed, and they threw open the spillways at full volume to prevent the water from overtopping – a potentially catastrophic event that would likely destroy the dam and create deadly flooding downstream.

Shortly after opening the spillways, sandstone colored water and chunks of cement began launching out of the outlet as cavitation – the hydraulic pounding of turbulent water – broke apart the poorly designed tunnels, stripping out the concrete and blasting apart the soft Navajo sandstone. Engineers frantically added plywood and metal plates to the top of the dam to hold back the rising waters.

By dumb luck alone, the water stopped just inches below the level of uncontrollable release and began to recede. Upon later inspection, house-sized craters found in the spillway tunnels bore testament to how close it came to losing the dam entirely.

The only upshot of the event was that the Colorado River through the Grand Canyon briefly experienced the type of flooding that once regularly defined the landscape. River runners lucky enough to ride the rapids at 92,000cfs still get a fiery glint in their eye and childlike grin when they recall the summer of 1983.

Water Conservation

Water is life in the desert, and water conservation is a perennial issue in and around the park. Every drop that visitors use on both rims is pumped up from Roaring Springs at the bottom of Bright Angel Canyon via an aging 12.5-mile pipeline that suffers assaults from rockslides and floods. In 2017 Grand Canyon Lodge had to cancel reservations while the park sunk $1.5 million into repairing the conduit to the North Rim, and they are now considering upgrading the entire system for around $120 million.

The tiny seeps and springs that leak out of the canyon walls are the epicenters of life and activity. These microwetlands support 500 times as many plant species as the surrounding hills, yet they make up less than 0.01% of the Grand Canyon's landscape. They are fed by a network of poorly understood underground aquifers that scientists are frantically studying to assess the immediate risk of pollution by nearby uranium mines and the long-term threat of depletion by population increases. If water use in the region doubles over the next 50 years – as many predict – these seeps may dry up as the aquifers are drawn down, leading to the collapse of vital riparian ecosystems and the species that depend on them.

CRYPTOBIOTIC CRUSTS

Watch where you step! That gray and black crust covering much of the desert sand is actually a fragile community of microscopic living organisms. Algae, fungi and cyanobacteria form a matrix that glues the soil particles together. This biological soil crust prevents erosion, creates places for vegetation to grow, stores water, and even fixes nitrogen for plants to feed on.

While extremely important, the magic shell is also easily destroyed by a careless footstep – not to mention bicycle, motorcycle and car tires. Once broken, the cryptobiotic crust can take decades to repair itself, or the ensuing erosion can destroy the entire community.

Air Pollution

To arrive at one the world's most scenic vistas only to find the view obscured by haze is a grim reminder of the wide-ranging impact humans have on the environment. Area coal-burning power plants provide the balance of the park's pall, while distant cities like Las Vegas and Los Angeles also contribute plenty of haze at times. Studies have found elevated levels of mercury, nitrogen, sulfur and related toxins in the water and soil – a result of pollutants settling out of the air.

While the park can do little about smog from far-away sources, it does actively work to reduce local emissions. A natural-gas bus system provides a convenient way for visitors to get to major points on the South Rim and is part of Grand Canyon's participation in the Climate Friendly Park's initiative. The park also works with other federal, state, and local agencies, as well as industry leaders to find ways to reduce air pollution throughout the Southwest, and the Clean Air Act requires the Environmental Protection Authority (EPA) to consult with the park before approving new potential sources of haze and pollution that may affect its viewshed.

Fishy Business

Visitors to Phantom Ranch may see crews of biologists and researchers wading up Bright Angel Creek electrocuting fish. As shocking as this may seem, it's for a good reason: non-native brown and rainbow trout have taken over the waterway and eat the native humpback chub.

The invasive fish were stocked in Grand Canyon through the 1950s before we knew their negative effects and appreciated how widely they roam; individuals tagged in Bright Angel have been recaptured 26 miles upstream.

The multi-year project is part of a wider effort by the National Park Service to restore the native fisheries, a task complicated by two major challenges. First, cold, clear water released from the bottom of Glen Canyon Dam suits invasive trout better than the native species which thrive in warm silty rivers. Second, the park is downstream of Lees Ferry where Arizona Game and Fish keeps stocking rainbow trout for recreational fishing. Anglers strongly oppose the park's proposal to kill brown trout at Lees Ferry (even though they also compete with prized blue-ribbon rainbows.)

Both agencies did jump on the discovery of a healthy breeding population of highly invasive green sunfish found just below Lake Powell in 2015. If left unchecked, the fish could wipe out all other species – native and non. An initial poisoning of the backwater worked, but the fish soon returned. Scientists suspect they're being sucked through Glen Canyon Dam as the water levels of Lake Powell drop to historic lows.

Native Americans of the Grand Canyon

Human habitation of the Grand Canyon region dates back at least 4000 years – according to carbon dating of split-twig animal figurines – and continues to the present day. Tribes whose reservations now border Grand Canyon National Park and who reside on the land surrounding the park include the Hualapai, Havasupai, Navajo, Hopi and Paiute peoples. It would be a mistake to generalize about American Indians in the region: each has its own traditions, sacred lands and specific (sometimes complicated) relationships to other tribes.

The Havasupai (Havsuw 'Baaja)

Well known for their beadwork and basketry, the Havasupai (whose name translates as 'people of the blue-green waters') share the Yuman language with the Hualapai. Both tribes are together referred to as Northeastern Pai. Their legends tell them that mankind originated on a mountain near the Colorado River. They left their Mojave relatives behind and headed to Meriwitica, near Spencer Canyon (a tributary of Grand Canyon). The Hualapai stayed near Meriwitica, but one story explains that a frog, enticed by the stream and lush vegetation, led the Havasupai east to Havasu Canyon. Archaeological records indicate that the Northeastern Pai arrived at the Grand Canyon around AD 1150, and the Havasupai have occupied Havasu Canyon since about that time.

At the bottom of Havasu Canyon, two Supai sandstone rock spires stand over the village of Supai. Known as Wii Gl'iiva, the spires – one male, one female – are believed to be guardian spirits watching over the Havasupai.

Today over 30,000 tourists visit Havasu Canyon every year, and the Havasupai's lives and economic survival are integrally related to the tourist industry that has developed in and around Grand Canyon National Park. They, along with the Hualapai, do not participate in the gaming industry. In Supai, the village at the bottom of the canyon, the Havasupai run a lodge and campground, as well as a small village store, serving the tourist industry.

The village's isolation probably magnifies the tension created by the outside influence of mainstream American culture on the younger generation of Havasupai. The traditional structure of Havasupai society, based on respect for tribal elders and the tribal council, remains in place despite such outside pressures – but as with much of life for many American Indians, this continues to be a struggle.

The Hualapai (Hwal' bay)

The Hualapai trace their origins to Kathat Kanave, an old man who sometimes took the form of a coyote and lived in Mada Widita Canyon (also known as Meriwitica), on the canyon's westernmost edge. He taught the Pai (literally 'The People') how to live in the canyon, explaining what herbs cured which ailments and how and what to plant. The Hualapai and Havasupai developed complex systems of irrigation and spent summers farming within the canyon, at places like Havasu Canyon and Indian Garden. During the winter, they hunted on the plateau.

RESERVATION ETIQUETTE

Visitors are usually welcome on American Indian reservations, as long as they behave in an appropriately courteous and respectful manner. Tribal rules are often clearly posted at the entrance to each reservation, but here are some general guidelines.

- Most reservations ban the sale or use of alcohol.
- As a rule of thumb: don't bargain. You can't know the larger effects you might have caused just to save a few dollars.
- Ceremonials and powwows are either open to the public or exclusively for tribal members. Ceremonials are religious events, and applauding, chatting, asking questions or trying to talk to the performers is rude. Photography and other forms of recording are rarely permitted. While powwows also hold spiritual significance, they are usually more informal.
- Modest dress is customary. Especially when watching ceremonials, you should dress conservatively; tank tops and short shorts are inappropriate.
- Many tribes ban all forms of recording, be it photography, videotaping, audiotaping or drawing. Others permit these activities in certain areas only if you pay the appropriate fee (usually $5 to $10). If you wish to photograph a person, do so only after obtaining his or her permission. A posing tip is usually expected. Photographers who disregard these rules can expect tribal police officers to confiscate their cameras and then escort them off the reservation.
- Don't enter private property unless invited. Don't climb on ruins or remove any kind of artifact from a reservation. Kivas (ceremonial chambers) are always off-limits to visitors. Off-road travel is not allowed without a permit.
- Activities such as backpacking, camping, fishing and hunting require tribal permits. On American Indian lands, state fishing or hunting licenses are not valid.
- It is considered polite to listen without comment, particularly when an elder is speaking. Be prepared for long silences in the middle of conversations; such silences often indicate that a topic is under serious consideration.

Through trade with other tribes, they acquired peaches, figs, wheat, melons, cattle and horses.

Nowadays the Hualapai Reservation, bordering a large section of the Grand Canyon's South Rim, stretches as far south as Route 66. The Hualapai (meaning 'people of the pine trees') counts itself among the few tribes in the Southwest that do not generate revenue from gambling; instead, they've tried their hand at tourism, most successfully through motorized rafting tours on this section of the Colorado River, and through tourism on the scenic West Rim (known as Grand Canyon West). If you plan to travel off Route 66 on the Hualapai Reservation, you must purchase a permit in tiny Peach Springs.

Like the Havasupai, the Hualapai are renowned for their basketry.

Wade deeper into the background of the Havasupai with the ethnography *I Am the Grand Canyon: The Story of the Havasupai People*, by Stephen Hirst, told largely in their own words.

The Navajo (Diné)

The Navajo people comprise one of the largest tribes in North America; about one of every seven American Indians are Navajo. Bordering the eastern edge of the national park, the 27,000-sq-mile Navajo Reservation is the biggest in the US. If you enter the park through the East Entrance, you'll pass through the Navajo Reservation; the tiny outpost of Cameron, also on the reservation, marks the intersection of Hwys 89 and 64, which leads to the East Entrance.

The Navajo Nation (also known as the Diné) has historically been adaptable to the ways of other tribes and cultures, which perhaps has

ETHICAL TOURISM

To varying degrees, the region's local tribes rely on tourism coming through the Grand Canyon National Park. You'll be contributing to the tribes' economies if you take tribal-run tours, stay at campsites or lodges on the reservations or purchase handicrafts and art directly from tribal members.

When visiting reservations, keep in mind that they are sovereign nations within the US and that tribal laws may apply (though federal laws supersede them). In addition to obeying stated rules and respecting tribal codes of etiquette, it's wise to take a cue from the tribespeople and consider the environment: be careful with water; leave no trace.

contributed to the nation's strength and size. But the Navajo people have certainly not been exempted from the poverty and historical struggle of all American Indian tribes.

The Navajo are renowned not only for their jewelry, pottery and sand paintings, but most famously for their weaving. Sought-after Navajo rugs, which can take months to complete, can be found for sale throughout the region, from Sedona to the South Rim. Most of the processes are still done by hand: carding the wool, spinning the thread, dying the threads with natural concoctions, and hand-weaving the designs themselves.

Between Cameron and the East Entrance of the park, Navajo stalls along the side of the highway sell jewelry and handicrafts. Some are preceded by hand-painted signs announcing 'Friendly Indians Ahead!' These are great opportunities to buy locally, and often directly, from the artisans.

The Hopi

East of the Grand Canyon lies the 2410-sq-mile Hopi Reservation, which is completely surrounded by the Navajo Reservation. The Hopi is Arizona's oldest tribe and is probably best known for its unusual, often-haunting kachina dolls.

According to Hopi religion, kachinas (*katsinam* in Hopi) are several hundred sacred spirits that live in the San Francisco Peaks north of Flagstaff. At prescribed intervals during the year, they come to the Hopi Reservation and dance in a precise and ritualized fashion. These dances maintain harmony among all living things and are especially important for rainfall and fertility. Kachina dolls, elaborate in design and color and traditionally carved from the dried root of the cottonwood tree, represent these sacred spirits.

While some kachina dolls are considered too sacred for public display or trade, Hopi artisans carve kachina dolls specifically to be sold to the general public. You can buy these, as well as pottery, basketwork and jewelry, at Hopi House in Grand Canyon Village; at the Watchtower at Desert View; at the Cameron Trading Post; and in the trading companies of Flagstaff.

On the Hopi Reservation, Old Oraibi is one of the oldest continuously inhabited villages in the US and site of the tribe's most sacred traditions. There is no official census data for the village, nor contemporary photographs, as photos and drawings are not allowed here.

The Paiute (Nuwuvi)

The Southern Paiute people occupy land north of the Colorado River in what is known as the Arizona Strip, and have traditionally used the canyon for hundreds of years. After contact and conflict with Navajo and Ute slavers, Spanish explorers, Mormon settlers and the US government, the Southern Paiute now live in scattered settlements and reservations in California, Utah, Nevada and Arizona.

One branch of this tribe, the Kaibab Paiute, occupies a reservation in northern Arizona, just west of Fredonia and south of Kanab, Utah. The tribe is largely involved in both agriculture and tourism and runs a visitor center and campground at Pipe Spring National Monument.

Survival Guide

Clothing & Equipment

Arriving outfitted with the proper clothing and equipment will keep you comfortable and safe on your adventures. Much of what is appropriate to bring depends, of course, on the season you're visiting and what activities you plan to pursue.

Plan carefully, particularly if you are going to explore the backcountry for the first time. Many first-time visitors are surprised by the weather, especially the extreme heat of summer and the high-country cold of the North Rim. Summer temperatures on the canyon bottom soar beyond 100°F (38°C), often higher, every day, and the interior remains stifling throughout the night. In the winter, it's not unusual to find mild and sunny skies on the South Rim, and a blinding blizzard 10 miles as the crow flies on the North Rim. November, March, April and even May snow is not unusual, and summer monsoons come out of seemingly nowhere mid-July through September. Hike prepared for dramatic shifts in weather regardless of the season.

When selecting clothing and equipment, a guiding principle should be the balance of safety and comfort with weight considerations. We've heard from rangers that it's not unusual to find abandoned tents and gear in inner-canyon backcountry, presumably left because they are too heavy to pack out, leaving the rangers to lug them up to the rim; lightweight gear should be a priority. In the summer, consider taking only a rain fly.

Think carefully about when, where and how long you are hiking. Plan, and pack, accordingly.

Clothing

Modern outdoor garments made from synthetic fabrics (which are breathable and actively wick moisture away from your skin) are better for hiking than anything made of cotton, but in cooler temperatures wool shirts, socks and sweaters are preferred.

Layering

To cope with changing temperatures and exertion, layer your clothing.

➡ Upper body: start with a base layer made of synthetic thermal fabric or merino wool; second layer is a long-sleeved shirt; third layer can be a fleece sweater or jacket that wicks away moisture. Outer shell consists of a waterproof and breathable jacket.

➡ Lower body: shorts will be most comfortable in midsummer, although some prefer long pants – light, quick-drying fabric is best. Waterproof overpants form the outer layer, and in the winter wear a wool base layer.

Waterproof Shells

Grand Canyon hikers should always carry a windproof, waterproof rain jacket, headwear and, in the cooler months, pants. Gore-Tex or similar breathable fabrics work best.

Footwear, Socks & Gaiters

➡ Some hikers prefer the greater agility that lightweight boots allow, while others insist on heavier designs that give firm ankle support and protect feet in rough terrain. Hiking boots should have a flexible (preferably polyurethane) midsole and an insole that supports the arch and heel. Nonslip soles (such as Vibram) provide the best grip.

➡ When considering what type and style of footwear to bring, weigh the advantages of heavier hiking boots with the burden of the added weight; a couple extra pounds on your feet can make a noticeable difference when tackling switchbacks out of the canyon.

➡ Ideally, purchase shoes in person rather than online so you can try on several options to see what works best with your feet.

➡ Try on hiking boots, preferably in the afternoon or evening, to allow for foot swell. Try boots on with whatever socks you plan on wearing; they should still offer plenty of toe room.

- Most hikers carry a pair of river sandals to wear around camp. River sandals are also useful when fording waterways.
- Merino wool socks that draw moisture away from your feet are another must; synthetic options can also work.
- Do not wait until the day before to purchase footwear, as you'll want at least a week or so to break it in.

Navigation

Route Finding

If backpacking beyond Grand Canyon's maintained and National Park Service (NPS) patrolled corridor trails, invest in a waterproof topographic map (www.grandcanyon.org). Even with a detailed map, however, some basic route-finding techniques can be helpful.

- Be aware of whether the trail should be climbing or descending.
- Check the north-point arrow on the map and determine the general direction of the trail.
- Time your progress over a known distance and calculate the speed at which you travel in the given terrain. From then on, you can determine with reasonable accuracy how far you have traveled.
- Watch the path – look for boot prints and other signs of previous passage.

Maps & Compasses

You should always carry a good map of the area you are hiking in, and know how to read it. Before setting off on your trek, ensure that you understand the contours and the map symbols, plus the main ridge and river systems in the area. Also familiarize yourself with the true north–south directions and the general direction in which you are heading. On the trail, try to identify major landmarks such as mountain ranges and gorges, and locate them on your map. This will give you a better understanding of the region's geography.

Buy a compass and learn how to use it. The attraction of magnetic north varies in different parts of the world, so compasses need to be balanced accordingly. Compass manufacturers have divided the world into five zones. Make sure your compass is balanced for your destination zone. There are also 'universal' compasses on the market that can be used anywhere in the world. Do not rely on digital compasses, as they are vulnerable to getting lost, broken or running out of batteries.

The following is a very basic introduction to using a compass and will only be of assistance if you are proficient in map reading. For simplicity, it doesn't take magnetic variation into account. We recommend you obtain further instruction before using a compass.

READING A COMPASS

Hold the compass flat in the palm of your hand. Rotate the bezel (rim) so the red end of the needle points to the N on the bezel. The bearing is read from the dash under the bezel.

ORIENTING THE MAP

To orient the map so that it aligns with the ground, place the compass flat on the map. Rotate the map until the needle is parallel with the map's north–south grid lines and the red end is pointing to north on the map. You can now identify features around you by aligning them with labeled features on the map.

TAKING A BEARING FROM THE MAP

Draw a line on the map between your starting point and your destination. Place the edge of the compass on this line with the direction-of-travel arrow pointing toward your destination. Rotate the bezel until the meridian lines are parallel with the north–south grid lines on the map and the N points to north on the map. Read the bearing from the dash.

FOLLOWING A BEARING

Rotate the bezel so that the intended bearing is in line with the dash. Place the compass flat in the palm of your hand and rotate the base plate until the red end points to N on the bezel. The direction-of-travel arrow will now point in the direction you need to walk.

DETERMINING YOUR BEARING

Rotate the bezel so the red end points to the N. Place the compass flat in the palm of your hand and rotate the base plate until the direction of travel arrow points in the direction in which you have been trekking. Read your bearing from the dash.

GPS

Originally developed by the US Department of Defense, the Global Positioning System (GPS) is a network of more than 20 earth-orbiting satellites that continually beam encoded signals back to earth. Small computer-driven devices (GPS receivers) can decode these signals to give users an extremely accurate reading of their location – to within 30m, anywhere on the planet, at any time of day, in almost any weather.

The cheapest hand-held GPS receivers now cost less than US$100 (although these may not have a built-in averaging system that minimizes signal errors).

CLOTHING & EQUIPMENT CHECKLIST

Though it's tempting to simply toss everything into the car at the last minute, taking time to think things through as you pack can save you a lot of headaches down the road. Organizing clothes and gear into packing cubes (Eagle Creek makes ultralight Specter Tech cubes of varying sizes) minimizes the frustration of digging for things while on the trail.

If hiking during the summer heat, consider hats and shirts with 25 to 50 UPF ratings that provide sun protection beyond standard materials.

Clothing

You will not need any cool-weather gear for inner-canyon hikes May through September, but be prepared for rain.

- ☐ broad-brimmed hat (one that ties under the chin is required for all mule trips)
- ☐ hiking boots, or sturdy trail-running shoes
- ☐ river sandals or flip-flops
- ☐ shorts and lightweight trousers or skirt
- ☐ sweater or fleece
- ☐ thermal underwear (synthetic or merino wool)
- ☐ T-shirt and long-sleeved shirt with collar (for sun protection)
- ☐ warm hat, scarf and gloves
- ☐ waterproof jacket, and pants in cooler months

Equipment

- ☐ backpack with a rain cover
- ☐ first-aid kit
- ☐ high-energy food and snacks
- ☐ DEET insect repellent
- ☐ map, compass and guidebook
- ☐ map case or clip-seal plastic bags
- ☐ pocket knife
- ☐ sunglasses
- ☐ sunscreen and lip balm
- ☐ survival bag or blanket
- ☐ toilet paper and trowel
- ☐ LED flashlight or headlamp with new batteries

Other important factors to consider when buying a GPS receiver are its weight and battery life.

Remember that a GPS receiver is of little use to hikers unless used with an accurate topographical map. The receiver simply gives your position, which you must then locate on the local map. More expensive receivers, however, can include topographical maps among other capabilities.

GPS receivers will only work properly in the open. The signals from a crucial satellite may be blocked (or bounce off rock or water) directly below high cliffs near large bodies of water or in dense tree cover and give inaccurate readings, and this includes canyon cliffs within Grand Canyon.

GPS receivers are more vulnerable to breakdowns (including dead batteries) than the humble magnetic compass – a low-tech device that has served navigators faithfully for centuries – so never rely on them entirely.

Equipment

It doesn't have to be fancy or high-end, but making sure you have the basic equipment will contribute greatly to a safe and comfortable journey.

Backpacking equipment is continually getting lighter, better designed and more comfortable. Be sure when selecting both day and overnight packs that your backpack can accommodate your gear.

- ☐ watch
- ☐ water bottle and reservoir (like a Camelbak)
- ☐ ziplock bags
- ☐ paracord or similar utility rope
- ☐ trekking poles
- ☐ water-purification tablets, iodine or filter
- ☐ safety mirror and whistle to attract attention in emergencies
- ☐ crampons (for winter hiking)

Overnight Hikes

- ☐ biodegradable soap
- ☐ cooking, eating and drinking utensils
- ☐ dehydrated food
- ☐ matches and lighter
- ☐ sewing/repair kit
- ☐ sleeping bag and/or liner, plus sleeping mat
- ☐ stove and fuel
- ☐ lightweight tent, tarp or rain fly
- ☐ toiletries and towel

Optional Items

- ☐ altimeter
- ☐ binoculars
- ☐ camera and/or cell phone
- ☐ portable power supply (like a solar charger)
- ☐ gaiters
- ☐ GPS receiver
- ☐ mosquito net
- ☐ notebook and pen
- ☐ swimsuit (for creeks – currents in the Colorado River can be deadly)
- ☐ tenacious tape (for patching jackets, tents etc)

Backpacks & Daypacks

➡ Look for a comfortable backpack that effectively distributes the weight between shoulders, spine and hips. Take plenty of time to try on backpacks and find one that fits to your body and is comfortable.

➡ Carefully consider the length of your trip before selecting a backpack.

➡ Internal-frame backpacks fit snugly against your back, keeping the weight close to your center of gravity. Look for one with good ventilation.

➡ Even if the manufacturer claims your pack is waterproof, use a super lightweight rain cover.

➡ For day hikes or side trips from camp, consider bringing daypacks that double as hydration systems (like Camelbaks); if using a reservoir system, you'll still want to bring a water bottle as a back up.

Tents

➡ A three-season tent will suffice for most backpacking expeditions. Winter overnight trips will necessitate a four-season tent for protection from the elements.

➡ The floor and the outer shell, or rain fly, should have taped or sealed seams and covered zips to stop leaks.

➡ Be sure to consider the weight.

HIKE SMART

Grand Canyon National Park's Hike Smart campaign, instituted in hopes of reducing the need for search and rescues and canyon deaths, strongly recommends the minimal amount necessary for safe below-the-rim summer hiking. Go to www.nps.gov/grca/planyourvisit/hike-smart.htm for details.

Sleeping Bag & Pad

➡ Three-season sleeping bags will serve the needs of most campers. Down fillings are warmer than synthetic for the same weight and bulk but, unlike synthetic fillings, do not retain warmth when wet.

➡ Mummy bags are the best shape for weight and warmth. Third-party European Norm (EN) temperature ratings (30°F or -0.1°C, for instance) show the coldest temperatures at which a typical adult should feel comfortable in the bag.

➡ An inner liner helps keep your sleeping bag clean, as well as adding an insulating layer. Silk liners are lightest.

➡ During the summer, the canyon floor is usually sweltering enough to forgo a sleeping bag altogether; backcountry campers might consider bringing just a sleeping-bag liner or a sheet. Some even soak a sheet in the river for the evaporative cooling effect.

➡ Cooler seasons, especially on the North Rim, call for both sleeping bag and sleeping pad for insulation from the cold ground. Inflatable sleeping pads work best; foam mats are a low-cost but less comfortable alternative.

Stoves & Fuel

The type of fuel you'll use most often will help determine what kind of camp stove is best for you. The following types of fuel can be found in the US, and local outdoors stores can help you choose an appropriate camp stove if you aren't traveling with your own. Fires are not allowed anywhere below the rim or beyond developed campgrounds above the rim.

White gas Inexpensive, efficient and readily available throughout the country, reliable in all temperatures and clean-burning. More volatile than other types of fuel.

Butane, propane and isobutane These clean-burning fuels come in nonrecyclable canisters and tend to be more expensive. Best for camping in warmer conditions, as their performance markedly decreases in below-freezing temperatures.

Denatured alcohol Renewable; the most sustainable alternative. Burns slowly but also extremely quietly.

Buying & Renting Locally

It can actually be a boon to buy or rent locally, as you can take advantage of local expertise on what works best in the region.

South Rim

In the park itself, **Canyon Village Market** (Map p76; ☎928-638-2262; www.visitgrandcanyon.com; Market Plaza, Grand Canyon Village; ⏰6:30am-9pm mid-May–Sep, 🚌Village) sells limited camping equipment and gear, and a couple of places offer a few camping necessities like flashlights, water-purification tablets and thermal blankets. The **Grand Canyon Association Park Store** (Map p76; ☎Grand Canyon Association 800-858-2808; www.grandcanyon.org; Grand Canyon Visitor Center Complex, Grand Canyon Village; ⏰8am-8pm Jun-Aug, shorter hrs rest of year; 🚌Village, 🚌Kaibab/Rim, 🚌Tusayan Mar 1-Sep 30) offers the best selection of trail guides and maps.

Outdoor stores in nearby Flagstaff sell and rent used and new camping equipment, and sell maps and detailed hiking guides.

Peace Surplus (Map p104; ☎928-779-4521; www.peacesurplus.com; 14 W Rte 66; ⏰8am-9pm Mon-Fri, 8am-8pm Sat, 8am-6pm Sun) Rental gear includes sleeping bags (summer/winter $3/7 per day) and tents (2/-4-person $7/9 per day).

REI (Map p100; ☎928-213-1914; www.rei.com/stores/flagstaff; 323 S Windsor Lane; ⏰9am-8pm Mon-Sat, 10am-6pm Sun) National chain with expansive selection of clothes and gear.

Babbits Backcountry Outfitters (Map p104; ☎928-774-4775; www.babbitts-backcountry.com; 12 E Aspen Ave; ⏰8am-8pm Mon-Sat, 10am-6pm Sun) Family-owned local institution with wide selection of gear for purchase and rent.

North Rim

The North Rim's **General Store** (Map p151; ☎928-638-2611; www.nps.gov/grca; ⏰7am-8pm mid-May–mid-Oct; 📶) sells a limited selection of camping gear, including fuel, sleeping bags and pads. Tiny **Willow Canyon Outdoor** (Map p162; ☎435-644-8884; www.willowcanyon.com; 263 S 100 E; ⏰7:30am-8pm) in Kanab, 80 miles from the park, sells outdoor supplies books and maps.

Directory A–Z

Accessible Travel

Around the Southwest, public buildings are required to be wheelchair accessible and to have appropriate restroom facilities. Telephone companies provide relay operators for those with hearing impairments, and many banks provide ATM instructions in Braille. On the South Rim, ATMs at Chase Bank and Maswik Lodge are equipped with Braille.

Many sites on the South Rim, including developed overlooks, museums and historic buildings, are readily accessible, and both Hermit Road (p64) and Desert View (p72) scenic drives offer multiple 'windshield' views clearly marked on the park accessibility map. On the North Rim, Point Imperial (p152) has a wheelchair-accessible viewing platform, and simply sitting on the back porch of Grand Canyon Lodge (p152) gives one of the most dramatic views in the park; for this reason, the North Rim makes an excellent choice for travelers with limited mobility. It is a quieter, calmer and easier to navigate than the South Rim as well, which makes it particularly suitable for elderly travelers.

Descending into the canyon is difficult for anyone with physical disabilities. The Bright Angel (p60; South Rim) and North Kaibab (p145; North Rim) trails are the least rocky, but still pose significant challenges. Use extreme caution. Certified service dogs are allowed throughout the South and North Rims, but to take one below the rim you must first check in at the Backcountry Information Center (p153).

For questions on traveling to the park with a hearing impairment, contact the park's **Deaf Services Coordinator** (☎928-638-7888).

Activities

Mule Rides (p71; South Rim) Provisionally accessible with advance notice. Contact the South Rim switchboard (928-638-2631), and they'll connect you with the barn to discuss your needs with the head wrangler.

Bus Tour (p72; South Rim) To secure a space on a wheelchair-accessible bus tour of Hermit Rd and Desert View Dr, call at least one week in advance.

Smooth Water Float (p72; South Rim) Specialized equipment can accommodate travelers with disabilities; call 800-922-8022 in advance.

White-water Rafting (p12) River concessionaires can sometimes accommodate people with disabilities, even on multiday white-water trips. Call Grand Canyon River Trip Information (☎800-959-9164) for details.

Ranger Programs (p72) To arrange for an American Sign Language (ASL) interpreter at regularly scheduled ranger programs, email the park (grca_information@nps.gov) three weeks in advance.

Rim Trail (Map p76; www.nps.gov/grca; Hermits Rest to South Kaibab Trailhead; 🚻; 🚌Village, 🚌Kaibab/Rim, 🚌Hermits Rest; Mar 1-Nov 30) The 2-mile paved stretch from Mather Point to Bright Angel Lodge passes historic buildings and museums in Grand Canyon Village Historic District.

Greenway Trail (p71; South Rim) On Hermit Rd, the 2.8-mile paved Greenway Trail winds along the rim from Monument Creek Vista past Pima Point, to Hermits Rest and about 2 miles from the Visitors Center east to the South Kaibab Trailhead.

Cape Royal Trail (p144; North Rim) A fairly level, 0.6-mile paved trail leads to several canyon viewpoints.

Accommodations

Lodges on both rims offer rooms compliant with ADA (Americans with Disabilities Act).

SOUTH RIM

El Tovar (p85)

Kachina and Thunderbird Lodges (p84)

Maswik Lodge (Map p76; ☎advanced reservations 888-297-2757, front desk & reservations within 48hr 928-638-2631, ext 6784; www.grandcanyonlodges.com; 202 South Village Loop Dr, Grand Canyon Village; r South/North $107/205; P❄@📶; 🚌Village)

Yavapai Lodge (p84)

NORTH RIM

Grand Canyon Lodge (p152)

Getting Around

NORTH RIM

➡ Public interior spaces at Grand Canyon Lodge (p152), the only lodge on the North Rim, are easily negotiable by people with limited mobility, and it's easy to arrange golf-cart shuttle to and from your cabin.

➡ The Visitor Center has one or two complimentary wheelchairs available on a first-come, first-served basis.

SOUTH RIM

➡ All shuttles can accommodate wheelchairs up to 30in wide and 48in long, but cannot accommodate scooters.

➡ The 'Scenic Drive Accessibility Permit' allows entrance for visitors with mobility issues to access roads otherwise closed to private vehicles and provides a temporary parking permit; available at entrance gates, park visitor centers and park hotel lobbies.

➡ Rent a wheelchair at Bright Angel Bicycles (p71).

Resources

➡ Download Lonely Planet's free Accessible Travel guides from http://lptravel.to/AccessibleTravel.

➡ A digital copy of the *Grand Canyon National Park Accessibility Guide* is available at www.nps.gov/grca/planyourvisit/accessibility.htm

Accommodations

Accommodations in the park range from historic lodges to rustic cabins to standard motel rooms (book 13 months in advance). There are developed campgrounds as well as backcountry campsites, where you can roll out your sleeping bag under the stars to experience an unforgettable inner-canyon sunrise. Casting a wider net opens up any number of accommodations options in nearby towns.

B&Bs

In the South Rim region, Williams, Sedona and Flagstaff have several B&Bs. Hosts tend to be knowledgeable about the area and offer great advice on things to see and do in their hometowns and at the canyon. Most don't welcome children.

Camping

➡ Car camping is only allowed at developed campgrounds inside the park.

➡ Vehicle-accessed campgrounds on the South Rim include Mather (p82), Trailer Village (p83) and Desert View (p82).

➡ North Rim Campground (p152) is the only car-camping site within the park on the north side, and DeMotte Campground (p159) lies just outside the park in the national forest.

➡ Camping inside the canyon requires a backcountry permit (p83) secured up to six months in advance.

➡ Dispersed vehicle-camping is allowed at previously impacted sites anywhere in the Kaibab National Forest, which borders both rims.

➡ Don't camp within a quarter-mile of the highway or any surface water, within a half-mile of any developed campground, or in meadows.

➡ Pay attention to fire restrictions – a more frequent occurrence in our warming climate.

Hostels

Hostels in the Grand Canyon region are limited, but those that exist provide a quality experience. Motel DuBeau (p105) and Grand Canyon International Hostel (p105) offer affordable digs in Flagstaff while the Grand Canyon Hotel (p97) in Williams offers hostel-style accommodations in addition to private rooms.

Hotels & Motels

This being Route 66 territory, a handful of roadside motor lodges have charm emanating from the walls, but still more have other things emanating as well. Chain hotels do provide a consistent level of quality, and there are some great historic hotels and independent options outside both rims. Most offer air-conditioning, wi-fi (sometimes for a small fee), telephones, TVs and complimentary parking.

Lodges

Inside the park, lodges are basically the park's hotels, where the rooms are comfortable enough but very basic. The exceptions are the South Rim's El Tovar (p85) and Bright Angel Lodge (p84) cabins. Phantom Ranch (p84) on the canyon bottom is a basic summer-camp affair, but feels like paradise after a long day of dusty hiking.

Resorts

In Sedona and Las Vegas, full-service resorts offer

SLEEPING PRICE RANGES

The following price ranges refer to a double room with bathroom in high season. Unless otherwise stated, tax is included in the price.

Resorts and lodges, particularly in and around Las Vegas and Sedona, often charge a mandatory resort fee. Expect to pay from $15 to $30 per day on top of the quoted daily rate, and always ask in advance.

$ less than $150

$$ $150–250

$$$ more than $250

luxury accommodations and amenities, beautiful surrounds, excellent restaurants and first-class service. Many offer on-site spas, activities and elegant pools.

Booking Services

Xanterra/Grand Canyon Lodges (p84) Concessionaire operating most of the South Rim lodges.

Delaware North (www.visitgrandcanyon.com) Reservations for Yavapai (the park's only pet-friendly lodge) and Trailer Village RV Park.

National Recreation Reservation Service (www.recreation.gov) For camping at Grand Canyon Village's Mather Campground (advanced reservations required March 1 to November 30).

Lonely Planet (www.lonelyplanet.com/usa/grand-canyon-region/hotels/a/lod/1334512) Recommendations and bookings around the park.

Last-Minute Accommodations

Because of the flexible cancellation policy, it's not unusual to secure last-minute rooms even during summer peak season. There's no waiting list, so keep trying. If all else fails, you can camp for free at just about any impacted site on the Kaibab National Forest on either rim.

SOUTH RIM

➡ For same-day reservations contact the concessionaire Xanterra (p84) that runs every lodge but Yavapai at ☎928-638-2631; for Yavapai (p84) call 928-638-6421.

➡ If you don't find a room on the South Rim, check motels in Tusayan (7 miles from the canyon rim), or the roadside motel in Valle, about 28 miles further south.

➡ In Cameron, 32 miles east of the East Entrance along Hwy 64 (but otherwise in the middle of nowhere), is the pleasant Cameron Trading Post & Motel which often has vacancies.

➡ Safest bets are further away in Williams (59 miles south of the rim) and Flagstaff (80 miles south), both of which offer pedestrian-friendly historic downtowns.

NORTH RIM

➡ To check for last-minute bookings at Grand Canyon Lodge call ☎928-638-2611.

➡ The closest accommodations outside of the park is Kaibab Lodge (p159), 18 miles north of the rim, or Jacob Lake Inn (p160), 44 miles north.

➡ If everything is booked, head to Kanab, a pleasant town about 80 miles north of the rim, where you'll find several motels with rates from $70 to $160.

> **BOOK YOUR STAY ONLINE**
>
> For more accommodations reviews by Lonely Planet authors, check out http://lonelyplanet.com/hotels/. You'll find independent reviews, as well as recommendations on the best places to stay. Best of all, you can book online.

Discount Cards

American Automobile Association (AAA) members can get hotel, museum, rental-car and other discounts by showing their cards – always ask about AAA discounts.

Park Passes

The Grand Canyon Annual and America the Beautiful passes are available at the park entrance stations. Details and links for advance purchase can be found online at www.nps.gov/grca/planyourvisit/fees.htm. It takes up to two weeks to receive your pass and there's an additional cost for shipping.

Grand Canyon Annual Pass ($60) Unlimited visits to passholder and accompanying guests arriving in a noncommercial vehicle, or family members arriving by train, shuttle, bicycle or on foot. Available in advance at www.yourpassnow.com/ParkPass/park/grca.

America the Beautiful Pass ($80) One year access for passholder and up to three adults; also includes all National Park Service (NPS), US Forest Service (USFS) and Bureau of Land Management (BLM) sites. Children under 16 free.

America the Beautiful Annual Pass for Military (free) Access to NPS, USFS, and BLM sites for active military personnel and dependents.

America the Beautiful Access Pass (free) Lifetime pass for US citizens or permanent residents with permanent disability; medical proof required. Admits passholder and up to three adults. Children under 16 free.

Senior Cards

Travelers aged 50 and older can receive rate cuts and benefits in many places. Inquire about discounts at hotels, museums and restaurants before you make reservations or purchase tickets.

American Association of Retired Persons (AARP; www.aarp.org) Members receive 10% discount at South Rim Lodges, 15% discount on Grand Canyon Railway, and varying discounts at area lodges, restaurants and attractions.

America the Beautiful Senior Pass ($80) Lifetime pass for US citizens or permanent residents aged 62 or older. Admits passholder and up to three adults plus children under 16 free. Annual senior pass available for $20.

Electricity

Type A
120V/60Hz

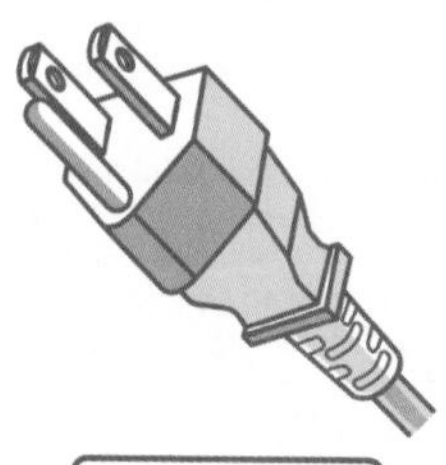

Type B
120V/60Hz

Etiquette

Etiquette at the Grand Canyon primarily relates to respectfully navigating the sometimes vast crowds at overlooks and on popular trails.

Overlooks When jostling to find the perfect spot to enjoy a canyon vista, be cognizant of fellow visitors taking photographs; stay out of frame of photographs and don't hog the best spot.

Share the Trail Turn with your pack to the canyon wall to allow faster hikers to pass; uphill travelers have the right of way. If faced with a mule train, follow the wrangler's directions.

Noise Canyon silence is as magnificent as its views; never blast music from speakers anywhere in the park, do not yell down (or up) a trail to a friend, and keep conversation levels low, especially after dark.

South Rim Shuttles Give up your seat for elderly visitors and people with a disability, as well as families with babies and young children.

Food

Except for the cafeteria in the Maswik, most park eateries require advanced reservations. Even then, you're booking atmosphere rather than a culinary experience, as the array of dining options are fairly predictable and uninspired.

Your best bet is to pack a picnic and strike out for a quiet overlook. If you're visiting the park for more than a day, invest in a small cooler. While the South Rim has a full-size grocery store, the North Rim offerings are more limited with the general store carrying a handful of basic snacks and staples, including wine and beer. The closest full grocery store is in Kanab, nearly two hours drive north.

EATING PRICE RANGES

The following price ranges are for a main dinner meal, not including tip.

$ less than $15

$$ $15–25

$$$ more than $25

Insurance

The US is an expensive country in which to get sick, crash your car or be robbed, so protect yourself. To insure yourself from theft from your car, consult your homeowner's (or renter's) insurance policy before leaving home.

Worldwide travel insurance is available at www.lonelyplanet.com/bookings. You can buy, extend and claim online any time – even if you're already on the road.

Internet Access

Expect all internet connections at the Grand Canyon to be slow, with limited bandwidth.

South Rim

Most South Rim hotel lobbies offer free wi-fi, sometimes for a small fee.

Grand Canyon Community Library (☎928-638-2718; Grand Canyon Village Historic District; ⏰10:30am-5pm Mon-Sat; 📶; 🚌Village (Village East stop)) Free wi-fi and computer terminals.

Grand Canyon National Park Research Library (☎928-638-7768; www.nps.gov/grca/learn/historyculture/reslib.htm; Park Headquarters, Market Plaza, Grand Canyon Village; ⏰8am-4:30pm Mon-Thu & every 2nd Fri; 📶; 🚌Village) Free wi-fi and computer terminals.

Canyon Village Market (Map p76; ☎928-638-2262; www.visitgrandcanyon.com; Market Plaza, Grand Canyon Village; sandwiches, pizzas $6-11; ⏰6:30am-9pm mid-May–Sep, deli to 8pm, shorter hrs rest of year; 🚌Village) Free wi-fi at the deli inside the supermarket.

Yavapai Lodge (Map p76; ☎advanced reservations 877-404-4611, reservations within 48hr 928-638-6421; www.visitgrandcanyon.com; Market Plaza, Grand Canyon Village; r $99-200; ⏰year-round; P❄@📶🐾; 🚌Village) Free computer terminal.

North Rim

General Store (Map p151; ☎928-638-2611; www.nps.gov/grca; ⏰7am-8pm mid-May–mid-Oct; 📶) Sporadically available free wi-fi.

Below the Rim

There is no internet access below the rim.

Legal Matters

If arrested, you have a right to an attorney; if you cannot afford one, one will be provided. US law presumes innocence until proven guilty. If you run into legal trouble, contact the Arizona chapter of the American Civil Liberties Union (ACLU; 602-650-1854; www.acluaz.org).

As anywhere in the US, you must be aged 21 to drink legally. Alcohol is prohibited on all American Indian reservations and cannot be transported on or through the reservations. The Hualapai and Havasupai Reservations border the national park within the canyon itself, and the region in general includes several reservations.

Maps

Do not hike below the rim beyond the three maintained corridor trails without purchasing an appropriately detailed topographical map. While several map apps are available as well, do not rely on these; if your phone gets lost, broken or runs out of batteries, you are left with nothing.

National Park Service (☎928-638-7888; www.nps.gov/grca) (www.nps.gov/grca/planyourvisit/maps.htm) For downloadable PDFs of official NPS maps of the region, scenic drives, corridor hiking trails and South Rim shuttles.

Grand Canyon Association (☎928-638-2481; www.grandcanyon.org) Best source for backcountry maps, including individual trail guides ($4.50) and waterproof National Geographic Trails Illustrated maps.

Money

ATMs

There are no ATMs below the canyon rim.

SOUTH RIM

Chase Bank (☎928-638-2437; Market Plaza, Grand Canyon Village; ⏰9am-5pm Mon-Thu, 9am-6pm Fri; 🚌Village) 24hr ATM at Market Plaza.

Bright Angel Lodge (p84) In the lobby.

Maswik Lodge (p227) In the lobby.

Desert View Market (Desert View, Desert View Dr; ⏰8am-8pm Mar-Sep, shorter hrs rest of year; 🚌Village) Market hours only.

NORTH RIM

General Store (Map p151; ☎928-638-2611; www.nps.gov/grca; ⏰7am-8pm mid-May–mid-Oct; 📶) Store hours only.

Roughrider Saloon (Map p151; ☎928-638-2611; www.grandcanyonforever.com; Grand Canyon Lodge; ⏰5:30-10:30am & 11:30am-10:30pm) Saloon hours only.

Tipping

Hotels $1 to $2 per bag is standard; gratuity for cleaning staff is generally $2 to $5 per day.

Restaurants and bars 15% to 20% of the before-tax total is expected.

Guided Trips It's customary to tip the trip leader, at your discretion; consider the length, party details and itinerary of your trip.

Opening Hours

Opening hours vary throughout the year. We've provided high-season opening hours; hours will generally decrease in the shoulder and low seasons. Note that North Rim services are closed October 15 through May 15.

Banks 10am–5pm Monday to Friday

Bars 5pm–11pm

Restaurants breakfast 6–10am, lunch 11am–2:30pm, dinner 5–9pm

Shops 9:00am–6pm

Photography

American Indian reservations generally do not allow photography of any kind; always ask before taking any pictures. The Hualapai and Havasupai Reservations lie within the Grand Canyon and border the national park, and several reservations surround the park.

Lonely Planet's *Guide to Travel Photography* is full of helpful tips for photography while on the road.

Post

The US Postal Service (www.usps.com) is inexpensive and reliable. Standard letters up to 1oz (about 28g) cost $0.50 within the US; $0.35 for postcards. Postcards and letters to destinations outside the USA cost a universal $1.15.

There is a **post office** (Map p76; ☎928-638-2512; Market Plaza, Grand Canyon Village; ⏰8:30am-3:30pm Mon-Fri; 🚌Village) on the South Rim, and a walk-up postal window on the North Rim.

Public Holidays

Public holidays do not affect park opening hours, but will affect businesses in gateway towns.

New Year's Day January 1

Martin Luther King, Jr Day 3rd Monday in January

Presidents Day 3rd Monday in February

Easter Late March or early April

Memorial Day Last Monday in May

Independence Day July 4

Labor Day 1st Monday in September

INTERNATIONAL VISITORS

Entering the Region

Your passport should be valid for at least another six months after you leave the US.

US Department of State (www.travel.state.gov) Up-to-date visa and immigration information.

Visa Waiver Program (VWP; www.dhs.gov/visa-waiver-program-requirements) Though most foreign visitors to the US need a visa, the VWP allows citizens of 38 countries to enter the US for stays of 90 days or less without first obtaining a visa. Go to the website for a list of participating countries and detailed information.

Electronic System for Travel Authorization (ESTA; https://esta.cbp.dhs.gov/esta) Visitors eligible for the VWP must apply for entry approval via ESTA; while it is recommended travelers apply at least 72 hours before travel, you may apply any time before boarding your flight and in most cases the process takes no more than half an hour.

In April 2018, the US Supreme Court heard challenges to the constitutionality of President Trump's executive ban on travelers from seven Muslim-majority countries; countries affected are Iran, Iraq, Libya, Somalia, Sudan, Syria and Yemen. For updated information on the status of these restrictions, go to www.travel.state.gov.

US Department of Homeland Security (www.dhs.gov) Clear details on requirements for travel to the US; follow links How Do I?/For Travelers/Visit the US.

US Customs and Border Protection (www.cbp.gov/travel/international-visitors) Customs and border regulations.

Embassies & Consulates

For contact information for embassies not listed here, go to https://embassy-finder.com.

Australian Consulate General (Los Angeles; 310-229-2300; http://losangeles.consulate.gov.au)

Canadian Consulate (Los Angeles; 844-880-6519; www.canada.cacanada-in-los-angeles)

French Consulate (Los Angeles; 310-235-3200; www.consulfrance-losangeles.org)

General Consulate of the Netherlands (Los Angeles; 310-268-1598, www.embassy-worldwide.com/embassy/consulate-general-of-netherlands-in-los-angeles-california-u-s/)

German Consulate (Los Angeles; 323-930-2703; www.germany.info/losangeles)

Columbus Day 2nd Monday in October

Veterans Day November 11

Thanksgiving Day 4th Thursday in November

Christmas Day December 25

Showers & Laundry

Camper Services Building (Map p76; 877-444-6777, late arrival 929-638-7851; www.recreation.gov; Market Plaza, Grand Canyon Village; campsites $18; year-round, required reservations accepted 6 months in advance for camping Mar 1-Nov 30; Village east-bound)

North Rim Campground (Map p151; 877-444-6777; www.recreation.gov; by reservation May 15–Oct 15, first-come, first-served Oct 16-31;)

Toilets

- On the South and North Rim, pocket maps given upon entrance show locations of restrooms.
- Public facilities can be found in park lodges and restaurants.
- Below the rim, there are pit toilets at corridor trail campgrounds and a few select spots; where toilet facilities are not available, you must pack out used toilet paper. Bring your own toilet paper as well as ziplock bags.

Tourist Information

Backcountry Information Center (928-638-7875; www.nps.gov/grca; Grand Canyon National Park, PO Box 129, Grand Canyon, AZ 86023; 8-5pm daily, seasonal variation) Backcountry maps, details and last-minute camping permits; headquarters on both the **South Rim** (Map p76; 928-638-7875; www.nps.gov/grca/planyourvisit/backcountry-permit.htm; Grand Canyon

Irish Consulate (Las Vegas; ☎702-889-2840; www.consulate-info.com/consulate/25968/ireland-in-las-vegas)

Japanese Embassy (Los Angeles; ☎213-617-6700; www.la.us.emb-japan.go.jp)

New Zealand Consulate General (Los Angeles; ☎310-566-6555; www.nzembassy.com/usa-los-angeles)

UK Consulate (Los Angeles; ☎310-789-0031; http://ukinusa.fco.gov.uk/la)

Telephone

CELL PHONES

You'll need a multiband GSM phone to make calls in the US. Installing a US prepaid rechargeable SIM card is usually cheaper than using your own network. They're available at major telecommunications or electronics stores in Flagstaff and Las Vegas. If your phone doesn't work in the US, these stores, as well as superstores, also sell inexpensive prepaid phones.

DIALING CODES

- US phone numbers begin with a three-digit area code, followed by a seven-digit local number.
- When dialing a number within the same area code, simply dial the seven-digit number; for long-distance calls, dial the entire 10-digit number preceded by ☎1.
- For direct international calls, dial 011 plus the country code plus the area code plus the local number.
- If you're calling from abroad, the US country code is ☎1.

Time

- Arizona is on Mountain Standard Time (MST) but does not observe Daylight Saving Time (DST).
- The Navajo Reservation *does* observe Mountain DST during the summer, putting it one hour ahead of Arizona and on the same time as Utah and New Mexico.
- DST starts on the second Sunday in March (clocks are set ahead one hour) and ends on the second Sunday in November (clocks are set back one hour).

Village; ⏲8am-noon & 1-5pm, phone staffed 8am-5pm Mon-Fri; 🚌Village) and **North Rim** (Map p151; ☎928-638-7875; www.nps.gov/grca; Administrative Bldg; ⏲8am-noon & 1-5pm May 15-Oct 15).

Bright Angel Transportation Desk (☎928-638-3283; Bright Angel Lodge, Grand Canyon Village Historic District; ⏲5am-8pm summer, reduced hrs rest of year.; 🚌Village) South Rim; books last-minute mule rides and Phantom Ranch, as well as guided bus tours and one-day smooth-water float trips.

Grand Canyon Association (GCA; ☎928-638-2481; www.grandcanyon.org) Nonprofit leg of the park; main on-site shop and tourist information sits next to the South Rim's NPS visitor center.

Grand Canyon National Park (☎928-638-7888; www.nps.gov/grca) Best source for all things Grand Canyon.

Grand Canyon River Permits Office (Map p100; ☎928-638-7843, outside the US 800-959-9164; https://grcariverpermits.nps.gov; 1824 S Thompson St, Suite 201, Flagstaff, AZ 86001; application fee $25; ⏲8am-4pm) Details on attaining permits for float trips through Grand Canyon.

Grand Canyon Visitor Center (Map p76; ☎park headquarters 928-638-7888; www.nps.gov/grca/planyourvisit/visitorcenters.htm; Grand Canyon Visitor Center Plaza, Grand Canyon Village; ⏲9am-5pm; 🚌Village, 🚌Kaibab/Rim, 🚌Tusayan, Mar 1-Sep 30) South Rim's NPS main visitor center.

Kaibab Plateau Visitor Center (☎928-643-7298; www.fs.usda.gov/kaibab; cnr Hwys 89A & 67; ⏲8am-5pm May 15-Oct 15) Information on Kaibab National Forest and North Rim; next to Jacob Lake Lodge, in Jacob Lake.

National Geographic Visitor Center (☎928-638-2468; www.explorethecanyon.com; 450 Hwy 64, Tusayan; ⏲8am-10pm Mar-Oct, 10am-8pm Nov-Feb) In Tusayan, just before entering South Rim.

MEDIA

Newspapers The weekly *Grand Canyon News* is available in print and online at at www.grandcanyonnews.com.

Podcasts and Video Grand Canyon National Park podcasts, webcam and digital photo archives are available for free at www.nps.gov/grca/learn/photosmultimedia; podcasts also available on iTunes.

Twitter The NPS runs an Official Twitter Feed (www.twitter.com/grandcanyonnps), the Grand Canyon Weather Feed (www.twitter.com/grandcanyonwx), and the River Permit Feed (www.twitter.com/GCRiverPermits).

North Rim Visitor Center (Map p151; 928-638-7888; www.nps.gov/grca; 8am-6pm May 15-Oct 15) Next to Grand Canyon Lodge.

Verkamp's Visitor Center (928-638-7146; www.nps.gov/grca/planyourvisit/visitorcenters.htm; Rim Trail, Grand Canyon Village Historic District; 8am-8pm Jun-Aug, reduced hrs Sep-May; Village, Train Depot or Village East stop) Small GCA visitor center on South Rim, next to El Tovar.

Volunteering

There are loads of opportunities to volunteer in and around Grand Canyon National Park, for one-day projects or longer-term endeavors. Among other things, volunteers work on trail maintenance, restore grasslands, pull invasive plants from the inner gorge, train to be an interpretive ranger and work with youth organizations.

Grand Canyon Field Institute (866-471-4435, 928-638-2485; www.grandcanyon.org/fieldinstitute) Partners with NPS to offer multiple single and multiday service-based trips, including family-friendly opportunities, on both the North and South Rims.

Grand Canyon Trust (Map p100; 928-774-7488; www.grandcanyontrust.org; 2601 N Fort Valley Rd, Flagstaff, AZ 86001) Single and multiday volunteer opportunities in Grand Canyon and the Colorado Plateau.

American Conservation Experience (Map p100; Flagstaff Office 928-226-6960; www.usaconservation.org; 2900 North Fort Valley Rd, Flagstaff, AZ 86001; 8am-5pm Mon-Fri) Restoration and conservation work in and around the park for adults aged 18 and older. In exchange for 40 hours work a week, volunteers are housed (often in on-site campgrounds) and fed.

National Park Service (877-444-6777, international 518-885-3639; www.recreation.gov, www.volunteer.gov) Apply online for National Park Service volunteer positions.

Student Conservation Association (703-524-2441; www.thesca.org) Opportunities throughout the USA, including the Grand Canyon, for high-school and college-aged students interested in hands-on conservation work.

Work

Work at the park tends to consist of low-paying service jobs; on the North Rim especially, where jobs are available from mid-May through mid-October only, jobs are mostly filled by young people. If working on the North Rim, shared accommodations and three meals are available for $13.75 per day, or RV hookup in the pet-friendly and wooded staff RV park for $4 per day, no meals. Laundry facilities are free. On the South Rim, jobs include dorm housing ($18 per week) and pay-as-you-go dining at the staff cafeteria.

Planning ahead is essential, whether you are applying for NPS or park concessionaire jobs – applications for summer jobs are typically due during December and January, though options can pop up as late as May. Non-US citizens must apply for a work visa from the US embassy in their home country before leaving. Visas vary, depending on how long you're staying and the kind of work you plan to do.

Cool Works (www.coolworks.com) Central resource for non-NPS jobs and volunteer opportunities in and around the Grand Canyon; provides current job listing for North Rim.

Grand Canyon National Park (928-638-7888; www.nps.gov/grca) Follow links to Get Involved/Work With Us for current information on NPS employment.

South Rim (www.grandcanyonlodges) Online application for employment at South Rim restaurants, shops and hotels; international applicants must be students and must have a J-1 Exchange Visitors Visa. See website for details.

North Rim (www.grandcanyonlodgenorth.com) Information on employment at the North Rim's Grand Canyon Lodge.

Transportation

GETTING THERE & AWAY

The most accessible area of the park is the South Rim, an easy 60-mile drive north of I-40 at Williams. Several regularly scheduled shuttles service the South Rim from Sedona, Williams, Flagstaff and airports in Phoenix and Las Vegas, and an historic train the Grand Canyon Railway (p238) runs daily between Williams and Grand Canyon Village.

Getting to the North Rim is more of a challenge. A **shuttle** (☎928-638-2820; www.trans-canyonshuttle.com; one-way rim to rim $90, one-way South Rim to Marble Canyon $80) runs from rim to rim mid-May to mid-November, but otherwise the only way to reach the North Rim is by car, foot or bicycle.

Flights, cars and tours can be booked online at lonelyplanet.com/bookings.

Air

If headed to the South Rim, fly into Phoenix (230 miles) or Las Vegas (273 miles); for the North Rim, fly into Las Vegas (266 miles). From these points, travelers can rent cars or make connections by bus or shuttle. Salt Lake City, Utah and Albuquerque, New Mexico offer alternative options, but they are a six- to eight-hour drive from the park.

Airports

McCarran International Airport (LAS; Map p124; ☎702-261-5211; www.mccarran.com; 5757 Wayne Newton Blvd; wi-fi) In Las Vegas, at the southern end of the Strip. There are ATMs, a full-service bank, a post office, first-aid and police stations, free wi-fi and slot machines with reputedly bad odds.

Sky Harbor International Airport (☎602-273-3300; http://skyharbor.com; 3400 E Sky Harbor Blvd; wi-fi) Located in Phoenix, this busy airport is 233 miles from the South Rim of the Grand Canyon and 357 miles from the North Rim.

Phoenix Mesa Gateway Airport (www.gatewayairport.com) Small and pleasant Phoenix airport with landscaped outdoor waiting areas past security. Services Allegiant Air and West Jet only, with flights primarily to regional airports in the American Midwest, the West and Florida.

Flagstaff Pulliam Airport (www.flagstaff.az.gov) The only commercial flights in or out of this regional airport are American Airlines flights to Phoenix and seasonal weekly flights to Los Angeles and Dallas.

Salt Lake City International Airport (SLC; ☎801-575-2400; www.slcairport.com; 776 N Terminal Dr; wi-fi) If combining a North Rim Grand Canyon trip with national parks in Utah, this makes a good option; it's a seven-hour drive from Salt Lake to the North Rim.

Albuquerque International Sunport (ABQ; ☎505-244-7700; www.abqsunport.com; wi-fi) Small and easy to navigate;

CLIMATE CHANGE & TRAVEL

Every form of transport that relies on carbon-based fuel generates CO_2, the main cause of human-induced climate change. Modern travel is dependent on aeroplanes, which might use less fuel per kilometer per person than most cars but travel much greater distances. The altitude at which aircraft emit gases (including CO_2) and particles also contributes to their climate change impact. Many websites offer 'carbon calculators' that allow people to estimate the carbon emissions generated by their journey and, for those who wish to do so, to offset the impact of the greenhouse gases emitted with contributions to portfolios of climate-friendly initiatives throughout the world. Lonely Planet offsets the carbon footprint of all staff and author travel.

it is a six-hour drive from here to the South Rim, and eight hours to the North Rim.

Airlines

DOMESTIC & CANADIAN

Air Canada (www.aircanada.com)

Alaska Airlines (www.alaskaair.com)

Allegiant (www.allegiantair.com)

American Airlines (www.aa.com)

Delta (www.delta.com)

Frontier Airlines (www.frontierairlines.com)

JetBlue (www.jetblue.com)

Southwest Airlines (www.southwest.com)

United Airlines (www.united.com)

US Airways (www.usairways.com)

West Jet (www.westjet.com)

FROM THE UK, IRELAND & EUROPE

Aer Lingus (www.aerlingus.com)

Air France (www.airfrance.com)

British Airways (www.britishairways.com)

Thomas Cook (www.thomascookairlines.com)

Virgin Atlantic (www.virgin-atlantic.com)

FROM AUSTRALIA & NEW ZEALAND

Air New Zealand (www.airnewzealand.com)

Qantas (www.qantas.com.au)

Land

Bicycle

South Rim - From Tusayan, bicyclists can enter the South Rim on the 6.5-mile paved Greenway Trail; otherwise, there are no devoted bike trails into Grand Canyon and bicyclists must share the busy road with motorized vehicles.

North Rim - The 44-mile road from Jacob Lake to the North Rim's Grand Canyon Lodge on the canyon rim makes a lovely high-country bike ride into the park.

ROAD DISTANCES

ROUTE	MILES
Albuquerque to South Rim	400
Las Vegas to South Rim	273
Las Vegas to North Rim	266
Phoenix to South Rim	230
Salt Lake City to North Rim	392
Los Angeles to South Rim	490

Bus & Shuttle

Arizona Shuttle (☎520-795-6771, 928-350-8466; www.arizonashuttle.com) Offers three daily scheduled shuttles for the 1½ hour trip between Grand Canyon's South Rim and Flagstaff (per person $32) or Williams (per person $24). Also provides scheduled runs between regional destinations including Phoenix Sky Harbour Airport. Direct pick-up available.

Grand Canyon Shuttle Service (Flagstaff Shuttle & Charter; ☎888-215-3105; www.grandcanyonshuttles.com) Runs 24-hour on-demand shuttles through Grand Canyon region, including but not limited to Flagstaff, Sedona, Williams, Phoenix, Page and St George (Utah), and both rims of Grand Canyon National Park; also offers rim-to-rim, Havasupai and West Rim service.

Greyhound (☎928-774-4573, 800-231-2222; www.greyhound.com; ⊙closed 5:30am-11am) Runs Flagstaff to Albuquerque (from $46, six to seven hours), Las Vegas (from $40, 5½ hours), Los Angeles (from $80; 11 to 13 hours) and Phoenix (from $19, 2½ to three hours).

Trans-Canyon Shuttle (☎928-638-2820; www.trans-canyonshuttle.com; one-way rim to rim $90, one-way South Rim to Marble Canyon $80) Connects the South Rim to Marble Canyon ($80; about three hours). Shuttles depart Bright Angel Lodge on the South Rim at 8am year-round; from May 15 to October 15, a second shuttle departs 1:30pm.

Tusayan Route Shuttle Bus (www.nps.gov/grca/planyourvisit/tusayan-route-purple.htm; ⊙8am-9:30pm Mar-Sep) Part of the Grand Canyon National Park free shuttle system, this seasonal shuttle runs every 20 minutes between Grand Canyon Visitor Center Complex and multiple stops in Tusayan.

Car & Motorcycle

Both the South and North Rim are surrounded by vast expanses of desert and high-mountain terrain; be prepared for long stretches with changeable weather and no services.

On the South Rim, the only fuel is at **Desert View Chevron** (Desert View Dr, Desert View; ⊙9am-5pm Mar-Oct, 24hr for credit-card service); otherwise, head to Tusayan, 7 miles from the South Entrance, or Cameron, 33 miles east of Desert View. Limited garage services are available at the **garage** (☎928-638-2631; S Entrance Rd; ⊙8am-noon & 1-5pm) in Grand Canyon Village.

On the North Rim, there's a seasonal **service station** (⊙8am-5pm, 24hr pay at the pump, May 15-Nov) by the campground with limited repairs and gas; outside the park, the closest services are the seasonal North Rim Country Store (18 miles) or Jacob Lake (44 miles).

FROM LAS VEGAS

It's an easy 4½ hour drive to either rim. The most direct route to the South Rim is Hwy 93 south to I-40, then east to Williams, where you'll turn north on Hwy 64 through Valle and Tusayan, and into the park.

To get to the North Rim, head north on I-15 into Utah. Just past St George, take

Hwy 9 east to Hurricane. You can either continue on Hwy 9 through Zion National Park, then connect with Hwy 89 down through Kanab and on to Fredonia via Hwy 89A/ Alt 89, or take Hwy 59/389 southeast to Fredonia and connect with Alt 89. Alt 89 heads southeast to Jacob Lake, where Hwy 67 (the only access to the park) leads 30 miles to the park entrance station and dead-ends 14 miles later at the canyon edge.

FROM PHOENIX

Take I-17 north to Flagstaff and continue on Hwy 180 north to the South Rim.

Another more scenic option is to take Hwy 60 northwest to Hwy 89 through the high-country town of Prescott, then connect with Alt 89, which winds northeast through forested mountains to Sedona. From there it's a short jaunt north through Oak Creek Canyon to Flagstaff. It is a beautiful drive, but traffic can be brutal in summer, particularly around Sedona.

If you're continuing to the North Rim from Flagstaff, take Hwy 89 north. About 60 miles north of Cameron, Alt 89 turns west through spectacular Lees Ferry and Marble Canyon to Jacob Lake.

AUTOMOBILE ASSOCIATIONS

American Automobile Association (www.aaa.com) Along with maps and trip-planning information, AAA members also receive discounts on car rentals, air tickets, hotels and attractions, plus emergency roadside service and towing. It has reciprocal agreements with international automobile associations such as CAA in Canada; be sure to bring your membership card from your country of origin.

Better World Club (www.betterworldclub.com) This ecofriendly association supports environmental causes in addition to offering emergency roadside assistance for drivers and cyclists, discounts on vehicle rentals (including hybrids and biodiesels) and auto insurance.

DRIVER'S LICENSE

Arizona recognizes foreign driver's licenses and does not require an International Driving Permit (IDP). However, an IDP, obtained in your home country, is recommended if your country of origin is a non-English-speaking one.

Some car-rental agencies require an IDP, so be sure to ask in advance.

RENTAL

Most car-rental agencies require renters to be at least 25 years old, and some have an upper age limit as well. When shopping around, always check with the agency itself. It's illegal to drive without automobile insurance, so consult your policy from your home country before leaving.

A number of major car-rental agencies operate out of the airports in Las Vegas, Phoenix, Albuquerque and Salt Lake City, but it is often cheaper to pick up from sites outside of the airports. You can also rent cars in Sedona and in Flagstaff. The car rental offices closest to the Flagstaff Amtrak station are Avis and Budget, an easy 1-mile walk from the station.

Alamo (☎888-233-8749; www.alamo.com)

Avis (☎800-633-3469; www.avis.com)

Budget (☎800-527-0700; www.budget.com)

Enterprise (☎800-736-8222; www.enterprise.com)

Hertz (☎800-654-3131; www.hertz.com)

National (☎877-222-9058; www.nationalcar.com)

INSURANCE

➡ Liability insurance covers people and property that you might hit. For damage to the rental vehicle, a collision damage waiver is available for about $20 per day. Collision coverage on your vehicle at home may also cover damage to rental cars; check your policy before leaving home.

➡ Some credit cards offer reimbursement coverage for collision damage if you rent the car with that credit card.

➡ Most rental companies stipulate that damage a car sustains while driven on unpaved roads is not covered by the insurance they offer. Check with the agent when you make your reservation.

ROAD RULES

Throughout the US, cars drive on the right side of the road. Apart from that, road

RV RENTAL

Recreational vehicles are a great way to travel the Grand Canyon region, where campgrounds are plentiful. If you need to rent a vehicle anyway, renting an RV can save money on accommodations. Rates vary by vehicle size, model and mileage; expect to pay at least $100 per day.

Apollo (☎800-370-1262; www.apollorv.com) With a branch in Las Vegas, Apollo rents everything from cozy campervans for two, to family-size motor homes.

Cruise America (☎800-672-8042; www.cruiseamerica.com) Rents nationwide and has offices in Phoenix, Flagstaff and Las Vegas.

Jucy (☎800-650-4180; www.jucyusa.com) Small campervans sleep two or four.

RIDING THE GRAND CANYON RAILWAY

On September 17 1901, the first Grand Canyon Railway train departed Williams to carry its pioneering passengers to the South Rim – and so began the modern era of the canyon as tourist destination. Instead of the hurdle of a long and arduous stagecoach ride, tourists could now travel to the canyon in relative comfort. By 1968, car travel had made the train obsolete. Only three passengers were on that year's final trip to the rim.

In 1989, Max and Thelma Biegert bought and lovingly restored the train, resuming passenger service after a 21-year absence. The Biegerts sold the company in 2007.

Today diesel locomotives make the daily journey to Grand Canyon Village. On a few select days each year, the railway runs a steam locomotive with engines powered by waste vegetable oil.

A 1952 parlor car doubles as a cafe, selling coffee, candy, box lunches, sunscreen, water and film.

Even if you're not a train buff, or if you generally shrink from traveling en masse, the train can be a lot of fun if you get into the spirit. A banjo player or other musician wanders the aisles, joking with passengers and strumming such folk classics as 'I've Been Working on the Railroad.' A mock horseback chase and train robbery enliven the return trip.

Packages are available through the Grand Canyon Railway Hotel in Williams, and lodgings at the rim. For reservations and details, contact Grand Canyon Railway.

Passengers can choose from the following classes of service. Prices quoted are for round-trip journeys:

Pullman Class (adult/child $67/32) The standard seats on the train are in these refurbished 1923 Harriman-style coach cars.

Coach Class (adult/child $82/51) Features 1950s-style cars with large windows and room for roving musicians and marauders.

First Class (adult/child $155/121) Has air-conditioning, spacious reclining seats, and snacks and beverages on offer in both directions.

Observation Dome (adult/child $184/153) With upper-level seating in a glass-enclosed dome, featuring snacks, beverages and a champagne toast on the return trip; not open to children under 16.

Luxury Dome & Luxury Parlor ($219) Incredibly comfortable cushioned window seats and an open-air rear platform; not open to children under 16.

rules differ slightly from state to state, but all require the use of safety belts as well as the proper use of child safety seats for children under the age of five.

➡ Speed limits vary; on rural interstates the speed limit is 75mph, but this drops down to 65mph in urban areas (55mph in Arizona).

➡ Pay attention to livestock- or deer-crossing signs – tangle with a deer, cow or elk and you'll total your car in addition to killing the critter.

➡ You can incur stiff fines, jail time and other penalties if caught driving under the influence of alcohol. The legal limit for blood alcohol level is 0.08% in Arizona and most other states.

Train

Amtrak (www.amtrak.com) The *Southwest Chief* stops at Flagstaff at 4:30am daily from Los Angeles (from $60; 11 hours) and at about 9pm daily from Chicago (from $134; 32 hours). From here, Amtrak connects to the South Rim via a 45-minute shuttle to the Holiday Inn Express in Williams and a connection on the Grand Canyon Railway. Alternatively, **Arizona Shuttle** (☎520-795-6771, 928-350-8466; www.arizonashuttle.com) departs daily from the Flagstaff Amtrak station to the South Rim ($32; 7:45am, 12:45pm, 3:45pm).

If headed to the North Rim, take the *Southwest Chief* to Flagstaff, rent a car, and drive four hours north, or take Amtrak's *California Zephyr* (connecting San Francisco to Chicago) to Provo, UT, rent a car, and drive six hours south.

Grand Canyon Railway (☎reservations 303-843-8724; www.thetrain.com; 233 N Grand Canyon Bvd, Railway Depot; round-trip adult/child from $67/32; ⏱departs 9:30am) has original 1923 Pullman cars chug the scenic 65 miles from Williams to the South Rim (from $67). Trains depart daily from Williams at 9:30am, arriving Grand Canyon 11:45am; return trip departs South Rim 3:30pm, arriving Williams 5:45pm. See website for overnight packages.

River

River trips access Grand Canyon National Park on the Colorado River primarily from Lees Ferry; from here, it is 225 miles to take-out at Diamond Creek. Motorized boats take a minimum of seven days to complete the trip, but half-trips that include hiking in or out from Phantom Ranch (p84) are available.

Dozens of companies offer three- to 18-day motorized and non-motorized river trips.

Permits

A river permit is required for all boat travel into and through Grand Canyon National Park. If you go with a commercial trip, your permit is included as part of the total cost.

The NPS grants permits for 12- to 25-day private, self-guided river access to the park from Lees Ferry to Diamond Creek. Permits are secured through a weighted lottery; every February, online applications are accepted for the following year. The NPS also allows two noncommercial trips per day to launch from Diamond Creek for two- to five-day river trips; there is no permit fee for these trips but there are land and launch access fees payable to the **Hualapai Tribe** (☎928-769-2636; www.grandcanyonwest.com; 900 Route 66, Hualapai Lodge; ⏲variable). Download and submit the *Diamond Creek to Lake Mead* application up to a year in advance.

For details go to www.nps.gov/grca/planyourvisit/whitewater-rafting.htm or contact the **Grand Canyon River Permits Office** (Map p100; ☎928-638-7843, outside the US 800-959-9164; https://grcariverpermits.nps.gov; 1824 S Thompson St, Suite 201, Flagstaff, AZ 86001; application fee $25; ⏲8am-4pm).

Boat Launch & Take-Outs

There are five active Colorado River launch and take-out spots providing access to Grand Canyon National Park.

Lees Ferry 45 miles southwest of Page, AZ and 130 miles north of Flagstaff, Lees Ferry is the official ground-zero launch-site for river trips through the park. There's a small campground and parking lot.

Phantom Ranch (river mile 89) Accessible by mule (from South Rim), foot, or boat only. Phantom Ranch (p84) offers dorm and cabin accommodations (available 15 months in advance by lottery reservation), and there is camping at nearby Bright Angel Campground (p146); advance backcountry permit required.

Whitmore Wash (river mile 188) Helicopter access only; services Bar 10 Ranch (www.bar10.com) on the canyon's north side.

Diamond Creek (river mile 225) Access to Diamond Creek is through Hualapai Tribal land only. A 21-mile dirt road leads from tiny Peach Springs down to the river; required permits ($30) available at Peach Springs Lodge (928-769-2230). The Hualapai run multiple daily rim-to-river helicopter rides as well as one- and two-day river trips. As a result, this river access is often loud and busy. The canyon south of the river is Hualapai land, while the canyon north of the river is Grand Canyon National Park.

Pearce Ferry (river mile 277) The official end of the Colorado River's Grand Canyon stretch, Pearce Ferry (Lake Mead) has a small marina and campground. Sits at the end of the 52 mile Pearce Ferry Rd, which veers of Hwy 93 about half-way between Las Vegas and Kingman, AZ.

GETTING AROUND

Bicycle

Bicycles are allowed on paved roads throughout the park, but there are no dedicated bike lanes.

South Rim

Because roads on the South Rim are so heavily trafficked, a great alternative is using bicycles. The Greenway Trail (p71), which winds through Grand Canyon Village and overlaps for a few miles with the paved Rim Trail, is an excellent way to get around the developed areas of the South Rim. Rent 'comfort cruiser' bikes at Bright Angel Bicycles (p71).

North Rim

On the North Rim, bicycles are allowed on blacktop roads only, except for the 17-mile dirt road to Point Sublime and the Bridle Trail from the campground to the lodge. You can fashion a terrific extended ride out to **Point Imperial** and on to **Cape Royal**, about 45 miles each way from Grand Canyon Lodge. The park's 35mph speed limit ensures slow traffic, and the pine-fringed road offers a good riding surface.

Boat

The only boat travel within the park is through multiday whitewater rafting trips (p38) along the Colorado River.

Bus

South Rim

Free shuttle buses operate every 10 to 15 minutes during the day, and approximately every 30 minutes during the hour before sunrise and after sunset. Note that the shuttle from one side of the Village to the other can take up to 45 minutes, and east- and west-bound shuttles make different stops; check park map for details. Shuttles can accommodate collapsible strollers and a limited number of bicycles.

Hermits Rest Route (March 1 to November 30) Accesses nine overlooks along the 7-mile Hermit Rd west from Grand Canyon Village. When the shuttle is in service, the road is closed to private vehicles. During this time, the only way to see the Hermit Rd overlooks is via shuttle, bicycle or on foot along the Rim Trail.

Village Route Services lodges and sights in Grand Canyon Village. You can drive throughout the village, but it's easier to park your car and take this shuttle.

Kaibab/Rim Route Stops at Pipe Creek Vista, South Kaibab Trailhead and Yaki Point.

Hikers' Express (www.nps.gov/grca/planyourvisit/hiker-express-shuttle.htm; Grand Canyon Village; ⏲departs 5am, 6am & 7am May & Sep, 4am, 5am & 6am Jun-Aug, 6am, 7am & 8am Apr & Oct, 8am & 9am Dec-Feb, 7am, 8am & 9am Mar & Nov) Early morning shuttle services South Kaibab Trailhead, departing two or three times every morning; it stops on the hour at Bright Angel Lodge, then continues to the Backcountry Information Center and Grand Canyon Visitor Center.

North Rim

The Grand Canyon Lodge offers a free **Hikers' shuttle** (Map p151) from the lodge to the North Kaibab Trailhead twice daily (5:45am and 7:10am) from May 15 to October 15. Call 928-638-2611 to reserve a spot at least 24 hours in advance.

There is no other shuttle service on the North Rim.

Rim-to-Rim

Trans-Canyon Shuttle (☎928-638-2820; www.trans-canyonshuttle.com; one-way rim to rim $90, one-way South Rim to Marble Canyon $80) From May 15 to October 16, the rim-to-rim shuttle ($90; 4½ hours) departs twice from each rim: from North Rim's Grand Canyon Lodge at 7am and 2pm; from South Rim at 8am and 1:30pm. Shuttle service is reduced to once daily October 16 to November 15, weather permitting. As long as you call at least 48 hours in advance, there will be space (shuttles are added as needed).

Car & Motorcycle

Hermit Rd is closed to private vehicles March 1 to November 30, and the road to the South Kaibab Trailhead and to Yaki Point is closed to private vehicles year-round. Fuel is available at the North Rim Campground (seasonal) and the South Rim's Desert View (self-serve year-round).

Road Conditions & Hazards

Check road conditions within the park by calling the automated information line 928-638-7888. For conditions in Kaibab National Forest (South Rim), call the **Tusayan Ranger Station** (Map p80; ☎928-638-2443; www.fs.usda.gov/kaibab; 176 Lincoln Log Loop); for conditions in Kaibab National Forest (North Rim), call the **Kaibab Plateau Visitor Center** (☎928-643-7298; www.fs.usda.gov/kaibab; cnr Hwys 89A & 67; ⏲8am-5pm May 15-Oct 15).

Ranging between 6500ft and 7500ft in elevation, roads in Flagstaff and environs may experience snow and ice from October through April. At elevations approaching 9000ft, roads along the North Rim are even more susceptible to weather. The drive up from deserts north and east of the park climb about 4000ft, and conditions change rapidly – you may start out in sunny, dry weather in Kanab or Lees Ferry and wind up battling rain, hail or snow in Jacob Lake. The forest service's dirt roads, particularly those in Kaibab National Forest, may be impassable after even light rain. Always check with a ranger before heading out.

You'll need a high-clearance 4WD vehicle to tackle both the 17-mile road to Point Sublime (a minimum two-hour round-trip) and the 60-mile dirt road to Toroweap. Absolutely do not attempt these drives without first telling someone where you're going, and take plenty of water.

If driving to Grand Canyon West on the Hualapai Reservation, be aware that nine of the 21 miles of Diamond Bar Rd are regularly graded but unpaved road. In wet weather, a 4WD vehicle is advisable. Be sure to start out with a full tank of gas and a good supply of water. Also on the Hualapai Reservation, Diamond Creek Rd is best traveled by 4WD with a plentiful supply of water. Even in the best of circumstances, this rough road leading directly to the Colorado River necessitates at least two creek crossings.

The main hazard to look out for is wildlife in and around the parks.

Parking

Several massive lots sit outside the South Rim's Visitor Center Complex; alternatively, the small parking lots outside Yavapai Geology Museum, El Tovar and Bright Angel are open to the public and are convenient to the rim. Most overlooks have parking.

On the North Rim, park at Grand Canyon Lodge or the North Rim Campground. There is a small lot by the North Kaibab Trailhead, as well at overlooks and other trailheads.

There is no added charge for parking anywhere in Grand Canyon National Park.

Taxi

A 24-hour **taxi** (☎928-638-2822; Tusayan & Grand Canyon South Rim; ⏲24hr) services the South Rim and Tusayan, just outside the park gates.

Health & Safety

Grand Canyon's desert environment and wilderness terrain brings health issues that can turn deadly quickly; understanding the dangers, being prepared and hiking smart will go a long way toward making your visit a safe and healthy one.

Visitors from lower elevations should allow several days to acclimatize before undertaking any strenuous activity at the Grand Canyon and, especially if heading to the North Rim, start hydrating to combat altitude sickness a week *before* arriving at the park.

BEFORE YOU GO

Health Insurance

Review the terms of health and emergency in your health-insurance policy before going on a trip; some policies don't cover injuries sustained as a result of dangerous activities. Double-check that emergency medical care – and emergency evacuation to your home country (if you're not from the US) – is covered by your policy.

Medical Checklist

You will find basic over-the-counter medicines and first-aid supplies on both rims, especially at the South Rim **grocery store** (Map p76; ☎928-638-2262; www.visitgrandcanyon.com; Market Plaza, Grand Canyon Village; ⏰6:30am-9pm mid-May–Sep, deli to 8pm, shorter hrs rest of year; 🚌Village), and the clinic on the South Rim has a limited **pharmacy** (☎928-638-2551; www.northcountryhealthcare.org; 1 Clinic Rd, Grand Canyon Village; ⏰8am-6pm mid-May–mid-Oct, reduced hrs mid-Oct–mid-May).

Your basic first-aid kit should include the following minimum:

- prescription medicines
- sunscreen (year-round for face) and lip balm
- insect repellent
- Band-Aids, bandages, nonadhesive dressings and adhesive tape
- sterile alcohol wipes
- antibacterial ointment (Neosporin)
- moleskin (if doing any hiking at all)
- tweezers
- ibuprofen and acetaminophen
- antidiarrhea medicine (Pepto-Bismol, Immodium)
- thermometer
- water-purification tablets, iodine or Steripen (if going into backcountry)
- calamine lotion and aloe vera (optional)

Further Reading

- *Backcountry First Aid and Extended Care,* by Buck Tilton (Falcon, 2007) Useful pocket-size guide.
- *Medicine for the Outdoors,* by Paul S Auerbach (Mosby, 2009) Brief explanations of myriad medical problems and practical treatment options.
- *Wilderness 911,* by Eric A Weiss (The Mountaineers Books, 2007) Step-by-step guide to first aid and advanced care in remote areas.

IN THE PARK

Availability & Cost of Health Care

Health care is available at the South Rim **clinic** (☎928-638-2551; www.northcountryhealthcare.org; 1 Clinic Rd, Grand Canyon Village; ⏰8am-6pm mid-May–mid-Oct, reduced hrs mid-Oct–mid-May); in Flagstaff you'll find several by-appointment, walk-in and urgent-care clinics, as well as the comprehensive **Flagstaff Medical Center** (☎928-779-3366; www.nahealth.com; 1200 N Beaver St; ⏰emergency 24hr).

There are no health-care services on the North Rim; the closest provider is the hospital in Kanab, Utah.

OVERNIGHT HIKING

Before departing for an overnight backcountry hike, give a contact person your itinerary, including your rim destination after the hike, the date of your return, and the permit holder's name. Upon completion of your hike, call your contact; if you do not return on schedule, they should call Grand Canyon Emergency at 928-638-2477.

Emergency rooms, located in regional hospitals, are required to treat all patients regardless of ability to pay. Clinics' policies vary; if you do not have insurance, and depending on the reason for your visit, they may ask you to pay up front.

Medical Services

In an emergency on either rim, dial 911; from your lodge or cabin, dial 9-911.

South Rim

North County Community Health Center (928-638-2551; www.northcountryhealthcare.org; 1 Clinic Rd, Grand Canyon Village; 8am-6pm mid-May–mid-Oct, reduced hrs mid-Oct–mid-May) Walk-in medical care and limited pharmacy.

Safeway (pharmacy 928-635-0500; 637 W Route 66; 5am-midnight) (Williams) Closest full pharmacy; 60 miles south.

Flagstaff Medical Center (928-779-3366; www.nahealth.com; 1200 N Beaver St, Flagstaff; emergency 24hr) Closest hospital; 80 miles south.

North Rim

Rangers provide emergency medical care, but there is no clinic.

Zion Pharmacy (435-644-2693; www.zionpharmacyut.com; 14 E Center St, Kanab; 9am-7pm Mon-Fri, to 2pm Sat) Closest pharmacy; 80 miles north.

Kane County Hospital (435-644-5811, emergency 911; www.kchosp.net; 355 N Main St, Kanab; 24hr) Closest hospital; 80 miles north.

Page Hospital (928-645-2424, emergency 911; www.bannerhealth.com; 501 N Navajo Dr, Page) It's 114 miles from the North Rim; closest hospital if driving between South Rim and North Rim.

Safeway (928-645-5714; 650 Elm St, Safeway; 9am-8pm Mon-Fri, to 6pm Sat, 10am-4pm Sun; Page) Local grocery store offers full pharmacy.

Below the Rim

There are no medical services below the rim. Emergency care is provided by NPS rangers.

Indian Garden (Map p80; Backcountry Information Center 928-638-7875; www.nps.gov/grca; Bright Angel Trail, 4.6 miles below South Rim) Ranger station staffed year-round.

Phantom Ranch (Map p80; 928-638-3283; www.grandcanyonlodges.com; bottom of canyon, 9.9 miles below South Rim on Bright Angel, 7.4 miles below South Rim on South Kaibab, 13.6 miles below North Rim on North Kaibab;) Ranger station staffed year-round.

Emergency Phones Connect to the park's 24-hour dispatch; located at Bright Angel Trail resthouses and the junction of the South Kaibab and Tonto Trails. Be warned, however, that these may not always work.

Common Ailments

Blisters

To avoid blisters, make sure your walking boots or shoes are well worn in before you hit the trail. Boots should fit comfortably with enough room to move your toes. Socks should fit properly and be specialized for walkers; be sure there are no seams across the widest part of your foot. Wet and muddy socks can cause blisters, so pack a spare pair. If you feel a blister coming on, treat it sooner rather then later by applying a bit of moleskin or duct tape.

Fatigue

More injuries happen toward the end of the day than earlier, when you're fresher. Although tiredness can simply be a nuisance on an easy hike, it can be life-threatening on narrow exposed ridges or in bad weather. Never set out on a hike that is beyond your capabilities on the day. If you feel below par, have a day off.

Don't push yourself too hard – take rests every hour or two and build in a good half-hour lunch break. Toward the end of the day, take the pace down and increase your concentration. Drink plenty of water and eat properly throughout the day – nuts, dried fruit and chocolate are all good energy-rich snacks.

Giardiasis

This parasitic infection of the small intestine, commonly called giardia, may cause nausea, bloating, cramps and diarrhea, and can last for weeks. Giardia is easily diagnosed by a stool test and readily treated with antibiotics.

To protect yourself from giardia, do not drink directly from lakes, ponds, streams and rivers, which may be contaminated by animal or human feces. Giardia can also be transmitted from person to person if proper hand washing is not performed.

For details and updated information on water treatment below the rim, go to www.nps.gov/grca/planyourvisit/safe-water.htm.

Knee Strain

Many hikers feel the burn on long, steep descents. Although you can't eliminate strain on the knee joints when dropping steeply, you can reduce it by taking shorter steps that leave your legs slightly bent and ensuring that your heel hits the ground before the rest of your foot. Some walkers find that compression bandages help, and trekking poles are very effective in taking some of the weight off the knees.

Travelers' Diarrhea

Serious diarrhea caused by contaminated water is an increasing problem in heavily used backcountry areas. Fluid replacement is the mainstay of management. A rehydrating solution is necessary for severe diarrhea, to replace minerals and salts. Commercially available oral rehydration salts (ORS) are very useful.

Environmental Hazards

For the casual park visitor, coping with environmental hazards requires little effort apart from keeping sufficiently hydrated and not goofing off on the rim. However, for those heading below the rim, preparation and responsibility for one's own safety are key to a safe adventure. Many emergencies below the rim occur because visitors overestimate their abilities and come underprepared to deal with the consequences.

Altitude Sickness

As the South Rim is more than 7000ft above sea level and the North Rim is about 8800ft at its highest point, altitude sickness is fairly common. It's characterized by shortness of breath, fatigue and headaches. Staying hydrated is one of the best preventive measures; any symptoms should be taken seriously.

Bites & Stings

Emergency services below the rim are limited to backcountry rangers; take precautions to avoid painful and potentially deadly bites and stings. Young children and the elderly are particularly vulnerable to extreme reactions.

SCORPIONS

While rarely fatal, the scorpion sting is extremely painful and can cause loss of muscle control and difficulty breathing. If stung, immediately apply ice or cold packs, immobilize the affected body part and go to the nearest emergency room.

SNAKES

Those bitten will experience rapid swelling, severe pain and possibly temporary paralysis. Death is rare.

To treat snakebite, place a light constricting bandage over the bite, keep the wounded part below the level of the heart and move it as little as possible. Attempting to suck out the venom and/or applying a tourniquet is *not* recommended. Stay calm and get to a medical facility for antivenin treatment as soon as possible.

TICKS

Wear long sleeves and pants to protect from ticks. Always check your body for ticks after walking through high grass or thickly forested areas. If ticks are found unattached, they can simply be brushed off. If a tick is found attached, press down around the tick's head with tweezers, grab the head and gently pull upward – do not twist it. (If no tweezers are available, use your fingers). Don't douse an attached tick with oil, alcohol or petroleum jelly.

Lyme disease, transmitted by ticks, is uncommon in Arizona, but you should consult a doctor if you get sick in the weeks after your trip.

Cold, Snow & Ice

South Rim snowstorms can come up out of seemingly nowhere as late as May and as early as October.

HYPOTHERMIA

This life-threatening condition occurs when prolonged exposure to cold thwarts the body's ability to maintain its core temperature. Hypothermia is a real danger for winter hikers. Remember to dress in layers and wear a windproof outer jacket. If possible, bring a thermos containing a hot (nonalcoholic) beverage.

TAP WATER

Tap water on both rims is drinkable, and you will find multiple water-bottle filling stations on both rims.

Water for all of Grand Canyon, however, is piped through an aging system from Roaring Springs, about 3500ft below the North Rim. Increasingly regular and unpredictable pipeline breaks result in sometimes extreme water restrictions on the rim and no water at all at below-the-rim sources. Both rims have reservoirs for such emergencies, but it can take days or weeks for pipelines to be fixed.

Do not assume that seasonal drinkable tap-water sources are available below the rim; they may be on your map, but that doesn't mean they will be working. It is absolutely imperative to bring plenty of water for any kind of hike, as well as a water-purifying system.

Hypothermia doesn't just occur in cold weather – dehydration and certain medications can predispose people to hypothermia, especially when they're wet, and even in relatively warm weather. Symptoms include uncontrolled shivering, poor muscle control and a careless attitude. Treat symptoms by putting on dry clothing, giving warm fluids and warming the victim through direct body contact with another person.

Flash Floods

Even if the sky overhead is clear, distant rainstorms can send walls of water, debris and mud roaring through side canyons without warning. Such flash floods have killed people caught in creeks and dry riverbeds. Never camp in dry washes, and be sure to check weather reports for the entire region before venturing into the canyon. This is crucial if you're planning on hiking through any slot canyons. Flash floods are most common during summer storms in July, August and September.

Heat

Absolutely do not underestimate the summer heat – temperatures routinely soar well past 100°F (38°C) below the rim.

PREHYDRATION

Since your body can only absorb about a quart of water per hour, it's highly beneficial to prehydrate before embarking on a long hike. To get a head start on hydration, drink plenty of water the days before your hike, and avoid diuretics like caffeine and alcohol.

DEHYDRATION & HEAT EXHAUSTION

The canyon is a dry, hot place, and even if you're just walking along the rim, lack of water can cause dehydration, which can lead to heat exhaustion. To prevent dehydration, take time to acclimatize to high temperatures, wear a wide-brimmed hat and make sure to drink plenty of fluids. Hikers should drink a gallon of water per day, and anyone overnight hiking below the rim should bring a water-purification system; corridor trails have potable water, but pipeline breaks are common and they cut off water supply without warning. It's also wise to carry water in your car in case it breaks down.

Take note if you haven't had to pee as often as usual, or if your urine is dark yellow or amber-colored. These are indicators of dehydration, which can rapidly spiral into more dire health concerns. Loss of appetite and thirst may be early symptoms of heat exhaustion, so even if you don't feel thirsty, drink water often and have a salty snack while you're at it. Add a little electrolyte-replacement powder to your water. Err on the side of caution and bring more water and food than you think you'll need – even if it turns out you don't need it, it could save someone else's life.

Characterized by fatigue, nausea, headaches, cramps and cool, clammy skin, heat exhaustion should be treated by drinking water, eating high-energy foods, resting in the shade and cooling the skin with a wet cloth. Heat exhaustion can lead to heatstroke if not addressed promptly.

HEATSTROKE

Long, continuous exposure to high temperatures can lead to heatstroke, a serious, sometimes-fatal condition that occurs when the body's heat-regulating mechanism breaks down and one's body temperature rises to dangerous levels.

Symptoms of heatstroke include flushed, dry skin, a weak and rapid pulse, poor judgment, inability to focus and delirium. Move the victim to shade, remove clothing, cover them with a wet sheet or towel and fan them continually. Hospitalization is essential for heatstroke.

HYPONATREMIA

While drinking plenty of water is crucial, it's also critical to supplement water intake with salty snacks and electrolyte drinks to avoid hyponatremia (a dangerously low sodium level in the blood that can lead to death). In the dry heat of the canyon, sweat can evaporate off of your skin so quickly that you may not notice how much you've perspired. Salt lost through sweating must be replaced in order to keep a balanced sodium level in the blood.

Symptoms of hyponatremia are similar to early signs of heat exhaustion: nausea, vomiting and an altered mental state. Give the victim salty foods and seek immediate help if their mental alertness diminishes.

SUNBURN

In the desert and at high altitude you can sunburn in less than an hour, even through cloud cover. Use sunscreen (with a SPF of 15 or higher), especially on skin not typically exposed to sun, reapply it regularly, and wear long sleeves. Be sure to apply sunscreen to young children and to wear wide-brimmed hats.

Lightning

Being below the rim does not protect you from lightning strikes. If a thunderstorm catches you on an exposed ridge or summit, look for a concave rock formation to shelter in, but avoid touching the rock itself. Never seek shelter under objects that are isolated or higher than their surroundings.

In open areas where there's no shelter, find a depression in the ground and take up a crouched-squatting position with your feet together; do not lie on the ground. Avoid contact with metallic objects such as pack frames or hiking poles.

HIKE SMART

Serious injury and death is a very real risk at Grand Canyon, and far too often visitors underestimate the dangers, especially those associated with below-the-rim hikes in the blistering summer months. In response, the NPS has instituted a park-wide Hike Smart campaign.

➡ Make the '2xdown = up' formula your hiking mantra. Generally speaking, it takes twice as long to wheeze back up the canyon as it does to breeze down. So if you'd like to hike for six hours, turn around after two. Most first-time canyon hikers slog uphill at about 1mph.

➡ Stay on marked trails, both for safety and erosion control. Nowhere is this more important than in the Grand Canyon, where hazards include stupefying drop-offs. It's also extremely difficult for rescuers to find a hiker who has wandered off-trail.

➡ Don't hike alone. Most of those who get in trouble in the canyon are solo hikers, for whom the risks are multiplied. Backcountry hikes are safer (and more enjoyable) with a companion.

➡ Given the altitude and extreme aridity, go slow to avoid overexertion. Ideally, you should be able to speak easily while hiking, regardless of the grade. Be sure to take a five- to 10-minute break every hour to recharge, in the shade if possible.

➡ Pay close attention to your intake of food and fluids to prevent dehydration and hyponatremia (low blood sodium level). One good strategy is to have a salty snack and a long drink of water every 20 to 30 minutes. In summer months each hiker should drink about a gallon of water per day, sipping constantly. Eat before you're hungry and drink before you're thirsty.

➡ In addition to sturdy, comfortable, broken-in boots and medium-weight socks, bring moleskin for blisters and make sure your toenails are trimmed. On long hikes, soak your feet in streams to reduce inflammation and safeguard against blisters (just be sure to dry them thoroughly before replacing your socks). After hiking, elevate your feet.

➡ Don't be overly ambitious. Particularly for novice hikers, it's a good idea to spend the first day or two gauging your ability and response to the climate and terrain. If you're planning long hikes, test your desert legs on a more level hike or a short round-trip of 2 to 4 miles, then work your way up to more difficult trails.

➡ Hike during the cooler early-morning and late-afternoon hours, especially in summer. Avoid trails between 10am and 4pm. Splash water on your face and head at streams and water sources, and soak your shirt or bandana to produce an evaporative cooling effect.

Should anyone be struck by lightning, immediately begin first-aid measures such as checking their airway, breathing and pulse, and starting burn treatment. Get the patient to a doctor as quickly as possible.

Rockfall

Always be alert to the danger of rockfall, especially after heavy rains. If you accidentally loosen a rock, loudly warn other hikers below.

Wildlife

For their own safety and yours, it's illegal to approach or feed any wildlife. In the canyon, always shake out shoes and sleeping bags to dislodge hiding scorpions. Also keep an ear out for rattlesnakes, whose rattle is a warning signal.

Elk and deer are common on the South Rim, and it's not unusual to see them lumbering through Grand Canyon Village or sidling up to a water-filling station trying to get to the runoff. On the North Rim, deer are ubiquitous. Less common but still Grand Canyon inhabitants are coyotes and mountain lions. The NPS advises visitors to stay at least 100ft (or two bus lengths) from large mammals.

Safe Hiking

It's easy to become complacent when hiking in the Grand Canyon, given the clearly marked trails and ease of descent. But hiking here can be serious business. On average, there are 400 medical emergencies each year on canyon trails, and more than 250 hikers need to be rescued at their own hefty expense. Incredibly, an average of 12 people die at the park every year, and almost every year people fall to their death while hiking along or into the canyon.

Time and again, hikers who have been rescued from the canyon say that their biggest mistake was underestimating how hot the canyon can be. The best way of ensuring a rewarding hike is proper planning. Learn about the trails, honestly assess your limitations and respect them.

Getting Lost

The park comprises 1904 sq miles of desert terrain, making it too easy to lose your way in its labyrinth of side canyons and sheer cliffs. It is imperative that you plan any hike carefully and appropriately. Whether backcountry hiking or driving in remote areas, always carry an adequate map, a generous supply of drinking water and electrolyte replacement.

Leave a detailed itinerary with a friend, listing routes and dates, as well as identifying details of your car. Cell phones won't get a signal inside the canyon and in most areas above the rim. For backcountry hikes, bring a topo map, know how to read it and never stray from trails under any circumstances.

If you do get lost, search-and-rescue operations may take days to find you. Stay calm and stay put, making your location as visible as possible by spreading out colorful clothing or equipment in an exposed place. Use a signal mirror (an old CD is a good lightweight substitute) and ration food and water. Do not attempt to blaze a shortcut to the river; people have died from falls, exposure or dehydration after stranding themselves on steep, dead-end ledges or ridges.

Rescue & Evacuation

Hikers should take responsibility for their own safety and aim to prevent emergency situations, but even the most safety-conscious hiker may have a serious accident requiring urgent medical attention. In case of accidents, self-rescue should be your first consideration, as search-and-rescue operations into the canyon are very expensive and require emergency personnel to put their own safety at risk.

If a person in your group is injured, leave someone with them while others seek help. If there are only two of you, leave the injured person with as much warm clothing, food and water as it's sensible to spare, plus a whistle and flashlight. Mark their position with something conspicuous.

Traumatic Injuries

If the victim is unconscious, immediately check if they are breathing. Clear their airway if it's blocked, and check for a pulse – feel the side of the neck rather than the wrist. Check for wounds and broken bones. Control any bleeding by applying firm pressure to the wound.

FRACTURES

Indications of a fracture are pain (tenderness of the affected area), swelling and discoloration, loss of function or deformity of a limb. Unless you know what you're doing, don't try to straighten an obviously displaced broken bone. To protect from further injury, immobilize a nondisplaced fracture (where the broken bones are in alignment) by splinting it, usually in the position found, which will probably be the most comfortable position. If you do have to splint a broken bone, remember to check regularly that the splint is not cutting off the circulation to the hand or foot.

Compound fractures (or open fractures, in which the bone protrudes from the skin) require urgent treatment, as there is a risk of infection. Fractures of the thigh bone also require urgent treatment as they involve massive blood loss and pain. Seek help and treat the patient for shock. Dislocations, where the bone has come out of the joint, are very painful and should be set as soon as possible.

Broken ribs are painful but usually heal by themselves and do not need splinting. If breathing difficulties occur, or the person coughs up blood, medical attention should be sought urgently, as this may indicate a punctured lung.

INTERNAL INJURIES

Internal injuries are difficult to detect and cannot usually be treated in the field. Watch for shock, which is a specific medical condition associated with a failure to maintain circulating blood volume. Signs include a rapid pulse and cold, clammy extremities. A person in shock requires urgent medical attention.

SPRAINS

Ankle and knee sprains are common injuries among hikers, particularly when crossing rugged terrain. To help prevent ankle sprains, wear boots that have adequate ankle support. If you suffer a sprain, immobilize the joint with a firm bandage, and if possible, immerse the foot in cold water. Relieve pain and swelling by resting and icing the joint, and keeping it elevated as much as possible for the first 24 hours. Take over-the-counter painkillers to ease discomfort. If the sprain is mild, you may be able to continue your hike after a couple of days.

Behind the Scenes

SEND US YOUR FEEDBACK

We love to hear from travelers – your comments keep us on our toes and help make our books better. Our well-traveled team reads every word on what you loved or loathed about this book. Although we cannot reply individually to your submissions, we always guarantee that your feedback goes straight to the appropriate authors, in time for the next edition. Each person who sends us information is thanked in the next edition – the most useful submissions are rewarded with a selection of digital PDF chapters.

Visit **lonelyplanet.com/contact** to submit your updates and suggestions or to ask for help. Our award-winning website also features inspirational travel stories, news and discussions.

Note: We may edit, reproduce and incorporate your comments in Lonely Planet products such as guidebooks, websites and digital products, so let us know if you don't want your comments reproduced or your name acknowledged. For a copy of our privacy policy visit lonelyplanet.com/privacy.

WRITER THANKS

Loren Bell

A heartfelt thanks to all the canyon veg-heads who are always up for brews and brats on a random Tuesday night. Also, a special thanks to Chalisa, Odin and Hawkeye for helping with the most crucial research. And finally to Kari: it's crazy to think that this is where it all began. Here's to moonlit hikes to granaries, being stuck in Lava left, and peanut butter on the esplanade. I'd do it all over again in a heartbeat.

Jennifer Rasin Denniston

Thank you to my husband Rhawn and my daughters Anna and Harper – I can't resist the quiet of the Canyon, and I couldn't do this project without you understanding that it always restores my spirit. To Buck, you have been an amazingly supportive, patient and kind editor – I had no idea that things would get a little crazy, and your calming and reassuring voice made all the difference. It's been great working with you. Thank you.

ACKNOWLEDGEMENTS

Climate map data adapted from Peel MC, Finlayson BL & McMahon TA (2007) 'Updated World Map of the Köppen-Geiger Climate Classification', Hydrology and Earth System Sciences, 11, 163344.

Cover photograph: Grand Canyon National Park, Tonda/Getty Images ©.

THIS BOOK

This 6th edition of Lonely Planet's *Grand Canyon National Park* guide was researched and written by Loren Bell and Jennifer Rasin Denniston, with additional research by Benedict Walker, as was the previous edition. The 4th edition was researched and written by Jennifer Rasin Denniston and Bridget Gleeson. This guidebook was produced by the following:

Curator Kathryn Rowan

Destination Editor Ben Buckner

Senior Product Editor Vicky Smith

Product Editor Kate Kiely

Senior Cartographer Corey Hutchison

Book Designer Mazzy Prinsep

Assisting Editors Janice Bird, Lauren O'Connell, Charlotte Orr, Ross Taylor, Fionnuala Twomey

Cover Researcher Fergal Condon

Thanks to Carolyn Boicos, Brendan Dempsey, Kristin Finley, Evan Godt, Melissa Malcolm, Tom Neubauer, Martine Power, Kirsten Rawlings, Sam Wheeler

Index

Map Pages **000**
Photo Pages **000**

Map Pages **000**
Photo Pages **000**

LONELY PLANET IN THE WILD

Send your 'Lonely Planet in the Wild' photos to social@lonelyplanet.com
We share the best on our Facebook page every week!

Map Legend

Sights

- Beach
- Bird Sanctuary
- Buddhist
- Castle/Palace
- Christian
- Confucian
- Hindu
- Islamic
- Jain
- Jewish
- Monument
- Museum/Gallery/Historic Building
- Ruin
- Shinto
- Sikh
- Taoist
- Winery/Vineyard
- Zoo/Wildlife Sanctuary
- Other Sight

Activities, Courses & Tours

- Bodysurfing
- Diving
- Canoeing/Kayaking
- Course/Tour
- Sento Hot Baths/Onsen
- Skiing
- Snorkeling
- Surfing
- Swimming/Pool
- Walking
- Windsurfing
- Other Activity

Sleeping

- Sleeping
- Camping
- Hut/Shelter

Eating

- Eating

Drinking & Nightlife

- Drinking & Nightlife
- Cafe

Entertainment

- Entertainment

Shopping

- Shopping

Information

- Bank
- Embassy/Consulate
- Hospital/Medical
- Internet
- Police
- Post Office
- Telephone
- Toilet
- Tourist Information
- Other Information

Geographic

- Beach
- Gate
- Hut/Shelter
- Lighthouse
- Lookout
- Mountain/Volcano
- Oasis
- Park
- Pass
- Picnic Area
- Waterfall

Population

- Capital (National)
- Capital (State/Province)
- City/Large Town
- Town/Village

Transport

- Airport
- BART station
- Border crossing
- Boston T station
- Bus
- Cable car/Funicular
- Cycling
- Ferry
- Metro/Muni station
- Monorail
- Parking
- Petrol station
- Subway/SkyTrain station
- Taxi
- Train station/Railway
- Tram
- Underground station
- Other Transport

Routes

- Tollway
- Freeway
- Primary
- Secondary
- Tertiary
- Lane
- Unsealed road
- Road under construction
- Plaza/Mall
- Steps
- Tunnel
- Pedestrian overpass
- Walking Tour
- Walking Tour detour
- Path/Walking Trail

Boundaries

- International
- State/Province
- Disputed
- Regional/Suburb
- Marine Park
- Cliff
- Wall

Hydrography

- River, Creek
- Intermittent River
- Canal
- Water
- Dry/Salt/Intermittent Lake
- Reef

Areas

- Airport/Runway
- Beach/Desert
- Cemetery (Christian)
- Cemetery (Other)
- Glacier
- Mudflat
- Park/Forest
- Sight (Building)
- Sportsground
- Swamp/Mangrove

Note: Not all symbols displayed above appear on the maps in this book

OUR STORY

A beat-up old car, a few dollars in the pocket and a sense of adventure. In 1972 that's all Tony and Maureen Wheeler needed for the trip of a lifetime – across Europe and Asia overland to Australia. It took several months, and at the end – broke but inspired – they sat at their kitchen table writing and stapling together their first travel guide, *Across Asia on the Cheap*. Within a week they'd sold 1500 copies. Lonely Planet was born.

Today, Lonely Planet has offices in Franklin, Dublin, Beijing and Delhi, with more than 600 staff and writers. We share Tony's belief that 'a great guidebook should do three things: inform, educate and amuse'.

OUR WRITERS

Loren Bell

North Rim, Around North Rim, Around South Rim When Loren first backpacked through Europe, he was in the backpack. That memorable experience corrupted his 6-month old brain, ensuring he would never be happy sitting still. His penchant for peregrination has taken him from training dogsled teams in the Tetons to chasing gibbons in the jungles of Borneo – with only brief pauses for silly 'responsible' things such as earning degrees. When he's not demystifying destinations for Lonely Planet, Loren writes about science and conservation news. He base-camps in the Rocky Mountains where he probably spends too much time on his mountain bike and skis. Loren also wrote the Understand Grand Canyon section and the Activities chapter.

Jennifer Rasin Denniston

South Rim Jennifer's love for travel began with a 10-week family trip through Europe when she was eight. By 21, she had traveled independently in Australia, New Zealand, Africa, China and the US, and soon after graduation from college she began writing for Lonely Planet. Though her professional career focuses on the US, with a graduate degree in American Studies and multiple Lonely Planet titles on US destinations, her personal travel focuses on extended travel with children and multi-generational travel. Today, she lives in Iowa with her husband and two daughters, and they spend their summers on the road. Jennifer also wrote the Plan Your Trip (except Activities) and Survival Guide sections.

Contributing Writer & Researcher

Benedict Walker A beach baby from Newcastle, Australia, Ben turned 40 in 2017 and decided to start a new life in Leipzig, Germany! Writing for Lonely Planet was a childhood dream for Ben: it was a privilege, a huge responsibility and a lot of fun. He's thrilled to have covered big chunks of Australia, Canada, Germany, Japan, Switzerland, Sweden and the USA. Come along for the ride on Instagram @wordsandjourneys. Ben researched and wrote the Colorado River chapter.

AVON LAKE PUBLIC LIBRARY
32649 ELECTRIC BOULEVARD
AVON LAKE, OHIO 44012

Published by Lonely Planet Global Limited
CRN 554153
6th edition – Mar 2021
ISBN 978 1 78868 068 4
© Lonely Planet 2021 Photographs © as indicated 2021
10 9 8 7 6 5 4 3 2 1
Printed in China

Although the authors and Lonely Planet have taken all reasonable care in preparing this book, we make no warranty about the accuracy or completeness of its content and, to the maximum extent permitted, disclaim all liability arising from its use.

All rights reserved. No part of this publication may be copied, stored in a retrieval system, or transmitted in any form by any means, electronic, mechanical, recording or otherwise, except brief extracts for the purpose of review, and no part of this publication may be sold or hired, without the written permission of the publisher. Lonely Planet and the Lonely Planet logo are trademarks of Lonely Planet and are registered in the US Patent and Trademark Office and in other countries. Lonely Planet does not allow its name or logo to be appropriated by commercial establishments, such as retailers, restaurants or hotels. Please let us know of any misuses: lonelyplanet.com/ip.

MAR 3 0 2021